SILENT WARRIORS

Merchant Navy memorial, Pier Head, Liverpool with the site of Cammell Laird Shipyard, Birkenhead, visible in the background.(© John Huxton)

SILENT WARRIORS

Submarine Wrecks of the United Kingdom

VOLUME THREE

PAMELA ARMSTRONG & RON YOUNG

This book is respectfully dedicated to
The men of the British Merchant Navy
Upon whose willing shoulders, the survival of this island has so often depended

First published 2010

The History Press
The Mill, Brimscombe Port
Stroud, Gloucestershire, GL5 2QG
www.thehistorypress.co.uk

British Library Cataloguing in Publication Data.
A catalogue record for this book is available from the British Library.

ISBN 978 0 7524 5542 6

Typesetting and origination by The History Press
Printed in Great Britain
Manufacturing managed by Jellyfish Print Solutions Ltd

CONTENTS

SUBMARINE

The ships destroy us above
And ensnare us beneath.
We arise, we lie down, and we move
In the belly of Death

The ships have a thousand eyes
To mark where we come...
And the mirth of a seaport dies
When our blow gets home

Rudyard Kipling

ACKNOWLEDGEMENTS

By its very nature, this book is a collective enterprise and could not have been written without the generous assistance of the following people:

Michael Lowrey
Simon Schnetzke and Horst Bredow of the Deutsches U-boot Archiv, Freundeskreis Traditionsarchiv (FTU)
Dr Axel Niestlé
Brian Head, Lt Cdr, RD★, RNR (ret.)
Dennis Feary
Oliver Lörscher
Bob Coppock, ex-FDS
J. Kevin Belcher for the splendid *U 995* photos
John Luxton of www.irishseashipping.com
Andy Mair
Darren Brown
Nelson McEachan and June Dillon and the staff at the UK. Hydrographic Office, Taunton
Howard Cock and the enthusiastic guys who run http://www.ubootwaffe.net
Donna and Mark Jones for helping me out with *Thetis*
Professor Eric Grove
Hubertus Weggelar
The late Dave Perkins
John Eade
Yves Dufeil, author, First World War U-boat and maritime researcher
Arie Visser
Terry Whalebone
Billy McGee
Roger Griffiths
Roger Jordan
Thomas Krispin
Jan-Olof Hendig, ship researcher
David Lee of the Birkenhead History Society
Maurice Voss, ship researcher
Herbert Karting
George Robinson
Davie McClymont
Jörn Jensen
René Alloin
Theodor Dorgeist of Westfalen Freiberuflicher,
Mr Heinz Thois, chairman of U-boat Memorial Foundation Council
Axel van Eesbreek
Captain W.L. Hume, MNI (ret.)
Jean Michel Forsans

Siri Holm Lawson of www.warsailors.com
The Volksbund Deutsche Kriegsgräberfürsorge
The Commonwealth War Graves Commission
Alain Croce
Rolf Kristensen
Mats Karlsson
Torsten Hagnéus
Trevor Hallifax
Deutsches Marinemuseum, Wilhelmshaven
The staff of the Bundesarchiv, Koblenz
Mikael Svensson, Göteborg, Maritime Museum
The staff of Birkenhead Library
The staff of the Holyhead Maritime Museum
The staff of Holyhead Library
The staff of the Mitchell Library, Glasgow
The staff of the Liverpool Maritime Museum
The Liverpool and Glasgow Salvage Association
The National Maritime Museum, Greenwich
The Liverpool Nautical Research Society
The Library of the Royal Naval Museum, Portsmouth
The staff of the National Archive, Kew
The Royal Naval Submarine Museum, Gosport

AN INTRODUCTION

Strolling at leisure along Liverpool Pier Head, you will pass several memorials. One, perhaps the most unassuming of the group, takes the form of a small cenotaph. It is Liverpool's tribute to the Merchant Navy. A simple inscription beneath the gilded badge reads: '*Dedicated to the men and women who gave their lives willingly for the freedom of others and have no grave but the sea.*'

The story that lies behind this simple memorial is an epic of world importance, for Liverpool was the gateway to the world. Britain had been reliant upon imported foodstuffs to feed her population since the 1890s. The politicians knew it, the Royal Navy knew it. German naval staff knew it too, and in both wars the latter continually sought means of exploiting this weakness to advantage. Dislocate or interrupt this transatlantic lifeline and there was every possibility that the ensuing socio-economic chaos would fatally undermine Britain's war effort, or at the very least erode her ability and inclination to prosecute the war. What follows is an attempt to sketch how submarine warfare touched the coastal fringes of western Britain, from Cape Cornwall to the Isle of Man, including the Bristol Channel, St George's Channel and the Irish Sea.

Prior to 1916 only the larger U-boats were capable of entering these waters, sometimes via the English Channel but more often than not by taking the long-haul *norweg* around northern Scotland. At times the U-boats threaded their way through the North Channel but many followed the west coast of Ireland before setting course for St George's Channel. For the first three years of the war, the U-boat incursions were mere probes. At 1400hrs on 29 January 1915, Hersing's *U 21* surfaced off Barrow-in-Furness and commenced a bombardment of Walney airship shed, the docks and the oil tanks. *U 21* remained on the surface for some time, in full view of astounded locals. The local battery commander had allowed the U-boat to approach because he mistook it for a Barrow-built submarine engaged in trials. To add further insult to injury, Hersing made his way to the Mersey roads where he sank (observing the German interpretation of the Prize Rules) *Ben Cruachan*, north-west of Morecambe Light, followed by *Kilcoan* and *Linda Blanche* off the Liverpool Bar Lightship.[1] On his return to Germany, Hersing was awarded the Iron Cross.

The Hersing raid inspired Schneider, the skipper of *U 24*, to mount his own private attack upon Cumbria. On 16 August 1915, *U 24* slipped into Partan Bay, Lowca. Taking up position just off Micklam Point, *U 24* commenced to bombard Harrington's coke works. A burning drum of Benzol spread fire to the loading tanks. Two 11,000-gallon Naphtha tanks were holed but failed to ignite. An estimated 900 windows were broken. Like *U 21* before her, *U 24* withdrew unscathed.

Further daring incursions followed in the form of rescue attempts staged off Great Orme's Head, near Llandudno. The captured Heinrich von Henning managed to persuade the KDM that he had priceless intelligence concerning the defences of Scapa Flow. Both *U 22* (Hoppe) and *U 38* (Valentiner) took part in these enterprising, but ultimately abortive, rescue bids in June and August 1915 respectively. Von Henning was destined to remain a prisoner throughout the First World War but the intelligence gathered would assist Gunther Prien in the Second.

These raids were all about tweaking the lion's tail and reminding the lion that there was very little he could do about it. This was not for want of trying. The Auxiliary Patrol improvised a mobile drifter net barrage between Tuskar Rock and the Welsh coast, followed by a second indicator net barrage between Dublin and Holyhead, designed to protect troopships. The nets proved impossible to maintain. They snagged on wrecks or were carried off by the current. Any U-boat commander worth his salt knew how to dive his boat under fixed nets. These early U-boat incursions damaged morale rather than *materiel*,

Hersing's 1915 bombardment of Barrow is commemorated in this propaganda postcard based on a painting by Willy Stower. (P. Armstrong)

but the introduction of the superior UBII- and UCII-type boats in the autumn of 1916, coupled with Germany's adoption of unrestricted submarine warfare announced on 31 January 1917, changed this scenario. The *KDM* now possessed boats capable of reaching these critical western waters and it was determined to harness U-boat potential to ruthless advantage. The U-boats now attacked with torpedoes from periscope depth and without warning. Now that the Prize Rules had been discarded, there was no longer any requirement to safeguard the crews and passengers. The muzzles were off and the hunters unleashed.

Fortunately for the British, Germany never did have sufficient U-boats to mount a viable blockade, but this knowledge would have offered scant compensation to the victims of unrestricted submarine warfare. Admiralty and Board of Trade stubbornly adhered to their 'safe route' system (Fig.1) which had been in operation since 1915. Approach 'A' directed inbound traffic towards Cornwall. Thereafter vessels could steam into the Bristol Channel or make their way along the south coast of England. Approach 'B' routed shipping through the south-western approaches, initially via Berehaven then into the Irish Sea, hugging the coast. Off Dublin, Liverpool-bound vessels would then shape course towards Anglesey. Approach 'C' funnelled ships through the North Channel, skirting the Isle of Man, then on to Liverpool. The system required that A/S units be concentrated in the 'safe zones' signified by dotted box lines in Fig.1. In reality these zones were death traps.

The zones were too large and A/S patrols were hopelessly overstretched. U-boats were frequently able to pounce without fear of retribution. Seamen's unions had long sought the introduction of convoy. Ship owners and the trade generally regarded convoy as an anathema. Convoy was equally unpopular with Admiralty because it threatened to tie up warships required as escorts. Ideologically it smacked of defence rather than attack. This combination of myopia, vacillation and downright greed would play directly into the hands of the *KDM*.[2]

The first known victim of unrestricted submarine warfare in British coastal waters was the little stone carrier *Essonite*, torpedoed off Trevose Head by *U 55* with the loss of ten lives on 1 February 1917. Many more followed her to the bottom as the new generation of boats took up station off the headlands of Pendine, Tintagel, Trevose and Hartland to wreak havoc amid the vulnerable Welsh collier trade. Lynas Point and the Anglesey Skerries were favoured ambush points within the Irish Sea. Both the High Seas and Flanders U-boats operated in these waters, notably *U 82, U 60, UB 73, UB 86, UB 109* and *UB 117*. The daring and the sheer horror encapsulated in submarine warfare have never been better captured than in Ernst Hashagen's *Winter in the Irish Sea*, his account of a foray made by *U 62* into Caernarvon Bay in December 1917:

Near Holyhead, shadows are slipping by. There's something there. But even with night-vision glasses we can discern little against the dark background. Now the coast falls back into a bay… Two vessels, long and squat, can now be seen – destroyers. The nearest is perhaps 2,000 yards away. Then a steamship, deep in the water: all

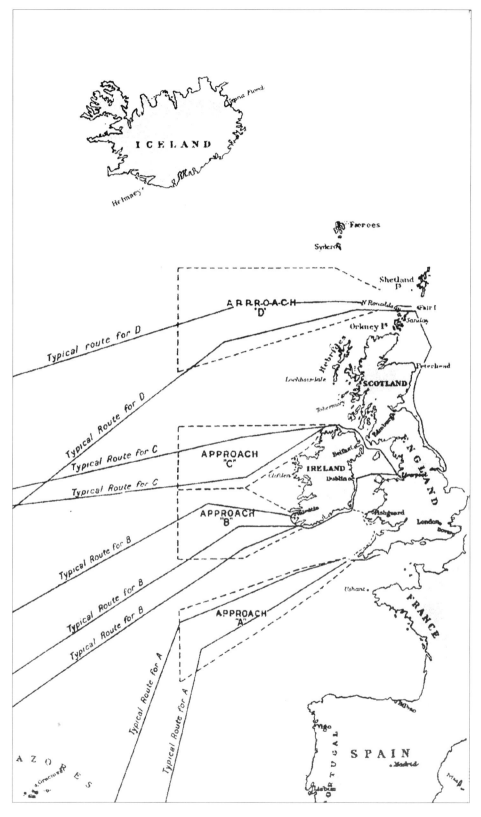

Fig.1: 'Safe Zones' 1915–1917.

The *Formby* memorial
erected on The Strand,
Waterford, Ireland.
(John Luxton)

are darkened, showing no lights. Astern of the ship indistinctly seen, are two little shapes – A/S boats? Can't make them out. The position of the destroyers makes a surface attack out of the question too.

We follow the ships for a considerable time, till we are off the Caernarvon Lightship. The convoy then disappears into the bay, and we decide to lie in wait at this landmark. Cautiously we edge past the lightship. Aft, in the cabin, a light is burning. No doubt they are sitting there, the old salts, huddled over their grog and cards. Or perhaps they are entering in their log-book all the calls for help that they have received that day… No need to trouble them. Navigation markers were, so to speak, neutral. They showed the way to friend and foe. Towards midnight a vessel passes, to the westward. We leave our station and creep nearer. She is a large, deep-laden ship, unescorted. It takes hours for us to haul sufficiently ahead to be able to carry out a surface attack. To get a safe shot, we must know the course and speed of the ship with fair accuracy. So first we run along for some time about a thousand yards from the ship and match our speed exactly with hers. It is by now so dark that, with the naked eye, only a vague mass can be made out beside us. Nine knots, we calculate from our own rate of revolutions. It is rather dreadful to be steaming alongside one's victim, knowing that she has only ten or perhaps twenty minutes to live before we blow her to pieces. A grim reflective mood dominates those of us on the bridge. The horror of war silences us. Every one of our orders, every movement, and every turn of a wheel is bringing death nearer our adversary. It's all so mechanical, is it maybe pre-ordained? Perhaps we have become a hand of Fate. I see Paulsen standing on the side of the bridge facing the ship, checking the settings on his sight with a pocket lamp. He shields it with his hands. You cannot be too careful.

'All hands at diving stations' reports Metzler. The off-duty watch has been asleep until this moment. Now somewhat confused, they stand at their motors and valves. 'What's up?' asks one of them, still half asleep. 'Surface night attack on a large ship.' 'Attacking in ten minutes,' whispers another… I check through everything again, try sighting the vessel at a thousand yards, but can see nothing more than a dark mass. It will, of course, be different at five hundred yards, for the shot. 'Attack commencing!' is passed by voice-pipe to all compartments. Down below, in the engine-room, the telegraphs ring: three times the pointer flies to 'Full Speed Ahead'. The face of Metzler, the engineer, lights up. He twists the valves open and hauls at the levers, signs, and directs. In the hellish din, not a word can be heard. Only by signs can one make oneself understood. The engines are working like furies: hammering, thundering, turning the screws with unleashed power. Enemy ahead! The boat is streaking through the night: burying her nose deep in the sea, then lifting it again to fling the spray over the tower.

Soon now the target must run on to the cross-wire of the sight. Huge and powerful she appears, bearing steadily on through the darkness. Already we can see the broad bow-wave, which she pushes before her, shining weirdly. 'Both bow tubes ready.' Nearer she comes, nearer, threatening, unreal. 'First tube, stand by.' I stand silently bent, my eye at the sight, and watch as the bow-wave goes by. Then all is black again. First comes the foremast, now the bridge, the funnel. 'Tube One, fire!!!'

Below in the tower, Bening presses a tiny knob, the electric firing gear for the torpedo. In the course of the years, we have learnt to work as one. There is no misunderstanding. At the moment that the command 'Fire!' rings out, the torpedo is already leaping from the tube and on its way. We fling the boat round to port to increase our distance from the explosion.

A silvery streak darts like a phantom.

On the tower, we all stare at the dark ship. Suddenly a gigantic tongue of fire in the night! Mighty, it stabs darkness. A powerful explosion follows. Our eardrums tremble. Our eyes are stung by the brilliance. We see the ship break into two pieces, with flames and smoke. The fore part goes down like a stone. The stern heaves up, glowing and hissing. The long muzzle of a gun shines in the light of the fire and seems to point at us in a last attitude of defiance. Too late! Once more, the flames blaze up, then everything fades into darkness. A single light is seen up the sea, flickering miserably. It is the vessel's night light buoy, which has released itself and now burns as a silent valediction above the unfortunate ship.

These events took place on the night of 15 December 1917. The ship in question was the 1,282-ton *Formby*, one of four ships *U 62* sank during this patrol.[3] *Formby* (Master Charles Minards) had left the Mersey earlier that day, bound for Waterford with a general cargo. Because the Clyde Shipping Co. rejected convoy, *Formby* sailed alone. Twenty miles WNW of Bardsey Island, *U 62* struck. The ship, her cargo and her entire crew simply disappeared. Censorship ensured that the loss was not reported in either the local or national press. To the City of London *Formby* was merely another ship to be crossed off Lloyd's List, but in the back lanes of Liverpool, Waterford and Glasgow, it was a time for mourning and the drawing down of blinds. Weeks later, a decomposed female body washed ashore in a lonely Pembrokeshire cove. Following a premonition, Stewardess Anne O'Callaghan had written her name in indelible ink on the reverse of her Sacred Heart medallion. Anne now rests in the consecrated ground of Newtown Cemetery near Waterford, the land of her forbears. She is the only member of the crew to have a grave. Capt Minards and the rest are remembered on the Tower Hill Memorial. The two Kilkenny men, Maurice and Walter Hennebry, were father and son.

FATALITIES OF SS *FORMBY*, 15.12.17

Burke, Edward, Able Seaman
Burns, John, Able Seaman, 30yrs
Butler, Maurice, Carpenter, 28yrs
Carpendale, George, Fireman, 35yrs
Clawson, James, Able Seaman, 56yrs
Coffee, Thomas Able Seaman
Condon, Thomas, Fireman, 50yrs
Connolly, William, Fireman, 26yrs
Connor, Christopher L/Seaman RN (DAMS), 47yrs
Cooke, Patrick, Fireman, 30yrs
Coutts, Daniel, Seaman RNR (DAMS)
Doyle, Patrick, Able Seaman, 35yrs
Eustace, Martin, Cattleman, 57yrs
Fortune, William, Able Seaman
Gillies, Archibald, 1st Mate
Hayes, John, Cattleman, 25yrs
Hennebry, Maurice, Donkeyman, 52yrs
Hennebry, Walter, Fireman, 28yrs

Hennessy, Edward, Winchman, 32yrs
Hurley, John, Able Seaman, 52yrs
Keating, Thomas, Able Seaman, 48yrs
Kiely, John, Fireman
Lemmon, John, 3rd Engineer, 21yrs
Lumley, William, 2nd Engineer, 31yrs
Manning, James, Cattleman, 50yrs
McGrath, John, Cattleman, 31yrs
Minards, Charles, Master, 62yrs
Moir, John, 1st Engineer, 51yrs
O'Brien, John, Cattleman
O'Callaghan, Anne, Stewardess
O'Connell, Daniel, Cattleman
Rankin, James, 2nd Mate, 26yrs
Sinclair, George, Service Steward, 28yrs
Sullivan, Jeremiah, Cattleman, 44yrs
Walsh, John, Fireman, 41yrs

Vessels like *Essonite* and *Formby* were fair game, but the U-boats were not averse to attacking hospital ships in these waters, Bristol being a centre for transporting casualties from Flanders. Even humane commanders of the calibre of Klaus Lafrenz, Werner Furbinger and Ernst Hashagen believed that the British misused hospital ships to transport troops and munitions. This belief stemmed partly from the sight of RAMC personnel dressed in khaki on deck and partly from German propaganda. However the recent discovery of 18-pounder artillery shells within the wreck of *Rewa* is incontrovertible evidence that a level of abuse was being perpetrated by the British. At any rate fears vouched for the safety of those hospital ships regularly sailing between Avonmouth and France proved justified following the sinkings of

Above: Surrendered UB III in Princes Dock, Liverpool, *c.*1921. (P. Armstrong)

Left: 'In circumstances which must be imagined for they cannot be described, *Inverdargle* blew up and sank.' (Reproduced courtesy of World Ship Society)

Rewa (*U 55*) in January and *Glenart Castle* (*UC 56*) in February 1918 in the Bristol Channel. Even more troubling was the dislocation of trade arising from the German blockade. Such a rate of loss was not just terrible, it was unsustainable. In April alone, *one in every four ocean-going British merchant ships failed to come home.* Most of these vessels were sailing to, or from, Liverpool, Bristol or Glasgow.

There were real shortages and prices rocketed in 1917. Rationing was introduced and the fat salvage bucket became a staple feature of the British home. A popular contemporary postcard portrayed a fat German military figure trapped in a bottle corked by a jolly British sailor, demonstrating that the British had not hitherto associated the word 'blockade' with starving civilians. With the onset of unrestricted submarine warfare, they tasted the other side of the equation. Calls to patriotism might see the urban populations through in the short term but none in authority knew how the British people might respond to a sustained starvation blockade. The Government made contingency plans for food riots and strikes. It was now horrifically apparent that Britain was unable to defend her merchant fleet. After all the Royal Navy had trained and organised for a swift and overwhelming Mahanesque fleet victory in the North Sea, not an attritional trade war fought in coastal waters. By the spring of 1917 it was clear that something must be done and done fast. Admiralty and Board of Trade were forced to think the unthinkable. From late July 1917 Atlantic traffic was organised into convoys[4] and the system was gradually extended. To paraphrase John Winton, the convoy system did not win the two world wars but at least it prevented them from being lost.[5]

One early outcome of the system was that it forced the U-boats to operate around the convoy dispersal zones, often uncomfortably inshore where A/S patrols were strongest. U-boat skippers were confronted by the frustrations and hazards of attempting to penetrate an escort screen to attack zig-zagging dazzle-painted steamers.[6] The Milford Haven convoy absorbed the Welsh colliers by shepherding them under escort to Weymouth, where a long-established escort system relayed them to France, or hustled them eastwards through the Channel. In effect convoy seized the initiative from the U-boats. It reduced the options available to a U-boat commander in terms of *when* to strike, *how* to strike and *where* to strike. Nevertheless by the close of 1917 there were still plenty of stragglers and independent vessels like *Formby* to keep the U-boats busy. There were minefields too.

The UC II mine-laying class of submarines were able to penetrate and foul the Irish Sea. The 5,039-ton *Kelvinia* was mined in the Bristol Channel as early as September 1916 on a field laid by *U 78*. Productive fields were also laid off Anglesey and the Isle of Man. Following the declaration of unrestricted submarine warfare, mining operations intensified. In March 1917 mines laid by *UC 65* in the Mersey roads claimed *Kelvinhead*. The liners *Lapland* and the American *New York* were both badly damaged by mines. There was a particularly distressing incident on 28 December 1917 when the Mersey Examination vessel *John H Reade* was mined in the Queen's Channel, courtesy of *UC 75* (*Oblt.z.s. Lohs* – see Vol.1). Thirty-nine died including sixteen river pilots.[7] Apart from the human cost, the commercial dislocation caused in Liverpool and Birkenhead was significant. The impact of the mining campaign was also felt in the roadsteads of Waterford and Queenstown (Cobh). *UC 44* was allegedly caught out by Admiralty subterfuge in the course of re-laying a field. Although the mining campaign slackened somewhat in July 1917, the UC missions continued but the crews paid for their audacity. By the autumn, western coastal waters swarmed with A/S vessels as the unfortunate crew of *UC 33* discovered when the bows of *P61* slammed into her pressure hull. *Oblt.z.s.* Arnold, another sole survivor, has left a graphic account of his boat's destruction.

By November 1917 the pendulum had begun to swing decisively in the Admiralty's favour as increasing numbers of veteran U-boats and their crews failed to return. A number of factors contributed, including the introduction of purpose-built A/S vessels equipped with hydrophones and reliable depth-charges. *U 87* – like *UC 33* – fell victim to the sharp bows of the new generation of purpose-built A/S vessels operating in western coastal waters. *U 61*, commanded by the highly capable Vicktor Dieckmann, may have shared this fate but decisive evidence is lacking. What is certain is that the sloop *Jessamine* destroyed *U 104* with depth-charges, leaving *MaschinistsMt* Karl Eschenberg as the sole survivor. His escape must rank among the most remarkable ever recorded. In a part of the country abounding in myth and legend, it is perhaps fitting to close this account of First World War U-boat activity with the story of the recently identified *UB 65*. Science may have led to the discovery and identification of *UB 65*, but she withholds her mysteries still and for many she will always be 'The Haunted U-boat'.

During the Second World War the U-boats returned to these waters. Two phases of the undersea war concern us here. The first was the opening gambit which occurred between the declaration of war in 1939 and the spring of 1940 when Dönitz masterminded a mining campaign designed to spread fear and chaos in British ports. The second phase unfolded during the end game, when Dönitz launched a last desperate campaign in British coastal waters. This second act saw the *Grossadmiral* playing for time to enable the *Elektroboats* to enter service.

In the early months of the Second World War, the men of the *Kriegsmarine* took up where their fathers had left off. The mining campaign was essentially a holding operation designed to mask the weakness in U-boat numbers while Dönitz built up his fleet in readiness for the Battle of the Atlantic. Until the fall of France, British maritime traffic was routed through the Bristol Channel, offering a tempting target for the adapted Type VIIAs of the Salzwedel Flotilla, notably *U 28*, *U 32* and *U 33*. Mine-laying was no easy task. For the TMB mines to be effective, it was required that they be placed in shallow water. Moreover the U-boat crews were acutely aware of ASDIC, the much-vaunted British wonder weapon. It remained to be seen how effective ASDIC would prove during this campaign.

On 15 September Paul Buchel of *U 32* transmitted back to Control: 'Following your orders I have fouled the British swine's (Churchill's) sea.'[8] Buchel was reporting that his boat had laid twelve TMB mines off Scarweather Light, Porthcawl, thus marking the start of a sustained mining campaign in the Bristol Channel/Irish Sea. Having laid their mines the boats were free to move on to a billet elsewhere, thus on 18 September Buchel sank the 4,863-ton *Kensington Court* in the south-west approaches. During this opening phase most U-boat interceptions were made in accordance with the Prize Regulations.[9] The dark nights which followed witnessed an intensification of mining operations and *U 33* (von Dresky) was in the vanguard:

Off Foreland Point on the British coast, U 33 laid 12 TMB mines in position AM 9947. The lay started at 0315 and ended at 0428. Afterwards U 33 sailed west to take advantage of the darkness and lay off Lundy. At 1710 three depth-charges were heard, with more at 1740 much closer. At 1.00, U 33 dived. At 2030 two destroyers were sighted. An attack was not possible as the torpedoes had not been loaded. (*KTB of U 33, 9 November 1939*)

The mines laid by *U 33* forced the temporary closure of Bristol. Tragically, not all the mines were swept and as late as 16 January 1940 this field claimed the 9,346-ton tanker *Inverdargle* [10] (Capt E. Skelley). The ship had sailed from Avonmouth bound for Trinidad with a cargo of 12,554 tons of aviation spirit. In circumstances which must be imagined, for they cannot be described, *Inverdargle* blew up and burned. There could be no survivors and her crew are remembered on Panel 58 of the Tower Hill Memorial. Records indicate they were drawn from homes as far apart as Port of Spain, Hull, Liverpool, Barbados and Glasgow. In essence these men represent a cross-section of the wartime British Merchant Navy.

FATALITIES OF *INVERDARGLE*, 16.1.40

Alves, James, Able Seaman
Annetts, James, Apprentice, 20yrs
Archbald, Carltan, Steward
Baptister Ramsay, M.V., Assistant Steward, 39yrs
Bennett, Arthur, Able Seaman, 42yrs
Bird, Edward Radio Officer, 31yrs
Brown, William, 3rd Officer, 23yrs
Bynoe, Lionel, Donkeyman, 34yrs
Carberry, Arnold, Boatswain, 51 yrs
Compton, Joseph, Able Seaman, 34yrs
Cross, Bertie, Quartermaster, 40yrs
Durant, Cleophas, Able Seaman, 41yrs
Edwards, James, 2nd Officer, 32yrs
Elder, Ernest, 6th Engineer Officer, 21yrs
Howard, Stanley, Apprentice, 19yrs
Hoyte, Joseph, Greaser, 34yrs
James, Herman, Pumpman, 40yrs
Lewis, Stephineal, Able Seaman, 29yrs
Lorde, George, Greaser, 33yrs
Lovell, Clayton, Mess Room Boy, 20yrs
Maynard, Thomas, Able Seaman, 30yrs

Mitchell, Cosmon, Able Seaman, 29yrs
Molyneux, Joseph, Greaser, 35yrs
Muir, John, 2nd Engineer Officer 45yrs
McMillan, Hugh, Steward, 34yrs
Nice, William, Chief Steward, 53yrs
Nicholson, Henry, Cook, 37yrs
Phillip, Cecil, Galley Boy, 19yrs
Quin, Harold, Chief Officer, 36yrs
Reynolds, Thomas, 4th Engineer Officer, 30yrs
Rice, Preston, Greaser, 36yrs
Rice, William, 5th Engineer Officer, 26yrs
Skelley, Evan, Master, 41yrs
Suttie, Alex, Chief Engineer Officer, 40yrs
Tandy, Henry, CPO, DEMS, 42yrs
Taylor, Ethelbert, Able Seaman, 30yrs
Trotman, Mcdonald, Assistant Cook, 23yrs
Walton, Harry, Apprentice, 17yrs
Welch, George, Able Seaman, 44yrs
White, William 3rd Engineer Officer, 45yrs
Wyke, Ivan, Carpenter, 28yrs
Yeates, Martin, Cabin Boy, 19yrs

As 1940 dawned, responsibility for mining British waters gradually passed to the *Luftwaffe* but in western waters the submarine mine-laying missions continued into the dark winter nights. On 5 December, *U 28* laid a field of twelve TMB mines off Swansea (AM9863). Operations were extended to the Mersey when the approach to the Queen's Channel (AM 9324) was mined by *U 30* (Lemp) on the night of 6 January 1940, with spectacular results. [11] On 2 March, *U 29* fouled the Bristol Channel off Nash Point (AM9810). Eight days later, navigating via the Morecambe Bay Lightship, *U 32* (Jensich) mined the channel north of Liverpool (AM 6986) adjacent to the field sown earlier by *U 30*. These mines once again forced the temporary closure of port installations at Liverpool and Bristol, bringing back painful memories of April 1917. The mining campaign subsided by the spring of 1940 as Dönitz evolved his wolfpack tactics in the mid-Atlantic. The limitations of ASDIC had been proved for all to see. Dönitz could plan in confidence. Intelligence gathered by the U-boats about western coastal waters was incorporated into *Kriegsmarine* Standing Order 481, C II (2b). The U-boats would return – it was only a question of *when*.

For the most part the Battle of the Atlantic was fought far from British shores, but that battle was largely won in the cramped bunker underneath Derby House, Rumford Street, Liverpool. Here the Combined Headquarters HQ of the Western Approaches was established. Admiral Noble, and later Admiral Horton, presided over a maritime spider's web, supported by a knot of stoic wrens. Convoy movements were plotted and U-boat activities monitored. Advanced communications systems linked the bunker with the Trade Division Office and the Submarine Tracking Room in Admiralty. In late 1942 the Western Approaches Tactical Unit (WATU) was established on the upper floor of Derby House with the aim of evaluating A/S tactics. Under Cdr Gilbert Roberts, procedure was analysed, codified and

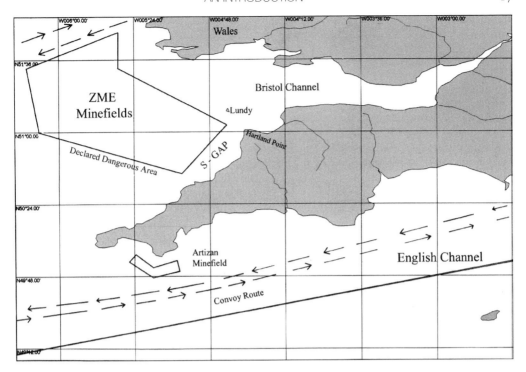

Fig.2:'Convoy Routes and Minefields late 1944 (after Admiralty 1144A).' (R.Young)

revised in the light of bitter experience.[12] It is often said that the Battle of the Atlantic was won as a result of allied superiority in terms of strategy, training, intelligence gathering and tactics. If this is true then much of the credit is due to Derby House and the City of Liverpool.

For the first few months of the Second World War, Admiralty had avoided defensive mine-laying in south-western waters on the grounds that the associated hazards and restrictions would hamper vital commercial operations. Indeed these waters had not been defensively mined during the First World War for these very reasons. The fall of France however brought the Bristol/St George's Channel sector within range of German aircraft. Admiralty therefore commenced routing the OB Atlantic convoys via the North Channel instead. OA coastal convoys now approached Milford and Bristol from the north. A large defensive minefield was laid from Saltees on the Irish coast, across the Bristol Channel to Trevose Head and thence to Hartland Point, coded 'ZME'. This field was internationally declared on 22 July 1940. Importantly, two swept channels were retained. The first (QZF15), used by coastal traffic, hugged the north coast between Trevose Head and Hartland Point. The second (QZF16), designated a 'secret gap' in Admiralty charts, provided transit route through St George's Channel (Fig.3). These swept channels would assume importance during the last phase of submarine warfare in coastal waters.

The first real incursion into the Bristol Channel since the winter of 1940 was made by U 667. Patrolling off Trevose Head on 8 August 1944, U 667 (Karl-Heinz Lange) attacked convoy EBC66, sinking the Ezra Watson and the corvette HMS Regina (Lt J.W. Radford, RCNR) as the warship was rescuing survivors. On 14 August U 667 struck off Hartland Point, this time sinking an American landing craft. The crew of U 667 did not live to enjoy reward as the boat was mined in the La Pallice roads but they had demon-strated it was possible to strike deep in commercially vital western coastal waters and escape unscathed. At this time the U-boats were suffering disastrous losses in attacking the post-D-Day Neptune supply lines (see Vol.2). With the French bases now under direct threat from the allied advance, the U-boats were withdrawn to Norway. The Channel coast was effectively beyond the range of the Norwegian boats but western coastal waters once again became an attractive proposition; BdU rightly deducing that, following the D-Day breakout, allied convoys would once again start using the St George's Channel route. A second great U-boat campaign in the Bristol Channel/Irish Sea was about to get underway.

BdU realised this campaign was likely to prove hazardous. The rules of the game had changed out of recognition since the happy times. The schnorchel-equipped U-boats would have to remain dived for most

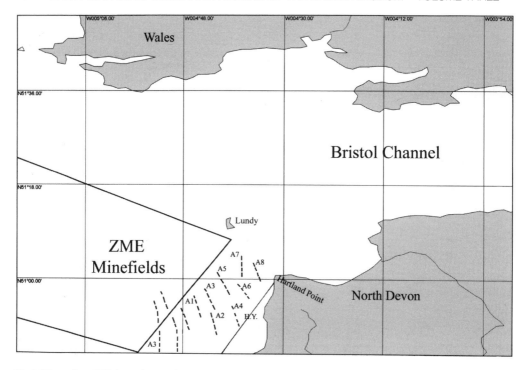

Fig.3: 'Operation CH' closes the 'Southern Gap'. (R.Young)

of the patrol, obtaining navigational fixes by periscope whenever the opportunity arose. Shallow coastal waters left little opportunity for the young crews to practice evasion techniques perfected by *experten* in the Atlantic. *BdU* assured crews that wreck-strewn coastal waters baffled ASDIC. This was partly true but the recently introduced 147B ASDIC set was capable of distinguishing a stationary target from a U-boat. Not everyone shared the optimism of *BdU*. Heinrich Lehmann–Willenbrock, commander of the 11th Flotilla (and model for Bucheim's immortal *Kaleun* in *Das Boot*), later admitted that sending crews on these futile patrols 'cut deep into his heart'. The equally sceptical Reinhard 'Teddy' Suhren, *FdU Nordmeer*, counselled young U-boat officers, 'Just make one attack then bugger off fast!'

On 29 October 1944 *BdU* issued all boats with a situation report on the Bristol Channel. The core of this intelligence, which was clearly based on a captured Admiralty chart of 1943, may be summarised as follows. The Germans were aware of the July 1940 minefield in the middle of the Bristol Channel.[13] The situation report clearly stated that this minefield had never been renewed and may even have been swept, however the presence of minefields inside the declared area was to be assumed. The situation report went on to provide details of the inshore channel, known on British charts as the 'Southern Gap'. The position of this swept channel was given as: 51°05' N 04°43'W as far as 51°02' N 04°32'W to 50°33'N 05°02'W to 50°35'N 05°15'W. *B dienst* added that three convoys per day might be expected here. Ultra decrypts had confirmed German intentions and Admiralty's mindset is evidenced in this communication between the Commander-in-Chief, Western Approaches and Admiralty dated 15 November 1944:

> Further consideration has been given to relative importance of A/S minefields in NW and SW approaches. Routeing of ocean convoys south of Ireland not only renders this more attractive but the U-boats' course of action can be predicted to some extent. In NW approaches mine-laying must follow rather than anticipate U-boat activities. Consider therefore as matter of policy that mine-laying operations should be for present concentrated in SW approaches. It is believed that U-boats will make use of shallow patches and banks to fix their positions without surfacing… the overall plan is to be named 'Operation CH'.

The first part of Operation CH was the laying of the CD (A) and CF fields covering the outer approach to the convoy route south of Ireland and a second field protecting the Labadie Bank. On 25 November 1944, *Apollo* and *Plover* commenced laying the 'HW' and 'HY' series of minefields off the north Cornwall/Devon/Somerset coast, in effect sealing off submarine access to the 'Southern Gap' (Fig.3). 'HW' consisted of three deep lines laid off Trevose Head. 'HY' introduced a further three deep fields between Trevose Head and Hartland Point. Work on the CH series of minefields commenced on 12 January 1945 when *Apollo* and *Ariadne* laid deep fields in the St George's Channel convoy route. These minefields were carefully planned to be deep enough not to hazard maritime traffic while simultaneously posing a deadly barrier to U-boats. Further fields were laid in the Irish Sea off Anglesey. At this point we must leave British coastal waters to briefly delve into the murky world of the *Abwehr*, the German espionage service.

A British-based German spy was apparently aware of 'Operation CH' and attempted to warn his masters, but Admiral Godt was not convinced by either his reports or his loyalties:

> The agent has now reported from England that new minefields, aimed at new types of submarine that do not need to surface, are being scattered in small groups close to the sea bed. As the mines are deep laid they are outside the declared mined zones and in swept channels to counteract submarines that are stalking convoys. Minelayers Plover and Apollo laid over 2,000 mines north of Ireland during September. Information was obtained from a member of the crew of an English minelayer. A further report showed that the above-mentioned minelayers are to lay similar minefields south of Ireland. Report is considered doubtful, as there is no proof that the agent is still reliable. He has already spent three years in England. He is suspected of being a double agent.

> *BdU Diary, 24 November 1944*

It has long been thought that the agent in question was Danish-born Wulf Schmidt, subject of the Gunter Peis book *The Mirror of Deception*. Schmidt, alias 'Agent 3725', operated under the name of 'Harry Smith'. Schmidt had indeed been 'turned' by MI5. According to Peis, double agent Schmidt: 'transmitted to Germany details of alleged minefields… As a result of this report some 3,600 miles were closed to

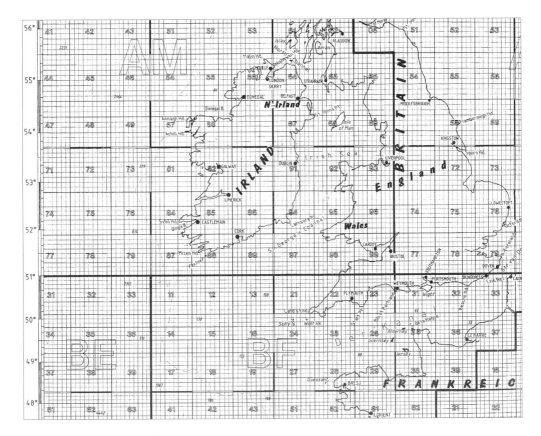

Kriegsmarine grid. (P. Armstrong)

German submarines.' In this instance the *Abwehr* agent may have been telling the truth. MI5 habitually fed him sufficient accurate information to maintain credibility with his *Abwehr* handlers. The implication is that the agent was referring to the imminent laying of the HW/HY minefields in the Bristol Channel. Dönitz temporarily suspended patrols in this sector until *U 1202* had provided a situation report on conditions within the Milford roads (AM 9816). By 2 January 1944 Thomsen and his crew had returned to file an upbeat report, having sunk the Liberty ship *Dan Beard* off Strumble Head on 10 December. For this achievement on this, his first patrol, and for the intelligence he had brought back, Thomsen was awarded a *Rittercreuz*. Digesting the contents of Thomsen's report, on 12 January the *BdU* Diary noted that the British had changed tactics:

> As a result of the submarine successes the enemy moved her route on 11 January to the middle of the Irish Sea (presumably only for single ships).
> South Route: AM 68128, AM 68774 (rendezvous for ships southbound from Liverpool), AM 94336, AM 95961
> North Route: Parallel to the former, but 8 miles to the east. Rendezvous for northbound convoys, 8 miles east of the south traffic rendezvous. All single ships are presumably using these routes.

Experiences of U 1202 in the Irish Sea [14]
A good area for operations, full of possibilities. Heavy convoy traffic, continuous single-ship traffic around points of concentration of convoy routes in AM 9470 – 9570 – 9250. Consequently these are the most favourable submarine stations.
Defence: Mediocre sea defences, aircraft over day and night: all the same, we managed to proceed off-shore, by Schnorchelling, and were never detected. Good conditions for navigation.

1. First passage is to follow the Irish coast 10 miles out, but the navigation part is considered difficult.
2. Second passage through the following positions:

Going south:
55.21 N/06.05 W
54.57 N/05.35 W
54.33 N/05.15 W
53.27 N/04.55 W
52.33 N/05.05 W
51.45 N/05.55 W
51.39 N/05.45 W
51.39 N/05.15 W

Then to Milford Haven:

Going north:
51.39 N/05.15 W
51.39 N/05.45 W
51.45 N/05.45 W
52.33 N/04.55 W
53.27 N/04.45 W
54.33 N/05.05 W
54.57 N/05.15 W
55.21 N/06.05 W

Third passage through:
54.33 N/05.15 W
53.45 N/05.25 W
52.45 N/05.35 W
52.03 N/05.35 W

NARA T-01022, PG 31752

'Barrow, where submarines are born…'
(P. Armstrong)

BdU transmitted these routes to U-boats on 12 January 1945. Seizing upon the *U 1202* report, it confidently dismissed the spy's minefield intelligence. In fact maritime traffic had been moved into the middle of the Bristol Channel not to escape the U-boats as German staff believed, but rather to avoid work in progress on the 'CH' minefields currently being laid across the sea lanes. Patrols in the Bristol Channel/St George's Channel and Irish Sea resumed. The crews of *U 400*, *U 325* and *U 1021* were destined to pay for this misjudgement with their lives. *U 242* was probably destroyed in one of the ZME/QZX fields.

U 1055 (Meyer) enjoyed a profitable patrol on 11 January, when it encountered a dispersing coastal convoy off Anglesey. Dönitz responded to this success by pushing more U-boats into western coastal waters. Once through the minefields, a U-boat could wreak havoc, as the story of *U 1302* illustrates. In this instance, success was short-lived, the crew of *U 1302* dying under the vengeful mortars of EG 25. *U 1051* 'gnatted' HMS *Manners*, before EG 5 detected then destroyed the U-boat. Similarly, *U 1276* succeeded in torpedoing HMS *Vervain* with significant loss of life. Moments later, the pursuing pack of convoy escorts latched onto the U-boat, shattering her with their first Hedgehog attack.

After torpedoing the carrier HMS *Thane* in the Firth of Clyde, *U 1172* slipped into the Irish Sea via the North Channel. When the promising Kuhlmann made an attack on a convoy off Anglesey, EG 5 quickly caught his scent. *U 1172* was cornered and 'Hedgehogged' on 21 January 1945. EG 8 pounced upon *U 1024* as she took up position to attack the inbound HX 346. In this instance *Kplt.* Gutteck managed to surface his boat and many of the crew survived. In each of these cases the U-boat was detected by ASDIC having first made, or in the course of attempting to make, an attack. The manually operated old '123' ASDIC sets of 1940 having been systematically refined, the newest ASDIC sets included recorders which indicated every contact with an underwater object, an automatic oscillator with a repeater on the bridge. Indeed most warships carried two oscillators, the second designed to calculate the trigonometrical equation required to determine depth versus range. Recently built ships were fitted with PPI (Plan Position Indicator) radar sets which enabled the hunter to see even the tip of a *schnorchel* mast, long before the submarine spotted the warship. The hopes placed in ASDIC were thus fully vindicated. The exception to this pattern was *U 246*. Although her probable wreck has been found close to the inbound convoy route north of Anglesey, the cause of this boat's destruction remains a mystery – a sad, anonymous little postscript to the undersea war.

Faced with these losses, *BdU* retreated into a fantasy world, refusing to acknowledge that the U-boat arm was now on the back foot. This denial was possible because it could rely absolutely upon the patriotism, courage and extraordinary *esprit de corps* of the *U-bootwaffe*:

'…and where they sometimes return to die…'. Note the relatively small space taken up by the pressure hull within the casing. (Both P. Armstrong)

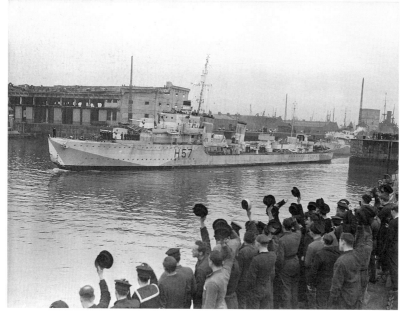

Hesperus returns to Gladstone Dock in triumph. Lower decks have been cleared to 'cheer in' the ship. (IWM A13983)

The submarine war cannot be allowed to cease, since once it has finally succumbed it would not be possible to take it up again. To parry with the enemy is, although a proverb, a tactical, technical, and above all a psychological necessity. The submarine arm has shown itself capable of withstanding the most difficult times. Once again she must carry her self-assertion into the battle with new weapons, even in the face of heavy loss, and without having abandoned the cause even temporarily.[15]

BdU Diary, p358, S14 summary

Aware that deadly new boats were in the offing, Admiralty expected to face a flotilla of Type XX1s by March 1945, but the U-boat men ordered to carry out the holding patrols in British coastal waters might have felt entitled to ask where these 'new weapons' actually were and when might they be expected to enter service?

The answer was that their pre-fabricated sections lay stacked in captured Strasbourg storage sheds, piled up forlornly in wrecked marshalling yards or strewn around canal banks. Accumulator batteries were scattered uselessly in the bombed-out factories of Hagen, Nürnberg and a dozen other devastated corners of the *Reich*. In short, the boats, or rather parts of them, were everywhere except where they were needed most. Even if sufficient Type XXI boats had entered service by March 1945 as the western

'…and the mirth of a seaport dies when our blow gets home…'. (P. Armstrong)

allies feared, they may conceivably have slowed American and British efforts but could have done absolutely nothing to stop the Russian juggernaut poised to roll up the eastern front. Only two Type XXIs actually saw service in March. Their design was flawed; only a handful would ever take to the water. The reality was that the image of these new war-winning submarines was a myth designed to keep Germans fighting. And perhaps the most damning indictment is that the men who sent young crews on suicidal patrols in British coastal waters in late 1944/1945 knew this to be the case.

Turning to look at our area, Milford deserves a special place in any account dealing with the undersea war. Many Q-ships operating in the Irish Sea were crewed by local reservists and the heroic HMS *Prize* (Vol.2) was based in the harbour. The authors were unable to locate a memorial to these men, said to be in St Katherine's Church. Pleasure boats now moor in a harbour once used by a flotilla of Auxiliary Patrol Vessels. There were plenty of U-boats out there in 1917–18. It is a little-known fact that during the First World War the French economy was dependent upon coal imported from Wales and that the colliers sailed via Milford in one of the earliest convoy experiments. In the Second World War, Milford was a vital convoy assembly port. In the months following D-Day, Milford played a leading role in maintaining the Neptune supply lines. The port served as a base for the mine-laying vessels *Plover* and *Apollo*, which proved so instrumental in defeating the U-boats during the inshore campaign of 1945.

Until its closure in 1926, Pembroke Dock was a Royal Dockyard, 'a town built to build ships', gun boats and armoured cruisers to be precise. Too small and specialised to handle battle-cruisers and battleships, the Yard did build a number of submarines including *J3*, *J4*, *H51* and *H52*, but it was a late entrant into submarine building and a depressing number of orders were cancelled. During the Second World War, Pembroke was a major Sunderland Flying Boat station, playing its own special role in the Battle of the Atlantic.

It is impossible to mention submarines without highlighting Britain's pre-eminent submarine builder, Vickers of Barrow. The Yard's rich story lies outside the remit of these pages. Sufficient to add that Devonshire Dock remains the place where British submarines are born and the both the Submarine Heritage Centre and Barrow Docks Museum are an absolute must for anyone interested in this subject. Submarines ended their careers here too. *U 3* foundered en route to be broken up at Preston, while *U9*, *U101*, *UC 52* and *UC 96* were slowly dismantled at Morecambe in the 1920s. Pembroke Dock and Newport's Cashmore Yard became famous for submarine-breaking, but a handful escaped this ignominious fate, *L1* and *E39* both being lost on their way to the scrap yard.

Inevitably this introduction returns to the Mersey, this time over the water at Birkenhead. A visitor who has just made the crossing to Woodside Ferry may be surprised to find a Jules Verne-like submarine replica at the Terminal approaches.

This is a model of *Resurgam* and a reminder that defeat was snatched from the jaws of victory when the little boat sank on her way to a display which may have proven once and for all that George Garrett was the most deserving recipient of the title 'Father of the Submarine'. Birkenhead and the little model of *Resurgam* help keep his achievements alive. Not far away can be found a genuine submarine, a U-boat no less. She may be sliced into three sections and so lack the sinister streamlined beauty of the Type VIIC/41, but as a reminder of the Battle of the Atlantic, *U 534* is as important to the history of Britain as the Tower of London and Hadrian's Wall. It is surely fitting that this unique Type IXC/40 should find a permanent home on the Mersey. The story of *U 534* lies beyond the scope of this book, but submarine and magnificent Visitor Centre cannot be recommended highly enough.

Of course our sketch is not yet complete. Three British submarines were lost in these waters from a combination of terrible error and wrenching bad luck. Journalists who regard 'friendly fire' as a recent phenomenon should study the case of *H5*. The boat was rammed and sunk all because a merchantman mistook her for a U-boat. The facts of her destruction were suppressed for several decades. Then there is the case of *H47*, sunk following an accidental collision with another submarine in 1929. One of the key players in this incident was 'Lucky Joe' Oram who, ten years later, was to be haplessly enmeshed in a yet greater tragedy.

For many years Birkenhead was of course synonymous with the Cammell Laird Yard. In its long history, the Yard built many fine, brave ships. Should the visitor head down Campbeltown Road (formerly Green Lane) he will pass a series of roads named after the Yard's notable ships. He will thus find 'Unicorn Way', 'Alabama Way', 'Valiant Way' and 'Ark Royal Way', but the visitor will look in vain for a road named after the most famous Cammell Laird vessel of them all, HM S/M *Thetis*.

Even after the passage of seventy years, mere mention of the name *Thetis* still strikes a chord with a wartime generation otherwise hardened to maritime tragedy. The *Thetis* incident has not lost its capacity to shock and anger in equal measure. Shock is understandable. The *Thetis* catastrophe was the first of its kind to be covered by the mass media. Everyone in the English-speaking world stopped, watched and waited in numbed silence as newsreel footage captured that stern protruding from the waters of Liverpool Bay, with salvation apparently within inches. To paraphrase the title of a successful play, the rescuers were close enough to touch, yet for the trapped men, rescue proved so very far away. The anger arises largely as a result of murky conspiracy theories which have dogged the events of June 1939. These theories take several forms but the dominant one alleges that on the brink of war, a mendacious British establishment opted to sacrifice the trapped men in order to preserve the integrity of the pressure hull. The *Thetis* disaster has generated books, plays and films. Seventy years on it is high time to re-assess events in Liverpool Bay on the basis of material fact. Incompetence and sheer bad luck all played their part but in this unflinching reappraisal, it is argued that events must be understood within the changing framework of Admiralty submarine rescue policy. Reliance upon DSEA to the exclusion of salvage was to prove a dangerously complacent strategy, turning the *Thetis* incident into the worst peacetime submarine disaster in British maritime history.

Back across the Mersey, the Liverpool known to the wartime generations is changing fast. Even the old sailor pubs have become gentrified. Tourists rather than war-scarred merchant ships now cram into the Albert Dock. Gladstone Dock in Bootle, once home to the convoy escorts, is now the P&O terminal, though here and there wartime buildings are still recognisable. When the escort groups steamed out, Gladstone Dock would reverberate to the strains of 'A Hunting We Will Go' blaring out on the tannoy system. On return, successful groups would steam up the Mersey in line ahead, saluted by the sirens of merchantmen and the ecstatic cheers of onlookers.

We end this introduction where it began, on the Liverpool waterfront. Standing before the Merchant Navy Memorial, the authors invite the reader to reflect on those footnotes of maritime history, the *Formby*s and the *Inverdargle*s and all the other ships that never made it home, their once boisterous crews reduced to faceless names on memorial tablets. The term 'unsung heroes' is a *cliché* but here it is apt. How else can we describe these querulous, exploited, scruffy, boozy, exasperating, stoic, brave, matchless mariners who sailed under the Red Duster and who stood between freedom and tyranny as surely as any branch of the armed services? Liverpool will always cherish their memory. So must we all.

CHAPTER ONE

WALES AND THE WEST

Let us begin this western odyssey by examining a mysterious quartet of U-boats lost off the coast of north Cornwall.

Note: Unless indicated otherwise, fatalities of British civilian vessels belong to the Merchant Navy while by default, British warship fatalities may be classified as Royal Naval in origin. To avoid repetition, technical specifications for Type VIIC U-boats are provided in Appendix 5.

U 325, KRIEGSMARINE U-BOAT

DATE OF LOSS: April 1945
DEPTH: 56m
REFERENCE: 50° 31.4'N, 05° 22.8'W
LOCATION: Off Padstow, north Cornwall

Type: VIIC/41 ocean-going attack boat *Builders:* Flender-Werke AG, Lübeck-Siems for *Kriegsmarine* *Ordered:* on 16 July 1942, within the batch of U 323 – U 328 *Keel laid:* as Yard No.327 on 13 April 1943 *Launched:* on 25 March 1944 *Commissioned:* by *Oblt.z.s.* Erwin Dohrn on 6 May 1944 *Feldpost No.:* M 14 243 *Badge:* Puss-in-boots

Erwin Dohrn was born in Kiel on 18 March 1920 and commenced his career within the Ordnance Branch in 1938, being promoted to *Oblt.z.s.* on 1 April 1943. Dohrn transferred to the seaman *laufbahn* on 15 July 1943.

U 325 was assigned to 4.U-Flottille at Stettin as *Ausbildungsboot* on 6 May 1944 until 30 November 1944, with Erwin Dohrn the only commander. The boat was fitted out with *schnorchel* equipment during October 1944. On 1 December 1944, *U 325* formally transferred to 11.U-Flottille at Bergen.

(1) On 1 December 1944, *U 325* departed Kiel and sailed to Horten, Norway, for frontline service, arriving on 4 December.

(2) *U 325* left Horten on 9 December, calling into Kristiansand. On 11 December she then sailed for the English Channel. After an unsuccessful patrol off Cherbourg, the boat returned to Norway, arriving at Trondheim on 14 February 1944.

FINAL PATROL

(3) The boat left Trondheim on 20 March 1945 for operations off the south-west coast of Britain. On 29 March *BdU* ordered U 325 to occupy grid square BE 3531 only for this instruction to be countermanded next day. On 31 March the boat was given revised orders to continue to grid square BE 31. North of Anglesey a Sunderland Flying boat of 201 Squadron (F/Lt K.H. Foster) apparently caught sight of a U-boat on 30 April. The U-boat was attacked three times, but no hits were recorded.

On 10 April *BdU* ordered *U 325* to patrol the coastal convoy route around Land's End from Bull Point to Lizard Head, with a projected arrival date at this billet on 16/17 April. *BdU* listed *U 325* as missing with effect from 7 April 1945. No explanation exists for the loss of *U 325* and her crew but analysis may bring us closer to a solution.[16]

'A submariner's constant dread'
preserved as a reminder at the
RN Submarine Museum.
(P. Armstrong)

U 325 reported in to *BdU* on 7 April 1945 from position 56° 00'N, 20° 00'W (AL61) on her way to
a billet 'off the Cornish coast'. Nothing further was heard from her. On 29 November 1944 Admiralty
reinforced the older ZME minefields with much deeper ribbons, known as the 'HW/HY A1–A8' series
(Fig.3), designed to destroy any U-boats tempted to sneak through the swept coastal channel or approach
headlands. In the post-war years, British naval intelligence linked the explosion in ZME 25 with the loss
of *U 1021*, which is certainly tenable, though destruction in one of the HW fields seems plausible too. It
is significant that Dr Niestlé argues the case for field A1.

FATALITIES OF *U 325*

Becker Alfred, Mt, 24yrs
Berndt Harry, Mt, 23yrs
Biernath Alfrons, Gft, 24yrs
Bischoff Hans-Erich, 1WO Ob/Tt, 28yrs
Bossbach Arnold, Ob/Gft, 20yrs
Briel Gerd-Heinz, Ob/Gft, 20yrs
Buscmann Horst, Ob/Gft, 21yrs
Buse Arthur, Ob/Gfr, 20yrs
Büttner Walter, Ob/Mt, 26yrs
Chilinski Emil, Ob/Gfr, 25yrs
Eickmann Karl, Ob/Gfr, 21yrs
Fabian Harry, Ob/Mt, 22yrs

Liere Wolf-Karl, Ob/Gfr, 22yrs
Lieske Walter, Mt, 23yrs
Michel, Hans Ob/Gfr, 21yrs
Müller Arnold, Gfr, 20yrs
Niklas Joachim, Lt. Ing, 24yrs
Olscewski Walter, Mt, 23yrs
Podszus Rudolf, Mt, 22yrs
Puls Siegfried, Mt, 24yrs
Ribbeck Heinz, Mt, 25yrs
Schlemmer Hermann, Gfr, 20yrs
Schlüter Heinz, Gfr, 20yrs
Schmidt Robert, Gfr, 20yrs

Grosse August, Mt, 23yrs
Hägele Karl, Gfr, 20yrs
Hausdorf Kurt, Gft, 20yrs
Heise Richard, Gft, 20yrs
Hilpert Heinrich, Ob/Masch, 28yrs
Hortian Hans, Ob/Masch, 26yrs
Jeske Richard, Ob/Gft, 20yrs
Kästle Johann, Gfr, 20yrs
Kimmling Arthur, ObStrm, 25yrs
Kratzke Werner, Ob/Gfr, 22yrs
Kreft, Gerhard Ob/Gfr, 23yrs
Kreutzer Dietrich, Mtr, 20yrs
Krüger Ernst, Haupt.Gfr, 25yrs

Schneede Hans, Mt, 25yrs
Schröder Bernhard, Gfr, 20yrs
Schuster Oktavian, Ob/Gfr, 25yrs
Schwarz Kurt, Gfr, 20yrs
Sicken Fritz, Gfr, 20yrs
Spanier Theodor, Ob/Gfr, 21yrs
Strauss, Martin, 2WO Lt.z.s, 22yrs
Stubner Rudolf, Gfr, 21yrs
Sufka Erich-Richard, Ob/Gfr, 22yrs
Utrecht Horst, Ob/Gfr, 24yrs
Vavru Otto, Mt, 23yrs
Wilhelm Lange, Gfr, 20yrs

WRECK SITE

The U-boat wreck at this location could conceivably be *U 325*, *U 1021* or *U 400*. Recognising a wreck as a late war Type VIIC is straightforward enough, positively identifying the individual submarine is quite another. The shattered and deteriorated wreck, which is possibly the remains of *U 325*, is orientated in an ESE to WNW (110/290-degrees) direction. It lies on a seabed of sand, in a general depth of 56m (183ft) (LAT). This position is just south of the plotted line of minefield (HW) A1. The vessel is upright, but the bows appear to have been blown off – a likely sign of mine detonation. The detached bow section is aligned with the rest of the boat. At the stern, the twin steel screws can be clearly seen (earlier Second World War U-boat propellers were made from bronze). The main section of the wreck is 28m in length, by 7m wide and 7m high at the conning tower. Large shoals of fish swarm around the wreck site which, of course, is a war grave.

NARA Series T-1022, Roll 3900, PG 30360- 30362, PG 31752,

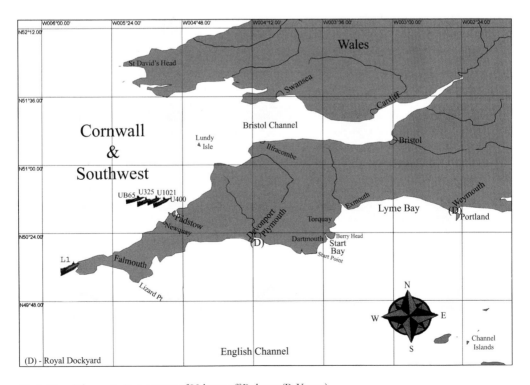

Fig.4: *L1* and the mysterious quartet of U-boats off Padstow. (R.Young)

U 1021, KRIEGSMARINE U-BOAT

DATE OF LOSS: Missing from 14 March 1945
DEPTH: 48m
REFERENCE: 50° 33.271'N, 05° 11.635'W
LOCATION: Off Padstow, north Cornwall

Type: VIIC/41 ocean-going attack boat **Builders:** Blohm & Voß Hamburg for *Kriegsmarine* **Ordered:** on 13 June 1942, within the batch U 1019 – U 1025 **Keel laid:** as Yard No.221 on 6 May 1943 **Launched:** on 13 April 1944 **Commissioned:** by *Oblt.z.s.* William Holpert on 25 May 1944 **Feldpost No.:** M 23 789

U 1021 was assigned to *31.U-Flottille,* Hamburg from 25 May to 30 November 1944, with *Oblt.z.s.* William Holpert the only commander. Interestingly Holpert was born in London on 11 June 1914, becoming a *kadet* in 1934. He served as *Signal-Ob/Mt* (Yeoman of Signals) on the light cruiser *Karlsruhe* from October 1939 to April 1940. After various courses, Holpert was promoted to *Oblt.z.s.* on 1 October 1943, U 1021 being his first U-boat command. On 1 December 1944, Holpert and U 1021 were formally assigned to *11.U-Flottille,* Bergen for operational frontline duties.
 (1) On 4 February 1945 U 1012 left Kiel and arrived at Horten on 8 February.
 (2) U 1021 departed Horten on 10 February 1945 and arrived at Bergen on 13 February.
 (3) On 16 February 1945, U 1021 sailed from Bergen, returning on 19 February.

FINAL PATROL
(4) Departing Bergen on 20 February 1945, U 1021 sailed for British coastal waters.
 On 1 March 1945 BdU ordered the boat to proceed towards the southern edge of AM 70. On 8 March U 1021 was ordered to transit between BF 2251 (Pentire Head) and BF 2371 (Bigbury Bay) prior to taking up patrol in BF 2198. Perhaps significantly, the boat failed to respond to a location request on 10 March, the projected date of arrival in her billet. She failed to return to Trondheim and was posted lost from 5 May. The Royal Naval Historical Branch calculated that U 1021 should have arrived in BF 2198 by 10 March and we must turn to British records for clues to her fate.
 It is known that on the afternoon of 10 March, the minesweepers *Concertator* and *Lorraine* attacked a periscope at 50° 36'N 05° 15'W without result. It is feasible that the boat in question was U 1021. In the immediate post-war period Admiralty assumed her loss had been due to a depth-charge attack carried out by frigates *Conn* and *Rupert* in the Minches on 30 March. However this location is well off track for U 1021 and this attribution seems unlikely in retrospect.[17] One further potential cause of loss must be considered. On 14 March 1945, *Rolfsborg,* a straggler from convoy TBC 95, reported a loud and unexplained underwater explosion at 50° 34'N 05° 47'W, very near the plotted position of ZME 25. Patches of oil were spotted and the absence of any other vessel led to the belief that an enemy submarine had been involved. ZME 25 consisted of 120 mines laid at a depth of 98ft along a line extending 3.04 miles 360° from 50°39.2'N 05° 07.7'W. The position is also close to the A3 (HW) minefield which according to 'British Mining Operations (BR1736(56)(1)' consisted of 156 Mk XVII and thirty-nine XVII mines orientated along a line extending for 3 miles in direction 182.5° from position 50°36.7'N 05°11.1'W at a depth of 70ft. This field, laid by HMS *Apollo* on 3 December 1944, was one of several minefields designed to close off the U-boat route through the swept channel coded 'Southern Gap' on 1940-43 charts. In 1990 the Naval Historical Branch in liaison with Dr Niestlé conceded that the wreck found off the north Cornish coast in the location given above is consistent with U 1021.

FATALITIES OF U 1021
Apel, Herbert, Bts.Mt, 22yrs
Bacht, Gerhard, Masch.Gfr, 20yrs
Biermann, Werner, San.Mt, 22yrs
Bösling, Karl-Heinz, Mtr.Gfr, 20yrs
Böttcher, Reinhold, Masch.Gfr, 20yrs
Braune, Werner, Masch.Gfr, 20yrs
Clemens, Peter, Mech.Ob/Gfr, 21yrs

Ludwig, Rudolf, Mtr, 20yrs
Maiwald, Kurt, Masch.Ob/Gfr, 20yrs
Mehlfeld, Harry, Masch.Gfr, 20yrs
Müller, Sebastian, Mech.Gfr, 20yrs
Piezonna, Heinz, Masch.Mt, 23yrs
Radde, Willi, Fk.Ob/Gfr, 20yrs
Reininger, Fritz, Ofk.Mt, 26yrs

TypeVIIC/41 boats laid up at Lisahally following surrender in 1945. Note *schnorchel* mast recesses and variations in radar antennae.The cylindrical life raft canisters provide a useful means of identifying late war U-boats. (P.Armstrong)

Dreyer, Hans-Joachim, Oblt.z.s., 22yrs
Fuhrmann, Horst, Fk.Ob/Gfr, 20yrs
Gartenschläger, Heinz, Bts.Mt, 25yrs
Gericke,Willi, Mech,Gfr, 20yrs
Glaser,Walter, Masch.Mt, 22yrs
Götz, Georg, Masch.Ob/Gfr, 20yrs
Grabozewski, Leo, Ob/Strm, 29yrs
Heymons, Oswald, Lt.z.s, 21yrs
Hilbeck,Walter Mtr.Gfr, 20yrs
Holpert,William, Ob/Lt.z.s, 31yrs
Ihlenfeldt, Helmut, Ob/Lt. Ing, 21yrs
Käsler, Kurt, Fk.O/Gfr, 22yrs
Keilhofer, Johann, Mtr.Gfr, 21yrs
Klein, Mathias, Mtr.Gfr, 20yrs
Kruchinski, Helmut, Mtr.Ob/Gfr, 20yrs

Rieth, Kurt-Georg, Masch.Mt, 26yrs
Rodinger, Justus, Ob/Gfr, 21yrs
Röscheisen, Heinz, Mtr, 21yrs
Rothe, Gerhard, Masch.Gfr, 20yrs
Ruthowski, Edmund Ob/Gfr, 21yrs
Sädler, Fritz,, Masch.Gfr, 20yrs
Schilde, Heinz, Masch.Mt, 24yrs
Schreiber, Jakob, Mtr.Ob/Gfr, 21yrs
Simianowski, Masch.Gfr, 22yrs
Sonntag, Kurt,Ob/Masch, 28yrs
Sonntag,Wolfgang, Masch.Gfr, 20yrs
Thormann, Gerhard, Mech.Mt, 25yrs
Wehling, Hans-Joachim, Ob/Masch, 30yrs
Weiß,Wilhelm, Masch.Mt, 23yrs

WRECK SITE

The wreck identified as *U 1021* is orientated in a SE to NW (155/335-degrees) direction. The location is indeed close to the plotted position of field A3. It lies on a firm seabed of sand, in a general depth of 48m (157ft) (LAT). The wreck is upright, but broken into two parts and listing about fifteen degrees to port. The bows are lying about 15m in front of the main section. Four pressurised life-raft recesses on the forward deck denote a late war boat. The hatches are all closed and the dual battery of anti-aircraft guns has been removed from what little remains of the *wintergarten*. The *schnorchel* has broken off and lies alongside. Close examination of this structure by Innes McCartney and Dr Axel Niestlé has identified a Type 1 model with ball float valve.Traces of anti-radar coating have been noted on this fitting. From the three U-boat candidates, only *U 1021* is known to have been fitted with this type of *schnorchel* and the life-raft recesses, enabling Dr Niestlé to finally confirm her identity. It is therefore probable that *U 1021* ran into the A3 minefield, blocking the former swept channel between Rumps Point and Tintagel Head in mid-March 1945. This wreck is of course a war grave.

NARA SeriesT-1022, PG 31752

U 400, KRIEGSMARINE U-BOAT

DATE OF LOSS: 17 December 1944
DEPTH: 55m
REFERENCE: 50° 31.401'N, 05° 22. 861'W
LOCATION: Off Padstow, north Cornwall

Type: VIIC ocean-going attack boat *Builders:* Howaldtswerke AG, Kiel-Gaarden for Kriegsmarine *Ordered:* on 25 August 1941, within the batch of U 399 – U 400 *Keel laid:* as Yard No.32 on 18 November 1942 *Launched:* on 8 January 1944 *Commissioned:* by *Kplt*. Horst Creutz on 18 March 1944 *Feldpost No.:* M 49 932 *Badge:* A stork in a cross standing in water, set within a shield

U 400 was assigned to 5.U-Flottille, Kiel from 18 March to 31 October 1944 as *Ausbildungsboot*, with *Kplt*. Horst Creutz the boat's only commander. Horst Creutz was born in Pankow, Germany on 19 May 1915 and commenced his naval career in 1935, serving on the heavy cruiser *Admiral Hipper* from December 1939 to March 1943. He was promoted to *Kplt*. on 1 December 1942. Creutz commenced U-boat training in March 1943, being assigned to the new *U 40* on 18 March 1944.

On 1 November 1944, *U 400* and Creutz were formally assigned to 11.*U-Flottille*, Bergen, for front-line operational duties.
(1) On 5 November 1944 *U 400* left Kiel, arriving at Aarhus, Denmark, on 6 November.
(2) Leaving Aarhus on 9 November, *U 400* arrived at Horten next day.
(3) On 15 November, the boat departed Horten for Kristiansand, arriving next day.

LAST PATROL

(4) Departing Kristiansand on 18 November, Horst Creutz was ordered to patrol British coastal waters. On 28 November 1944 *BdU* ordered the boat to square AM 70. On 4 December 1944, *U 400* was ordered to patrol along the coastal convoy route off Land's End as replacement for *U 680*. The boat was expected to have reached her billet in BF22 by 16 December. *BdU* anticipated that Creutz would turn helm for home on or around 30 December but it is worth noting that no position report was made from this boat, even when one was explicitly requested by *BdU* on 8 January 1945. The boat was officially posted as missing with effect from 3 January.

It is possible that *U 400* reached her patrol area. A U-boat sighting as early as 10 December caused Admiralty to route vessels in the Bristol Channel outbound for Milford to proceed via the Mumbles or the Barry Roads. *U 400* was expected to operate around the south Cornish coast and the Plymouth roads, however she may have approached north Devon and the Hartland Point region to obtain a navigational fix.

FATALITIES OF *U 400*

Bauer, Willi, Mtr.Ob/Gfr, 21yrs
Bonneß, Wilhelm, Ob/Masch, 27yrs
Brune, Wolfgang, Mech.Gfr, 26yrs
Bublitz, Hans, Masch.Ob/Gfr, 20yrs
Cappel, Otto, Ob/Bts Mt, 25yrs
Creutz, Horst, Kplt., 30yrs
Dipp, Wilhelm, Fk.Mt, 22yrs
Dlugosch, Gotthard, Ob/Strm, 27yrs
Dorr, Helmut, Mtr.Ob/Gfr, 21yrs
Ebert, Herbert, Mtr.Ob/Gfr, 20yrs
Eichelmann, Gerhard, Masch.Ob/Gfr, 20yrs
Eichler, Kurt, Fk.Ob/Gfr, 20yrs
Engel, Bruno, Masch.Gfr, 21yrs
Engelhardt, Alexander, Mtr.Ob/Gfr, 21yrs
Enskat, Erich, Mtr.Gfr, 20yrs
Frahm, Günter, Masch.Ob/Gfr, 21yrs
Gärtner, Gerhard, Mech.Gfr, 20yrs

Himpel, Ingomar, Mtr.Gfr, 20yrs
Huhn, Friedrich, Mtr.Ob/Gfr, 20yrs
Ingerling, Georg, Masch.Ob/Gfr, 21yrs
Jakesch, Otto, Fk.Ob/Gfr, 21yrs
Kamphausen, Herbert, Masch.Mt, 24yrs
Klein, Ulrich, Fk.Ob/Gfr, 21yrs
Kleinmann, Ernst, Ob/Masch, 30yrs
Kunze, Werner, Masch.Gfr, 24yrs
Küpper, Horst, Masch.Gfr, 20yrs
Labuhnm, Kurt, Masch.Ob/Gfr, 22yrs
Laue, Werner, Masch.Mt, 23yrs
Leistner, Heinz, Mech.Mt, 25yrs
Lipinski, Alfons, Masch.Mt, 25yrs
Maas, Wilhelm, Bts.Mt, 26
Naumann, Hermann-Berhard Lt.z.s, 22yrs
Növe, Horst-Erich, Lt. Ing, 22yrs
Rosen, Wilhelm, Masch.Mt, 21yrs

Gier, Helmut, Masch.Ob/Gfr, 21yrs
Graßhoff, Werner, Masch.Mt, 22yrs
Gründinger, Josef, Mtr.Ob/Gfr, 20yrs
Häger, Hilmar, Mech.Ob/Gfr, 20yrs
Hanke, Wilhelm, Mtr.Ob/Gfr, 20yrs
Helwich, Kurt, Ob San.Mt, 26yrs
Herold, Franz, Mtr.Ob/Gfr, 20yrs
Hertlein, Johann, Mtr.Gfr, 20yrs

Rudolph, Paul, Masch.Ob/Gfr, 22yrs
Schmid, Adolf, Masch.Mt, 25yrs
Schön, Walter, Lt.z.s, 21yrs
Schröder, Ernst, Fk.Mt, 25yrs
Schulze, Alfred, Obts.Mt, 26yrs
Seibert, Helmut, Masch.Ob/Gfr, 21yrs
Strobl, Richard, Masch.Ob/Gfr, 22yrs
Willms, Ubbo, Mtr.Ob/Gfr, 20yrs

WRECK SITE

The wreck of *U 400* is orientated in an east to west (080/260-degrees) direction. It lies on a seabed of sand, in a general depth of 55m (180ft) (LAT). The position of this wreck corresponds to the southern extremity of minefield (HY) A1, laid at a depth of 70ft by *Apollo* on 29 November 1944. As for the wreck itself, it is upright and intact, but has a 10m hole through the pressure hull on the starboard side, abaft the conning tower, most probably caused by a mine exploding. The fact that the conning tower hatch is closed and the *schnorchel* extended, all points to the boat having been mined. It is known that *U 400* was equipped with an old Type 1 folding *schnorchel* and this is still present. Interestingly, although deck guns were phased out of Type VIIC production, a large circular gun mounting plate can be found on the deck. As *U 325* was never fitted with such a plate, Dr Niestlé has been able to identify this wreck as *U 400*. *U 400* had been fitted with a prototype Type 43, 3.7cm AA-gun. While the mounting plate is present, the gun itself has disappeared. This wreck is of course a war grave.

NARA Series T-1022 Rolls 4066,3981, PGs30358–30362
Additional information provided by Mr Bob Coppock, Royal Naval Historical Branch (FDS) and Dr Axel Niestlé.

UB 65, SM IMPERIAL U-BOAT

DATE OF LOSS: July 1918
DEPTH: 54m
REFERENCE: 50° 40.107' N, 005° 02.123' W
LOCATION: 7 miles off Padstow, north Cornwall

Type: UBIII coastal torpedo attack boat *Builders:* AG Vulcan, Hamburg for Kaiserliche Deutsche Marine *Ordered:* on 20 May 1916, within the batch of UB 60 – UB 65 *Keel laid:* as Yard No.90 *Launched:* on 26 June 1917 *Commissioned:* by *Oblt.z.s.* Martin Schelle on 18 August 1917

TECHNICAL SPECIFICATIONS

Hull: double *Surface displacement:* 508 tons. *U/Dt:* 639 tons *LBDH:* 55.52m × 5.75m × 3.68m × 8.25m *Machinery:* 2 × 550ps MAN diesels *Props:* 2-bronze. *S/Sp:* 13.3 knots. *Op/R:* 8,420-n.miles @ 6 knots *Sub/R:* 55-n.miles @ 4kts *U/Power:* 2 × 394ps electric motors gave 8kts *Batteries:* AFA lead/acid/accumulators *Fuel/Cap:* 32 & 36 tons *Armament:* 4-bow & 1-stern 50.04cm torpedo tubes *Torpedoes:* 10 × 50.04cm (19.7in) *Guns:* 1 × 105mm (4.13in) forward deck gun *Ammo:* 160 rounds of 105mm *Mines:* none *Diving:* max-op-depth 50m (164ft) & 30-sec to crash-dive *Complement:* 3-officers & 31-ratings.

UB 65 was formally assigned to the German-based V.U-Flottille at Bremerhaven from 30 September 1917, with *Oblt.z.s.* Martin Schelle the commander from 18 August 1917.

(1) On 10 October 1917 *UB 65* sailed from Bremerhaven for patrol around the Hebrides, via the Shetlands, returning to base on 4 November 1917 after an uneventful patrol.

(2) Leaving Germany on 6 December 1917, *UB 65* sailed for operations in St George's Channel, via the Straits of Dover. On 12 December, some 40 nautical miles off Tuskar Rock, Schelle captured and sank the 992-ton Swedish barque *Belleville* (1877 – Aktieb. Bellville, Hall Shipping Co., Landskrona)

Left: UB 65 under construction at Wilhelmshaven and minus her upper casing. Note how unlike the design of British submarines, the conning tower is enveloped within the pressure hull. (U-boot Archiv)

Below: The fore-ends of a UB boat, crowded abode of the 'Lords'. (P. Armstrong)

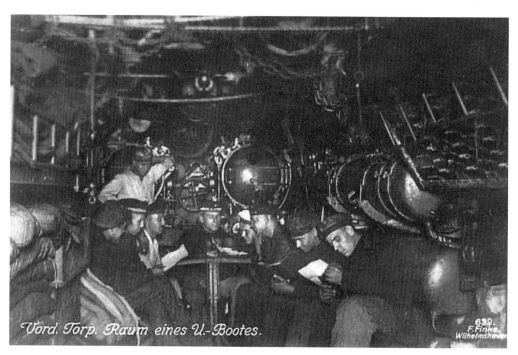

with explosives. *Belleville* was carrying pitch from Fleetwood to Cadiz. Later that day, the defensively armed merchantman *Charleston* (1908 – Furness, Withy & Co. Ltd, West Hartlepool) was captured in St George's Channel, 30 miles west of the Smalls. Two DAMS gunners were taken prisoner before the vessel was scuttled with explosive charges. The vessel was carrying stores and coal from Cardiff to Berehaven in Ireland.

In St George's Channel on 14 December, some 27 miles from Bardsey Island, the 1,418-ton Norwegian steamer SS *Nor* (1901 – D/S A/S Nor, Bergen) was sent to the bottom with a torpedo. *Nor* had been en route from Caen to Glasgow in ballast at the time. From her crew of eighteen, two men, Anders Hovde (20) and Karl Danvik Andersen (28), died. Next *UB 65* confronted a warship.

The 1,290-ton 'Anchusa' Class sloop HMS *Arbutus* (1917 – Cdr Charles Oxlade, RD, RNR) was based at Milford Haven as a 'convoy sloop'. Her role was to carry out A/S sweeps in advance of expected convoy arrivals. On 15 December 1917 *Arbutus* was steaming in company with the American destroyer, USS *O'Brien* when a warning was transmitted at 0930hrs that a U-boat had been spotted in the sector. *Arbutus* was detached to investigate and at 1500hrs the Admiralty trawler *Okino* confirmed by wireless transmission that a U-boat was indeed prowling 16 miles WSW of the Smalls Lighthouse. When a submarine was spotted Cdr Oxlade ordered his men to action stations. At 1600hrs, as *Arbutus* approached the location of the sighting at 51° 31'N 5° 55'W, a torpedo detonated on her port side, flooding the boiler and engine rooms in minutes.

With the ship still underway, a disturbance in the water was thought to be the submarine. Cdr Oxlade ordered that the 'D' depth-charge be dropped, set for 80ft. There were cheers when a significant amount of oil was spotted on the surface following detonation. Oxlade and his crew were in no condition to chase submarines however. Faced with steady flooding, he had no option but to order his crew to abandon ship. During this time, the American destroyer circled the stricken *Arbutus*, protecting her from further torpedo attacks.

Lt Alfred Eastley:

> It was the general opinion that the ship might crack in half at any time. The captain wished us to leave him and of course we vigorously protested. When the last of the men had been evacuated we insisted on standing by with the captain, or as an alternative course persuade him to leave the ship with us. Ultimately it lay between the Navigator and myself as to who should remain with the captain and it was decided by the toss of a coin that the Navigator should remain. Previous to leaving I pointed out to the captain that there was no boat or raft left in the case of the ship sinking. I embarked in the gig leaving the captain and Lt Stewart alone on the bridge.

ADM 137/3292

A short time later HMS *Arbutus* broke up and sank, taking her captain and Lt Stewart with her.

FATALITIES OF HMS *ARBUTUS*, 15.12.17
Bunker, Samuel, Stoker PO, 23yrs
Croskery, John, Stoker PO, 25yrs
Halliwell, Thurston, Steward 2nd class, 18yrs
Jones, George, Stoker 1st class
Oxlade, Charles Herbert, (RD) Cdr
Phillips, William, Stoker 2nd class, 19yrs
Pickett, George, Stoker, RNR, 20yrs
Rowley, Walter W.J., Painter 2nd class
Stewart, Charles, Act/Temp Lt, RNR

Two days later, a destroyer attacked *UB 65*. The depth-charges badly damaged the periscope, forcing Schelle to abort the patrol. *UB 65* returned to Germany on 29 December 1917.

(3) *UB 65* left Helgoland in convoy with *U 104* on 2 February 1918 and the minesweepers parted company south of Horn's Riff. The patrol was aborted and the two boats returned to base the following day, travelling via the Skagerrak but *UB 65* put into Wilhelmshaven.

(4) On 19 February 1918, *UB 65* sailed from Helgoland for operations in the Irish Sea, via the *norweg*. On 2 March and 20 miles ESE of Tuskar Lightship, Schelle torpedoed the 1,150-ton Norwegian SS *Havna* (1908 – Aktieselskapet Havna, Kristiania): *Havna* was transporting iron ore from Seville to Maryport and she sank like a stone. From her crew of eighteen the following men died:

FATALITIES OF SS *HAVNA*, 2.3.18
Ahlfeldt, Karl, Donkeyman from Sweden
Burger, Frederick, Cook from Holland
Frantzen, Halfdan, 1st Mate

Johnson, Albert, Stoker from Sweden
Monsen, Magne, 1st Engineer from Bergen
Pedersen, Alf, Sailor from Kristiania
Rylander, Karl, Sailor from Sweden
Svendson, Waldemar, Sailor from Sweden
Terpet, Nils, Sailor from Hirthals/Denmark
Voetetz, Henrik, Engine Boy from Holland
Roadley, Charles, Signalman (DAMS) RNVR, 23yrs

On 15 March 1918, the U-boat arrived back at Helgoland. *UB 65* and the crew formally transferred to II.U-*Flottille* at Helgoland on 18 April 1918.

(5) Departing Helgoland on 22 April 1918, *UB 65* once again sailed for operations in the Irish Sea. On 4 May, Schelle tangled with a couple of armed merchants in St George's Channel, off the Skerries. The 449-ton *M.J. Headley* (1891 – Calico Printers Assoc. Ltd, Manchester) was steaming to Cork from Runcorn, loaded with sulphur phosphate. Her chief engineer William Pearn died of a heart attack during the engagement but the ship reached Holyhead in a damaged state.[18]

The second ship was 4,316-ton *Pensilva* (1913 – Pensilva SS Co. Ltd, Falmouth), which also returned the fire. Fearing the engagement would attract every A/S vessel in the sector, *UB 65* eventually broke off the fight, leaving the steamship damaged but seaworthy.

Two further ships were attacked on 8 May. The 335-ton British coaster SS *Elizabetta* (1911 – James Henry Monks (Preston) Ltd, Liverpool) was damaged by shell fire, about 15 miles off Lucifer Light-vessel. The ship was transporting burnt-ore from Dublin to Cardiff at the time of the attack. *Elizabetta* was forced to put into Milford Haven to assess the damage.

The other ship was the 586-ton wooden-hulled Danish barque *Thoralf* (1896 – Sejlskibsselskabet Bark 'Thoralf' A/S, Copenhagen), which was commanded by Capt Simon Peter Andersen of Thurø. The barque was carrying 591 tons of logwood from Black River, Jamaica to Fleetwood when she was attacked at 0700hrs, 20 miles south-east of Coningbeg Lightship. A torpedo streaked past 3ft aft of the rudder. Capt Anderson ordered the sail reduced and boats launched. Minutes later *UB 65* surfaced, Schelle doubtless concluding *Thoralf* was not worth wasting a second torpedo and that bombs must suffice. The sailing ship's crew had by this time taken to the lifeboats in anticipation of what was to follow. Hailing them with a loudspeaker, Schelle ordered the crew to go alongside. The master and four seamen were taken on board the U-boat. *Thoralf* was looted then burned down to the waterline. A black sailor was seized but the remainder was allowed back into their lifeboats. A passing steamship spotted the forlorn men and landed them at Queenstown. The fate of the Jamaican is unknown.

Schelle wisely withdrew from the sector and by 13 May, on her return journey up the Irish coast, *UB 65* encountered an inbound convoy 35 miles off Lough Swilly. Schelle fired a torpedo at the 4,981-ton steamer *Esperanza de Larringa* (Master T. Newton, 1907 – Miguel de Larrinaga SS Co. Ltd, Liverpool). The ship was carrying general cargo from Galveston, Texas and Newport News, Virginia bound for Manchester. Chief Engineer Harry Westhorpe reboarded the vessel with four firemen. Working waist deep in water and oil, they managed to start the engines and keep them running. The damage to *Esperanza de Larringa* was not fatal and the depth-charge onslaught which followed prevented Schelle from finishing her off. The ship was beached in Swilly Bay.

UB 65 returned to Helgoland on 19 May.

FINAL PATROL

(6) *UB 65* sailed from Helgoland on 2 July 1918 for operations in her customary billet of the Bristol Channel, St George's Channel and the Irish Sea. Once again the *norweg* route was taken. On 4 July, *UB 65* transmitted the reported sighting of a British submarine in the North Sea, probably *G6*.

Schelle possibly sank the 185-ton Portuguese *Maria Jose* off Lundy Island on 14 July but it is far more likely that this sailing boat was *destroyed* by *UB 108,* the implication being that Schelle and his crew were already dead by this time, for after 4 July the trail goes dead. Nothing was ever heard from the U-boat or her crew again. For decades it was thought that American records held the key to her fate. The USN submarine *L2* (Lt P Foster) investigated a mysterious buoy off Cape Clear at 1830hrs on 10 July 1918, in location 51° 07'N, 09° 42'W. As the American submarine approached, a violent explosion was followed by a 'geyser' of water. As it subsided, a periscope was allegedly spotted. Now certain he was looking at a U-boat, Foster prepared to ram. Then the periscope disappeared. For about twenty minutes the hydrophone operator reported HE, thereafter, silence. In the years that followed, some authorities assumed the mystery U-boat had been the missing *UB 65*, possibly destroyed by a torpedo malfunction. Spindler certainly considered this a plausible explanation. They were wrong. In recent years a First World War UB III class U-boat was discovered following a survey off Padstow. In 2003, Innes McCartney dived this wreck. Evidence enabled Innes and Dr Axel Niestlé, to positively identify it as *UB 65*.

FATALITIES OF *UB 65*

Baar, Albert, Heizer	Knof, Arthur, Matrose
Bauer, Paul, Heizer	Kroll, Eduard, MaschinistenMt
Bock, Richard, Matrose	Külpmann, Joseph, Matrose
Brose, Anton, Steuermann	Luding, Karl, MaschinistenMt
Baar, Paul, Heizer	Münchmeyer, H., Lt. zur See
Deutschbein, F., Ob/Masch.Mt	Rediek, Otto, Matrose
Dietrich, Eugen, Ob/Heizer	Reinken, Bernhard, Ob/Matrose
Eggers, Willi, MaschinistenMt	Richters, Friedrich, Matrose
Elsner, W, MaschinistenMt	Sander, Paul, U-MaschinistenMt
Eppel, Ludwig, Heizer	Schein, Hans, U-BootsmannsMt
Fassbender, P., Heizer	Schelle, Martin, Ob/Lt. zur See
Glogau, Paul, F.T.Mt	Schmidt, Fritz, Ob/Matrose
Hall, Joseph, Heizer	Schnabel, Franz, Marine Ingenieur der Reserve
Hardenberg, P., Matrose	Schug, Johann, Matrose
Hess, Alfred, Matrose	Siegel, Eduard, Heizer
Jüngst, Friedrich, F.T.Gast	Steinfeld, P., Maschinist d.Seew.II
Karrenbauer, Heizer	Vespermann, E., Ob/Matrose
Kist, August, Ob/Heizer	Wende, Hermann, MaschinistenMt
Klusmann, W., Heizer	Wilsky, Karl, Masch.Anw

WRECK SITE

The wreck lies on a seabed of sand and shingle, in a general depth of 60m (196ft). It is intact and upright, with the propellers, deck gun and conning tower all in place. Age has taken its toll on the casing which is rapidly disintegrating. As mentioned, the submarine featured in a television documentary in the 'Wreck Detectives' series. The propellers were found to be engraved with U-boat numbers enabling Dr Axel Niestlé to identify it as *UB 65* but the cause of destruction proved more mysterious. The absence of any obvious damage to the hull and structure is consistent with the lack of any recorded A/S confrontations during the period concerned. Nor is there any evidence of explosion, either internal or external. The bow tube doors appear to be closed: with the exception of the closed fore-end hatch, the remaining hatches are open. A diving accident remains a strong probability. The UB III class were prone to a sudden loss of buoyancy in the stern but the pattern of open and closed hatches suggests that whatever overcame *UB 65*, the problem affected the bow section first. One scenario is that the boat was operating 'conned down' to avoid being spotted. It is possible that the submarine encountered a fresh water layer, became bodily heavy and plunged without warning. The effect of salt water cascading through open hatches can be imagined. The crew may have made an escape attempt via the conning tower and engine room hatches but this attempt was doomed by virtue of the depth and the hostile conditions. This is, of course, pure speculation. The end of *UB 65* remains as enigmatic as her spectral crewman.

Sailors are notoriously superstitious. They react to weather portents, they treasure cauls and some believe in ghosts. According to some *UB 65* was haunted. Legend has it that *UB 65* was cursed from the outset. When the boat was under construction a girder slipped from its cradle, mortally injuring one man and maiming a second. A few months later, a second accident occurred. Deadly chloride fumes overcame three engineers who were testing the boat's dry cell batteries. On returning from her patrol in October 1917, a torpedo explosion alongside fatally wounded her *IIWO* and the ghost stories began in earnest. A hideously disfigured phantom was glimpsed on patrol, standing on the bow casing as the boat was diving. A smell of decomposition was permanently present in the fore-ends. Even when the boat was in dock, the ghost was seen flitting through the compartments. One version has it that Schelle himself saw the ghost. Rumour spread throughout the Flotilla to the extent that the authorities were forced to step in to quell the tales. The submariners were forbidden on pain of punishment to mention the ghost but a Lutheran minister was brought in to perform an exorcism all the same. It did little good because as we know, the doomed submarine was lost with all hands on her sixth patrol.

That is the ripping yarn, what follows are the facts. There is not the slightest grain of evidence in support of any of the salient points of the story. Michael Lowrey scrutinised the KTB of *UB 65* and found no reference to any torpedo explosion, plus, refits were of a standard duration. Bendert is equally silent on the matter. German sources affirm there were no accidents during her building. No sailors were swept overboard and no officer died in an explosion. *IWO* Adolf Eckoldt left for another boat and survived the War, *Lt. z. S.* Henry Münchmeyer (appointed April 1918) and *LI* Fritz Schnabel (appointed October 1917) were lost on the last patrol. Some have suggested that the ghost story and attendant portents of disaster may have in some way resulted from a crisis of morale within the riven *KDM* of 1918. However this theory is undermined by the fact that until August 1918, the dominant belief in Germany and beyond was that Ludendorff was winning the war. Evidence indicates that morale amongst U-boat crews remained remarkably high in spite of the losses. The legend is post-war and does not appear in German accounts. Some detect the fertile imagination of Lowell Thomas. At any rate the story appears in countless anthologies.

With or without a resident phantom, the wreck of SM *UB 65* is now protected by law and no diving is allowed without special permission. Besides you might wind up with company that you didn't bargain for...

Norwegian Maritime Declarations 1914-1918
ADM 137/3292

L1, HM SUBMARINE

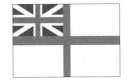

DATE OF LOSS: 28 March 1930
DEPTH: 1-2m
REFERENCE: 50° 07.10'N, 05° 42.08'W
LOCATION: Penanwell beach, under Carn Gloose

Type: L1 Class (Emergency war programme L1-L8) Pennant: L1 **Builders:** Vickers of Barrow **Keel laid:** 18.5.16 **Launched:** 10.5.17 **Commissioned:** 10.11.17

One of the first 'L' boats on sea trials; note the civilian personnel. (P. Armstrong)

Hull: Admiralty Saddle Tank *Surface displacement:* 891 tons *U/Dt:* 1,074 tons *LBD:* 70.4m x 17.2m x 4m *Machinery Props:* 2 x Vickers/Admiralty diesel engines 2 x electric motors BHP Surface: 2,400 hp/1,600 hp knots Sp: 17/10.5 knots BHP Submerged: 1,600 *Op R:* 3,800nm *Armament:* Group I had six X 18in torpedo tubes (four bow, two beam tubes, ten torpedoes carried in total. *L1* had the beam tubes removed after the war *Guns:* As completed *L1* and *L2* were equipped with 1 x 3in quick-firing gun, later replaced by a 4in gun at bridge deck level *Complement:* 35

(Source: BR3043, Ch 11)

By 1916 Admiralty was favouring saddle tank-types of submarine construction but seeking a design which would deliver higher speeds. Two experimental elongated 'E' class submarines were ordered from Vickers in February 1916 and, named *E57* and *E58*. By the time of completion both vessels had evolved into a new type named the 'L' Class. These boats were later renamed *L1* and *L2*.

Commanding Officers
08.06.17 – 09.09.18 Lt-Cdr Reginald Darke
09.09.18 – 11.11.18 Lt Cromwell Varley (see *H5* entry)

1st Lieutenants:
28.06.17 – 11.11.18 S-Lt Jocelyn S. Bethell

Third Hands:
26.07.17 – 01.01.18 Lt Gerald Portch
01.02.18 – 01.07.18 Lt Benjamin Bolt
01.08.18 – 01.09.18 Lt Charles St John
12.10.18 – 11.11.18 Lt William Mackenzie

Engineers:
01.06.17 – 30.05.18 Art.Eng. John Hird
01.07.18 – 11.11.18 Art.Eng. Alfred Nash

L1 was initially stationed at Berehaven, Ireland to operate with the Ambrose Flotilla as part of Jellicoe's energetic A/S campaign (see *H5* entry).

26.02.18 – 06.03.18
L1 left Berehaven with *E54* for 'QF' patrol (a billet patrolling Lat. 50°00'N and between Long. 07°W,08°W) On 1 March the boat was redirected to position 51°55'N,13°50'W where Darke was to investigate reports of two U-boats engaged in cable-cutting. There were no sightings and *L1* returned to Berehaven with *E54*.

14.03.18 – 22.03.18
Once again *L1* left Berehaven in company with *E54* and American boat *AL3*, this time for a 'QA' patrol (parallel of Lat. 51°35' N and between Long. 06°W, 07°W)
    On 21 March *L1* was fired upon in error by two Auxiliary Patrol trawlers in position 51°35' N,06°46'W. The boat returned to Berehaven undamaged.
    On 31 March 1918 L1 was assigned to Blockhouse with HMS *Ambrose*, *L7* and *E54*. For the remainder of the War, *L1* was engaged in A/S patrols in the English Channel.

08.05.18 – 15.05.18
L1 left Portsmouth for East Northern-patrol (between Lat. 50°35'N,50°25'N and between Long. 00°16'W,00°25'W). Boat returned to Portsmouth, no sightings.

01.06.18 – 08.06.18
L1 left Portsmouth for another East Northern-patrol, returned to Portsmouth, no sightings.

The Rover's Return. *L1* aground at Carn Gloose. (P. Armstrong)

19.06.18 – 26.06.18
The boat left Portsmouth for East Northern-patrol, returned to Portsmouth, no sightings.

01.07.18 – 07.7.18
The boat left Portsmouth for patrol with a trawler escort. The Log describes an encounter on 2 July at 0130hrs when the boat was 2 miles east of Owers Light-vessel: 'Sighted enemy submarine about one point on port bow steering N70. Proceeded to attack. 0145hrs Fired starboard lower torpedo 0201hrs Two depth charges dropped by trawler escort.'

L1 missed *UB 57* (*Oblt.z.s.* Lohs). Lohs evaded *L1* and HMT *Sweeper* and was oblivious to the torpedo attack. This was *L1*'s one and only attack in anger.

13.07.18 – 20.07.18
L1 left Portsmouth for yet another East Northern-patrol. The boat returned to Portsmouth, no sightings.

25.07.18 – 01.08.18
L1 left Portsmouth for another routine East Northern-patrol. On 27 July the boat was chased by HMT *Curran, P 40* and *Joseph Coates*. Fortunately *L1* was able to identify herself before a sustained depth-charge attack developed. The boat returned to Portsmouth, with no further sightings. The war might be over but for *L1* and her crew, the adventure was about to begin.

In March 1919, *L1* sailed with HMS *Ambrose* and *L3, L4, L7, L15* and *L9* to form the nucleus of the 4th Submarine Flotilla based at the China Station. The boats reached Bombay on 27 October 1919 and by November had arrived at the fabled anchorage of Wei Hai Wei on the Shandong peninsula (aka Port Edward). By maintaining an essentially flag-waving flotilla in the China seas, Admiralty hoped to impress the Chinese while simultaneously countering any belligerent ambitions on the part of the Japanese and Bolshevik Russians. Traditionally the 4th Flotilla submarines wintered at Hong Kong. In spring the boats cruised the South China seas, alternating between Singapore, Borneo and the Philippines. The 4th Flotilla boats habitually spent summer at Wei Hai Wei, before making a courtesy visit to Japan in the autumn. There were variations to this pattern as *L1*'s log reveals.

On 17 May 1920 the boat sailed to Chifu with her consorts. On 21 June she left Chifu for Kobe. On 30 June 1920 *L1* left Kobe for Port Hamilton. On 5 July 1920 the boats were joined by *Titania*. By 21 August the 4th Flotilla boats visited Amoy before returning to Hong Kong.

On 3 May 1921, *L1* left Wei Hai Wei to visit Shanghai in company with *Titania, L19, L20* and *L33*. The Singapore cruise began early that year, *L1* leaving Amoy for Swatan on 9 November 1921 and arriving at Singapore on 24 January 1922. Visits to Penang, Sarawak, Kuobing and Manila followed in succession, with the boats returning to Hong Kong in early April 1922. In 1923, *L1* was officially assigned to the Reserve Flotilla at Hong Kong.

In early 1925, *L1* participated in a series of courtesy visits which took her to Singapore in February, Surabaya on 13 March and Manila on 30 March, thence back to Wei Hai Wei. In August 1925 there were brief calls at Chifu and Tsingtao before the boat wintered at Hong Kong again. On 16 March 1926, *L1* left Hong Kong for Singapore. On 7 April she was at Penang, arriving at Singapore on 17 April in company with HMS *Ambrose*. At this juncture the cash-strapped Admiralty had little use for veteran submarines and in August 1926 it announced that the older 'L' Class boats were to be paid off, starting with *L9*. On 15 March 1928, *L1, L2, L4, L5, L7* and *L8* were recalled to Blockhouse with HMS *Ambrose*. By 3 May, *Ambrose* and the doomed boats had reached Aden. On 14 May, they arrived at Port Said. On 1 June, the 'L' boats called at Malta, followed by Gibraltar three days later. On arrival at Portsmouth on 19 June 1928, the boats were divided between Chatham and Blockhouse, being maintained in an efficient condition in readiness for scrapping. *L1* was among those boats sent to languish at Chatham.

FINAL PATROL

L1 was finally sold to the Cashmore Yard, Newport, as scrap in March 1930. The stripped out boat was under tow from the tug *Eastleigh* en route between Chatham and Newport, when the tow parted off Cape Cornwall on Friday 28 March 1930.

Three days later the old submarine rolled ashore between Inner Greeb Reef and the Brisons. The coast guard reported her to be badly holed and partially flooded. The torpedo tubes and conning tower were salvaged but the rest was abandoned to the elements. Endlessly battered by the tides, the wreck slowly broke up. Steel ribs, plates, valves, pipes and hand wheels can still be seen amid the gullies and shelving rocks.

ADM 173/6858-6997
Additional information supplied by Olli Lorscher and Dennis Feary.

E39, HM SUBMARINE

DATE OF LOSS: 13 September 1922
DEPTH: 5–10 m
REFERENCE: 51° 41.425' N, 005° 09.364' W
LOCATION: Watwick Reef, Pembrokeshire

Type: British 'E' Class over-seas submarine of Group-III (E21 – E56) *Pennant No.:* E39 *Builders:* Palmers' S.B. & Iron Co. Ltd at Jarrow-on-Tyne for Royal Navy *Ordered:* for 1914 Emergency War programme *Keel laid:* in December 1914 *Launched:* on 18 May 1916 *Commissioned:* on 13 October 1916

TECHNICAL SPECIFICATIONS

Hull: Admiralty saddle-tank-type *Surface displacement:* 662 tons *U/Dt:* 807 tons *LBD:* 55.168m × 6.86m × 3.81m *Machinery:* 2 × 800bhp 8-cylinder Vickers-Admiralty diesels *Props:* 2-bronze *S/Sp:* 15.25kts *Op/R:* 3,225-n.miles @ 10kts *Sub/R:* 85-n.miles @ 5kts *U/Power:* 2 × 420hp electric motors providing 9.75kts *Batteries:* 2 × 112-cell (224) Exide accumulators *Fuel/Cap:* 41.67 tons in 8 tanks & 5.28 tons of 'lubricating oil' in 2 tanks *Armament:* 5 × 45.72cm torpedo tubes (2 bow, 2 beam & 1 stern tube) *Torpedoes:* 10 × 45.72cm (18in) *Guns:* 1 × 5.44-kilo Quick-Firing (12-pounder) on a disappearing mount forward of the conning tower *Diving:* max-designed depth 60.96m (200ft) *Complement:* 3 officers & 27 ratings

Some of this Class were fitted with a 0.91-kilo (2-pounder) pom-pom gun.
Source: BR 3043, Ch 4.

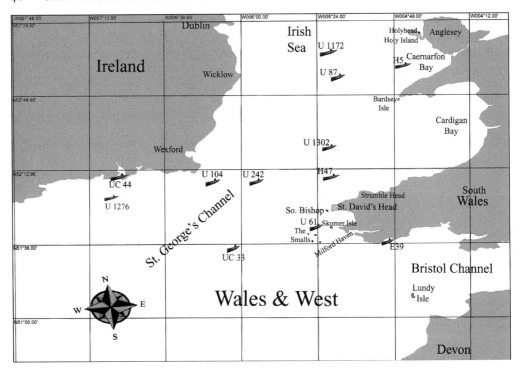

Fig.5: 'St George's Channel and the Irish Sea.' (R.Young)

Commanding Officers (dates before 1919 from nominal list):
Lt George Sarsfield Walsh 1.9.16 – 1.12.16
Lt Frederick Kennedy from 1.12.16 – (Date unknown)
Lt Tom Bellairs from 31.8.18 – 26.9.18
Lt Maurice Bailward from 26.9.18 – 18.9.19

First Lieutenants of *E39*:
01.09.16 – 29.11.16 – Lt John Aitchison
29.11.16 – 01.10.17 – Lt Lawrence Bayley
01.11.17 – 30.05.18 – Mate James Asby
01.07.18 – 12.10.18 – Lt Arthur Sayle
06.11.18 – 11.11.18 – Lt Wilfred St Malleson

Third Hands of *E39*:
01.09.16 – 01.03.18 / Lt Arthur Sayle
01.04.18 – 11.11.18 / Lt Frank Smith

Upon commissioning, *E39* served with HMS *Lucia* and the 10th Flotilla (Tees) from October 1916 to March 1917. Her logs reveal monotonous anti-submarine and blockade patrols off Horns Riff, Kattegat and the Norwegian coast. Several U-boats were sighted but no attacks were made. Life took a slightly more exciting turn when she left for Scapa Flow in November 1917. From Scapa she sailed in company with HMS *Intrepid* and *E 44* to Alexandrovsk, carrying out ten Arctic patrols. On one occasion she penetrated an ice field to seize an armed German sealing vessel, escorting her back to base. In 1919 *E39* joined the 7th Flotilla operating from Reval as part of the British 'intervention force'. In September 1919 she made the long journey home to Devonport and the 2nd Flotilla. By 1920 *E39*'s operational life was over and she was laid up in Group H reserve at Portsmouth. Now surplus to requirements, on 13 October 1921 the boat was sold for scrap to the South Wales Salvage Co. of Llanelli. The old girl had her own ideas.

FINAL PATROL

On 13 September 1922, the steam-tug *Joffre* was towing *E39* from Blockhouse to the breaker's yard when the tow parted. *E39* became hopelessly wedged on Watwick Reef, near St Anne's Head, where she remained for several decades. In 1968 the Pembrokeshire Underwater & Salvage Co. removed most of the pressure hull, tubes and conning tower.

WRECK SITE

The remains of *E39* lie on a seabed of sand, in a general depth of 5m (16.4ft) (LAT). The wreck has been crudely salvaged with explosives. The hull has now totally collapsed and the wreckage is dispersed. All that remains are some twisted steel plates and ribs, festooned in fishing gear and seaweed fronds. The wreckage projects up to 2m from the sea bed. Underwater visibility is usually very poor.

ADM 153/1567 – 1587, ADM 137/626 – 628 ADM 137/871 ADM 137 / 1925
Thanks to Ollie Lörscher for additional information.

U 61 SM IMPERIAL U-BOAT

DATE OF LOSS: 26 March 1918
DEPTH: 65m
REFERENCE: 51° 49.725' N, 005° 31.612' W
LOCATION: 9.22-n.miles SW of St David's Head and 6.5 miles NE of The Smalls in St George's Channel

Type: Mittel-U class (improved Type *U 27*) ocean-going torpedo attack submarine **Builders:** AG Weser, Bremen for Kaiserliche Deutsche Marine **Ordered:** on 6 October 1914, within the batch of *U 57* – *U 62* **Keel laid:** as Yard No.216 on 22 June 1915 **Launched:** 22 July 1916 **Commissioned:** by Kplt. Vicktor Dieckmann on 2 December 1916

TECHNICAL SPECIFICATIONS

Hull: double **Surface displacement:** 768 tons **U/Dt:** 956 tons **LBDH:** 67m × 6.30m × 3.7m × 8.05m **Machinery:** 2 × 1,200ps Maschinefabrik-Augsburg-Nürnberg (MAN) diesels **Props:** 2-bronze **S/Sp:** 16.5kts **Op/R:** 11,400-n.miles @ 8kts **Sub/R:** 55-n.miles @ 5kts **U/Power:** 2 × 600ps electric motors gave 8.4kts **Batteries:** AFA lead/acid/accumulators **Fuel/Cap:** 76 + 52 tons **Armament:** 2-bow & 2-stern 50.04cm torpedo tubes **Torpedoes:** 7 × 50.04cm (19.7in) **Guns:** 1 × 105mm (4.13in) forward-facing deck gun **Ammo:** 276-rounds of 105mm **Diving:** max-op-depth 50m (164ft) & 30-sec to crash-dive **Complement:** 36

U 61 was formally assigned to the *II.U-Flottille* at Helgoland on 15 February 1917. Kplt. Vicktor Dieckmann was assigned to the boat as commander from 2 December 1916. Dieckmann, born 1 September 1887, had been promoted to Kplt. on 19 April 1916. A highly able commander (see *UB 27*, Vol.1), he was to make seven war patrols with this boat:

1) The first war patrol of *U 61* began on 1 March 1917, when the boat sailed from Helgoland via the *norweg* then down the Atlantic coast of Ireland, thence to the western entrance of the English Channel. On 3 March while crossing the North Sea Dieckmann captured the 1,874-ton Danish SS *Rosborg* (1907 – Aktieselskabet Dampsk. Selsk. Dannebrog, Copenhagen) at 54° 40'N 00° 15'W. The steamer was transporting maize from Baltimore to Aarhus, Denmark. Her route took her via Kirkwall in the Orkneys, which made her fair game for the U-boat. Although the ship was ultimately dispatched with a torpedo, Dieckmann appears to have made his challenge under the Prize Regulations. The Norwegian steamer *Edvard Grg* was similarly disposed of by bombs and boarding party.

As the boat picked its way down the Irish coast the 2,287-ton Norwegian barque *Spartan* (1891 – Bech's Rederi A/S, Tvedestrand) was intercepted on 9 March. This time Dieckmann opted to send his victim to the bottom using explosive charges. The steel-hulled sailing ship was en route from New York to Rotterdam with general cargo. Next day *U 61* torpedoed and sank SS *Angola* (1906 – Empreza

Duty watch loading torpedoes ashore – an essential task hated by all submariners. This photograph was taken of a Flanders Flotilla UBIII boat in late 1917. Note the UB boat painted with eyes in the manner of North Sea fishing vessels. The G7 torpedo being loaded here remained in service, albeit subject to numerous modifications, throughout both wars. (Johan Ryheul, Marinekorps Flandern Archive)

Nacional de Nav., Lisbon) 112 miles SW of Bishop Rock. The Portuguese steamer had sailed from Cardiff for Lisbon with coal.

Three days later *U 61* entered one of Admiralty's 'safe zones' some 14 miles off the Blasket Islands where victims came thick and fast. On 13 March at 0015 Dieckmann torpedoed the defensively armed, 3,626-ton SS *Northwaite* (1905 – Raithwaite SS Co. Ltd, Cardiff). The ship was transporting a cargo of phosphate from Sfax in Tunisia to Dublin. The thirty-two strong crew were picked up by Royal Navy trawlers and landed at Berehaven.

By this stage Dieckmann and his crew were getting into their stride, which was rather unfortunate for the crew of the defensively armed 3,765-ton steamer *Luciline* (1899 – Luciline Navigation Co. Ltd, London). The ship was carrying a cargo of 4,900 tons of liquid naphtha (rock oil) from New York to Le Havre. As the ship was sailing in a small convoy, this time Dieckmann attacked with a torpedo fired from periscope depth. At 0305hrs his torpedo struck home. The effects were quite devastating as noxious fumes billowed from the shattered containers in the hold. Those lifeboats not destroyed in the explosion, were quickly launched but the master returned in order to search for the for the ship's steward, who was missing. Tangled wreckage and escaping gas prevented access to the man's cabin and the steward was reluctantly given up as lost. The master returned to the lifeboat only to discover that the naphtha fumes had affected his men who, with classic bad timing, were delirious, 'acting silly and talking a lot of gibberish'. They managed to overturn the lifeboat. Thirteen drowned as a result but the remainder managed to clamber into another boat, although the fourth engineer died of heart failure. The escorting trawler picked up the survivors and took the ship in tow. *Luciline* was eventually beached at Ventry Harbour on the Dingle Peninsula. Note the international character of her crew.

Opposite: Submarine *D3* rescues the crew of HMS *Warner* – a dangerous operation with a U-boat known to be lurking nearby. The rescue took place at dusk on 13 March 1917. Just one year later, on 12 March 1918, *D3* was herself bombed in error by a French airship. This time there was no kind hand to rescue her crew and the boat was lost with all hands. (P. Armstrong)

FATALITIES OF *LUCILINE*, 13.3.17

Bilbag, Louis, Fireman, 23yrs
Cordin, Hdolyn, Fireman, 33yrs
De Nally, Sailor, 22yrs
Diaz, Francisco, Fireman, 36yrs
Farren, A., Sailor, 25yrs
Flaherty, John, Fireman/Trimmer, 23yrs
Gavatz, Luis Fireman/Trimmer, 30yrs
Gonzalez, Jose, Fireman, 23yrs
Johnson, Benjamin, 3rd Engineer, 20yrs
Jurgenstein, George, 4th Engineer, 37yrs
Marcus, John, Steward, 26yrs
Miyagawa, M., Cook, 47yrs
Sina, Bernardina, Sailor, 21yrs
Yaminishl, J., Fireman, 29yrs

At this juncture *U 61* was reduced to one elderly bronze stern torpedo and the boat had not even reached its patrol billet. Then, at 0900hrs (CT) look-outs on *U 61* spotted what appeared to be an old steamer 50 miles west of the Shannon estuary. Dieckmann closed the vessel at periscope depth. Caution was justified. Although he did not know it, Dieckmann was about to confront HMS *Warner* (Capt T. Biddlecombe) otherwise known as Q 27.

Warner, a former passenger-cargo ship, had been requisitioned from Clyde Shipping Co. in January 1917. She had been sent to patrol this as part of the ongoing A/S campaign in the safe zones. This was her first patrol. The *KTB* reveals that the crew of *U 61* was suspicious from the start. As a precautionary measure the vessel was sailing East and according to Dieckmann, 'zig-zagging erratically'. The submarine commander noted that his victim carried a large crew for such a small vessel. The steamer was unusually small for these waters. Most telling of all, she appeared to be following the dived U-boat. Dieckmann had reason to believe his submarine was being stalked by a Q-ship, although it is clear that the crew of *Warner* was in fact oblivious to his presence. The stern tube of *U 61* was brought to readiness and at 0940hrs the steamer executed a change of course which presented Dieckmann with the opportunity to strike.

The torpedo struck *Warner* on the port side, aft. Two men died in the resultant explosion. The vessel began to settle by the stern. There was no panic. While boats were being lowered, the guns were manned in the event of the U-boat breaking surface. Suddenly there was a second explosion, not a torpedo but an exploding boiler. The captain and First Lieutenant Milne, who had been surveying the damage at the time, were killed by flying shards of metal. At this point *Warner* broke in two. As the bow section sank, the resultant suction dragged down one of the lifeboats. As it resurfaced, the men scrambling in the water somehow managed to right it and tumble in. In all twenty-four men clambered onboard.

Dieckmann noted with satisfaction that three minutes after the torpedo detonation, the steamer had sunk. Eager for information, and one suspects, a human trophy, he surfaced and approached the survivors. The Germans seized Lt Yuile RNR (Navigation Officer), CPO Tel Sims, a steward, an AB and one stoker. Satisfied with his haul, Dieckmann then made off. At dusk, the submarine *D3*, engaged on an A/S patrol in the same sector, spotted the lifeboat and transmitted a request for assistance. Two days later the survivors of HMS *Warner* were finally brought ashore. The saga underlines the point that Admiralty was unwise to persevere with Q-ship operations now that the *KDM* was aware of the ruse.

FATALITIES OF HMS *WARNER*, 13.3.17

Branch, Charles, Greaser, 27yrs
Biddlecombe, T.W.R., Cdr, RAN, 36yrs
Denton, William, O/S, 18yrs
Gray, Herbert, Armourer's Crew, 20yrs
Jones, David, AB, 21yrs
Mildren, Jesse, Pte RMLI, 24yrs
Milne, Robert, Act/Temp/Lt, RNR, 25yrs
O'Brien, Michael, O/S
Rigby, Charles Arnour, O/S

Rogers, Edward, AB, 27yrs
Stafford, Albert, O/S, 24yrs

U 61 returned to Helgoland via the *norweg*, arriving back in Germany on 18 March. The boat moored alongside *U 53* and the artist Claus Bergen captured her return in one of his striking drawings.

(2) Leaving Helgoland on 11 April 1917, *U 61* travelled via the *norweg* for operations in the south-western approaches. The 3,730-ton SS *Aburi* (1907 – African SS Co., London, Master W. Heaton) was torpedoed on 17 April. The attack took place 125 miles from Tory Island. The ship has recently left Liverpool bound for Senegal. The torpedo exploded against No.2 hold, flooding the engine room. *U 61* surfaced then commenced shelling the stricken ship. One lifeboat was destroyed by the explosion while two others were swamped. Eventually two boats were successfully lowered. Two days later the survivors were picked up but by this time sixteen had died of exposure.[19]

KNOWN FATALITIES OF *ABURI*, 14.4.17

Brown, Charles, Fireman, 38yrs
Croll, Henry, Carpenter, 59yrs
Davies, J., Trimmer, 23yrs
Dennes, Charles, Steward, 19yrs
Dixon, Sam, Fireman, 23yrs
Grogan, Henry, AB & Quartermaster, 68yrs
Huxtable, Tom, Chief Steward, 37yrs
Lewis, Sam, Fireman, 24yrs
Lopez, Jose, Fireman, 34yrs
Lundberg, Quartermaster, 62yrs
Marsh, Arthur, Assistant Steward, 42yrs
Morris, Henry, 4th Engineer Officer, 26yrs
Philip, George, Cabin Bedroom Steward, 19yrs
Renner, Coffa, Trimmer, 22yrs
Roach, William, Greaser/Fireman, 37yrs
Roberts, William, Fireman, 23yrs
Sango, Tom, Cook, 39yrs
Spicer, William Coath, Quartermaster, 50yrs
Stanley, Robert, Trimmer, 22yrs
Stephens, George, 4th Mate, 23yrs
Wadsworth, John, Greaser/Fireman, 44yrs
Will, Tom, Fireman, 45yrs
Wood, George, Greaser/Fireman, 57yrs

Next day it was the turn of the 1,923-ton defensively armed SS *Castilian* (1890 – Ellerman Lines Ltd, London). The ship had been bound from Liverpool to Genoa with a general cargo when *U 61* struck 110 miles north-west of Tory Island. At 1300hrs *Castilian* was hit by a torpedo. Many of the crew were thrown into the water and several died from exposure. Survivors were rescued by *Manchester Corporation* and landed in Lough Foyle.

FATALITIES ON *CASTILIAN*, 18.4.17

Cooper, George, Assistant Cook, 17yrs
Cullen, Henry, Greaser/Fireman, 29yrs
Deroo, Gustave, Chief Steward, 39yrs
Fisher, Niel McGregor, 3rd Engineer, 26yrs
Heyes, Thomas, Chief Engineer, 42yrs
Hughes, Edgar, Sailor, 21yrs
Hughes, William, Able Seaman, 64yrs
Sodergren, Alexander, Lamps, 34yrs
Thomas, William, Mess Room Steward, 16yrs
Wirtan, Erik, Boatswain (Bosun), 41yrs

Dieckmann continued his rampage without interference from the Royal Navy. On 19 April he attacked the defensively armed steamship *Annapolis* (1911 – Furness, Withy & Co. Ltd, Liverpool) of 4,567 tons, 74 miles off Eagle Island at 54° 55'N 11° 45'W. The ship was inbound from Halifax to Liverpool with a general cargo. This time the damage was not fatal and it was left to *U 69* (Kplt. Ernst Wilhelms) to administer the *coup de grace* next day.

The crew of the Norwegian barque *Skjold* (1891 – O. Gotaas, Kristiania) was more fortunate when they ran into *U 61* off Fastnet Rock on 21 April. Dieckmann did not consider the 1,592-ton ship to be worth a torpedo. The crew was given time to evacuate then the barque was blown up with explosives. It is believed that *U 61* also accounted for the 4,778-ton steam tanker *Telena* (1895 – Anglo-Saxon

Petroleum Co. Ltd, London). *Telena* was shipping benzene from Philadelphia to Queenstown when the U-boat struck her with a torpedo, 170 miles WNW of Fastnet.

The flavour of Dieckmann's method of attacking minor targets can be tasted in this extract from the log of the 1,405-ton steel-hulled Danish barque *Calluna*, which had the misfortune to be intercepted by *U 61* on April 23, while voyaging from Aalborg to New York via Cardiff (1891 – Rederiselskabet 'Limfjorden', Aalborg) with a cargo of chalk.

Extract from ship's log:

> Monday, 23. April 1917, noon Position: 48° 51'N, 8° 38'W, course true SW, 4 knots, wind ESE 2, clear.
> At 5.45 p.m. ordinary seaman Alfred Nørreskov from foretop reported submarine at starboard bow, which immediately started gunfire without warning. We lowered sails to stop speed, put to the wind and boarded both boats, rowed about 300 feet astern, waited there until ship sunk. The submarine fired about 12 shots and another 5 or 6 before we had our boats in the water. She then sent three men with her own boat, which put bombs on board as she would not sink by shellfire. Our ship sank bows first at 6.20 p.m. The submarine came from the north-west and steered back the same way. We set course north, with our boats for the Irish coast.
> Wednesday, 25 April 5.30 a.m., met SS *Peninsula*, Captain. J.B. May, at 50° 14'N, 9° 49'W, who took both boats together with crew on board. We arrived Falmouth 26th, 2 p.m., where the whole crew went ashore. Signed: A. Barrit, 2nd mate: Carl Petersen, AB: Alfred Nørreskov, O.S. I. H. Weibøl, master.'
> ('Samling av Søforklaringe over Krtisgforliste Dansk skibe', page 33)

The 2,463-ton steamer *Lena* (1904 – Whitefield SS. Co. Ltd, Cardiff), on the other hand, received a torpedo when south-west of the Scilly Isles at 48° 45'N, 08° 30'W on the same day. The ship was en route for Huelva from Bristol with a cargo of Government stores. She was armed and Dieckmann was not about to risk his U-boat. All hands were lost.

FATALITIES OF *LENA*, 23.4.17

Armston, Charles, Steward, 55yrs	Lima, Manuel, Fireman, 26yrs
Beckson, J., Able Seaman, 31yrs	Miller, William Seaman, RNR, 19yrs
Brito, Jose, Fireman, 45yrs	Mitchenson, Robert, Master, 46yrs
Carter, Henry, Mess Room Steward, 16yrs	Moyse, George, Able Seaman, 31yrs
Diamentina, Jose, Fireman, 39yrs	Neville, William, 1st Mate, 54yrs
Dost, Muh Subnan, Fireman/Trimmer	Piloto, M., Donkeyman, 34yrs
Du Rees, Philip, Cook, 30yrs	Ramos, A., Fireman/Trimmer, 40yrs
Gerada, George, Fireman/Trimmer, 23yrs	Rodrigues, M., Donkeyman, 40yrs
Gould, Francois, Able Seaman, 34yrs	Townsend, J., Boatswain (Bosun), 54yrs
Jackson, Ernest, L/Boatswain, 39yrs	Townsend, William, Acting L/Seaman, RNR, 25yrs
Jellings, Arthur, 1st Engineer, 20yrs	Wallace, William, 34yrs
Jones, William, 2nd Engineer, 54yrs	Walsh, W., Able Seaman, 50yrs
Leo, T., Able Seaman, 26yrs	

And so the pattern continued. *Metropolis* (1887 – A/S Metropolis, Kristiansand), a 1,811-ton iron-hulled Norwegian barque transporting oil from Philadelphia to Le Havre, was captured on 23 April 1917 and scuttled with explosives in the Atlantic at 48 °30'N, 11° 15'W.

Next day, on 24 April, *U 61* opened fire with her deck gun at the armed 2,009-ton steamship *Thirlby* (Master T. Hill, 1898 – Sir R. Ropner & Co. Ltd, West Hartlepool). *Thirlby* was travelling in ballast from Gibraltar to Dunkerque, when no fewer than three successive torpedoes were fired at her between 0730hrs and 0815hrs. Each torpedo was dodged by judiciously altering course and speed. When the U-boat surfaced astern to continue the chase, Hill responded with gunfire. For Dieckmann and his crew it was all very frustrating. Sad to relate, *Thirlby* survived this encounter only to fall victim to *UC 31* on 2 July 1917 with the loss of two crew members.[20]

Crossing the North Sea, *U 61* chanced upon the 198-ton wooden-hulled Norwegian schooner *Jarstein* (1909 – A/S Motorseil, Lillesand) on 30 April, 80 miles off Egerä light. She was in ballast and bound from Anstruther, Scotland to Lillesand in Norway. The vessel was abandoned then sunk by gunfire. A short time later, *U 61* nearly fell victim to a torpedo herself when the British submarine *J6* (Vol.1) managed to get a shot on target. The torpedo narrowly missed *U 61* and the U-boat arrived safely back at Helgoland on 2 May 1917.

(3) On 7 June 1917, *U 61* once again left Helgoland for a patrol in the south-west approaches via the *norweg*. It will be recalled from Vol.1 that Norwegian shipping was one of the first to benefit from the convoy system, this method having been adopted in April 1917 following the Longhope Conference. Lerwick (later Methil) was the focus of these traffic movements. Shipping would be escorted the length of the east coast swept channel as far as Lerwick, prior to making the crossing to Bergen, shepherded by destroyers.

The 2,245-ton Swedish SS *Ada* (1881 – A/B Ada, Stockholm) had recently made the crossing from Copenhagen to Bergen and thence to Lerwick. Capt Erik Wilhelm Ternström now prepared to join the next southbound convoy that would take him to his destination of Blyth. Like many merchant skippers he chafed under the petty stipulations imposed by naval personnel who organised the convoy sailings. Capt Ternström had not endeared himself to the Royal Navy when *Ada* became wedged in the Lerwick harbour boom. It was almost as if the ship did not want to make the journey ahead of her. Perhaps deep in her fabric she knew the fate that awaited her, 45 miles to the south where *U 61* was waiting for the convoy. The southbound convoy consisted of ten merchant ships, mostly Scandinavian in origin. The escort included two destroyers and six armed trawlers. The merchant crews enjoyed far more cordial relations with the trawler crews who were largely drawn from east coast reservists, mostly fishermen. The convoy moved off at 1000hrs on 7 June 1917, with the ships organised in two lines, with SS *Ada* number three in the port column. At 1600hrs on 9 June, the fussy destroyers suddenly became animated, signalling warnings that U-boats were suspected to be in the area. At 1630hrs Capt Ternström observed the wake of a torpedo heading straight towards the starboard side.

The torpedo detonated in the boiler room, instantly killing three men. The resultant explosion rendered the lifeboat on the starboard side into a splintered wooden skeleton, dangling from the davits. The force of the explosion shattered the superstructure. The stanchions supporting the navigation room below the bridge collapsed like a pack of cards. The port lifeboat was being lowered but Capt Ternström hesitated, then dashed back inside the wrecked navigation room to recover a Gladstone bag which had been a family heirloom for generations. In the bag lay a gold watch that had belonged to the captain's Uncle Robert. Uncle Robert had in turn rescued the watch from his own ship, just before it had sunk. Bag in hand, Capt Ternström leapt from the stricken ship. He was still clutching the bag when his crew dragged him, sodden and frozen, into the lifeboat. A short time afterwards the survivors were taken onboard HMT *Sealion* (Capt Treacher) and relayed to Aberdeen. The Gladstone bag and the gold watch is still a treasured family heirloom. From a crew of twenty-three men and three women, the following died:

FATALITIES OF *ADA* 9.6.17
Andrén, Knut, 19yrs
Dahlöf, Carl, 23yrs
Nordlöf, Eric, 39yrs

The fact that a second ship, the 1,590-ton *Dana*, was sunk in the same attack is eloquent testimony of Dieckmann's skill in that he was capable of targeting and hitting two different ships with one single torpedo salvo – without the benefit of tube-angling gear. Realising he had stirred a hornet's nest, Dieckmann left the area. He is credited with having shelled БЕТТИ (*Betty*) (1898 – Russisch-Baltische Dampfs. Ges., Riga) a Russian steamer of 2,683 tons, off North Rona on 10 June. The ship was carrying coal from Cardiff to Murmansk when she was sunk. A second collier was sunk by Dieckmann later that day when *U 65* confronted the 3,511-ton SS *Ribera* (1915 – Humphries (Cardiff) Ltd, London). The ship was en route from Penarth to Archangelsk, Russia when Dieckmann made his attack 70 miles from Cape Wrath.

On 14 June the 299-ton three-masted Russian barquentine *Widwud* (1903 – P. Anderson's Erben & P. Osolin, Riga) was transporting timber from Mobile, Alabama to Britain, when she was damaged by shell fire from *U 61*, 40 miles WNW of the Skelligs. Under Capt P. Melbard she survived to be towed into Castletown. She would not survive a future encounter with *U 104* (Kurt Bernis) on 16 April 1918, however.

The rampage of *U 61* in Western waters was far from over. On 16 June *U 61* shelled the armed 3,012-ton steamer *Falloden* (1903 – Pyman, Watson & Co. Ltd, London) en route from Cork to Cherbourg

U 61 unleashed! Note the exposed helmsman's platform in front of the conning tower. (U-boot Archiv)

with a cargo of hay. The ship was beached at Queenstown but like *Widwud* she was doomed to be sunk in a future encounter; in *Falloden*'s case with *UC 71* (Ernst Steindorff) on 28 December.

The 1,012-ton armed steamer *Raloo* (1898 – Shamrock Shipping Co. Ltd, Belfast) was sunk 6 miles from Coningbeg Light-vessel on 17 June. She was steaming at 10 knots on passage from Newport, Monmouth for Cork and carrying a crew of sixteen and a cargo of coal, when a torpedo struck amid-ships at 2150hrs.

The crew abandoned ship in the boat at 2220hrs but the master, Capt J. McBride, Greek fireman Evanelous Anastasia Sytzioukis and John Sutherland (DAMS gunner) were found to be missing. Just after the lifeboat cleared the sinking ship, a second torpedo was fired at 2300hrs by the unseen *U 61*. The survivors safely reached Coningbeg Light-vessel.

The armed 4,054-ton steam tanker *Batoum* (1893 – Associated Oil Carriers Ltd, Swansea) was torpe-doed and sunk on 19 June. She was proceeding at 9 knots on passage from New Orleans to Queenstown with a cargo of oil when a torpedo detonated abaft the engine room at 0710hrs, John Fleming, donkey-man, being killed in the subsequent explosion and flooding. A USN torpedo boat destroyer landed the forty-one survivors at Queenstown.[21]

On 19 June, off the west of Ireland, Vicktor Dieckmann attacked the 6,381-ton steamer *Nitonian* (1912 – Fredk. Leyland & Co. Ltd, Liverpool) with gunfire, but the ship reached Liverpool safely. *Nitonian* (Master D. Lawton) succeeded in keeping her stern turned towards her assailant, like *Thirlby* constantly changing speed and course to confuse the German gunners. The pursuit commenced at 1119hrs and by 1150hrs *U 61* did succeed in getting a shot on target with the result that *Nitonian* caught fire. As the U-boat drew closer, she was treated to a broadside from the steamer. The engagement continued until

1400hrs, when the U-boat broke off. At 1648hrs *Nitonian* was met by a destroyer and escorted into Lough Swilly where her damage was patched. *U 61* arrived at Helgoland on 25 June, returning via the *norweg*.

(4) *U 61* sailed from Helgoland on 23 July 1917 for a patrol in the Bay of Biscay via the *norweg* and consecutive British safe approach zones D, C and B (Fig.1). En route, in Approach C/Alpha, Dieckmann torpedoed but only damaged the 5,588-ton SS *Comanchee* (1912 – Anglo-American Oil Co. Ltd, Newcastle) off the North Channel. The ship, on passage from Liverpool for New York in ballast, was forced to put into Lough Swilly for repairs. *Comanchee* had been lucky but fortune did not smile down on the 2,416-ton French steamship *Libia* (1889 – Cie. Française de Navigation, Marseille). The French merchant was torpedoed 70 miles west of Penmarc'h on 2 August 1917 and was lost with all hands.

The 2,234-ton British steamer *Countess of Mar* (1916 – Gascony SS Co. Ltd, London) was on passage from Bilbao for Cardiff with iron ore, when *U 61* sank the vessel on 4 August, 55 miles off Bayonne. The ship's master, George Dobbie, had been credited with ramming a U-boat on 6 May 1917. It was believed that the U-boat had been badly damaged, leading to Master Dobbie's award of the DSC:

KNOWN FATALITIES OF *COUNTESS OF MAR*, 4.8.17

Charalamboas, Donkeyman, 33yrs	Marsh, Thomas, Steward, 22yrs
Conrorakes, N., Fireman, 21yrs	Maydwell, Chas, Ordinary Seaman, 22yrs
Cooper, William, 1st Mate, 29yrs	Michell, G., 3rd Engineer, 30yrs
Dobbie, George, Master (DSC)	Murray, John, L/Deckhand RNR (DAMS), 21yrs
Everett, Samuel, Able Seaman, 34yrs	Piggford, Alfred, 1st Engineer, 66yrs
Gritenez, Mauel, Fireman, 29yrs	Pringle, John, 2nd Engineer, 26yrs
Harris, William, Fireman, 18yrs	Redmore, Thomas, Ship's Cook, 23yrs
Larsen, L., Fireman, 24yrs	Valliano, C., Able Seaman, 53yrs
Litschin, A., Sailor, 24yrs	Watkins, William, Mess Room Steward, 18yrs
Marsh, Thomas, Boatswain (Bosun), 22yrs	Withey, Charles, Deckhand RNR (DAMS), 24yrs

Two more victims rapidly followed: the 902-ton French steamer *Sauternes* (1900 – Worms & Cie., Havre) torpedoed and sunk without warning on 4 August, 15 miles off Cap Ferrat, followed by the Spanish fishing smack *Campo Libre* next day. A similar fate overtook the 3,678-ton American steam freighter *Campana* (1901 – Standard Oil Co. (New Jersey). *Campana*, in ballast, was en route from La Rochelle to Huelva in Spain when she was captured and scuttled with explosives in the Bay of Biscay, 143 miles west of Ile de Ré (46° 08'N 05° 30'W) on 6 August.

U 61 did not have everything her way. Later that same day the U-boat tangled with a French Q-ship, *Jeanne et Genvieve*, coming under sustained depth-charge attack, Dieckmann being forced to display all his guile in order to escape the ship's attentions. Undaunted, *U 61* sank with explosives the 3,276-ton Italian collier *Trento* (1899 – Soc. Anon. Ilva, Genoa) 50 miles WSW of Ushant: the vessel was hauling coal from Cardiff to Torre Annunziata, Italy. *U 61* returned to Helgoland by the same route, arriving on 14 August 1917.

(5) On 22 September 1917, *U 61* left Helgoland for operations off the Atlantic coast of Ireland, once again sailing via the *norweg*. Dieckmann torpedoed and sank the 3,503-ton SS *Elmsgarth* (1896 – Garth SS Co. Ltd, Newcastle). The steamer was armed for defence and carrying a cargo of sugar from Kingston, Jamaica and Matanzas in Cuba to Liverpool. The attack took place 50 miles off Tory Island. The *Elmsgarth*'s master, Capt C. Wheeler was taken prisoner.

The Coningbeg Light-vessel was a favourite ambush point for U-boats. The armed 4,313-ton SS *Rhodesia* (1900 – Franco-British SS Co. Ltd, Cardiff) was torpedoed and sunk without warning on 11 October while transporting oil and bitumen from Tampico, Mexico to London.

FATALITIES OF *RHODESIA*, 11.10.17

Jacquin, Leon, Fireman, 25yrs
Musgrave, Thomas, 2nd Engineer, 65yrs
Okivera, Juan, Fireman, 24yrs
Tabares, Miguel, Fireman/Trimmer, 27yrs

The American destroyer USS *Cassin* chanced upon *U 61* on 15 October. Naturally Dieckmann dived in the hope of giving the warship the slip but the Americans were eager for action, having been previously engaged in dull troopship escort duties. More experienced hunters would have zig-zagged, maintained a healthy speed and summoned reinforcements but the American warship steered a straight course and slowed down to give their hydrophone operator the chance to locate the U-boat. The wily Dieckmann needed no second chance. As the warship slowly turned, so he brought his bows to bear. At 1330hrs *Cassin* was rocked by an explosion, port side, aft.

The explosion killed Gunner's Mate First Class Osmond Ingram outright and wounded nine other men. The detonation also severely damaged the rudder. The destroyer commenced to circle slowly and helplessly. Two factors prevented Dieckmann from delivering the *coup de grace*: firstly his men had difficulty keeping depth faced with such a heavy sea and secondly, *Cassin*'s gunners opened fire as soon as they spotted *U 61*'s periscope at 1430hrs. Dieckmann withdrew. Later a couple of British destroyers coaxed the listing *Cassin* into Newport. The warship returned to escort duties in July 1918, one of very few vessels to have escaped the clutches of Vicktor Dieckmann and *U 61*. On the return leg *U 61* was ordered to return via the Baltic, because the British had fouled the Helgoland Bight. Observing these instructions, the boat passed through the Skagerrak and Kiel Canal to Wilhelmshaven, where *U 61* tied up on 28 October 1917.

(6) *U 61* departed Helgoland for operations on 23 December 1917. The billet was off the south coast of Ireland/Irish Sea but in contrast with previous patrols, *U 61* slipped through the perilous Dover Straits. The crew spent a dismal Christmas on the bed of the English Channel. On 27 December the prolific Dieckmann torpedoed and damaged the American Q-ship USS *Santee* off Queenstown.[22]

The 2,756-ton defensively armed steamer *Birchwood* (1910 – Birchwood SS Co. Ltd, Middlesbrough) was torpedoed and sunk 25 miles east of Blackwater Light. The ship had been en route from Glasgow to Devonport with coal.

The armed 2,220-ton SS *Rose Marie* (1916 – Rodney SS Co. Ltd, Newcastle) was torpedoed and sunk on 5 January, 13 miles off North Arklow Light-vessel. The ship was sailing from Scapa Flow to Barry in ballast. One man died.

Next day Dieckmann torpedoed the 1,049-ton *Halberdier* (1915 – Fisher, Renwick Manchester-London Steamers Ltd, Manchester) 27 miles off Bardsey Island. The ship was transporting a general cargo from Manchester to London.

FATALITIES OF *HALBERDIER*, 6.1.18

Bowden, Francis, Fireman, 32yrs
Dalby, Edwin, Steward, 33yrs
Griffith, Lewis Robert, 1st Engineer, 60yrs
Hall, Frederick Richmond William, L/Seaman RNVR (DAMS), 23yrs
Higgins, William Adam, AB RNVR (DAMS), 20yrs

Later the same day *U 61* sank the 4,186-ton defensively armed SS *Spenser* (1910 – Liverpool, Brazil & River Plate Steam Navigation Co. Ltd, Liverpool). *Spenser* was hauling general cargo from Buenos Aires to Liverpool when she was sunk by torpedo, 28 miles off Bardsey.

U 61 arrived back at Helgoland on 14 January 1918, having returned via the safer *norweg*.

FINAL PATROL

(7) *U 61* departed Helgoland on 14 March 1918 via the familiar *norweg* for operations in the Irish Sea. On 23 March Dieckmann is known to have torpedoed and sunk the 6,515-ton armed British steamer *Etonian* (Master J. Gardner, 1898 – Fred Leyland & Co. Ltd, Hull (Liverpool). The ship was bound from Liverpool to Boston, Massachusetts with general cargo. This attack took place 34 miles off the Old Head of Kinsale. Although listing badly, the ship was later reboarded. Unfortunately she was too badly flooded to make it back to port.

FATALITIES OF *ETONIAN*, 14.3.18

Craig, J., Horseman
Finlayson, Kenneth, Seaman RNR (DAMS)
McGee, William, Fireman, 45yrs
McKay, Thomas, Sailor, 18yrs
Rudholm, Emil, Sailor, 50yrs
Scarisbrick, Richard, L/Signalman, RNR, 25yrs
Wolfunberg, Alfred, Horseman, 24yrs

The next set of casualties included Dieckmann and his crew because at this point they simply disappear from history. Authorities such as Admiral Spindler and Robert Grant attribute the loss of *U 61* to an attack made on a U-boat on 26 March in St George's Channel. This sector had been Dieckmann's hunting ground in the past and it is credible to suggest he would have been in this area on the date of the attack. Spindler and Grant based their attribution on the Monthly Anti-Submarine Report issued by Admiralty. On the face of it the Anti-Submarine Report seems very convincing with a description of oil patches, underwater explosions, human remains and debris liberated from the wreck. Let us now examine the evidence in greater detail by turning to the unadorned log of the Milford-based HMS *P51* (Lt W. Murray RNR).

Log P51, 26.3.18
20.30   Smalls abeam – 2 miles 51°48'N, 05°32'W.
20.45   Sighted enemy submarine 2 points on port bow, 3 – 400 yards
*   Helm jammed at 20 degrees of starboard. In consequence forced to turn 32 points and missed submarine*
20.55   Dropped 3 DCs in vicinity submarine submerged and probably destroyed him as air rising in vicinity.

Firstly it must be observed that evidence for the presence of a U-boat is strong. The U-boat was less than 300 yards away. It has been proven by post-war investigation that depth-charges of this period were rarely potent unless used in large numbers on the direct track of the submarine. Yet we see from the log that *P51* dropped just three depth-charges in darkness. While a direct hit cannot be ruled out, this would have been incredibly lucky given the circumstances, as the U-boat had ten minutes to take evasive action. Although the log refers to air rising in the vicinity, it is obvious that the convincing descriptions which feature so prominently in the official release, are not evidenced by this primary source. It is feasible these descriptions have been omitted on grounds of brevity but it is far more likely that they are the embroidery of an Admiralty propaganda machine, eager to make an interception in coastal waters seem like a confirmed kill. Doubt is now cast over the certainty that a U-boat was destroyed in this action and the claim begins to unravel further when it is considered that no wreck has been discovered in this location to date. It is possible that *P51* did indeed attack *U 61*. It is equally plausible to suggest that the U-boat escaped only to be lost elsewhere on the *norweg*, cause unknown.[23]

FATALITIES OF *U 61*

Binder, Paul, Ob/Matrose
Bullrich, Ernst, Oblt. zur See
Böhm, Wilhelm, Heizer
Böhm, Alfred, Ob/Matrose
Dieckmann, Victor, KpLt.
Eichmann, K., Ob/MaschinistenMt
Endres, Friedrich, F.T.Gast
Eppel, Gerd, Heizer
Fromme, W., MaschinistenMt
Färber, August, MaschinistenMt
Gauss, Oswald, Ob/Masch.Anw
Geilke, Hermann, Ob/BootsmannsMt
Gross, Friedrich, Lt zur See der Reserve
Gruber, Albert, MaschinistenMt
Hellmann, G., Ob/Heizer
Herfurth, Karl, Heizer

Knauer, Reinh, Matrose
Krummhaar, C, BootsmannsMt
Lünstedt, Paul, Ob/BootsmannsMt
Matte, Otto, Ob/Matrose
Norrmann, Karl, Matrose
Otto, Max, Ob/MaschinistenMt der Reserve
Paszek, Stanislaus, Ob/Matrose
Rehm, Heinrich, Maschinist
Schellenwald, F.T.Mt
Schmidt, Stefan, Ob/Heizer
Schroweg, F., MaschinistenMt
Schumann, M., BootsmannsMt
Sievers, Karl, Ob/Heizer
Spiel, Richard, Ob/Heizer
Strobel, Alois, Marine Ob/Ing
Tammen, Johann, Heizer

Hirche, Karl, Steuermann
Jahnke, Wilhelm, BootsmannsMt
Jahre, Wilhelm, F.T.Gast
Jennessen, Karl, Heizer
Kettmann, G., MaschinistenMt

Thienat, Karl, Ob/MaschinistenMt
Vahldick, Rudolf, Heizer
Wegener, Paul, Matrose
Wilke, Larl, MaschinistenMt
Winkler, Friedrich, Matrose

WRECK SITE

No wreck has yet been located. There is one candidate near the location of the attack which may (or may not be) *U 61*. It is orientated in an ENE/WSW direction (060/240-degrees). It lies on a seabed of fine sand, gravel, mud and shells, in a general depth of 65m (213.2ft) (LAT). The wreck appears to be upright and reasonably intact. The height is over 7m amidships. Little else is known about this vessel but if it does turn out to be *U 61* it follows that it will be classified as a war grave.

ADM 53/56577 ADM 137/2961 ADM 137/2962 NARA T-1022, Roll 34

(*Ada* account courtesy of Eva Ternström-Lidbetter-Sessions, daughter of Capt Erik Wilhelm Ternström: *Memoirs of a Swedish Seafaring Family* ISBN 1 8507.)

UC 33, SM IMPERIAL U-BOAT

DATE OF LOSS: **26 September 1917**
DEPTH: 83m
REFERENCE: 51° 52.999'N, 06° 13.933'W
LOCATION: 34-n.miles W of St David's Head, in St George's Channel

Type: UCII coastal mine-laying boat *Builders:* AG Vulcan, Hamburg for Kaiserliche Deutsche Marine *Ordered:* on 29 August 1915, within the batch of UC 25 – UC 33 *Keel laid:* as Yard No.72 *Launched:* on 26 August 1916 *Commissioned:* by *Kplt.* Martin Schelle on 25 September 1916

TECHNICAL SPECIFICATIONS

Hull: double *Surface displacement:* 400 tons *U/Dt:* 480 tons *LBDH:* 49.45m × 5.22m × 3.68m × 7.46m *Machinery:* 2 × 250ps MAN diesels *Props:* 2-bronze *S/Sp:* 11.6kts *Op/R:* 10,040-n.miles @ 7kts *Sub/R:* 53-n.miles @ 4kts *U/Power:* 2 × 230ps electric motors gave 6.6kts *Batteries:* lead/acid/ accumulators *Fuel/Cap:* 41 + 14 tons *Armament:* 2-external 50.04cm torpedo tubes at the bow, one either side of the mine chutes & 1 stern internal tube *Torpedoes:* 7 × 50.04cm (19.7in) maximum *Guns:* 1 × 88mm (3.46in) forward deck gun *Ammo:* 133-rounds of 88mm *Mine tubes:* 6 mines: 18 × UC200 *Diving:* max-op-depth 50m (164ft) & 33-sec to crash-dive *Complement:* 3 officers & 23 ratings

Some boats carried an extra dismantled stern torpedo, others lashed two additional torpedoes to the deck.

    Kplt. Martin Schelle (see *UB 65*) commanded the boat from 25 September 1916. After some initial training, *UC 33* was formally assigned to the Germany-based I.U-Flottille at Brunsbüttel on 16 December 1916. Schelle made the following war patrols with the boat:

    (1) On New Year's Eve 1916, *UC 33* left Germany and operated around Shetlands and Orkney, followed by the Scottish east coast, however after an uneventful patrol. *UC 33* returned to Brunsbüttel on 7 January 1917.

    (2) Leaving Germany on 7 February 1917, *UC 33* laid mines and patrolled off the south coast of Ireland, travelling via the hazardous Dover Strait. The day after leaving port, Schelle snared his first prey off Hoofden when the 153-ton Dutch trawler *Derika* was sunk by explosives. On 11 February, a torpedo fired at an unknown steamer in the western exits of the English Channel, missed its target. That same evening, *UC 33* began laying mines off Queenstown. Four more were laid off the Old Head of Kinsale with four further mines laid off Galley Head. During this final lay a premature detonation rocked the boat and caused some damage, leaving several fuel bunkers leaking. Repairs were duly carried out but

UCII boat in dry dock. Note the six wet-storage mine chutes in the bow section. The lower ends of these chutes were open to the sea for ease of mine dispatch. The two perforated external torpedo tubes are apparent. A simple mass-produced purpose-built design, *UC 33* and her sisters wrought havoc on the west coast of Britain. (Bundesarchiv, Koblenz)

the damage justified an early return to base. On the return leg via the *norweg*, on 14 February, *UC 33* was 30 miles off Fastnet Rock when she came upon the British 1,992-ton, four-masted barque *Eudora* (1888 – T. Shute & Co., Liverpool). The vessel, which was en route from Buenos Aires to Queenstown with maize, was stopped and sunk by gunfire. The crew was allowed to safely abandon ship. *UC 33* arrived back in Germany on 21 February 1917.

The ability of German U-boats to mine western coastal waters came as an unpleasant shock to the British. One of the mines laid by *UC 33* off the Daunt Light-vessel sank the 1906 built, 242-ton RN trawler *Clifton* (Lt E. Garrod RNR) on 18 February. The former Grimsby boat had been requisitioned in December 1914 as Admiralty Trawler No.954. At 0645 *Clifton* detonated the mine and disintegrated, leaving Lt Clemens as the sole survivor.

FATALITIES OF HMS *CLIFTON*, 18.2.17
Baskcomb, Harry, 2nd Hand, RNR, 32yrs
Cook, James, Deckhand, RNR, 34yrs
Flynn, Thomas, Trimmer, RNR
Garrod, Edward, Skipper, RNR
Glavin, William, L/Smn, RNR, 41yrs
Harrington, Patrick, Deckhand, RNR, 19yrs
Lamont, Donald, Deckhand, RNR, 18yrs
Pask, Reginald, Deck Hand, RNR, 24yrs
Railton, John, Trimmer, RNR, 22yrs
Robson, Thomas, Engineman, RNR
Rollinson, John, Engineman, RNR
Robson, Thomas, Enginman, RNR
Todd, George, O/Telegraphist, RNVR, 24yrs
Whalley, Thomas, Trimmer RNR

On 24 February 1917, the 437-ton RN yacht *Verona* (Cdr Charles Wilson RNR) joined *Clifton* on the seabed. *Verona* was unfortunate enough to trigger one of the mines laid by *UC 33* off Tarbet Ness during her December patrol. The mine exploded at 0817hrs abreast the funnel. The force of the explosion rent the ship in half. She was observed to sink stern first at 57° 51.40'N 03° 38.40'W. There were no survivors from her crew of twenty-four.

FATALITIES OF HMS *VERONA*, 24.2.17
Bibby, Harold, Temp/Lt RNR, 24yrs
Bragg, Reginald, Steward
Doyle, Harry, Sub-Lt, RNR, 33yrs
Duck, Frederick, Assistant Steward, 35yrs
Kesson, William, 3rd Engineer, 22yrs
Laurenson, Robert, Seaman, RNR, 22yrs
Lowe, William, Sig, RNVR, 31yrs
Marett, Joseph, Fireman, 35years
McIntosh, Alister, Sig, RNVR, 31yrs
McLaren, Charles, Fireman
Malcolmson, William, L/Smn, RNR, 24yrs
Noble, Thomas, Temp/Asst Paymaster RNR, 24yrs
Noel, Phillip, Able Seaman
Phillips, Edgar, Assistant Cook, 37yrs
Ruthin, Samuel, Petty Officer, RNR, 41yrs
Powell, James S., Fireman, MMR, 33yrs
Salmon, George, Cook, MMR
Shepard, Thomas, Assistant, Cook, MMR, 30yrs
Steady, William, Able Seaman, MMR, 47yrs
Stephen, Alexander, Carpenter, MMR
Stewart, Thompson, 2nd Engineer, MMR, 50yrs
Thorne, Ernest, Greaser, MMR
Weaver, Walter, Fireman
Wilson, Charles, (ret.) Cdr, RNR

(3) *UC 33* left port on 7 April 1917 and made a minelaying expedition to the south coast of Ireland. Between 13 and 15 April, groups of mines were laid off the Coningbeg Lightship, south of Rame Head and south-east of Ballycotton Lighthouse. On 13 April the 1,456-ton steamer *Bandon* (1910 – City of Cork Steam Packet Co. Ltd, Cork, Capt P. Kelly) had been on passage from Liverpool to Cork with a general cargo when at 1610hrs a mine detonated on the port side of the engine room. While some authorities attribute her destruction to an attack made by *UC 33*, *Bandon* almost certainly struck a mine laid by *UC 44* in March. For the crew of *Bandon*, the source of destruction was academic for the ship sank too quickly for the men down below to escape and from a crew of thirty-two, just four survived. Eventually rescued by a motor launch, the survivors were landed at Dungarry.

FATALITIES OF *BANDON*, 13.4.17
Courtney, John, Able Seaman, 45yrs
Bird, Charles, Able Seaman, 36yrs
Collins, Batt, Trimmer, 41yrs
Crone, Caleb, Cook, 31yrs
Curtin, Patrick, Fireman, 36yrs
Dowling, Michael, 2nd Engineer, 48yrs
Edwards, Martin, L/Seaman RNR (DAMS)
Martin, Charles, Fireman, 32yrs
Mercer, Robert, 1st Engineer, 67yrs
McCarty, Jeremiah, Able Seaman, 30yrs
MacCashin, Charles, Steward, 35yrs
O'Brien, 2nd Mate, 53yrs
O'Callaghan, John, Fireman, 37yrs
O'Keefe, Patrick, Fireman, 37yrs

Ferns, Edward, 1st mate, 49yrs

O'Keefe, Robert, Cattleman, 49yrs

Higgins, Patrick, Fireman, 43yrs

O'Sullivan, William, Cattleman, 45yrs

Lacey, James, Trimmer, 34yrs

Paterson, John L., Able Seaman, RNVR (DAMS)

Leahy, Feremiah, Fireman, 52yrs

Sullivan, John, Able Seaman, 37yrs

Long, Jeremiah, Fireman, 34yrs

Thompson, Joseph, Able Seaman, 36yrs

Louro, Simon, Able Seaman, 48yrs

Wafer, John, Able Seaman, 24yrs

Mahoney, George, Fireman, 43yrs

Walsh, John, Fireman, 42yrs

Two steam trawlers, *Jedburgh* (1897) and *Yeovil* (1898), were captured on 21 April about 35 miles off Foula Island and sunk by gunfire: unfortunately Charles Joseph Hamilton, a deckhand on the *Yeovil*, was killed.

UC 33 returned to Helgoland on 25 April 1917.

There were subsequent victims of *UC 33*'s mines including the 4,011-ton SS *Hermione* (1891 – British & South American Steam Navigation Co. Ltd). In addition to 4,000 tons of general cargo, *Hermione* was transporting fifty-seven live horses from Buenos Aires to Liverpool for war work. The mine detonated beneath her hull at 0910hrs on 14 April. As flooding continued unabated, the boat began to settle. In common with most merchant ships at this time, *Hermione* was fitted with a gun of questionable efficacy, though in this instance it was fired to attract attention from shore. An SOS message was transmitted then the engine was stopped and the vessel abandoned by her forty-three-strong crew. Royal Navy trawlers rescued the crew and by 1000hrs *Hermione* was in tow with a skeleton crew aboard, heading for Waterford Harbour. The horses and cargo were removed but *Hermione* proved to have been too badly damaged. She sank off Dunmore Pier and was slowly scrapped in situ.

The 225-ton *Loch Eye* (William McLeod RNR) was working off Dunmore on 20 April when she detonated a mine. The section of trawlers was in line ahead, with *Loch Eye* fourth in the column, when the explosion took place one mile off Hook Point. *Loch Eye* sank rapidly by the stern taking half the crew with her.

FATALITIES OF HMT *LOCH EYE*, 4.4.17

Anderson, Thomas, Engineman, RNR, 36yrs

Baxter, Albert, Trimmer, RNR

Farquhar, George, Engmn, RNR

Keech, Reginald, Ordinary Seaman, RNCVR, 16yrs

Milne, James, Trimmer, RNR

Nightingale, Willie, Ordinary Seaman, RNCVR

Pirrie, Robert, Deck Hand, RNR, 36yrs

One of the mines laid by *UC 33* destroyed the 396-ton steam coaster *Lodes* (1898 – M.A. Morris, Middlesbrough) off Ballycotton on 5 May. The vessel was en route from Newport to Cork with coal when she was blown in two. Only two of her crew of nine survived.

FATALITIES OF *LODES*, 5.5.17

Horrocks, Joseph, Fireman

Kavanagh, Thomas, Able Seaman, 41yrs

Kearon, John, Mate, 53yrs

Lennon, Patrick, 2nd Engineer, 46yrs

Thompson, James, Chief Engineer, 71yrs

Waters, Michael, Fireman, 34yrs

Willoughby, John, Master

(4) *UC 33* departed Germany on 13 May 1917 and proceeded to the south coast of Ireland for mine-laying operations. On 17 May, six mines were laid off Capel Island. The remaining twelve should have blocked the entrance to Waterford Harbour but Schelle wisely abandoned this part of his mission due to a leaking oil tank. Returning via the *norweg* and the Færoe Banks, Schelle captured and sank five Danish fishing vessels with scuttling charges on 23 May: the *Beinir*, *Brittania*, *Else*, *Streymoy* and *Margrethe*. Two British steam trawlers were also captured and sunk with explosives on 23 May: the 209-ton *Olearia*

(1899) had left Grimsby for the fishing grounds when she was sunk, 65 miles off Sudero, Færoe Isles, followed by the *Sisapon* (1905), 60 miles off the north end of Sudero. On 24 May Schelle captured and sank three more Danish fishing cutters with explosives off the Færoe Bank: the *Bresti*, the *Isabella Innes* and the *Traveller*. The 110-ton *A.H. Friis* (1903), a Danish sailing boat, was transporting 192 tons of salt from Setubal, Portugal to Trangisvaag, in the Færoes, when she was captured on 24 May and sunk about 35 miles from Sudero.

On 25 May, two more vessels were destroyed: the 358-ton Norwegian coaster *Glyg* (1889 – Gjerdsø & Bakkevig m fl., Haugesund), under the command of Capt Ole Martin Pedersen Veluren, was captured and sunk with explosives approximately 17 miles NNW of Muckle Flugga. The crew abandoned ship and survived. The *Glyg* was voyaging from Fraserburgh, Scotland to Akureiri, Iceland with salt and empty barrels. The 1,378-ton steel-hulled Norwegian barque *Whinlatter* (1887 – Skibs A/S Oslo, Kristiania) was captured and sunk by explosive scuttling charges at 61° 04'N 02° 53'W: she was transporting wood from New Orleans to Copenhagen.

UC 33 arrived back at Helgoland on 28 May.

(5) Departing Helgoland on 24 June 1917, *UC 33* sailed to the Shetlands to lay mines off Lerwick. On 28 June and some 65 miles from Sumburgh Head, the British fishing smack *Corona* was captured and sunk by gunfire. The next day, two more British fishing boats were intercepted and sunk by gunfire off Rattray Head: the *Gem* and *Manx Princess*.

Schelle now turned to larger targets. The somewhat ironically named 1,064-ton Swedish steamer *Germania* (1908 – Rederi A/B Svenska Lloyd, Göteborg), was torpedoed and sunk about 40 miles east of the Orkneys on 30 June while on passage from Göteborg to Hull with general cargo and timber.

The career of HMS *Cheerful* came to an unhappy end thanks to *UC 33*. On 30 June the 1897 vintage HMS *Cheerful* (Lt H. Bond RNR) was escorting an inbound convoy of nine ships through Bressay Sound. Unbeknown to the crew, warship and charges had strayed over a mine outside the limits of the swept channel. Just before midnight *Cheerful* was abreast the rear-most ship and heading for Kirkabister when she detonated one of *UC 33*'s mines. The explosion occurred under the boiler room, tearing the 370-ton destroyer in two. Both fore and aft sections remained afloat for about twenty minutes, allowing for the rescue of eighteen men. Now only too aware of the mine menace, Admiralty developed a siege mentality. Only constant sweeping could guarantee safety in British coastal waters. The subsequent inquiry highlighted the imperative for escorts to keep within the limits of swept channels at all times.

FATALITIES OF HMS *CHEERFUL*, 30.6.17

Antrichan, Robert, Stoker 1st class
Bailes, Percy, AB, 21yrs
Bodin, Hugh, Signalman, RNVR
Breitnauer, Walter, AB
Bridges, Walter, Stoker 1st class
Carpenter, Henry, AB, 35yrs
Chalmers, David, Stoker 1st class, 23yrs
Collings, Henry, Stoker 1st class, 16yrs
Collyer, Henry, Cook's Mate, 23yrs
Cuttance, Gabriel, Tel., 21yrs
Darbon, Daniel, AB, 19yrs
Dixon, Robert, Stoker 1st class, 19yrs
Dunn, James, Stoker 1st class, 24yrs
Dyson, Louie, Stoker 1st class, 26yrs
Eason, Daniel, Stoker 1st class, 27yrs
Flindall, Arthur, L/Stoker, 29yrs
Green, Albert E., Stoker PO, 34yrs
Hanks, Edgar R., Stoker 1st class, 28yrs
Hickman, William, Stoker 1st class, 24yrs
Hinds, William, Stoker 1st class
Herberts, Sydney, L/Signalman

Hutchison, John, Stoker 1st class, 19yrs
Joslin, Sidney, Stoker 1st class, 24yrs
Lewis, John, Stoker 1st class
Liddle, Thomas, Stoker Petty Officer
Macro, Fredenck, ERA, RNR, 31yrs
Main, Alexander, ERA 4th class, 37yrs
McGrady, William, Stoker 1st class, 26yrs
Mokler, Walter, Officer's Steward 2nd class, 23yrs
Moore, W., L/Tel., 24yrs
Morgan, George, L/Seaman, 31yrs
Oliver, Bernard, Stoker, 1st class, 23yrs
Payne, Edwin, Stoker 1st class, 23yrs
Perrin, James, L/Seaman
Rowley, Ben, Stoker 1st class
Scovell, Ernest, AB, 23yrs
Tanner, Arthur, L/Stoker, 25yrs
Taylor, Edward, Stoker 1st class
Virgo, Albert, Stoker 1st class, 22yrs
Williams, William, L/Stoker, 39yrs
Woodcock, Albert, Stoker, 34yrs

On 1 July, *UC 33* sank the 108-ton British sailing vessel *Ariel* with bombs at 57° 54'N, 01° 12'W: she was delivering coal and oil from Leith to Lerwick. On the voyage home on July 6, two Dutch fishing cutters, *Groen van Frinsterer* (M.A.103) and *Piet Hein* (M.A.16) were stopped then sunk by grenades. Next day the Montrose drifter *Southesk* (1912) detonated a mine and sank in Auskerry Sound at 59° 03'N 02° 34'W.

FATALITIES OF HMD *SOUTHESK*, 7.7.17
Bremner, William, Deckhand, RNR
Copland, James, Trimmer, RNR
Cormack, William, 2nd Hand, RNR
McLean, A., Deckhand, RNR

The 477-ton steel-hulled Norwegian barque *Skjald* (1877 – O. Gotaas, Kristiania, was the last victim of this patrol. The ship was transporting pit props from Fredrikshald in Norway to Blyth when she was captured and blown up with explosives.

   UC 33 returned to Germany on 8 July 1917.

   Oblt.z.s. Alfred Arnold assumed command of the minelaying boat on 20 July 1917 while Schelle took over the new *UB 65* (see entry). Arnold had previously commanded the minelayer *UC 49* and was consequently familiar with these waters.

   6) *UC 33* left Helgoland under Arnold on 5 August 1917 for a patrol on the south coast of Ireland. *UC 33* sailed via the English Channel to lay a minefield off Queenstown on 11 August. Two days later, Arnold made a torpedo attack on the 3,919-ton steamer *Akassa* (1910 – Elder Line Ltd, Liverpool). *Akassa* was outbound, carrying a general cargo from Liverpool bound for Sierra Leone. The attack took place 8 miles off Galley Head with the ship sailing at her top speed of 13 knots. Arnold's torpedo detonated in the engine room at 0747hrs. The crew abandoned ship immediately. Haste was fully justified because at 0815 *Akassa* rolled over and sank.

FATALITIES OF *AKASSA*, 13.8.17
Davies, Tom, Trimmer, 21yrs
Harrison, M., Fireman, 22yrs
Kwofie, Ben, Fireman, 35yrs
Morrison, T., 2nd Engineer, 29yrs
Newton, Joseph, Greaser/Fireman, 48yrs
Quayson, T., Trimmer, 23yrs
Seabreeze, Fireman

The 3,808-ton SS *Spectator* (1914 – Charente SS Co. Ltd, Liverpool) was 11 miles south-east of Galley Head on 19 August. The ship was inbound from Zanzibar to Liverpool with a general cargo and had recently dispersed from a convoy. Because a U-boat was known to be operating in the area, the torpedo boat USS *Paulding* was assigned to escort her into the Mersey roads. Both vessels were proceeding at 9.5 knots and zig-zagging when Arnold's torpedo struck portside between Nos two and three holds at 1018hrs. The explosion blew the forward lifeboats apart and destroyed the wireless aerials. Flooding spread to the engine room and the crew was unable to close the engines down. With the ship slowly settling the order was given to abandon ship. *Spectator* sank at 1026hrs and *Paulding* landed the crew at Queenstown.

   Arnold and *UC 33* returned to Germany on 26 August 1917.

FINAL PATROL
(7) After departing Helgoland on 16 September 1917, *UC 33* set off for a mine lay off Waterford. On 23 September *UC 33* was engaged mining the Waterford roads at a depth of 20m when she became entangled in A/S nets. Although *UC 33* managed to withdraw, in the process the starboard propeller and hydroplane became ensnared and the resultant damage prevented the boat from making an emergency dive. Early in the morning of 26 September 1917 visibility was quite poor with a sea fret lingering as *UC 33* sailed through St George's Channel, when the 6,430-ton British oil tanker *San Zeferino* (1914 –

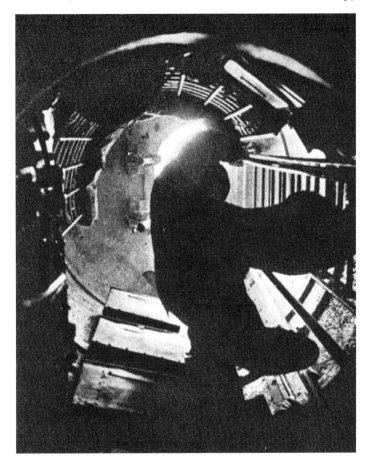

The conning tower hatch – a means of escape but no place for the faint-hearted. (P. Armstrong)

Eagle Oil Transport Co. Ltd, London) hove into view at 51° 52'N 6° 25'W. In spite of the presence of an escort and the earlier damage to *UC 33*, Arnold decided the tanker was too inviting a target to pass. The torpedo struck home but *San Zeferino*, in ballast, remained afloat and did not burn.[24] The ship survived to be towed into Milford.

FATALITIES OF *SAN ZEFERINO*, 26.9.17

Fell, Charles, 2nd Engineer, 32
Hale, Alfred, Fireman, 23
Patrick, Arthur, 5th Engineer, 32

After firing the torpedo at *San Zeferino*, Arnold turned and tried to make his escape on the surface. The gunners of *P61* had the U-boat in their sights.

The British view – the log of HMS *P61*, 26.9.17:

> At 6.26 enemy submarine of UC type appeared on surface starboard bow distant 1,000 yards.
> We opened fire with 12-pounder. One shell struck at point blank range forward of conning tower.
> At 6.30 P61 rammed enemy at full speed of 20kts abaft conning tower. A loud explosion followed and submarine sank stern first. Two men came to surface.

Some accounts state that as *P61* turned in to ram at maximum speed, her engines were shut down moments before the impact so that her bows would be driven downward to reinforce the impact on the U-boat. There is no evidence of this in the ship's log. *Oblt.z.s.* Arnold, the sole survivor of *UC 33*, refused to talk to British naval intelligence, but wrote this letter to *Oblt.z.s.* Klatt via the Red Cross:

I could see the patrol boat through the deadeye and he was bearing down on us fast. Then impact. The boat rolled right over. Water poured in through a great gash in our side. I ordered all tanks to be blown but we had shipped too much water. The engine room and the control room were virtually flooded. Batteries short-circuited and our lights went out at twenty metres.

The whole of the conning tower filled with water, which rose up to my hips. She sank with appalling rapidity, the lights went out immediately and everything was smashed in an instant. I was hurled backwards and could not stand upright. I was tearing at the hatch clips but I could not get it to open. I was clinging to the ladder with a stoker below me. Water continued to enter the conning tower via the speaking tube and cables. I tried to help the stoker into the conning tower but the water swept him away from my grasp and off the ladder. By this time the water in the conning tower was level with my chest. The war pilot helped me with the hatch clips, our last chance. Then came an uprush of extremely cold air as the hatch flew open. The sudden upward pressure jammed me against the war pilot. I dragged myself down in order to resist the pressure till he got out. I let go and whizzed [sic] upwards for two minutes in the middle of a giant air vortex. Twenty minutes later I was picked up but the navigator died shortly afterwards.

FATALITIES OF *UC 33*, 26.9.17

Behrends, Heinrich, Ob/MaschinistenMt
Calbecki, Erich, F.T.Gast
Cordes, Eito, Ob/Heizer
Distelrath, J., Heizer
Driestmann, Wil. Ob/Matrose
Hahlweg, W., Lt. zur.See.de Reserve
Hiering, Franz, Ob/Heizer der Reserve
Husemann, E., Ob/Matrose
Jost, Karl, Matrose
Kohlhaas, Johann, Matrose
Küchler, Friedrich Marine Ing Ober Asp
Leimbrink, Franz, Heizer
Lucke, Bernhard, Matrose
Ludwig, Josef, MaschinistenMt

Lutter, Franz, BootsmannsMt
Rahner, K., MaschinistenMt
Romkowski, F., Ob/MaschinistenMt
Röding, Hermann, F.T.Gast
Sager, W., Steuermann der Reserve
Simon, W., MaschinistenMt der Reserve
Viebahn, Karl, Heizer
Wagner, Georg, Heizer
Wildtraut, Heinrich, Heizer
Wittkuhn, Otto, MaschinistenMt
Woelke, Franz, Ob/Matrose
Wolter, August, Steuermann der Reserve
Zuchaschewski, Matrose

WRECK SITE

The wreck believed to be *UC 33* is orientated in a NE to SW (046/226-degrees) direction and lies on a seabed of sand, gravel and shells, in a general depth of 83m (272.3ft) (LAT). It is intact, stands 5.5m high and is lying on its port side. The conning tower has collapsed, but the two propellers are still in place and the deck gun has fallen over to the seabed. The wreck, which is of course a war grave, is covered in colourful anemones and soft corals.

ADM 137/3897, ADM 137/3673 ADM 137/2961 ADM 137/2962 NARA T-1022, Roll 85

H47, HM SUBMARINE

DATE OF LOSS: 9 July 1929
DEPTH: 74m
REFERENCE: 52° 08.506' N, 05° 19'.780' W
LOCATION: 15 miles W of Strumble Head and 12 miles N of St David's Head, Pembrokeshire and southern end of Cardigan Bay

Type: 'H21' Class coastal defence submarine of the Group III (*H47* and *H50*) **Builders:** Beardmore, Dalmuir for Royal Navy **Ordered:** for 1917 Emergency War Programme **Keel laid:** 20 November 1917 **Launched:** on 19 November 1918 **Completed:** 25 February 1919

TECHNICAL SPECIFICATIONS

Hull: single **Surface displacement:** 410 tons **F/L:** 440 tons full-load **U/Dt:** 500 tons **LBD:** 52.35m (171.9ft) × 4.67m (15ft-4in) × 3.42m (11ft-3in) **Props:** 2-bronze **Machinery:** 2 × 4-stroke 8-cylinder, air-injection NELSECO (New London Ship & Engine Co. of Groton, Connecticut, USA) diesels, 240bhp at 375rpm each continuous, with 480hp max (MAN & Vickers licensed the diesels) **S/Sp:** 13kts max as designed, but sea-speed of 11.5kts **Op/R:** 1,375-n.miles @ 10kts, 2,985-n.miles @ 7.5kts or 1,100-n.miles @ full power **Sub/R:** 10-n.miles @ 9kts, or 130-n.miles @ 2kts **U/Power:** 2 × Electric Dynamic Co. (Bayonne, New Jersey, USA) electric motors rated 320bhp continuous or 620bhp maximum (for less than 1 hour) gave 9 kts max **Batteries:** Exide 120-cells **Fuel/Cap:** 16 tons **Armament:** 4 × 53.34cm bow torpedo tubes **Torpedoes:** 8 × 53.34cm (21in) **Guns:** 1 × 7.62cm (3in) deck gun **Diving:** max-op-depth 54.86m (180ft) **Complement:** 22

H47 commanders with dates of appointment:

Lt Charles Ralfe Thompson – 1 December 1918 (Thompson was destined to become Churchill's ADC)
Lt Denis Ward Granet – Wednesday, 24 September 1919
Lt Henry Kelsall Beckford Mitchell – 14 February 1921
Lt John Gilbert Sutton – Saturday, 7 January 1922
Lt William Theodore Fredrick Annesley Voysey – 25 August 1923
Lt Thomas Mark Taylor – 4 November 1923
Lt Victor Cyril Dorman-Smith – 3 January 1925
Lt Frank Edmund Getting – 1925[25]
Lt Geoffrey Healet – 18 November 1926
Lt Alfred Maguire – 4 July 1927
Lt-Cdr Evelyn Seacombe Felton – 10 April 1928

Following an initial brief spell attached to HMS *Thames* at Campbeltown with the 'Periscope School', *H47* was then transferred to 6th Submarine Flotilla at Portland for training duties, attached to HMS *Vulcan*.[26] Unlike the well-travelled *E39* and *L1*, the Portland-based *H47* rarely strayed beyond the south coast, except for annual exercises and an occasional refit. On 4 May 1920 the boat was at Torquay, returning to Portland on 6 May.

On 22 September 1921, the boat returned to Torquay and Falmouth on exercise.

In July 1922 the boat took part in training exercises off Torquay. A further series of exercises took place on 16 October at Dartmouth.

In October 1925 the boat was temporarily attached to the 5th Flotilla and following North Sea exercises took part in a courtesy visit to Antwerp, in company with *M1* and *M3*.

On 1 January 1924 the boat took part in the solemn sail past to commemorate the dead of *L24* (see Vol.2).

On 3 June 1924 *H47* was at Pembroke on exercise in the Irish Sea. These evolutions were followed by a visit to Swansea, with *H32*, *H49* and *Vulcan*. On 9 June 1924 the boat was on exercise off Falmouth. On 11 September 1924 the boat was based in Penzance while exercises took place off the Scillies and Falmouth.

On 6 December 1926 the boat was involved in a minor collision with her stablemate *H32*, requiring a refit at Sheerness commencing 11 January 1927. By June of that year *H47* took part in a courtesy visit to Danzig in company with *Alecto* and boats of the 3rd Flotilla. On 27 February 1927 the boat visited Dover. In July 1927 the boat was involved in exercises off Portland and Devonport. For the next two years *H47* and *Alecto* exercised in the Irish Sea. On 3 July 1929, *H47* and her consorts put into Holyhead. The boat was now under the command of Lt Robert Gardner, appointed to the boat on 11 April 1929. As a midshipman of sixteen, Gardner had been wounded at Jutland. In June 1927 he left the cruiser *Cambrian* to enter submarines. Robert Gardner had later been appointed to *L24* only to leave that boat a matter of days before her subsequent loss.

FINAL PATROL

In order to understand the circumstances of this accident, it is necessary to turn to another British submarine in transit, *L12* (Lt-Cdr Harry Oram). *L12* was assigned to the 5th Flotilla, Portsmouth. Annual

Last known photograph of *H47*. (P. Armstrong)

HMS *L12*. (P. Armstrong)

summer exercises had recently taken place off Lamlash on Arran. The boats involved were: *H23*, *H43*, *H31*, *H34*, *H44*, *H49*, *R4*, *L6*, *L11*, *L12*, *L14*, *L22* and *L25*. Now, on 9 July, the twenty-seven-year-old instructor, Harry Kendall Oram, was returning to St Ives with *L12* and his class of young officers. Some distance behind trailed *L14*, which had been slowed by reason of a defective bearing.

A real sailor who had served his apprenticeship in tall ships, Oram, known as 'Joe', wrote a minor classic, *Ready for Sea*, which chronicled his early years in windjammers sailing round the Horn. Oram had been in the thick of the Jutland action on HMS *Obdurate* and he had been present on the bridge of *K6* during the 'Battle of May Island'. Now Lt-Cdr Oram was in command of the officer training course at Blockhouse. In some ways he was old school but as a trainer of men Harry Oram was in many ways ahead of his time, developing heretical ideas which threatened to put him at variance to his brother officers. Oram reasoned that the future of the Royal Navy depended upon the Senior Service evolving into a meritocracy and that meant broadening the gene pool in terms of officer recruitment. Royal Navy wardrooms should no longer be the exclusive preserve of public school-educated scions drawn from county families. If a man from a humble background otherwise had the ability to become an officer, authority should back him to the hilt. Furthermore, Oram believed in throwing his trainees in at the deep end. Many years later, Oram summed his training philosophy up with these words, which may have some bearing on the drama about to unfold:

> You cannot train someone for watch officer duties if he knows there is someone else doing the watching for him. What you can do is train him up to the point where he has enough confidence to deal with normal situations by himself and enough common sense to shout for help when he needs it. Nothing is ever lost by asking for help.

At 0600hrs Oram took over on the bridge as officer-on-watch. Visibility was moderate and conditions were reasonably calm with a light south-westerly wind. *L12* was 40 miles north of St David's Head when at 0730hrs a third submarine was spotted by lookouts off the starboard bow, on a bearing of 240 degrees. This submarine was none other than *H47*.

Lt-Cdr Oram:

> From 0730 to 0750 I observed the bearing of H47 to be definitely drawing aft…the situation at 0750 was perfectly normal…H47 distant two miles, fifty degrees on starboard bow, bearing drawing aft and slightly converging…in view of subsequent events it is clear that H47 could not have cleared L12's bows, providing the existing courses and speeds were maintained. By the instructions laid down in the Signal Manual, and the customs of the service, H47 as a junior approaching a senior officer had to ask permission before passing through the line. The course and speed of L12 and L14 was therefore not altered.

At 0750hrs one of the trainees, Sub-Lt Wise, took over the watch from Oram. Before leaving the bridge, Oram drew the trainee's attention to *H47*, which was by now on a bearing of 252-degrees at 2 miles distance. Oram had taken the precaution of verbally ordering that whenever one of the training class assumed watch duties, one of the boat's qualified watch keepers was to be close at hand 'to advise, instruct and if necessary take over from the officer on watch in case of emergency'. Following this order, *L12*'s Navigator, Lt Claude Keen RNR, made his way to the bridge.

Although a qualified watch keeper, Lt Keen was himself still under training at this time and was not an experienced submariner. By 0800hrs both submarines were steering southwards on a parallel course some 15 miles west of Strumble Head, with *L12* drawing slightly ahead of *H47*. At this moment the officer on watch, Lt Wise, indicated to Keen that if *H47* was to maintain her current course and speed, the boats would end up on a converging course. If this dangerous situation was to be avoided, *L12* must alter course accordingly.

Lt Keen agreed:

> I arrived on the bridge at 0802 and looked at the land and the chart because it was not familiar to me. While I was so engaged Lt Wise told me 'we should have to get out of the way of H47'. I looked at H47 and thought he was probably right and then rang down to tell the captain that H47 was trying to cross our bows. I decided to alter course to conform to the Rule of the Road. I gave the order 'Port 20' to pass under the stern of H47.

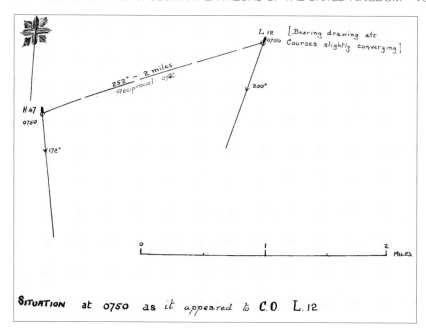

SITUATION at 0750 as it appeared to C.O. L.12

Fig.6: 'Situation at 0750.'

At 0804 Lt Keen passed this message to the control room via AB Arthur Sampson: '*ASK THE CAPTAIN IF WE CAN EASE DOWN AS H47 IS TRYING TO CROSS OUR BOWS.*'

There was no response, so minutes later a second message was sent down to Oram: '*ASK THE CAPTAIN TO COME TO THE BRIDGE AS H47 IS GETTING VERY CLOSE.*'

It was rather unfortunate that simultaneously a second message was received from *L14* requesting Oram's permission to slow down, owing to a hot bearing. At this time Oram was in the wardroom, eating his breakfast while studying a chart held by First Lt Lipscomb in readiness for a scheduled change of course.

Lt–Cdr Oram:

> At about 0806 AB Sampson came with a message from the bridge about L14's reduction of speed. I sent back a reply approving a reduction in speed for L12 and proceeded to go to the bridge. When in the crew space, I heard two blasts on the whistle and felt the engines stop. I hastened up the conning tower. Before I reached the bridge I felt the motors running astern. When I took over I realised that collision was inevitable and ordered, 'Collision stations. Close watertight doors'.

Oram's assent to a speed reduction had been duly relayed back to the officers on the bridge. Lt Keen now took matters into his own hands by issuing the order to 'Slow Both'. However the distance between the two submarines had now closed to an alarming 800 yards. Keen had calculated that as long as *H47* maintained her speed, collision might be avoided. To his horror, he now noted that *H47* had actually stopped engines. Worse still, her bow was swinging towards *L12*. Keen responded by altering course to starboard in the hope that any collision impact might be reduced to a glancing blow.

THE COLLISION

What had happened to *H47*? At 0803, following *L12*'s alteration of course to starboard, Lt Gardner had issued two instructions. First, he had ordered *H47* to go full astern. When impact seemed inevitable, Gardner followed with, 'COLLISION STATIONS!' *H47*'s whistle was blown but the frantic efforts made to avoid an impact proved in vain. At 0810hrs the two submarines collided, the bow of *L12* penetrating an estimated 2ft into the port side of *H47*, abaft the forward control room bulkhead, at a time when the off-duty watch were enjoying breakfast. Although the fore-endsmen managed to shut the bulkhead door, within fifteen seconds *H47* began to list sharply to starboard. She sank in twenty seconds, the inrush of water trapping most of the crew. PO Tel Cleburne had been in the control room when the violent inrush of water slammed him back against the bulkhead. As the boat careered towards the bottom, an escape of air powered Cleburne up the conning tower, and deposited him in the sea. Elation at his own survival was tempered by the knowledge that the very air bubble that had saved his life had signified the extinction of his boat-mates. Sydney Cleburne already enjoyed a charmed existence, having previously served in *M1* only to be drafted two days before she was lost (Vol.2).

L12 was also in serious trouble. As she dipped by the bows, the bridge party consisting of Oram, PO Wheeler, AB Sampson and L/Sig Bull were tipped into the sea.

Lt-Cdr Oram:

> I was sucked completely under for some seconds and when I did pop up found some difficulty in orientating myself. I trod water, anxiously scanning the surface of the sea for members of my crew who had been swept off the bridge but there was quite a chop and heads were difficult to spot.

AB Sampson, key witness to the messages that had passed between Lt-Cdr Oram and Lt Keen, died of exposure shortly after being hauled aboard *L14*, while L/Sig Bull drowned. Fortunately the lower conning tower hatch had been closed by CPOs Betty and Jolley before *L12* plunged. All watertight doors had not been shut, only the stern compartments had been secured. The crew quickly recognised the danger as chlorine gas began to billow from the saturated batteries. Lt Lipscomb and ERA Hoggett showed great presence of mind. First Lipscomb ordered every man to don a gas mask. Next he ran the battery fans to disperse the gas. *L12* took on a forty-five-degree angle. Although badly affected by gas, ERA Hoggett manually released the drop-keel. *L12* now levelled out. Disorientated by their experiences, the crew mistakenly believed the boat had struck the seabed. Only when they read the depth gauges did they realise the boat was actually on the surface. Indeed, some time passed before CERA Jenkins gave the order to open the engine room bulkhead door. As the crew of *L12* clambered out on deck, there was a surreal sight. Stoker PO Hicks of *H47*, who had been on the bridge at the time of the collision, was discovered clinging to the bows of *L12*, having jumped over the side at the moment of impact. When *L12* plunged 60ft, he had somehow managed to cling to the jumping wire.

Lt-Cdr Oram:

> Sub Lt Miers[27] went onto the bridge and found Stoker PO Hicks in a state of shock. Whether this was the result of his watery ordeal or whether the sudden appearance of L12's crew momentarily convinced them that they were all on their way to Davy Jones locker, he never disclosed. Miers attended to the poor chap and it was from him that First Lieutenant Lipscomb learned that L12 had sunk H47.

Apart from Hicks and Cleburne, only Lt Gardner survived to be rescued by *L14*. After picking up this pathetic knot of survivors, *L14* put into Milford Haven to effect emergency repairs. The boat arrived at Blockhouse on 13 July. The Secretary to the Admiralty announced to Parliament that attempts at salvage had been abandoned because of bad weather and strong currents in the Irish Sea. There were pragmatic reasons too. The small submarine was probably too badly damaged to justify repair and return to service. At sunset on 11 July a memorial service was held on board HMS *Rodney*. An inquest was held on the body of AB Sampson at Milford next day.

How could two of HM submarines have been allowed to collide with such catastrophic consequences? The actions of Lt-Cdr Oram, Lt Keen of *L12* and Lt Gardner of *H47* in the moments leading up to the collision now came under scrutiny. Heads must roll, but whose? The first of three courts martial commenced at Portsmouth on 26 July 1929 presided over by Capt Somerville DSO. The prosecuting council for the courts martial faced by Keen and Gardner was Reginald Darke of the Blockhouse staff. Darke, who we briefly met earlier in command of *L1*, rejoiced in the sobriquet of 'Reg the Hatchet'. Among those sitting in judgement was Capt Max Horton DSO. Square in Admiralty sights was Lt Keen RNR. There was a widespread belief in naval circles that RNR personnel always suffered harsher treatment at the hands of courts martial compared with that meted out to regular RN officers. Capt Oram certainly doubted that Keen had received fair treatment and recorded this view in *The Rogues Yarn*.

In his defence Keen maintained that the decisions he had taken were the correct ones at the time. Had *H47* held her course instead of stopping engines, *L12* would have cleared *H47* by a margin of 4-600 yards. Lt Keen had merely judged the situation to the best of his ability and acted accordingly. The court was unimpressed:

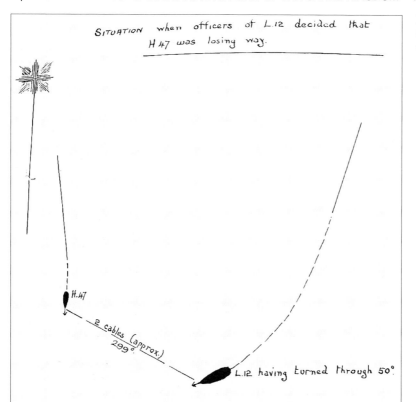

SITUATION when officers of L.12 decided that H 47 was losing way.

H.47

2 cables (approx.)
299°

L.12 having turned through 50°

Fig.7: 'Situation at 0803 – Boats on converging course.'

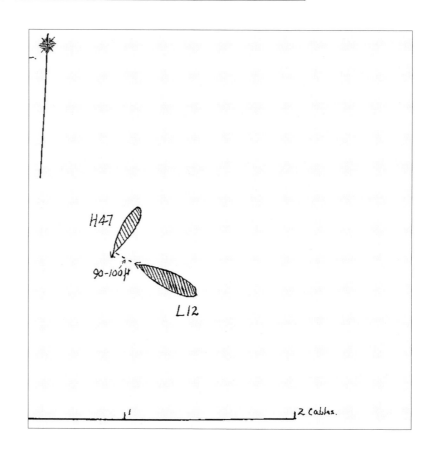

H47

90-100ft

L12

2 Cables.

Fig.8: 'Collision inevitable?'

The court finds that…he did not take the best action for avoiding H47 and having committed submarine L12 to a turn, did not make full use of the engines and helm. Secondly of negligently performing the
duty imposed on him as Officer of the Watch…the court having found the charges proved, judges the said
Lieutenant Claude Stanley Griffiths Keen to be dismissed from His Majesty's Ship *Dolphin* and to be severely
reprimanded, 26 July 1929.

The next man to face naval justice was Lt Gardner. A popular officer, his career to date had been exem-
plary. When his court martial commenced on 2 August 1929, Lt Gardner faced four charges under
sections nine and twenty-eight of the Naval Discipline Act. Firstly, that he had negligently or by default
lost his submarine *H47*; secondly, that he had negligently or by default hazarded his submarine; thirdly,
that he had not handled his submarine in such a manner to avoid the consequences of the negligent
navigation of *L12*. Finally Lt Gardner faced the charge that he had not handled *H47* in such a manner
so as to minimise the 'negligent navigation' of *L12*. Gardner's court martial was presided over by Capt J.
Cunningham MVO. Much discussion centred on the wisdom of Lt Gardner's actions in putting *H47*'s
engines on full speed astern, while simultaneously ordering the helm turned hard a port. Capt Darke,
prosecuting counsel, alleged that by maintaining a course and speed which brought *H47* unduly close to
L12, without first ascertaining that *H47* could safely pass astern, Lt Gardner had failed to take sufficient
steps to prevent a collision.

Gardner was exonerated on two of these charges only to be found guilty of '*not handling* H47 *in such
a manner as to avoid the consequences of the negligent navigation of* L12'. Gardner was also held responsible
for '*not handling* H47 *in such a manner as to minimise the negligent navigation of* L12'. When the proceedings
were over, one much-decorated veteran submarine commander present in court turned towards the
men sitting in judgement and observed loudly: 'And we thought all the idiots were in the army!'

Lt Gardner's response was to quit the Submarine Service though he opted to remain in the Royal
Navy. On 22 October 1929 he was appointed to the sloop *Daffodil*. On 15 April 1931 Gardner was promoted to Lt-Cdr and in January 1925 he was serving in a training capacity at HMS *Pembroke*.

It remained to be seen whether the court would see fit to punish Lt-Cdr Oram. His court martial was
held on 12 August. Oram faced two charges. Firstly, that he had 'negligently or by default suffered *L12* to
be hazarded' and that he had 'left the bridge in charge of a sub-lieutenant under training in submarines
when the situation had been one that demanded his personal attention on the bridge on account of H47
being on a converging course'.

The second charge was that Oram had omitted making a proper bridge hand-over to Lt Keen, as the
latter was forced to take over watch officer duties from Sub-Lt Wise, the officer under instruction. Oram
pleaded 'not guilty' to both charges.

Lt-Cdr Oram maintained that nothing had been amiss at the time of his hand over to Sub-Lt Wise at
0750hrs. More controversially, he denied receiving the 0804hrs message from Lt Keen. It will be recalled
that the men on the bridge had been concerned that *H47* was attempting to cross *L12*'s bows. In his
testimony Lt Keen had maintained that this crucial message had been passed down to the wardroom
by AB Sampson. Here Oram's version of events differed from that of Lt Keen. According to Oram, AB
Sampson had merely brought a message from *L14* requesting permission to reduce speed because of an
overheating bearing. In response to this question Lt-Cdr Oram had nodded, 'Yes, certainly'. Oram maintained he had been unaware that *H47* *was* bearing down fast. He had no reason to think that his boat
was in danger. Signalman Simpson, who had been on the bridge, testified that Keen had indeed sent the
message: 'Ask the captain if we can ease down, *H47* is trying to cross our bows.'

At 0806hrs, a second verbal message had been passed down to the wardroom. Lt Keen had ordered AB
Rogers to 'Ask the captain if we can ease down, as *H47* is crossing our bows'. AB Rogers maintained that
not only had he repeated this message to Lt-Cdr Oram, but the captain had nodded his head in consent.
AB Rogers, who had been control room messenger between 08 and 12, unequivocally testified that Lt-Cdr
Oram's assent had been given and duly relayed back to the bridge. In other words, if Rogers' version
of events is accepted, by 0806hrs Oram must have been aware of the seriousness of the situation. Oram
maintained he had no knowledge of the message referred to by Simpson and Rogers and could give no
explanation as to how he had failed to receive the information about *H47* attempting to cross *L12*'s bows.

The testimony of First Lt Frank Lipscomb (who, it will be recalled, had been studying a chart in the
wardroom with Oram) was now pivotal to the outcome. Lipscomb, whose heroism that day had been
roundly praised, corroborated the evidence of Oram. Under oath he maintained that the only message passed to the captain had been the one from AB Sampson and that Oram had left immediately for

the bridge. Lipscomb's testimony proved decisive. The court found the case against Oram 'not proven' resulting in his complete exoneration. For the remainder of his naval career, he would be known by the wardroom sobriquet of 'Lucky Joe'.

Towards the end of his life Oram entrusted a series of taped interviews to teacher Wendy Harris, published as *The Rogues Yarn*. Oram emerges as a perceptive man with an admirable respect for 'lower deck' potential. A chapter of the book is devoted to the *H47* incident and it is clear that he was profoundly affected by the loss of so many lives. Oram regarded his crew as 'family' and later became godfather to the son of his lost signalman, Charles Bull. The book contains a sad little postscript concerning CERA Harry Hoggett, who the reader may recall had been one of the heroes of *L12*. Hoggett had joined the navy as a boy sailor of fifteen in 1917. Rising to the rate of CERA, he remained in submarines during the Second World War only to die in *Tarpon* in May 1940. This is not the last we shall hear of Lt-Cdr Oram. Ten years after the loss of *H47* 'Lucky Joe' would become forever associated with one of the worst submarine disasters in British maritime history.

The *H47* crew is commemorated by a stained-glass window in St George's Hall, Chatham. In reference to the accident in the Irish Sea, the striking image portrays a green-clad St Patrick driving out snakes.

FATALITIES OF *L12*, 9.7.29
Bull, Charles, L/Sig
Sampson, Arthur, AB
Wheeler, Horace, PO

FATALITIES OF *H47*, 9.7.29
Bain, David, AB
Bickmore, Noel, Lt
Crew, John, Stoker
Crimmins, Benjamin, Stoker
Ditcher, John, ERA
Elliott, Edmund, P O
Goodlet, John, CERA
Harris, Tom, L/Sig
Hartland, Sydney, AB
Hawley, Frederick, AB
Henderson, Clifford, L/Stoker
Legg, Alfred, ERA
Maccabee, Edward, L/Stoker
Mann, Cyril L/ Sig
McSweeney, John, Stoker (Material in Submarine Museum)
Pike, Lionel, ERA
Robbins, Percy, PO
Spencer, Nat, L/Smn
Stone, Arthur, LTO
Taylor, Alfred, Tel
Wise, William, L/Tel

WRECK SITE
This wreck, although not positively identified to date, is most probably that of HM S/M *H47*. The wreck in question lies in a general depth of 74m (LAT) on a seabed of coarse sand, gravel and pebbles. The wreck appears to be upright, is intact and orientated in a north/ south direction.
ADM 156/100

Although there is no wreck and the sinking did not occur in British waters, the story of the next submarine's demise is too compelling to ignore.

UC 44, SM IMPERIAL U-BOAT

DATE OF LOSS: 4 August 1917
REFERENCE: 52° 09'N, 06° 59'W
LOCATION OF WRECK: Duncannon Pier, Ireland

Type: UCII coastal mine-laying boat *Builders:* AG Vulcan, Hamburg for Kaiserliche Deutsche Marine *Ordered:* on 20 November 1915, within the batch of *UC 40 – UC 45 Keel laid:* as Yard No.77 on 1 February 1916 *Launched:* on 10 October 1916 *Commissioned:* by *Kplt.* Kurt Tebbenjohanns on 4 November 1916

TECHNICAL SPECIFICATIONS

Hull: double *Surface displacement:* 400 tons *U/Dt:* 480 tons *LBDH:* 49.45m × 5.21m × 3.68m × 7.46m *Machinery:* 2 × 250ps diesels *Props:* 2-bronze *S/Sp:* 11.7kts *Op/R:* 9,410-n.miles @ 7kts *Sub/R:* 60-n.miles @ 4kts *U/Power:* 2 × 230ps electric motors gave 6.7kts *Batteries:* lead/acid/accumulators *Fuel/Cap:* 41 + 14 tons *Armament:* 2 external 50.04cm torpedo tubes at the bow, one either side of the mine chutes & 1 stern internal tube *Torpedoes:* 7 × 50.04cm (19.7in) maximum *Guns:* 1 × 88mm (3.46in) forward deck gun *Ammo:* 133 rounds of 88mm *Mine tubes:* 6 *Mines:* 18 × UC200 *Diving:* max-op-depth 50m (164ft) & 33-sec to crash-dive *Complement:* 3 officers & 23 ratings. Torpedo load as designed: a torpedo in each tube plus a reload for the stern tube. Some carried a dismantled stern tube, others two additional torpedoes lashed to the deck. *UC 44* was formally assigned to the Germany-based *I.U-Bootflottille* at Brunsbüttel on 1 January 1917, with *Kplt.* Kurt Tebbenjohanns the Commanding Officer from 4 November 1916

(1) On 3 February 1917, *UC 44* sailed from Brunsbüttel for operations against allied shipping off the northern isles and the Scottish east coast. On 6 February, *UC 44* first laid two mine barriers off Lerwick, consisting of three and four mines; then on the 8 February, two more barriers consisting of four mines in each group, were laid in the Cromarty Firth. Three remaining mines were laid at the entrance to Kirkwall on 9 February. With the minelaying over, *UC 44* was free to rampage through the fishing grounds of northern Britain.

On 11 February Tebbenjohanns captured and sank the 129-ton Shields trawler *Ashwold* (1894) with bombs, taking the skipper prisoner. Overnight Tebbenjohanns sailed north. Next day, off North Ronaldsay, the 198-ton British trawler *Dale* (1900) was captured then sunk by explosives; the skipper was also taken prisoner. Later that day, some 39 miles off Dennis Head, Aberdeen, the 835-ton Swedish coaster *Adolf* (1872 – Angf. Akt. Adolf, Göteborg) was sunk with bombs. *Adolf* was carrying a general cargo between Warkworth and Gothenburg. Once again Tebbenjohanns took the master captive. Seventy-five miles south of Fair Isle, *UC 44* seized the British trawler *King Alfred* (1899) on 13 February, sinking her with charges. Next day two more fishing vessels were sunk with charges, the 221-ton *Belvoir Castle* (1899) and the 144-ton *Mary Bell* (1898) some 50 miles off Aberdeen. The masters were once again taken prisoner and a somewhat crowded *UC 44* returned to base on 16 February.

On 9 March, the 440-ton Class 'B' destroyer HMS *Albacore* (1908) raised anchor from her berth in Kirkwall to investigate reports of a U-boat operating off Auskerry. At 0444hrs *Albacore* struck one of Tebbanjohan's mines. The mine detonated on the bow, starboard, fatally close to the forward mess deck where the off-duty watch was sleeping. The signallers on watch were blown into the sea with the wireless transmitter. Neither they, nor the equipment, could be recovered in the darkness. Mr Baker (Gunner) AB Double and Telegraphist Moore showed great courage in leading a party of stokers below decks to search for survivors. When daylight came it was apparent that the ship forward of the bridge had sheared off. *Albacore* was towed back to Kirkwall and those who could be found were buried at Lyness.

FATALITIES OF HMS *ALBACORE*, 9.3.17

Davies, Norman, Sig, RNVR, 20yrs
Dowdall, Joseph, AB, 35yrs
Elsey, Lawrence, AB, 24yrs
Halfhead, Herbert, AB, 29yrs

Flanders Flotilla hardware on display. Two of the boats belong to the UCII class and are distinctive by reason of their raised fore-decks and pronounced torpedo tube bulges. These external bulges were necessary to provide room for the internal mine wells. The raked bows indicate the UCs belong to the *UC 40–UC 79* marque as older models had a distinctive rounded bow. (Johan Ryheul, Marinekorps Flandern Archive)

King, Herbert, AB
McCullock, William, Chief Stoker, 33yrs
Murphy, William, Sig, RNVR, 26yrs
Patton, William, AB, 33yrs
Payne, Charles, L/Sig
Pledge, Bruce, Petty Officer
Robinson, Bertie, AB
Saunders, A., Stoker 1st class
Sedwell, John, Stoker 1st class
Stevens, W., Able Seaman
Thompson, Robert, L/Seaman, 25yrs
Turner, William, AB, 35yrs

On 29 March the 234-ton iron coastal steamer *Ruby* (1882 – W. Cooper & Son, Kirkwall) was carrying a crew of seven and a general cargo from Leith to Kirkwall when she detonated a mine and sank a couple of miles from Auskerry, Orkneys. A deckhand, who was the only survivor, was working in the galley when at 1010hrs a violent explosion caused the ship to disintegrate without time to lower a lifeboat. He described how he jumped into the sea and swam towards an empty floating barrel. A patrol vessel picked him up thirty minutes later and landed him at Kirkwall.

FATALITIES OF *RUBY*, 29.3.17

Marwick, James, Fireman, 42yrs
Mason, William, Master
Rendall, George, Mate, 23yrs
Rendall, John, Fireman, 23yrs
Rendall, Steward, Able Seaman, 30yrs
Sevis, George, Engineer, 41yrs

(2) On 1 March 1917, *UC 44* sailed for mining operations off the south coast of Ireland, taking the direct route through the English Channel. On 5 March Kurt Tebbenjohanns captured then burned out the Portuguese sailing ship *Guadiana* (1916 – J. Mourao, Oporto) using an incendiary device. The small vessel was transporting mahogany to England at the time of this interception. Tebbenjohanns laid small minefields off Mine Head, Queenstown and Waterford on 6/7 March.

The Queenstown minefield soon bore vicious fruit. The 5,694-ton SS *Westwick* (1916 – Westwick SS Co. Ltd, Sunderland) detonated a mine one mile south of Roche Point on 7 March. The inbound ship had been transporting maize from Baltimore to Hull when the mine detonated. The crew abandoned ship leaving *Westwick* drifting in the Cork roads. The crew of thirty-eight was rescued by the Cork harbour examination vessel. Meanwhile *UC 44* had moved on to patrol off Fastnet Rock, where she shelled and dispatched the 1,577-ton Norwegian steamer *Adalands* (1880 – Aktieselskapet 'Adalands' Alf Monsen, Tønsberg) later that day. The vessel was voyaging between Dakar and Hull with a cargo of groundnuts.

UC 44 had an encounter with the famous Q-ship, HMS *Penshurst* (Vol.2) on 8 March. *Penshurst* spotted the surfaced boat in a heavy sea. The Q-ship was slowly bringing her broadside to bear when the astute Tebbanjohanns' suspicions were aroused. Tebbanjohanns dived and withdrew. This was to be the first of several encounters between *UC 44* and special service vessels.

Tebbanjohanns sank two steamers on 12 March off Kinnaird Head. The first victim was the 914-ton Norwegian steamer *Marna II* (1883 – Aktieselskapet 'Marna' Martin Pedersen, Mandal) which was transporting a general cargo from Leith to Bergen. This ship was sunk by torpedo but the second vessel, the 1,073-ton collier *Lucy Anderson* (1904 – Roberts & Cooper Ltd, Hull) was shelled to destruction some 55 miles off Noss Head. A couple of trawlers were seized off Rattray Head next day, the 227-ton *Nuttalia* (1899) and the 167-ton *Navenby* (1891). While *Navenby* was sunk with explosives, *Nuttalia* was towed back to Wilhelmshaven as a prize of war when *UC 44* returned on 15 March.

(3) *UC 44* sailed out from Wilhelmshaven on 13 April 1917 for a minelaying mission off the east coast of Scotland and northern England. Next day near the Dogger Bank, Tebbanjohanns seized then sank the Boston steam trawler *Dalmatian* (1900) with charges. Tebbanjohanns left the crew in a lifeboat but this later overturned and all hands drowned.

FATALITIES OF *DALMATIAN*, 14.4.17

Braime, Fred, Fireman
Corbin, Frederick, Deckhand
Draper, G., 2nd Hand
Norton, John, 1st Engineer
Priestley, Walter, Deckhand
Richards, J., Steward
Spink, James, 2nd Engineer
Webb, Charles, Skipper
Wisking, Thomas, Deckhand

That same day, Tebbenjohanns sank Boston steam trawler *Sutterton* (1893) with explosive charges off St Abbs Head at 55° 45'N, 00° 15'W. Tom Haddinott, a fireman, died. The 157-ton Dutch sailing vessel *Heikina* was shelled and sunk with all hands on 15 April.

Tebbenjohanns approached the Durham coast to lay mines off Sunderland on 16 April. *UC 32* (Vol.1) had recently been lost here and the crew of *UC 44* can only have regarded its orders with trepidation. Having mined off Roker, *UC 44* moved north to mine the Tyne roads. The collier *Poltava* (1889 – Kaye, Son & Co. Ltd, London – Crown nominees) struck one of those mines on 19 April and sank 3 miles off Souter Point. As *UC 44* made her way up the Northumbrian coast, she disposed of the trawlers *Edith* (1899) and *Grecian* with explosives off the Farne Islands.

On 21 April 1917, *UC 44* torpedoed and sank the 701-ton Norwegian steamer *Peik* (1910 – Dampskipsselskapet Aktieselskapet Asnæs, Sandefjord). *Peik* (Capt Alfred Olsen) was transporting a mixed cargo from Newcastle to Arendal, Norway. It was 1600hrs and she had just passed Coquet Island when the torpedo exploded against the engine room. All fifteen crew were rescued by a passing trawler and landed at the Tyne. As the men evacuated *Peik*, the U-boat's periscope was clearly seen. As *Peik* was clearly marked as a Norwegian ship, there was shock in neutral circles that she had been attacked but

Incendiary device used by U-boats to administer the *coup de grace* or to dispatch minor targets considered unworthy of a torpedo. This contraption was recovered from *UC 44*. (IWM)

the recent declaration of unrestricted submarine warfare underlined that all vessels trading with Britain would be considered as valid targets.

By 23 April Tebbanjohanns had sunk two fishing boats. *Nightingale* (1892) was captured and sunk by explosive charges, while *Auriac* (1890 – T.C. Steven & Co., Leith) was sunk with gunfire off St Abb's Head. *UC 44* had suddenly appeared a quarter of a mile distant and opened fire with the deck gun. The first shot hit the ship and the second one wounded the helmsman but just as Capt Jones ordered his vessel to stop, a third shell exploded near the bridge. Numerous shells began raining down all around the ship. The master had little option but to tell his men to take cover. Minutes later, an explosion killed Boatswain William Leask. Fourteen of the crew later escaped in the lifeboat. It was claimed that when *UC 44* closed on the lifeboat Capt Jones asked Tebbanjohanns for bandages to aid the wounded but the U-boat man allegedly ignored him. Fishing boats picked up the survivors and took them to St Abbs. Two Danish steamers were destroyed on 23 April: the 1,564-ton *Scot* (1895 – Aktieselskabet Dampskibsselskabet Scot, Aarhus) on passage from Copenhagen to Burntisland, when *UC 44* captured her off St Abb's Head, later destroying her with explosives.

The 991-ton *Baron Stjernblad* (1890 – Det Forenede Dampskibs Selskab, Copenhagen) was torpedoed off St Abb's Head on 23 April prior to being finally dispatched with gunfire. The ship was transporting 500 tons of general cargo from Hull to Copenhagen.

UC 44 returned to Helgoland on 25 April 1917.

(4) On 14 May 1917 *UC 44* departed for mine-laying operations off the south coast of Ireland. Tebbanjohanns is credited with sinking the 1,126-ton Norwegian steamer *Turid* (1905 – A/S Dampskipsselskapet Turid, Trondheim) off Peterhead on 28 May. *Turid* was delivering herring and wood pulp from Trondheim to Grimsby: all the crew survived.

UC 44 arrived back at Helgoland on 30 May.

(5) Leaving Helgoland on 23 June 1917, *UC 44* sailed for to the west coast of Ireland via the English Channel. Off St Catherine's Point on the Isle of Wight on 25 June, *UC44* became embroiled in an indecisive exchange of fire with the Q-Ship schooner HMS *Glen* (1897). This engagement ended when the U-boat dived and left the area. *UC 44* safely reached her mining billet in the Shannon estuary on 28 June. One group of mines was laid in the Shannon while a second deposit was made in Dingle Bay, near Inishtearaght.

On 30 June Tebbenjohanns made a surface interception against the 2,345-ton Norwegian barque *Asalia* (1892 – Thv B. Herstein & Sønner, Kristiansand). As *Asalia* was transporting a highly volatile cargo of 16,325 barrels of oil/petroleum, her crew required little persuasion to take to the boats. This encounter took place approximately 170-nautical miles west of Fastnet lighthouse. At least the crew of *Asalia* survived, the crew of the 3,133-ton Italian steamer *Phoebus* (1894 – Soc. Anon. Ilva, Genoa) was not so fortunate. It is believed that Tebbanjohanns torpedoed Phoebus on 1 July with the loss of all hands, off Berehaven. The ship had been carrying a cargo of iron ore from Almeria to Vickers of Barrow and she sank like a stone.

At 1500hrs on 2 July, *UC 44* surfaced to intercept a seemingly innocent five masted barque off the south-east Irish coast. The Q-ship *Gaelic* opened fire, fatally wounding *IWO Oblt.* Felix Pantel. Tebbanjohanns managed to submerge before the boat was disabled. Felix Pantel died during the night and was buried at sea off Bantry Bay.

An interesting encounter took place on 6 July 1917 when *UC 44* was on its return journey. Tebbenjohanns attacked a small Lerwick-bound convoy at 1020hrs (CT) off the Pentland Firth. The location given in the *KTB* was 58° 35' N, 00° 45' W. His target was apparently a small steamer of 1,000 to 1,500 tons. The *KTB* reported a detonation ninety seconds following the torpedo launch. Some confusion surrounds the identity of this vessel as we shall see. At 0830 HMS *Itchen* (Lt Cavaye), previously instrumental in the destruction of *UC 39* (see Vol.1), was zig-zagging on the starboard side of the convoy. The destroyer had just steadied on a new course when a torpedo was spotted. There was insufficient time to take avoiding action, with the result that the torpedo struck port side aft, killing several men. A second, larger explosion, possibly depth-charge detonations, followed, resulting in massive structural damage. Fortunately the escort trawler *Gardenia* was able to draw alongside and rescue most of the crew. Several hours later, HMS *Itchen* rolled over and sank by the stern. The report into the sinking maintains that the torpedo had actually been fired on the port side (i.e. opposite side to *Itchen*) of the oncoming convoy and that it had streaked past the target only to hit the escort instead. For decades the sinking was attributed in British records to *U 99* but Michael Lowrey concludes that the probability is that Tebbenjohanns attacked a steamer but fortuitously bagged a destroyer instead.

FATALITIES OF HMS *ITCHEN*, 6.7.17
Collins, Dennis, Stoker 1st class
Frampton, William, L/Stoker
Hedges, Stanley, Stoker 1st class
H Maund, Reginald G., Able Seaman
Revell, Alfred, Able Seaman, 32yrs
Sutton, Walter J., Able Seaman, 33yrs
Wright, Ernest B., ERA
Hicks, Edwin J., Mate RN, 32yrs

UC 44 headed back home, arriving at Helgoland on 8 July 1917.

FINAL PATROL
Patrick Beesley in 'Room 40' claims that *UC 44* fell victim to an elaborate ambush laid by British naval intelligence. For some time the decoders of 'Room 40' in Admiralty had been able to piece together a picture of German activity from an array of fragmentary decryptions. Likewise German radio intelligence assiduously monitored British transmissions, having earlier broken the Admiralty code themselves. 'Room 40' discovered that as soon as British minesweepers transmitted a signal advising that a recently fouled sector had been cleared, a UC boat would be immediately dispatched to relay the mines. The British now attempted to turn this intelligence to their advantage.

On the night of 14 June 1917, the Irish port of Waterford was mined by *UC 42* (Muller). The authorities closed the port to maritime traffic and although located, the nine mines were not swept. A fake 'mines cleared' message was, however, transmitted. German radio intelligence duly detected this transmission and *UC 44* was despatched to carry out the next mine lay off Waterford.

UC 44 departed Helgoland on 31 July 1917, arriving off Waterford on the evening of 4 August. The log book indicates that at 2044hrs *UC 44* approached the mining position with Newton Point bearing 336 degrees and Hook Point at forty-eight degrees. At this juncture Tebbanjohanns dived the boat and lay her on the bottom in twelve fathoms at 2242hrs. Just before midnight *UC 44* surfaced to lay a four-mine group in 10m of water at the harbour entrance. At 0030hrs *UC 44* had just dropped the fifth mine in a five-mine group. What follows is Tebbenjohann's post-war account translated from *U-Boote Westwarts*:

> On the evening of 4 August we arrived off Waterford. Because it would be several hours before the tide was favourable for mine-laying, I kept the boat on the bottom. Shortly after midnight we surfaced. It was a crystal clear, moonlit night with a mirror flat sea and no wind. The Waterford light was working and I had an exact position fix. We dove to lay the nines in two groups, one of four and one of five. During the mine-laying, I personally plotted the course and recorded the mines positions. I had just given the order to drop the ninth mine, and had received the reply, 'mine dropped', when the boat was shaken by a powerful explosion. The lights went out and there was a strong odour of sulphur. The explosion threw me against the bulkhead, cut my eyelid and room momentarily stunned me. I never lost consciousness. Two ratings took refuge with me in the conning tower, and from beneath us in the control room I could hear water rushing in and I could feel the boat sinking. It hit bottom hard, but there was no sound from the crew. Not a sound. I closed the hatch into the control room...

UC 44 had sunk to the bottom of the Waterford roads and the predicament of her crew was dire:

> It was absolutely black in the conning tower, but I tried to contact the crew through the speaking tube. I knew that the boat was lost and the entire crew, except for we three, were dead. We were jammed tightly in the cramped confines of the conning tower with the water rising slowly. We could not see it, but we could feel it rising around our feet. It was so dark that we could not see each other, which is probably good because that meant that we could not see the fear on our faces. I knew our exact position, and I knew that the chances of us swimming to shore were very small. In any event, I was not sure that we could survive the escape from the boat. I have a strong fear of drowning, but as we stood there in total darkness I had the urge to at least try. There was, after all, nothing to lose.
>
> We took our positions on the ladder leading to the conning tower hatch. The explosion had ripped open the stern and the entire boat was flooded except for our portion of the conning tower. That worked in our favour because the steadily rising water was compressing the air inside the conning tower and soon it would equal the outside water pressure.
>
> I loosened the upper hatch and it sprang open. We were blown through the opening and I tried to control my ascent so that I would not rise too quickly. Despite the endless time it took for me to reach the surface, I never had a problem with running out of breath. My lungs automatically adjusted to the diminishing water pressure as I rose, and a constant stream of air issued from my mouth. What we all did wrong was that none of us had shed our clothes before we opened the hatch.
>
> We all three men surfaced in a tight group, and I pointed toward the light tower at the Waterford entrance and told them, that was their goal. But the current was setting us away from the lighthouse, and after several minutes of fruitless swimming, I told them to swim with the current toward the shore. That was the last I saw of them. For a while I heard one of them calling for help and then the calling ceased. I was having my own problems.
>
> I was developing cramps and my clothing was dragging me down. I was a good swimmer but my clothes were getting too heavy. I now realized what fools we had been to have not shed our clothes while we were still inside the U-boat. It would have been so easy. But now I had to struggle out of my sea boots, my heavy watch coat and my sweater. Finally I was down to my undershirt, trousers and socks. I remembered to unhook my Iron Cross First Class from my coat and shoved it into my trousers pocket.
>
> After an hour and a half two men in a rowboat pulled me out of the water and took me to Waterford. At the time they believed I was a neutral seaman or an Auxiliary Patrol member whose ship had hit a mine. They had rowed out looking for survivors after hearing the explosion just after midnight. If I had any thoughts of escaping disguised as a neutral seaman those hopes were dashed in the morning. I was lying in bed when a man entered the room with two constables. The man had my Iron Cross in his hand.'

The wreck was salvaged on 7 September 1917, examined then towed into Dunmore on September 23. To paraphrase the famous inscription, War sent *Maschinist* Walter Richter to sleep for eternity at the *Deutsche Kriegsgraberstatte* at Glencree. At least one unidentified body was washed ashore at Slade but it

The salvaged *UC 44*. Note extended periscope and external torpedo tube bulge. The extensive damage to the conning tower was caused during the recovery operation. (P. Armstrong)

appears the nineteen badly decomposed bodies recovered from within the wreck on September 28/29 were immediately buried at sea.[28]

Was *UC 44* the victim of an Admiralty ruse? There is no hard evidence to prove that the boat detonated one of the mines laid earlier by *UC 44*, indeed Grant convincingly deconstructs these myths in 'U-boat Hunters'. The premature dissolution of soluble plugs would claim *UC 42* off Cork in September and it is possible that *UC 44* too may have fallen victim to one of her own mines.[29] The stern abaft the aft bulkhead was wrecked and the area beneath the *maschinenraum* betrayed evidence of blast damage. Eight mines were recovered in the vicinity but the missing ninth was assumed to be responsible for the sinking. At any rate divers cut their way into the wreck on 7 August 1917 and damage discovered was consistent with the boat having been mined.

One extremely important consequence of salvage was the discovery of intact confidential papers and equipment. These papers included orders issued on January 1917 following Germany's adoption of unrestricted submarine warfare. Orders specified that the Channel route must be used but sufficient fuel reserves should be maintained to enable a return journey via the *norweg* should this be required. Passage through the Channel was carefully described. The boat should navigate via the North Hinder Light-vessel followed by Buoy 2501 then by way of the light buoy in the Dover Straits. The U-boat should transit at night following the current. If nets were encountered, the boat should submerge to 40m and dive under them. Hydrophone reception was believed to be poor below 30m. Patrols could thus be outwitted by diving below 20m when conditions allowed, by proceeding slowly on one motor, by closing down pumps and auxiliary machinery, followed by frequent alterations of course. The *UC 44* haul also included a copy of the general cipher or *AFB* dated 31 May 1917 to 20 January 1918 and a chart which divided British coastal waters off into squares, anticipating the *Kreigsmarine* grid of the Second World War. In addition, a flotilla list dated 8 February, together with a most useful summary call signs dated 1 May 1917, was handed to the boffins in Room 40.

FATALITIES OF *UC 44*, 5.8.17

Bartz, John, Matrose
Bendler, Wilhelm, Lt zur See der Reserve
Bienert, Fritz, Ob/MaschinistenMt
Borgwaldt, K., Heizer

Kersten, Heinrich, Heizer
Klein, Karl, MaschinistenMt
Krämer, A., F.T.Ober Gast
Lehmann, R., Ob/MaschinistenMt d.S.I

Bürger, Otto, Ob/Matrose
Böttcher, A., BootsmannsMt der Reserve
Clasen, H., Masch.Anw
Düsing, August, Ob/Matrose
Fahnster, Johann, Ob/MaschinistenMt
Fehrle, Erwin, Heizer
Giesenhagen, K., F.T.Gast
Golombowski, T., Heizer
Heuer, Otto, BootsmannsMt
Horand, Hans, Ob/BootsmannsMt
Idselis, Michael, Matrose

Müller-Heye, D, MaschinistenMt
Pabsch, J., Ob/BootsmannsMt der Reserve
Richter, W., Masch.Anw
Rottschalk, Walter, Matrose
Rösler, P., MaschinistenMt
Schickendanz, W., Ob/Heizer
Schülter, J., Steuermann d.Res
Schmitz, F., MaschinistenMt
Seifarth, Helmut, Marine Ing Ober Asp
Zielosko, Emanuel, Matrose

WRECK SITE

The wrecked boat was towed into Duncannon on a barge then beached near the East Pier on September 28. The stern was taken away as scrap to aid the war effort but some accounts say that *UC 44* remained there until 1960, a playground for curious local children. Photographs show three sections, resembling pieces of boiler. A small portion was still visible up to 1995, when it was decided to extend the rock-wall over her remains to form a hard standing for fishing gear. In a very real sense *UC 44* has become an integral part of the Irish coast.

NARA T 1022, Roll 47, PG61957 ADM 116/1632, ADM 137/645, ADM 137/3897, ADM 137/2961 ADM/137/3217

U 1276 KRIEGSMARINE U-BOAT

DATE OF LOSS: 20.2.45
DEPTH: 75 m
REFERENCE: 51° 47.952' N 07° 07.524'W
LOCATION: 20 miles south-east of Dungarvan

Type: VIIC/41 ocean-going attack boat *Builders:* Bremer Vulkan Vegesacker Werft *Ordered:* 1 June 1942 *Keel laid:* as Yard No.70 on 13 July 1943 *Launched:* on 25 February 1944 *Commissioned:* by *Oblt.z.s.* Karl-Heinz Wendt on 6 April 1944 *Feldpost No.:* M 07 089

U 1276 trained with *8. U Flotille* at Danzig from 6 April 1944 to 31 October 1944.

Movements prior to first wartime patrol:

(1) *U 1276* left Kiel under the command of Karl-Heinz Wendt on 4 November 1944, arriving at Horten, Norway on 11 November 1944.
(2) 15 November 1944, *U 1276* left Horten under the command of *Oblt.z.s.* Karl-Heinz Wendt, arriving at Kristiansand on 17 November 1944. At 2148 *U 1276* was slightly damaged by a mine explosion in AN 3561, hence the return to port. The mine caused damage to the stern tube, casing and ballast tanks.
(3) *U 1276* departed from Kristiansand on 19 November 1944, arriving at Farsund on 20 November.
(4) *U 1276* left Farsund on 16 January 1945 arriving at Bergen on 17 January.
(5) On 19 January 1945, *U-1276* left Bergen under the command of *Oblt.z.s.* Wendt and returned on 22 January 1945.

FINAL PATROL

U 1276 left Bergen on 28 January 1945 for her first real patrol, a billet in the Bristol Channel/Irish Sea. Although nothing more was heard from *U 1276* until the events outlined below, it is highly likely that the submarine followed the course taken by *U 1202* given in the introduction. Now we must move forward in time to 20 February because fate was to bring *U 1276* into the path of an oncoming convoy.

The Dive Panel of *U 995*, identical to that fitted in *U 1276*. These colour-coded red or green valves controlled the rate of flooding or the venting of tanks, thus determining rate of dive or ascent. The crucial role of handling these valves was given to a trusted *unteroffizier* who closely followed the commands of the *LI*. Diving entailed flooding tanks from the bow, moving aft, the usual sequence being opening Nos 5, 4 and 3. When the boat reached the requisite angle of dive, the stern tanks, Nos 1 and 2, were opened. Once the desired depth was reached, the valves were shut and, with the assistance of the hydroplanes, the boat levelled out. (Kev Belcher)

Convoy HX 337, consisting of sixty-nine ships, organised in eight columns, had sailed from St Johns on 11 February. As it entered the home strait, the convoy was joined by escorts comprising EG 22, EG 23 and EG 26. Acutely aware of the danger posed by U-boats, several warships preceded the convoy as an ASDIC screen fanned out ahead. 2,000 yards astern, the Corvette HMS *Vervain* (Lt-Cdr R. Howell) trailed the convoy, while HMS *Peacock* (Lt-Cdr S. Harries) was 4,000 yards astern of the port wing column. HMS *Amethyst* (Lt-Cdr N. Scott-Elliot, DSC) was keeping pace astern of the starboard wing. Unbeknown to the escorts, that afternoon *U 1276* was watching the progress of HX 337 from periscope depth nearby.

At 1249hrs when HMS *Vervain* was 120 degrees/20 miles from Minehead Light at 51° 47'N, 07° 46'W, her ordered world suddenly exploded. A torpedo had detonated port side forward and *Vervain* settled quickly by the bows. The rescue vessel *Bory* steamed in to pick up thirty ratings and three officers. Capt Howell and the following men perished:

FATALITIES OF HMS *VERVAIN*, 20. 2. 45

Balderson, John, Sick Berth Attendant, 39yrs
Baptie, John L., Ordnance Mechanic 4th, 33yrs
Bissett, William, O/Signalman
Blazier, Frank, AB, 22yrs
Bloomer, Stewart, O/S, 18yrs
Blower, Clifford, Lt, RNVR, 32yrs
Browne, John, O/Smn, 23yrs
Bulmer, James, AB, 24yrs

Lisney, Ronald, Stoker, RNPS, 21yrs
Maclouglin, Frank, L/Supply Assistant
Maher, Ernest, AB, 21yrs
Marsh, Donald, Tel., 18yrs
Moon, Harry, Act/L/Stoker, 28yrs
O'Connell, Vincent, O/S
O'Connor, William, Act/AB, 19yrs
Pleasance, Stuart, AB, 20yrs

The *TDC* of *U 995*. The *Torpedovorhaltrechner* was (for its time) a sophisticated analogue computer fitted in U-boats like *U 1276*. Once sights were 'On', data relating to range, heading, bearing, speed of a target, referenced with the U-boat's own position, was fed into the computer by the *Obersteuermann*. The *TDC* responded by producing an attack solution calculation within seconds. The protective cover of this display version has been removed to show its internal workings. (Kev Belcher)

Cartwright, Harry, O/S, 18yrs
Corke, Ronald, O/S, 18yrs
Cremins, Edward, AB, 21yrs
Dawson, Stanley, Act/L/Sig, 23yrs
Doig, Frederick, Sig
Eden-Smith, Waller, Ty/Sub Lt, RNVR, 38yrs
Greenhalgh, Maurice, Stoker 1st class, 19yrs
Greenwood, Thomas, Ordinary Coder, 18yrs
Hammer, Harry, L/Steward, 27yrs
Hancocks, Eric, AB, 19yrs
Harrold, Dennis, Stoker 1st class
Hart, Herbert, Stoker 2nd class
Hawkesworth, Geoffrey, Lt, RNVR, 33yrs
Howell, Robert, Ty/Act/Lt-Cdr, RNVR, 39yrs
Hurst, Philip, AB, 31yrs
Isted, Robert, AB, 24yrs
Jones, Thomas, AB, 30yrs
Keatinge, Roland, Act/L/ Seaman, RNR, 33yrs
Lawson, George, Stoker 1st class, RNPS, 28yrs
Leicester, Alfred, Steward
Levi, Joseph, Coder, 20yrs
Lindsay, Clifford, Stoker 2nd class, 19yrs

Price, Francis, AB, 20yrs
Prince, Robert, L/Seaman
Procter, Arthur, AB, 19yrs
Proudley, Kenneth, AB, 23yrs
Roberts, George, Steward, 19yrs
Rodgers, Ben, L/Stoker, RNPS, 27yrs
Roy, William, Stoker 1st class, 19yrs
Scott, Thomas, Able Seaman, 19yrs
Shaw, Ernest, O/S, 19yrs
Shore, John, Act/L/Seaman, 21yrs
Simpson, Alexander, Stoker 1st class
Smith, John Patrick, Sig, RNVR
Swatton, Peter, AB
Thorp, Leslie, O/S, 19yrs
Wakefield, Charles, AB
Wells, David, AB, 21yrs
Whalen, Wallace, Act/L/Seaman, 25yrs
Wharton, Alan, AB, 19yrs
Whitfield, Thomas, O/S
Whittet, William, AB, 32yrs
Withers, William, AB
Worton, James, Tel., 19yrs

Bows of *U 995*. A product of technological evolution from the UB III, the sinister beauty of the Type VIIC/41 is here seen to advantage. The wafer-slim bows and elegantly tapering stern were designed to present a minimal ASDIC target for hunters, an advantage lost in shallow British coastal waters. (Kev Belcher)

The remaining warships 'boxed' the location of the attack. At 1305hrs *Amethyst* picked up a strong ASDIC contact: Report of Cdr Paterson, HMS *Exe*:

> ASDIC contact was obtained at range 1,800 by Amethyst, range 1,600 yards by Peacock. Peacock heard 'HE' on the bearing on which the contact was initially obtained and estimated the U-boat was sailing at 5 knots, course 060 (i.e. towards the convoy). Set 147B was most effective in both ships. Amethyst obtained depth of 50' on run in for her Hedgehog attack. Peacock attacked with a full pattern set to 250 and 385' i.e. on the bottom. After these attacks the Group circled the contact which was held on the bottom. Peacock obtained an ES trace giving length 150' and 25' high, lying on a course of 070 degrees, suggesting that the U-boat was broken in half. The 147B trace clearly showed a stream of oil up from the contact following the first attack.

Cdr Paterson suggested that having made its attack, the U-boat, perhaps overawed by the strength of the ASDIC screen, had dived under the convoy, rising to periscope depth in the hope of finding a straggler. In the hazy visibility, the U-boat commander did not see the warships *Amethyst* and *Peacock* until too late. The reports into the incident strike a congratulatory note with regard to the destruction of the U-boat but there is also disquiet as to why the ASDIC screen did not locate the U-boat prior to the attack. The 'Gnat Panel' later sat to determine whether *Vervain* had been the victim of a *Zaunkonig* but dismissed this theory. The convoy moved on but EG 32 revisited the scene to carry out a 'can opener', sending this message to Capt (D) Liverpool: 'Consider U-boat probably sunk. Hedgehog from first attack by Amethyst exploded within four seconds and produced immediate heavy air bubbles, diesel oil and wreckage. Picked up navigator's book in German including sights and positions, also four German-made sea boots.'

Stern of *U 995*.
(Kev Belcher)

A jacket was also recovered bearing the name and service number of *Fk O/Gfr* Helmut Meyer, known to have been serving on *U 1276* at the time of her loss. This find was somehow forgotten and for years the Naval Historical Branch believed that *U 1276* had fallen victim to a Liberator attack off Bergen on 3 April 1945. There is now no doubt that Wendt and his crew had been responsible for the sinking of HMS *Vervain* only to perish with his crew in the fierce retribution which followed.

FATALITIES OF *U 1276*, 20.2.45

Bals, Albert, Masch.Mt, 24yrs
Bauske, Albert, Mtr Gfr, 20yrs
Bisowski, Horst, Masch Ob/Gfr, 21yrs
Detjen, Heinz, Masch Ob/Gfr, 21yrs
Gäbel, Walter, Ob/Masch, 29yrs
Hanysek, Josef, Mtr H/Gfr, 24yrs
Hennes, Hubert, Fk Ob/Gfr, 21yrs
Herrmann, Franz, Mtr Gfr, 20yrs
Hupke, Kurt, Mtr Ob/Gfr, 19yrs
Huth, Fritz, Ob/Strm, 25yrs

Nachtigall, Heinrich, Mech.Ob/Gfr, 20yrs
Pietschmann, Hans, Masch.Ob/Gfr, 20yrs
Regner, Heinz, Mech.Ob/Gfr, 20yrs
Reinhold, Gunter, Masch.Ob/Gfr, 21yrs
Richer, Walter, Masch.Mt, 25yrs
Rössger, Helmut, Ob/Masch, 29yrs
Rothbauer, Josef, Ob/Masch.Mt, 25yrs
Rothe, Joachim, Ob/Ltz.S, 24yrs
Reinhard, Rudolph, O/Lt Ing, 23yrs
Sarembe, Walter, Mtr Ob/Gfr, 20yrs

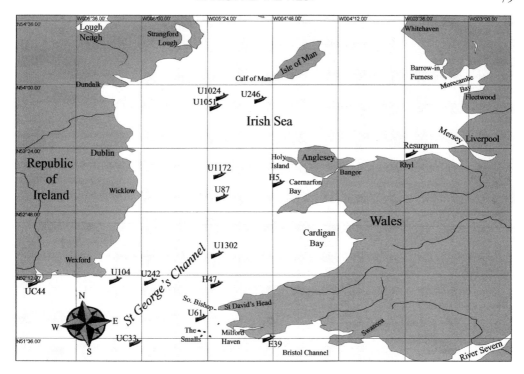

Fig.9: 'Submarine wrecks in the Irish Sea.' (R.Young)

Jansen, Ernst, Mtr Ob/Gfr, 20yrs

Jordan, Gerhard, Mtr Ob/Gfr, 20

Kassel, Eberhard, Ltz.S, 21yrs

Kehrer, Georg, Mtr Ob/Gfr 21yrs

Klomki, Kurt-Eduard, Mtr Ob/Gfr, 20yrs

Klöpping, Albert, Mtr Ob/Gfr, 22yrs

Koch, Peter, Ob Fähnr.Ing, 21yrs

Könitz, Werner, Fk Mt, 23yrs

Lamm, Kurt, Bts Mt, 23yrs

Mainka, Erich, Mech.Gfr, 20yrs

Mark, Peter, Ob/Fähnr.Ing, 21yrs

Melcher, Josef, Mtr Ob/Gfr, 22yrs

Meyer, Helmut, Fk Ob/Gfr, 22yrs

Michelbach, Friedrich, Ob/Mech.Mt, 25yrs

Mönch, Emil, Masch.Ob/Gfr, 23yrs

Schäfer, Willi, Masch.Ob/Gfr, 23yrs

Shabbat, Walter Masch Mt, 25yrs

Schmalfuß, Hans, Fk Gfr, 20yrs

Schmitt, Albert, Masch.Ob/Gfr, 20yrs

Schöpke, Werner, Masch.Ob/Gfr, 22yrs

Sellhorn, Hans, O Ltz.S, 25yrs

Saddleback, Hans Masch.Gfr, 25yrs

Skindoris, Erich Ob/Strm Mt, 26yrs

Stein, Günter, Masch.Ob/Gfr, 22yrs

Susat, Karl, O/Masch.Mt, 26yrs

Tetzlaff, Rudolf, Masch.Gfr, 22yrs

Volk, Heinz, Masch O/Gfr, 21yrs

Wendt, Karl-Heinz, Oblt.z.s, 25yrs

Wolff, Hans-Heinrich, O/bSanMt, 23yrs

WRECK SITE

Fishermen had long reported a 'fastener' in this location but Gavin Tivy and Pat Waide of the Ardmore Diving Centre confirmed the wreck of *U 1276* in 2006. The boat is lying upright, orientated in an E/W direction and is reasonably intact, though the casing is deteriorating. Wreathed in nets, the conning tower poses a significant hazard to the unwary. It seems likely that three Hedgehog mortars exploded forward of the conning tower, resulting in immense damage to the officer's quarters, the tube space and the control room. The crew in the forward section would have died quickly. All hatches are closed. *Schnorchel* and periscopes are retracted, which is evidence that Wendt and his crew were expecting retribution. Hydroplanes are set for eternity at hard-a-dive. It is not clear whether damage to the stern is evidence of a second mortar explosion or the result of depreciation. The *wintergarten* has collapsed alongside, burying the guns under a tangle of metal rails, crushed ammunition lockers, ventilation tubing and valve covers.

Not too far away, in the autumn of 2007, the same divers found the badly broken, net-ensnared wreck of HMS *Vervain*.

NARA T-1022, Roll 3463, PGs 30358-30359, 31752 ADM 199/2062, ADM 217/136 D/NHB/9/2/17s/28,11,90

U 104, SM IMPERIAL U-BOAT

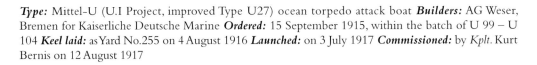

DATE OF LOSS: 25 April 1918
DEPTH: 59m
REFERENCE: 52° 00.467' N, 06 °27.217' W
LOCATION: 10.53 nautical miles SSW of Carnsore Point, Wexford in St George's Channel and 42.7 nautical miles WNW of St David's Head

Type: Mittel-U (U.I Project, improved Type U27) ocean torpedo attack boat *Builders:* AG Weser, Bremen for Kaiserliche Deutsche Marine *Ordered:* 15 September 1915, within the batch of U 99 – U 104 *Keel laid:* as Yard No.255 on 4 August 1916 *Launched:* on 3 July 1917 *Commissioned:* by *Kplt.* Kurt Bernis on 12 August 1917

TECHNICAL SPECIFICATIONS
Hull: double *Surface displacement:* 750 tons *U/Dt:* 952 tons *LBDH:* 67.58m × 6.31m × 3.8m × 8.0m *Machinery:* 2 × 900ps Maschinenfabrik-Augsburg-Nürnberg diesels *Props:* 2-bronze *S/Sp:* 16.5kts *Op/R:* 10,100-n.miles @ 8kts *Sub/R:* 45-n.miles @ 5kts *U/Power:* 2 × 600ps electric motors gave 8.8kts *Batteries:* AFA lead/acid/accumulators *Fuel/Cap:* 46 + 68 tons *Armament:* 2-bow & 2-stern torpedo tubes *Torpedoes:* 7 × 50.04cm (19.7in) *Guns:* 1 × 105mm facing forward & 1 × 88mm 5m aft of conning tower *Ammo:* 220-rounds of 105mm *Diving:* max-op-depth 50m (164ft) & 45-sec to crash-dive *Complement:* 35

On 1 October 1917, *U 104* was formally assigned to *II.U-Flottille* at Helgoland, with *Kplt.* Bernis the commander from 12 August 1917. Bernis made the following patrols with *U 104*:
   (1) On October 17 1917, *U 104* departed Helgoland and proceeded for operations off the north-west of Ireland, travelling via the *norweg*. On 26 October, the 4,366-ton British steamer *Sapele* (1904 – British & African Steam Navigation Co. Ltd, Liverpool) was torpedoed and sunk without warning, 100 miles off Tory Island. *Sapele* was sailing between Liverpool and Sierra Leone with a general cargo. The following men died of exposure while waiting for rescue:

FATALITIES OF *SAPELE*, 26.10.17
Elobe, Peter, Fireman, 28yrs
Lamptey, Robert, Greaser, 23yrs
Lawson, Tom, Trimmer, 21yrs

U 104 arrived back in Germany on 4 November 1917.
   (2) *U 104* departed Helgoland on 4 December for a patrol in the Bay of Biscay, transiting via the *norweg*.
   On 15 December Bernis torpedoed and sank the 1,235-ton Norwegian SS *Maidag* (1916 – Aktieselskapet Nordsjøen, Kristiania), 25 miles south of Longships Light-vessel. *Maidag* (Capt K. Reff) was bound from Newport, Monmouth to Bordeaux with a cargo of coal. Two of her crew of sixteen were wounded but three drowned:

FATALITIES OF *MAIDAG*, 15.12.17
Berg, Trygve, Sailor
Martinsen, Georg, Stoker, 18yrs
Diaz, Antonio, Stoker, 19yrs

The 1,507-ton Norwegian SS *Spro* (1882 – Aktieselskapet Frogner, Kristiania) was transporting coal from Barry to La Pallice when Bernis torpedoed her on 21 December, 4 miles south-west of Iles des Glenans, Brittany. From a crew of nineteen, the following were lost:

FATALITIES OF SPRO, 21.12.17
Henriksen, Johannes, Stoker
Jacobsen, Ingvald, Stoker
Jacobsen, Einar, Sailor
Jacobsen, Herman, 1st Engineer
Jørgensen, Søren, 2nd Engineer
York, Hans Hansen, 2nd Mate
Olsen, Paul, 1st Cook
Pettersen, Wilhelm, 2nd Cook
Torkildsen, Olaf, Messboy
Myhren, Jens, Sailor
Johansson, Ernst, Sailor
Larsen, Karl, Donkeyman

Off Audierne Bay at position: 47° 53'N, 04° 32'W, the *Ajax* (1889 – Dampskibsselskabet Selsk. Ajax, Helsingør), a 1,018-ton Danish steamer, was unsportingly torpedoed and sunk while carrying iron ore from Bilbao to Cardiff on Christmas Day 1917.

U 104 returned to Helgoland on 1 January 1918.

(3) Leaving Germany on 2 February 1918, *U 104* sailed for Ushant and the Irish Sea via the *norweg*. At 1900 on 2 March 1918, *U 104* sank the armed 1,330-ton SS *Kenmare* (1895 – City of Cork Steam Packet Co. Ltd, Cork), 25 miles off the Skerries, Anglesey. *Kenmare* was carrying a general cargo from Liverpool to Cork. The ship sank immediately; only the chief officer and five other men survived by clinging to floating wreckage for twelve hours. They were later rescued by the SS *Glenside* and landed at Dublin.

From the crew of thirty-five the following men were lost:

KNOWN FATALITIES OF KENMARE, 2.3.18

Ahern, Michael, Fireman, 26yrs	Keenan, John, Greaser, 63yrs
Aston, Albert Edward Able Seaman RNVR 22yrs	Kemp, Oscar, Cook, 47yrs
Blacklock, Peter, Master	Lyons, William, Fireman, 24yrs
Bowen, Stephen, Quartermaster, 59yrs	McCartie, Percival, Able Seaman, 20yrs
Coleman, Michael, Fireman, 41yrs	McLaughlin, Robert, Fireman, 34yrs
Corcoran, Patrick, Greaser, 30yrs	Moore, William, Able Seaman, 26yrs
Delea, Michael, Able Seaman, 64yrs	Murphy, Thomas, 1st Engineer, 34yrs
Fennesay, Patrick, Able Seaman, 55yrs	O'Driscoll, Michael, Fireman, 40yrs
Fitzgerald, James, Trimmer, 41yrs	O'Keefe, John, Fireman, 26yrs
Good, John, Able Seaman, 21yrs	Ogle, Thomas Hugh, 2nd Engineer, 23yrs
Grant, Geoffrey, Quartermaster, 51yrs	Shaw, Allen Charlesworth, 3rd Engineer, 20yrs
Johnstone, Robert, 2nd Mate, 33yrs	Macaulay, John, Leading Deckhand, RNR

On 9 March 1918 *U 104* put into Wilhelmshaven.

FINAL PATROL
(4) On 11 April 1918 *U 104* left Wilhelmshaven for operations in the Irish Sea, once again via the *norweg*. The objective of thirty-one-year-old Bernis was to harass Holyhead-Dublin maritime traffic. Next day *U 104* captured and sank the 578-ton barque, *Njaal* (1881 – Lindström & Co., Mariehamn, Russia) off Flekkefjord in Norway. The vessel was engaged in hauling coal from West Hartlepool to Marviken in Norway.

As mentioned previously it is believed that *U 104* finally sank *Widwud* (see *U 61*) off north-west Ireland on 16 April 1918, all eight crewmen being rescued by the destroyer HMS *Pigeon*. There was more easy prey to be had among the independent sailings. As *U 104* made her way down the Atlantic coast of Ireland, her look-outs spotted the 503-ton British coaster SS *Fern* (1900 – Laird Line Ltd, Glasgow) 5 miles off Kish Light-vessel. Little *Fern* was carrying a general cargo from Dublin to Heysham in Lancashire. Despite the small size of this vessel, Bernis opted for a torpedo attack with predictably devastating consequences. It is believed that all hands died.

KNOWN FATALITIES OF *FERN*, 22.4.18

Doherty, Hugh, Winchman, 44yrs
Doherty, John Francis, Cabin Boy, 18yrs
Gregory, W.J., Leading Seaman RNR, 26yrs
McKechine, Angus, Chief Officer, 41yrs

On 23 April Bernis decided to take on a warship, in this case the Queenstown-based, four-stack USS *Cushing*. The torpedo attack failed leaving the initiative with the destroyer which countered with depth-charges. *U 104* escaped but apparently suffered damage in the form of a ruptured external oil tank which left a surface trail. The U-boat was now seriously damaged, deep inside enemy dominated waters. The sea was calm and visibility moderate with a bright moon – extremely hazardous for a vulnerable submarine. The U-boat crept away from the scene then surfaced to caulk leaking seams. Repairs were still ongoing when the sloop *Jessamine* (Cdr S. Geary-Hill) spotted *U 104* at 0130hrs on 25 April. The officer-on-watch, Lt Marshall-Reay, brought the crew to 'Action Stations' then turned the helm and ratcheted-up speed in readiness to ram.

The British view: log of *Jessamine* 25.04.18:

0145   *Sighted stopped submarine on port bow at 51° 59N, 6° 26W.*
        Full speed. Shaped course to ram.

MaschinistMt Karl Eschenberg, aged twenty-two, was in the U-boat's fore-ends with eleven other torpedo men:

> We spotted the British ship coming towards us at speed just 450 metres away. The alarm sounded. We turned and commenced diving at once. I think we got to thirty metres when the first depth-charge exploded under our stern, which was forced up violently. The boat was at ninety-eight metres when the second depth-charge forced the stern right back down again. We began to go down stern first. As we sank deeper the seams started to give and water flooded in. We could hear her ribs crack all right. The air pressure rose alarmingly making it difficult to breathe, not to mention the fumes rising from the bilges. We managed to close the bulkhead door to the control room but we could do little about the terrible pressure. I recall air was making a terrible screaming noise as it entered through the voice pipes and cables – at least I think it was high pressure air.

Log of *Jessamine* continued:

0203   *Jessamine passed along starboard side dropping dcs in quick succession, set for 150ft. Course altered to port.*

A third depth-charge exploded at 164ft which caused sufficient damage to bring about an attempt to blow all tanks from the fore-ends. Unfortunately the submarine's stern tanks were already ruptured. The bows shot up to 32ft but the stern was inclined sharply downwards. HMS *Jessamine* dropped her last depth-charge then circled to examine the results. Her guns were trained on a large disturbance in the water, some 200 yards away.

Log of *Jessamine* continued:

'*Course altered to port and 1 round fired at disturbance in water. Voices heard.*'

Karl Eschenberg again:

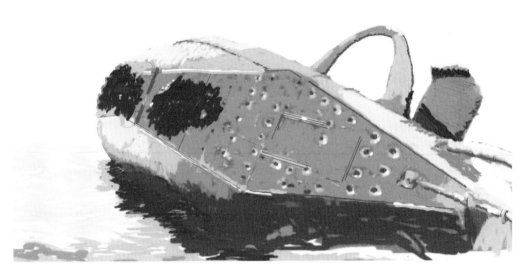

Wreck of *U 104* drawn by Pamela Armstrong.

All eleven of us crowded under the hatch, but it became increasingly difficult to remain upright against the angle of the deck and the water surging in. It was hard to concentrate on removing the clips. I don't know what happened next but I do recall the mighty inrush of water, which forced some of my colleagues over. My face was battered off the hatch coaming. Next I knew I was on the surface with the taste of blood in my mouth.

Eschenberg was carried to the surface in a maelstrom of escaping air, oil and general debris. He tore off his waterlogged clothing and cried for help. Luckily *Jessamine* caught him in her searchlight beam and her crew plucked the German petty officer from the sea. The sloop remained on the scene for some time, but Karl Eschenberg was the only survivor from *U 104*. With a confirmed U-boat sinking, Geary-Hill was awarded a DSC while Marshall-Reay received a DSO for his role. A British prize court presented the crew of *Jessamine* with a bounty of £5 per German killed, calculated on an estimate of the number of crew on board the U-boat.

FATALITIES OF *U 104*, 25.4.18

Apitz, Otto, Heizer
Bamberg, Max, Heizer
Bernhard, E., Heizer
Bernhart, Th., Matrose
Bernis, Kurt, Kplt.
Bloy, Reinhold, Ob/Heizer
Braune, Gustav, MaschinistenMt
Budziss, Alf, Matrose
Bölke, August, MaschinistenMt
Deutrich, Rud, Heizer
Erdmann, Fr, Heizer
Fischer, Konrad, F.T.Gast
Förster, Johann, Lt. zur See

Koennecke, G., Ob/Mt
Kubitza, Joseph, MaschinistenMt
Loibel, Xavier, BootsmannsMt
Lutz, Albert, Heizer
Löscher, Emil, Matrose
Muchow, Franz, Mt
Nielsen, Christ, Ob/Heizer
Nölting, Otto, Matrose
Oehlert, Warner, Marine Ob/Ing
Reihn, Alex, Ob/Matrose
Rund, H., Maschinist
Schalk, Gustav, Masch.Anw
Schrott, Hans, MaschinistenMt

Golz, Wilhelm, Matrose
Harder, Hans, Steuermann
Hauschildt, A., Heizer
Jacobsen, Georg, Ob/MaschinistenMt
Keller, W., BootsmannsMt
Kirchbach, Ed, Matrose
Kluge, Arthur, Ob/Matrose

Speckmann, W., F.T.Gast
Taege, W., MaschinistenMt
Thaer, Werner Oblt.zur see
Voigt, Heinrich, Heizer
Weberling, P., F.T.Mt
Wisskirchen, J., Ob/MaschinistenMt
Wittig, N., MaschinistenMt der Reserve

WRECK SITE

The wreck is orientated in a SE to NW (132/321-degrees) direction and lies on a seabed of sand and shells in a general depth of 59m (193.5ft (LAT). It is intact, lies on its side and is partially buried. The bow section has completely broken down, the conning tower has now become detached and lies a short distance to the south. The two propellers are still attached. Live shells have broken from their lockers and lie strewn a few metres forward of the conning tower.
ADM 53/45363 ADM 186/38 ADM 137/2964 NARA T-1022, Roll 10

U 242, KRIEGSMARINE U-BOAT

DATE OF LOSS: 5 April 1945
DEPTH: 94m
REFERENCE: 53° 42.362'N, 04° 56. 966'W
LOCATION: 20 nautical miles WNW of St David's Head, in St George's Channel

Type: VIIC ocean-going attack boat *Builders:* F. Krupp Germaniawerft AG, Kiel-Gaarden for *Kriegsmarine* *Ordered:* on 10 April 1941, within the batch of U 241 – U 246 *Keel laid:* as Yard No.676 on 30 September 1942 *Launched:* on 20 July 1943 *Commissioned:* by *Oblt.z.s.* Karl-Wilhelm Pancke on 14 August 1943 *Feldpost No.:* M 29 339

Karl-Wilhelm Pancke was born in Husum on 4 October 1915, commencing his naval career in 1938. He first served as VP Cdr 11 Harbour Defence Flottille between May 1940 and October 1940. On 1 August 1943 Pancke was promoted to *Oblt.z.s.* (R).

U 242 was assigned to *5.U-Flottille* in Kiel as *Ausbildungsboot* from 14 August 1943 until 31 May 1944. *Oblt.z.s.* Pancke commanded the boat until February 1945 and made the following patrols:

(1) On 21 May 1944 *U 242* left Kiel for the transfer to Stavanger in Norway, where she arrived on 25 May and formally transferred to *3.U-Flottille* on 1 June for frontline duties. *U 242* joined the *Mitte* group organised to counter any invasion of Scandinavia. The group consisted of twenty-two non-*schnorchel* boats based at Bergen, Stavanger and Kristiansand. Following the news of the Normandy landings, they were brought to instant readiness.

(2) *U 242* sailed from Stavanger on 6 June to participate in a reconnaissance line of eleven boats stationed between Trondheim and Lindesnes. Orders prevented them from surfacing except to recharge batteries. By the time *U 242* put into Bergen on 26 June, there were two fewer thanks to radar-equipped allied aircraft.

(3) Pancke left Bergen with *U 242* on 27 June 1944 and arrived at Stavanger later that day.

(4) On 28 June *U 242* left Stavanger, arriving at Kristiansand later that day.

(5) On 29 June *U 242* sailed out of Kristiansand and two days later on 1 July, arrived at Kiel. Here, she came under the control of the *5.U-Flottille* (nominally a training unit) between 6 July and 31 July, detailed for operations in the Gulf of Finland.

(6) On 11 July 1944, *U 242* departed Kiel and sailed to Estonia, arriving at the port of Reval on 14 July. On 1 August 1944 the boat and crew formally transferred to *8.U-Flottille*, Danzig for frontline service.

(7) Departing Reval on 17 July 1944, *U 242* sailed to Finland and arrived at the advanced base (doubtless ironically) code-named 'Grand Hotel' later that day. Pancke made three, two-day patrols from Grand Hotel on Patrol: (8) from 18 to 20 July, (9) 21 – 23 July and (10) 24 – 26 July, returning to Grand Hotel each time.

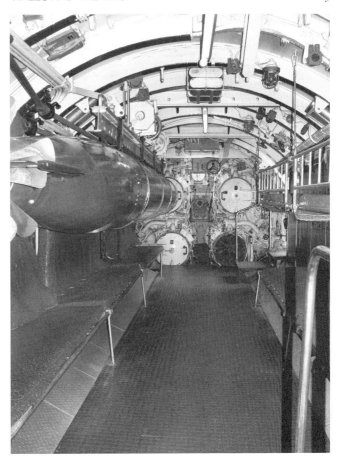

The fore-ends of *U 995* housed the torpedoes. A G7(e) torpedo is on display, slung and armed ready for loading. The torpedoes were actually fired from a panel within the *Zentrale* but controls were duplicated at a secondary station between the tubes so the *Mechaniker* could take over should circumstances dictate. (Kev Belcher)

(11) *U 242* embarked on a four-day patrol on from July 26 to 30.

(12) On 1 August *U 242* left Grand Hotel and put into Helsinki that same day.

(13) On 23 August 1944, *U 242* sailed to the Eastern section of the Gulf of Finland and put into Grand Hotel on 26 August. In position 60° 04'N, 29° 00'E on 25 August, Pancke fired torpedoes at the stationary 600-ton Soviet survey vessel *KKO-2* and the 500-ton Soviet barge *VRD-96 Del'fin*.

(14) From 29 August to 1 September Pancke made a three-day patrol from Grand Hotel.

(15) On 3 September *U 242* sailed from Grand Hotel to Reval, arriving the same day.

(16) *U 242* departed Reval on 12 September and sailed to 'Baltisch Port' later that day.

(17) Leaving 'Baltisch Port' on 21 September, *U 242* patrolled and laid mines off Porkkala, before putting into Windau on 28 September. On 28 October 1944, a mine laid by *U 242* near Obbnäs, North beacon off Porkkala on 21 September, sank the 1,495-ton Finnish steamer *Rigel* (1937 – Finska Ångfartygs A/B, Helsingfors) in grid position AO3513 (59° 57'N, 24° 21'E). *Rigel* had been voyaging from Mäntyluoto to Leningrad.

(18) *U 242* sailed from Windau on 30 September 1944 and arrived at Pillau on 2 October.

(19) Pancke made a four-day active service patrol with the boat from Pillau between 5 and 9 October 1944.

(20) On 10 October, *U 242* sailed to Danzig, where she arrived the following day.

(21) *U 242* departed Danzig on 12 January 1945 and sailed to the Finnish coast where a radio operator was landed on 23 January, along with explosives and a wireless set. Following a reconnaissance in the southern part of the Gulf of Bothnia, *U 242* put into Kiel on 30 January.

Oblt.z.s. Heinrich Riedel assumed command from 16 February 1945. Riedel was born on 30 December 1921 in Rienberg, Moldau and commenced his naval career in 1939. He served as *IIWO* on *U 612* between March 1942 and August 1942 before being promoted to *Oblt.z.s.* on 1 December 1943.

Just add men. The fore-ends was also home to the 'Lords', the *matrosen* who lived, ate and slept upon the torpedoes – which were frequently preferable to the bunks (which in any case could only be rigged once the torpedoes had been fired). The notable absence of '*Eels*', coupled with the relaxed atmosphere, indicates this propaganda image was taken on a return journey. (Bundesarchiv)

U 242 then formally joined *5.U-Flottille* for more training with the new CO.

(22) On 23 February Riedel took *U 242* from Kiel to Horten, arriving on 25 February.

(23) Leaving Horten on 28 February *U 242* moved down to Kristiansand, arriving next day, 1 March 1945.

FINAL PATROL

(24) On 4 March 1945, *Oblt.z.s.* Riedel left Kristiansand with *U 242* for operations in the Irish Sea. At 2319 on 17 March *BdU* ordered the boat to enter the Irish Sea. On 19 March the boat was urged to transmit a *passiermeldung*. This was done from AM 46 early the following morning, off the west coast of Ireland. *U 242* was expected to set return course for Trondheim at the end of the third week of April.

It is accepted that *U 242* sank after detonating a mine in Barrage QZX in St George's Channel, with the loss of all hands. The crew of HMS *Willow* witnessed the explosion at 52° 01. 24'N, 05° 47. 06'W, 0715hrs on 5 April and investigated the incident:

HMS Willow was proceeding on course 117 degrees at sixteen miles when an underwater explosion was felt. Despite the poor light, a mushroom of water ten feet high was seen, bearing 160-degrees, distance five-cables. Course was altered immediately and at 0720hrs Willow was in the centre of a spreading patch of oil. At 0722, gun crews trained on a cylindrical object, which appeared in the ever-increasing circle of oil. This was found to be an iron cylinder three feet 6in long and two feet 6in in diameter with a large clamped lid. Attempts to recover samples were unsuccessful. A lookout reported seeing a waistcoat with a row of pearl buttons floating past.

FATALITIES OF *U 242*, 5.4.45

Beck, Edmund, Ob/Gfr, 21yrs
Beck, Rudolf, Mt, 26yrs
Belles, Hans, Ob/Gfr, 22yrs
Böhmer, Horst, Ob/Gfr, 20yrs
Böhnke, Ewald, Mt, 22yrs
Buntrock, Gerhard, Ob/Gfr, 21yrs
Crell, Arthur, Mt, 24yrs
Demsky, Willy, Ob/Mt, 26yrs
Dosse, Bruno, Stab.Ob/Masch 30yrs
Dressel, Paul, Ob/Masch, 27yrs
Friedrich, Heinz, Mt, 23yrs
Gebel, Heinz, Mt, 24yrs
Giebel, Horst, Mt, 24yrs
Gstöttner, Johann, Haupt.Gfr, 22yrs
Hammer, Oskar, Ob/Fahnr, 21yrs
Handsteiner, Ludwig, Ob/Gfr, 20yrs
Harms, Dietrich, Gfr, 19yrs
Heintz, Alfred, Ob/Gfr, 21yrs
Hottinger, Kurt, Ob/Gfr, 21yrs
Huhndorf, Erhard, Ob/Gfr, 21yrs
Hundert, Walter, Ob/Gfr, 21yrs
Kuhlenbach, Erich, Ob/Mt, 30yrs

Lüders, Otto, Ob/Gfr, 22yrs
Müller, Horst, Ob/Gfr, 21yrs
Munck, Wilhelm, Mt, 22yrs
Neumann, Leo, Gfr, 20yrs
Nichnerewitz, Franz, Ob/Gfr, 22yrs
Nolzen, Wolfram, Ob/Gfr, 21yrs
Ockelmann, Günther, Ob/Gfr, 20yrs
Otterbeck, Arthur, Ob/Strm. 3WO, 31yrs
Pinkwart, Helmut, Ob/Gfr, 21yrs
Pultar, Gerhard, Mt, 21yrs
Riedel, Hans, Ob/Lt Ing 30yrs
Riedel, Heinrich, Ob/Lt zur See
Rönisch, Hans, Haupt.Gfr, 23yrs
Runte, Herbert, Oblt.z.s. 1WO, 21yrs
Sass, Otto, Ob/Gfr, 22yrs
Seiser, Franz, Haupt.Gfr, 21yrs
Trapp, Heinz, Gfr, 20yrs
Troll, Herbert, Ob/Gfr, 21yrs
Voss, Fritz, Ob/Gfr, 22yrs
Wahn, Gustav, Ob/Mt, 27yrs
Wiels, Heinrich, Ob/Gfr, 24yrs
Winkel, Horst, Ob/Gfr, 23yrs

WRECK SITE

The condition of this wreck is mysterious and no description was available. Another wreck standing 5m high, intact and upright, lies at 52° 01.546' N, 05° 48.210'W and in a depth of 98m (LAT). The seabed is comprised of sand and shells, but tidal streams are quite severe. *U 242* was fitted with a 3-16-2 bow slot pattern.

ADM 199/2062, NARA T-1022, ROLL 3900, PG31752

U 1302, KRIEGSMARINE U-BOAT

DATE OF LOSS: 7 March 1945
DEPTH: 83m
REFERENCE: 52° 19.772' N, 005° 17.731'W
LOCATION: 19.8-n.miles NNW of Strumble Head, near Fishguard, Wales

Type: VIIC/41 ocean-going attack boat *Builders:* Flensburger Schiffbaugesellschaft, Flensburg, Germany for *Kriegsmarine* *Ordered:* 2 April 1942, within the batch of U 1301 – U 1304 *Keel laid:* Yard No.495 on 6 March 1943 *Launched:* 4 April 1944 *Commissioned:* by *Kplt* Wolfgang Herwartz 25 May 1944 *Feldpost No.:* M 38 782

Wolfgang Herwartz was born in Hildesheim on 25 June 1917, commencing his naval career in 1937. A secondment to the *Luftwaffe* between October 1939 and June 1943 intervened before Herwartz commenced his U-boat training. Herwartz was promoted to *Kplt.* on 1 August 1944.

U 1302 was assigned to 4.*U-Flottille* at Stettin as *Ausbildungsboot* from 25 May 1944 to 31 December 1944. During her training period, one of the crewmen suffered a fatal accident. On 1 January 1945 boat and crew formally transferred to 11.*U-Flottille* at Bergen for frontline service.

(1) On 22 January 1945, *U 1302* sailed from Kiel to Horten, Norway, arriving on 25 January.

FINAL PATROL

(2) *U 1302* departed Horten on 3 February 1945 on her first and last wartime patrol in British coastal waters. On 20 February the boat was on passage off the west coast of Ireland. The boat entered the Irish Sea via St George's Channel. On 28 February Herwartz torpedoed and sank the 646-ton British motor-vessel *Norfolk Coast* (1937 – Coast Lines Ltd, Liverpool) off Strumble Head at position 51° 58'N, 05° 25'W. The ship was on passage from Cardiff for Liverpool with general cargo. The Canadian corvette HMCS *Moosejaw* (*K164*) (Lt A. Harvey) rescued the master, Capt Thomas Humphreys, four crewmen and one DEMS gunner, landing them at Fishguard. It is not clear why Herwartz should have attacked such an insignificant vessel.

FATALITIES OF MV *NORFOLK COAST*, 28.2.45

Bennett, Bernard, Able Seaman, 24yrs
Charman, Archibald, 2nd Officer, 49yrs
Galton, Edward, 3rd Engineer Officer, 26yrs
Johnson, John, Mess Room Boy, 19rs
McDowell, Ephriam, Able Seaman, 35yrs
Roper, N., Ty/Act/Petty Officer (DEMS) 36yrs
Sullivan, Michael, Lamp Trimmer, 36yrs
Walker, Richard, Able Seaman RN (DEMS), 35yrs

U 1302 remained in St George's Channel and on 2 March Herwartz turned to larger prey when the thirty-nine ship strong convoy SC 167 hove into view. Herwartz selected the 4,536-ton MV *King Edgar* (1927 – King Line Ltd, London) and the 3,204-ton SS *Novasli* (1920 – Skibs Aktieselskapet Novasli) as suitable targets. At 1812hrs with the convoy at position 52° 05'N, 05° 42'W, Herwartz made his attack.

King Edgar was on passage from Halifax, Nova Scotia bound for Swansea. Her cargo consisted of 1,667 standards of lumber, 2,038 tons of plywood and 500 tons of lead and zinc. One torpedo sent her to the bottom but one of the escorting frigates, HMS *Nyasaland* (*K.587*) (Lt-Cdr J. Scott) was able to rescue Capt Arthur Warren Wheeler, thirty-two crewmen and nine DEMS gunners.

KNOWN FATALITIES OF *KING EDGAR* 2.3.45

Ogden, Robert, Senior Ordinary Seaman, 32yrs
Taylor, William, Greaser, 32yrs
Roper, Norman, Ty Act PO RN (DEMS), 36yrs

Novasli received a torpedo in the stern which blew her rudder and screw off. A great rent opened up amidships. With the engine room flooding, the crew abandoned ship to be rescued by the escorting trawler *Helier II* (FY-312). A handful, including Capt Midthassel, the first mate, radio operator, a steward and a mess boy remained on board, in the hope of saving the ship. Although taken in tow, the engine room flooding proved uncontrollable. Nine hours after the attack the skeleton crew was forced to abandon its task. *Novasli* was abandoned to the waves. Thankfully no lives were lost from this vessel.

Herwartz had pushed his luck and now the hunters were at his heels. EG18 was heading for the scene, cutting off any line of escape to the south. 25 EG was also probing hard among the headlands. On 7 March, the Canadian 25 EG gained contact north-west of Dinas Head. The frigate *La Hulloise* (Lt-Cdr John Brock RCNVR) obtained both radar and ASDIC contacts on the U-boat's *schnorchel* and periscope at position 52° 19'N, 05° 23'W. The warship fixed a searchlight on the spot. Interestingly the U-boat made no attempt to evade, being seemingly oblivious to the approaching danger. *La Hulloise* was unable to attack, having already expended her supply of depth-charges. *Strathadam* (Lt-Cdr I. Quinn) and *Thetford Mines* (Lt-Cdr J. Allen) were plentifully supplied and they carried out an attack in calm seas and excellent visibility.

Report of Lt-Cdr J. Brock of *La Hulloise*:

At 2026 La Hulloise gained ASDIC contact bearing 205 degrees at 2,800 yards. The contact, which was promising, was closed, a radar contact being obtained at 1,800 yards on the same bearing...HE was reported.

The stern, or *hecktorpedoraum*, of *U 995* identical to that of *U 1302*. The second, smaller tube seen on the right is the *pillenwerfer* or 'pill chucker' used for firing a soluble decoy device. Unfortunately for the U-crews, by 1945 the escort groups could tell the difference between a decoy and the real thing. (Kev Belcher)

The bearing was illuminated by searchlight, which revealed a periscope and schnorchel...Strathadam gained firm ASDIC contact and at 2112 fired Hedgehog projectiles, two of which exploded 2.5 seconds after hitting the water, producing a tremendous explosion and a blue green flash immediately followed by air bubbles. It was thought the air bubbles were caused by the U-boat trying to surface. The position was illuminated and a black hulk was seen to emerge momentarily. A second Hedgehog attack was made at 2128. Further attacks were made at 2206 and 2225.

Attacks continued until 1617hrs on 8 March resulting in considerable oil and wreckage. Among the objects released during the 'can opener' were: tins, foodstuffs, a writing pad, a jacket sleeve, a sock, a postcard of Vienna Cathedral, a piece of engine room blackboard, shattered wood used as decking, an emergency ration kit, shoes, part of a *Drager* set, a German prayer book and a harmonica. There were no survivors.

FATALITIES OF *U 1302*, 7.3.45

Böhme, Heinz, Masch.Gfr, 20yrs
Braun, Günter, Fk.Ob/Gfr, 20yrs
Büschleb, Karl, Mtr, 21yrs
Deubel, Armin, Mtr.Gfr, 20yrs
Döring, Siegfried, Masch.Ob/Gfr, 20yrs
Drews, Heinz, Fk.Ob/Gfr, 21yrs
Eichler, Alfred, Bts.Mt, 22yrs
Eineinkel, Heinz, Fk.Mt, 22yrs
Frankenstein, Kurt, Ob/Strm, 25yrs
Franz, Philipp, Masch.Mt, 26yrs

Lackenberger, Karl, Fk.Mt, 26yrs
Liepelt, Joachim, Masch.Mt, 22yrs
Matthes, Werner, Masch.Mt, 25yrs
Meyer, Georg, Ob/San.Mt, 30yrs
Miblitz, Heinz, Mech.Gfr, 21yrs
Müller, Egon, Mech.Ob/Gfr, 22yrs
Myszka, Bernard, Mtr.Ob/Gfr, 22yrs
Nielsen, Sören, Mtr.Ob/Gfr, 20yrs
Ortner, Johann, Masch.Ob/Gfr, 21yrs
Ranft, Oskar, Ob/Masch, 29yrs

Goßmann, Werner, Masch.Mt, 22yrs

Gröniger, Hans, Ltz.s, 21yrs

Hans, Bernard, Mtr, 20yrs

Handrack, Werner, Masch.Gfr, 20yrs

Heise, Hermann, Masch.Gfr, 20yrs

Hengels, Nikolaus, Mtr.Ob/Gfr, 21yrs

Hentzschel, Walter, Mtr.Ob/Gfr, 20yrs

Hering, Heinz, Mtr.Ob/Gfr, 20yrs

Herwartz, Wolfgang, Kplt, 28yrs

Hübner, Manfred, Masch.Mt, 23yrs

Jäger, Ernst, Masch.Gfr, 20yrs

Janzen, Josef, Masch.Ob/Gfr, 20yrs

Joos, Erwin, Mtr.Ob/Gfr, 19yrs

Krause, Otto, Mtr.Ob/Gfr, 23yrs

Reimer, Engelbert, Ob/Mech.Mt, 23yrs

Schneider, Hans, Masch.Gfr, 20yrs

Schöneberg, Rolf, Masch.Ob/Gfr, 21yrs

Schulz, Friedrich Ob/Masch.Mt, 24yrs

Schürkämper, Herbert, Masch.Ob/Gfr, 20yrs

Sielig, Heinz, Mech.Ob/Gfr, 20yrs

Sokolis, Reinhold, Mtr.H.Gfr, 22yrs

Stengel, Imanuel, Mtr.Ob/Gfr, 20yrs

Stubauer, Franz, Masch.Ob/Gfr, 21yrs

Sumann, Gerhard, Mtr.Hpt Gfr, 23yrs

Vigehls, Rudolf, Ob.Bts.Mt, 28yrs

Wachenberg, Karl-Anton, Ob/Masch, 31yrs

Wackerbarth, Wilhelm, Ob/Strm, 29yrs

Zembsch, Hans, Lt Ing, 22yrs

Post-war Canadian accounts assert that during the attack, the commander of EG 18 (who held seniority over EG25's Lt-Cdr Howard Quinn) attempted to take charge of the hunt, only to be warned by the Canadians, 'that he would have to come in shooting'.[30] There is no evidence of this in contemporary records, leaving a suspicion that events may have been clouded by subsequent nationalistic fervour.

WRECK SITE

The wreck, possibly that of *U 1302*, is orientated in an east to west (090/270-degrees) direction and lies in a 3m scour, on a seabed of coarse sand, shell and gravel, in a general depth of 83m (272.3ft) (LAT). The wreck is upright and stands 6m high, but appears broken, according to the survey. The surface in this particular area is subjected to strong tidal streams and massive over-falls, which can be very dangerous.

ADM 1/30389 NARA T-1022, Roll 3900, PG30877

H5, HM SUBMARINE

DATE OF LOSS: 2 March 1918

DEPTH: 51m

REFERENCE: 53° 05.483' N, 004° 41.975' W

LOCATION: 10.56-n.miles WNW of Llanddwyn Light and 9.82-n.miles SSW of Holy Island in Caernarvon Bay

Type: 'H1' Class coastal defence submarine of Group I **Builders:** Vickers Yard, Montreal, Canada in 1915 (Subsidiary of Vickers Ltd, Barrow-in-Furness) **Ordered:** for 1914 Emergency War Programme **Keel laid:** 11 January 1915 **Launched:** 1 April 1915 **Completed:** 10 June 1915

TECHNICAL SPECIFICATIONS

Hull: single **Surface displacement:** 364 tons **U/Dt:** 434 tons **LBD:** 45.79m (150ft-4in) × 4.80m-beam (15ft-9in) × 3.75m-draught (12ft-4in) **Props:** 2-bronze **Machinery:** 2 × 4-stroke 8-cylinder, air-injection, NELSECO (New London Ship and Engine Co., Groton, Connecticut, USA.) diesel engines with horizontal valves & each developed 480bhp at 350rpm (Diesels were built under license by MAN & Vickers) **S/Sp:** 13kts max as designed **Op/R:** 1,600-n.miles @ 10kts **Sub/R:** 10-n.miles @ 9kts, or 130-n.miles @ 2kts **U/Power:** 2 × Electric Dynamic Co., Bayonne, New Jersey, USA, each rated @ 320bhp continuous (620bhp maximum for less than 1 hour) gave 10kts max **Batteries:** Gould storage batteries of 120-cells, divided into 2-sections, capacity amounted to 3,800AH **Fuel/Cap:** 16 tons **Armament:** 4 × 45.72cm bow torpedo tubes, arranged in pairs, one above the other **Torpedoes:** 8 × 45.72cm (18in) **Guns:** none **Diving:** max depth 54.86m (180ft) **Complement:** 22 **Cost:** contract price for each Canadian boat was $600,000

In 1914 Britain embarked on a major submarine expansion. Negotiations took place with the Bethlehem Steel Works, USA for a batch of 'H' boats to be designed by the Electric Boat Company of America. Some of these patrol boats were already in service with the US Navy, earning praise for their underwater handling. Standardised, cheap and capable of being mass produced in a relatively short period of time, they were an attractive proposition for Admiralty. British sailors would later nickname the 'H' boats 'Ford submersibles' because of their conveyor-belt-style production. On 10 November 1914 a contract was signed with Bethlehem Steel Works for twenty boats, 'ten to be delivered during the war and ten afterwards'. Because of trade limitations production of the first batch was switched from the US to Canada. Vickers Montreal built *H1* to *H10* using components manufactured in the US by EBCO and its subsidiaries, NELESCO and Electric Dynamic Co. Boats from *H1* to *H4* were commissioned into the Royal Navy, crossing the Atlantic under their own power in June 1915, thus undertaking the first transatlantic journey ever made by a submarine. Once fitted with deck guns, these boats were destined for Mediterranean flotillas. *H5* to *H10* made the Atlantic crossing escorted by the cruiser HMS *Carnarvon*. It was planned to deploy these boats in home waters with the 8th Submarine Flotilla at Harwich (see Vol.1).

Lt Cromwell Hanford Varley was assigned to the command of *H5* on 16 May 1915. During the 1916 shelling of Yarmouth (see Vol.1), *H5* was stationed off the Cross Sands Light-vessel. Later that day, *H5* was despatched with three 8th Flotilla submarines to intercept the German High Seas Fleet, Varley being the first to sight the warships. One aspect of *H5* took a little adjusting to. The aft periscope was fitted within the control room (albeit mounted higher than was the case in British submarines) but the fore periscope was operated American-style (and German) from *within* the conning tower. Varley was at periscope depth, manoeuvring *H5* into a satisfactory torpedo attack position when the enemy fleet suddenly broke off the bombardment, leaving the scene at full speed. It later transpired that the attack periscope mounted within *H5*'s conning tower had been spotted. Unbeknown to Varley and his crew, British aircraft were also in pursuit of the enemy warships. Failing to spot the enemy, they chanced instead upon the surfaced *H5*. *H5* therefore had the doubtful distinction of being the first British submarine to encounter 'friendly fire' from allied aircraft. In this instance the aerial attacks were ineffective.

Along with the rest of the 8th Flotilla, *H5* spent the remainder of the year in fruitless blockade patrols in the southern half of the North Sea. Surveillance was an integral element of these patrols and orders dictated that any attacks upon U-boats should only take place at the end of the patrol in order to avoid compromising the presence of the boats. This was a sensible strategy but it made for boring fruitless patrols.

In July 1917, *H5* was given a billet off the island of Terschelling, aimed at monitoring movements around the Helgoland Bight. On 11 July Varley decided to re-interpret his orders, or as he put it in his report 'use his initiative', by relocating to the island of Borkum, which *H5* reached at 0200hrs on 12 July. Next night the boat surfaced to charge batteries and repair the periscope standard, when at 2225hrs a destroyer was sighted. 'Crom' Varley had no other option but to dive. The repair crew and lookouts quickly scrambled below, leaving everything on deck. The destroyer steamed on, oblivious to the submarine's presence. Unfortunately all the tools and periscope parts were lost. The periscope would now have to be turned manually. Rather than abandon the patrol, Varley was determined to continue his watch, sensing that something was about to happen. Once the enemy warship had left the scene, *H5* resurfaced and continued charging. Another enemy destroyer was sighted within minutes. This time the distance was great enough to enable *H5* to remain surfaced. At 0100 the boat dived within sight of the Wangerooge lights, then slowly crept towards the Aussen (Outer) Jade Lightship, at the entrance to the Ems Estuary.

Sure enough, a flotilla of *G101* destroyers passed by. Varley attempted to attack but the combination of unwieldy periscope allied with the speed of his quarry, resulted in all torpedoes missing their targets. Fortunately the destroyers remained oblivious to the enemy submarine in their midst. Unperturbed, Varley took up position at periscope depth just outside the Ems entrance. At 1000hrs on 14 July a surfaced U-boat was spotted leaving the Ems and heading in *H5*'s direction. *U 51* (*Kplt.* W. Rumpel) was one of a number of U-boats on passage between Helgoland and Wilhelmshaven for refit. Conditions were not ideal for making an attack. The roadstead was predictably shallow, the heavy sea rendered depth-keeping extremely difficult and periscope operation required the combined efforts of Varley, his outside ERA and a stoker. At 1142 the distance had closed sufficiently for Varley to fire a couple of torpedoes. Seconds later there was a detonation just forward of the U-boat's conning tower. A column of smoke rose high into the air. *U 51* had been rent asunder. Running on the surface some 2 miles astern *Kplt.* Hans Rose, the skipper of *U 53* also witnessed this explosion and German A/S units were soon steaming to the scene. Nevertheless, Varley, intent on obtaining debris as evidence of his 'kill', surfaced

H5 off the Donegal coast, late 1917. (P. Armstrong)

H5. Before any detritus could be recovered, gunfire from German destroyers persuaded Varley to take the boat back down to periscope depth.

Forced to leave the scene of his attack without the commission-saving evidence he needed, Varley made the following entry in his log:

> After torpedoing the submarine, I proceeded four miles north and lay on the bottom in 18 fathoms. Many vessels were heard in close proximity. Several explosions, one very heavy. On one occasion a sweep wire scraped the whole length of the boat along the port side and a vessel was heard to pass directly overhead.

U 51 had been torpedoed on her own doorstep but the crew had not all perished. Eighteen men, including the skipper, chief engineer, the navigator, the senior *Maschinist*, six *Unteroffiziere*, three *Funker* and five *Matrosen*, had taken refuge in the forward torpedo room. Unfortunately just six of these men were equipped with *Drager* sets. Three other crewmen were trapped in the aft-torpedo room, the control room between, having completely flooded. A further knot of men survived in the engine room. Eleven hours after *U 51* sank to the bottom, two men from the forward torpedo room, *Maschinisten* Mysk and Pieper, made their escape and bobbed to the surface. Neither had breathing equipment but they did possess rubber life-vests. In his subsequent debriefing, Mysk testified that the air purification and auxiliary systems had broken down and by 2300hrs many of the trapped men were already dead.

Meanwhile within the engine room, *Heizer* Adolf Kössinger, *Maschinist Maat* Sobirey and *Oberheizer* Böttercher struggled to flood the compartment. Kössinger later described how the trapped men had been unable to find the emergency lightswitch, as its position differed from the location given in the blueprints. By the time it was located, water was lapping over a metre above the deck-plates. To stay clear of the frigid water, Kössinger, Böttercher and Sobirey clambered up the engine room hatch ladder. Pressure duly equalised, *Drager* sets were donned and Böttercher and Kössinger succeeded in opening the hatch about 5cm. At this point the exhausted Sobirey became hysterical. Finally with Böttercher forced to restrain Sobirey by holding his head in an arm lock, up they went. Just before 0300hrs the men reached the surface but Sobirey continued to panic, seizing hold of Böttercher's hair, wrenching out his mouthpiece. Böttercher was forced to push Sobirey away. By the time a drifter had reached them, Sobirey had drowned, leaving the two *heizen* as the sole survivors from the engine room of *U 51*.

Propaganda shot of Ensign Childs
on the bridge of *H10*.The doomed
officer was older than most of his
counterparts, a factor which led
to much (unfounded) lower-deck
speculation about his real role on
H5. Note the canvas screen on the
bridge. (IWM HU 067304)

As he set course for home, 'Crom' Varley faced a few problems of his own. He had disobeyed orders; the chart track provided ample proof. He knew he had destroyed a U-boat but lacking any evidence, critics would merely conclude that the sinking was a fabrication designed to draw some of the heat from his misdemeanour, or as he phrased it in his report, his 'slight transgression from orders'. Following Varley's return to Harwich Capt (S), in naval parlance, 'read his horoscope'. Lt Arthur Forbes (see Vol.1) was now given command of *H5*.Varley would remain under a cloud for several months until supporting evidence of the sinking of *U 51* reached Admiralty. Now lauded for his initiative, an abrupt reversal of fortune witnessed the award of a DSO.[31] Fate would shortly deal a rotten card to Varley's old boatmates however.

Under her new skipper *H5* continued operating off Dogger Bank, Helgoland, the Ems and Amrum. There were many sightings but Lt Forbes made no attacks. In March 1917 *H5* was dispatched to Queenstown, Ireland with a view to intercepting U-boats on passage via the *norweg*, as part of Jellicoe's answer to U-boat attacks in western waters. From May 1917 Admiralty consolidated this policy by stationing a flotilla of submarines at Berehaven in Bantry Bay, Ireland, alongside HMS *Vulcan*.[32] A second flotilla of submarines deployed further north at Killybegs (Buncrana) under HMS *Platypus*. *H5* alternated between these bases, patrolling off the sharp headlands of County Mayo and Donegal. On 23 August 1917 the boat was engaged in a routine patrol off the approaches to the North Channel. *H5* was surfaced and charging batteries when a suspicious vessel was spotted. The ship's log takes up the story:

0820 sighted object at 55° 56'N, 8° 54'W. Dived and proceeded to attack same.

0837 Object proved to be enemy s/m. Got tubes ready. Manoeuvred to get in a shot

0927 Fired port upper tube and starboard lower

0928 Fired port lower and starboard upper. Missed with both

The target was the surfaced *UB 61* (Theo Schultz). In order to avoid the torpedoes streaking towards his boat, Schultz was forced to make such a violent turn of the helm that two men were lost overboard and drowned.

In the autumn of 1917 it was decided to increase the strength of the Berehaven Flotilla to six 'E' class, six 'D' class and two 'H' class submarines. *H5* spent September 1917 engaged in A/S patrols operating from Killybegs. These patrols were interspersed with exercises in the North Channel involving *E54*, *E48* and *E32*. December 1917 saw *H5* extend her radius of operations to Fastnet and The Smalls.

On Christmas Day 1917, at 1352, Forbes sighted a U-boat at 51° 31'N, 6° 20'W. The range proved too great to close. At any rate no attack was made.

On 23 January the boat took part in A/S exercises using stablemate *L1* (see entry) as a target. In fact this was training for the 'GF' A/S operations planned for early in the new year. The *Vulcan* and *Platypus* submarines were ordered to patrol between 54 and 57 degrees NW of 90 degrees West. An optimal seven submarines would be operating off the Irish coast with an eighth given a billet in the Irish Sea at any one time.[33] Because of the secrecy attending these operations, convoy escort ships and merchants were not informed that British submarines were operational in their area. For *H5* and her crew, the consequences were to be fatal. Meanwhile the Americans were coming. In January 1918 the USS *Bushell* docked in Berehaven with a brood of seven 'AL' class boats of the US Navy. As part of the working up exercises it was decided to send a selection of young American officers on 'makee learn' trips with the British submarines engaged in G/F patrols. On 25 February Ensign Earle Childs of the US Navy noted enthusiastically in his diary, 'This afternoon I went over onboard HMS *Vulcan* to see the captain of the H5'.

FINAL PATROL

On 26 February 1918, *H5* and her crew of veterans, plus Lt Childs, sailed from Berehaven for a patrol in the Irish Sea. Wild rumours circulated at the time that Lt Childs was a scientist, appointed to the boat to carry out secret tests. Lt Forbes had been issued with instructions to patrol a line extending 10 miles east from Caernarvon Bay Light-Ship, along latitude 53° 06' N, between longitude 4° 30'W and 4° 50'W. *H5* was expected to return to port by 0900hrs on 2 March but she failed to appear. What follows is an extract from a report written by Capt Martin Nasmith VC[34] (in command of the Berehaven Flotilla – See *Thetis* entry) to Vice Admiral Sir Lewis Bayly (Admiral Commanding Western Approaches) written on 7 March 1918:

> I regret to report that Submarine H5 having failed to return from patrol is considered to have been lost with all hands. It is further considered that she was the Submarine referred to in the following message from Vice Admiral, Milford Haven: observing that her line of patrol was in Lat. 53° 6'N. between Long 4° 30' and 4 °50'W. 'Message begins: Master of SS *Rutherglen* reports that his Vessel rammed Submarine 2030, 2 March when in position Lat.53°4'N. Long 4° 40'W. Submarine was crossing bow at considerable speed. After collision cries were heard and men seen in the water, also there was a strong smell of petrol vapour. Forepeak of Rutherglen is flooded. Ends.'
>
> Her Commanding Officer, Lt AW Forbes DSO was an officer of considerable submarine experience and one for whom I had the greatest admiration and in whom I placed complete confidence. I am convinced with my knowledge of this Officer that he at all times took every possible step, first for the destruction of the enemy, and secondly for the safety of his ship and that whatever the circumstances of the collision, that no possible blame can be attributed to him. He was specially noted for the command of one of our larger submarines and his loss to the Service together with that of his men, who have performed excellent work in these waters, is very much felt. It is deeply regretted that Ensign EWF Childs, USN of US Submarine AL2 who was making an instructional cruise in H5, was also lost.
>
> With regard to the SS *Rutherglen*, it is submitted that she should not be informed that the rammed submarine was British but should receive the usual reward for sinking the enemy, since the success of the campaign must largely depend upon immediate hostile action being taken by any merchant vessel finding herself favour-

ably situated for attacking a submarine. The question of recognition between merchant vessels and allied
submarines is not considered feasible and the risk of such an accident happening on a dark night, although
deeply to be regretted, must be accepted as a necessary war risk.

And the final twist of fate came on 28 July 1919, when a British prize court awarded the crew of *H5* a
£175 bounty for sinking *U 51*. This figure was based on a payment of £5 per German crewman killed.
U 51 was actually carrying a crew of thirty-six, so the prize court slightly under-paid the bounty but by
that time it hardly mattered: the much-decorated crew of *H5* was already dead. At any rate the master
of *Rutherglen* and his crew received the bounty offered to any merchant ship which succeed in sinking
a U-boat. In retrospect in can be observed that any U-boat would have blown *Rutherglen* apart, long
before her crew sighted the submarine.

The reader may like to reflect on the wisdom of this 'necessary war risk'. Accounts of British submarines having been attacked by bounty-hungry allied merchant vessels (known to submariners as 'Fritz
Hunters') are legion. Two examples will suffice here. On 10 May 1916 *G10* was deliberately run down
by a Norwegian merchant[35] in the Blyth roads. Fortunately the boat was able to regain the surface after
a struggle. On 31 March 1918 *H9*[36] narrowly escaped the attentions of the SS *Benarty* off the Haisboro'
Light-vessel. Both attacks took place in coastal waters close to British submarine bases. It can be seen
that the policy of encouraging merchants to ram U-boats placed allied submarines in peril. On the other
hand, officialdom evidently believed that by encouraging merchants to take up the initiative at a time
when U-boats were running rampant, the guarantee of a bounty gave a much-needed fillip to morale.
This particular morale-booster led to the death of a fine body of men.

PO Wall DSM: 'This particular
morale booster led to the death of
a fine body of men.' (P. Armstrong)

The *H5* relatives, if they were told anything at all, were simply informed that the boat had been 'mined'. The story of *H5*, which began so gallantly in Montreal, ended in the unforgiving seas off Holyhead. It is one of the least known, yet surely one of the saddest stories in this series.

FATALITIES OF *H5*, 2.3.18

Alford, Henry, Stoker 1st class, 27yrs
Anson, Sir John, Lt, 21yrs
Ashmore, Ernest, Stoker 1st class, 36yrs
Bluett, Sydney, ERA 3rd class, 23yrs
Burgess, Nathaniel, Lt, Navigator, RNR, 28yrs
Childs, Earle, Ensign, USN Liaison Officer
Colbran, Charles, PO, 34yrs, DSM
Darvill, Frederick, PO, 28yrs, DSM
Elliott, Charles, AB, 28yrs
Forbes, Arthur, Lt DSO
Heath, George, ERA 4th class, 23yrs
Heath, Herbert, L/ Stoker DSM
Hibbert, Frederick, Stoker 1st class, 25yrs
Hurst, Stephen Charles, AB, 21yrs

Kelly, James, AB, 22yrs
Layzell, Frederick, AB, 22yrs
Lewis, John, AB, 32yrs
Lloyd, Thomas, Stoker PO
Newman, Percy J. ERA 3rd class, 25yrs
Payne, Percy E.E., Sig, 22yrs
Roberts, Harold B., Stoker 1st class
Rowe, John H., PO, 27yrs
Smith, Alfred, CERA 1st class, DSM
Smith, George, Stoker Petty Officer
Snowden, Harry, Wireless Tel Op, RNR, 32yrs
Thompson, James, Boy Tel., 17yrs
Wall, Frederick, PO, 34yrs, DSM

Ensign Earle Wayne Freed Childs, a 1915 graduate of Annapolis, was the first American to die as part of a world conflict. A copy of his diary can be seen at the RN Submarine Museum. The other victims of *H5* are commemorated on the Portsmouth and Chatham Naval Memorials. PO Wall DSM, aged thirty-four, had been in submarines for most of his adult life. He held both the Long Service and Good Conduct medals. Boy Tel. Thompson by contrast, was just seventeen years old. (An analysis of the *H5* crew profile can be found in the section dealing with RN rates and organisation.)

In 1990 diver Keith Hurley of Chester chanced upon a wreck whilst clearing an obstruction in Caernarvon Bay but other accounts credit divers Ron Mahoney and John Lee with the discovery. The toy-like dimensions signified that *H5* had been found.

WRECK SITE

The wreck is orientated in an east to west (090/270-degrees) direction, with the bows to the west. It lies in a scour, on a seabed of sand, in a general depth of 51m (LAT). The wreck is intact, standing upright, but leaning with a 15/20-degree list to port. The partially buried bow is mutilated beyond recognition, though the hydroplanes are in place. The wreck evidence is consistent with *H5* having been surfaced at the time of ramming. The conning tower hatch gapes open. Abaft the conning tower is a large gash, obviously caused by the impact. Resultant flooding would have been immediate and overwhelming in such a small boat. The periscope standard lies in an extended position, suggesting that the boat had not been long surfaced prior to the impact. The casing has largely rotted away, leaving the pressure hull colonised by large orange plumose anemones and inhabited by fish shoals and crabs. The wreck of HM S/M *H5* was designated as a Protected Military Wreck under the Protection of Military Remains Act 1986. Although it is now illegal to dive within 300m of the wreck site, at the time of writing there is evidence on YouTube that *H5* is being illegally dived. The 'POMRAD' Act makes it illegal to conduct any operations (including any diving or excavation) within the controlled site that might disturb the remains unless licensed to do so by the Ministry of Defence.

On 2 March 2002, eighty-four years after her loss, a moving double service was held at St Cybi's Parish Church, Holyhead on Anglesey with a second simultaneously held over the wreck site. Wreaths were scattered at the location and the national anthems of Wales, Britain and the US were all played in tribute. To ensure these brave men will not be forgotten, in recent years a plaque was erected to the memory of the *H5* dead in the appropriate setting of Holyhead Maritime Museum.

ADM 137/2577-2598, NARA T-1022, Roll.19 ADM 137/2071, Admiralty Technical History, Vol.1

U 87, SM IMPERIAL U-BOAT

DATE OF LOSS: 25 December 1917
DEPTH: 97m
REFERENCE: 52° 56.634' N, 005° 05.548'W (conning tower and stern section)
REFERENCE: 52° 56.523' N, 005° 05.481'W (bow section in 95m)
LOCATION: 14.3-n.miles WNW of Penrhyn Mawr, Lleyn Peninsular, Wales in St George's Channel

Type: MS (U.I Project, improved Type *U50*) ocean torpedo attack boat *Builders:* Kaiserliche Werft, Danzig for Kaiserliche Deutsche Marine *Ordered:* 23 June 1915, within the batch of U 87 – U 92 *Keel laid:* as Yard No.31 on 28 October 1915 *Launched:* on 22 May 1916 *Commissioned:* by *Kplt*. Rudolf Schneider on 26 February 1917

TECHNICAL SPECIFICATIONS

Hull: double *Surface displacement:* 757 tons *U/Dt:* 998 tons *LBDH:* 65.80m × 6.19m × 3.9m × 8.70m *Machinery:* 2 × 1,200ps MAN diesels *Props:* 2-bronze *S/Sp:* 15.6kts *Op/R:* 11,380-n.miles @ 8kts *Sub/R:* 56-n.miles @ 5kts *U/Power:* 2 × 600ps electric motors gave 8.6kts *Batteries:* AFA lead/acid/accumulators *Fuel/Cap:* 54 + 79 tons *Armament:* 4-bow & 2-stern 50cm torpedo tubes *Torpedoes:* 12 × 50.04cm (19.7in) *Guns:* 1 × 105mm (4.13in) 5m forward of the conning tower & 1 × 88mm (3.46in) about 5m aft *Ammo:* 220-rounds *Diving:* max-op-depth 50m (164ft) & 45-sec to crash-dive *Complement:* between 36 & 39.

Kplt. Schneider commanded the boat from 26 February 1917 until 13 October 1917.

Following her training period *U 87* was formally assigned to *III.U-Bootflottille* at Wilhelmshaven on 24 April 1917.

Oblt.z.s. Karl Klotz was appointed *IWO* from February 1917 and *Oblt.z.s.* Ernst Wodrig served as *WO* from February 1917. *Marine Ob/Ingenieur* Karl Hilgenberg was *LI* of *U 87* from October 1916.

(1) *U 87* departed Ems (Borkum) on 20 May 1917 for operations in the south-west approaches, sailing via the *norweg*. It was an interesting passage. The Dutch steamer *Bernisse* (1915 – P. A. van Es & Co., Rotterdam) of 951 tons was damaged by a torpedo on 23 May, 16 miles south-east of Nony Head, while transporting groundnuts from Rufisque, Senegal to Rotterdam.[37] Next came the 958-ton Dutch cargo vessel *Elve* (1916 – P.A.van Es & Co., Rotterdam), also on passage from Rufisque, Senegal for Rotterdam with groundnuts. This vessel was captured and sunk off northern Scotland at 59°41'N 03°07.5'W. Following a failed torpedo attack on the Q-ship *Merope*, Schneider wisely withdrew into the North Channel where less resistant targets might be expected.

On 26 May, Schneider captured, shelled and sank the 1,943-ton Russian barque *Lucipara* (1885 – Mathias Lundqvist, Vårdö, Åland). The vessel was on passage between Ardrossan and Brazil when its journey was cut short. The crew abandoned ship and rowed to shore without fatalities. Later that day, a second barque, the *Saint Mirren* (R. Thomas, Glasgow) was captured off Inishtrahull then sunk by gunfire. As the ship was conveying patent fuel from the Clyde to Santos, Brazil, compliance with Schneider's orders to abandon ship was therefore the wisest option.

Four days later *U 87* had reached her billet. The 2,821-ton SS *Bathurst* (Master J. Jones) inbound to Hull with a cargo of mahogany logs and palm kernels from West Africa, sailed in company with the armed 3,331-ton steamer *Hanley* (1902 – Lewis SS Co. Ltd, Cardiff). *Hanley* had been in the final leg of a journey between Argentina and Falmouth, when at 1415 she was intercepted under the Prize Regulations, some 90 miles off Bishop Rock. The crew abandoned ship but the attack cost the life of Fireman/Trimmer Bengradi. At 1450, *U 87* appeared and commenced to open fire at *Bathurst* at a range of 2,000yds. Once Bathurst was abandoned, Schneider dispatched her with a torpedo.

Schneider torpedoed the 3,583-ton Italian steamer *Eliofolio* (1897 – D. & E. Fratelli Bozzo, Genoa) on 2 June, which apparently sank with all hands; this attack taking place 130 miles west of Ushant. The vessel was carrying a cargo of ore from Italy to Britain which explains a rapid sinking. Later that day, a torpedo damaged the 6,670-ton French steamship *Mississippi* (1912 – Cie. Générale Transatlantique, Havre), voyaging from Havre for New Orleans. The ship limped into Brest on 4 June.

U 87 put into Emden on 9 June 1917. The remainder of *U 87*'s patrol was without incident.

The camouflaged *U 87* lying at Uto-Werft, Wilhemshaven. (U-boot Archiv)

(2) On 1 July 1917, *U 87* left Emden again for operations in the south-west approaches. On 4 July, 85 miles off Færoe Isle, Schneider captured the 151-ton fishing vessel *Loch Katrine*, dispatching her with gunfire. There was no excursion into the North Channel while en route and *U 87* reached her billet on 8 July.

On 8 July Schneider encountered the 5,871-ton armed steamship *Valetta* (1913 – Valetta SS Co. Ltd, Glasgow). *Valetta* was bound for Dublin from Montreal with flour and wheat, when *U 87* torpedoed her 118 miles from Fastnet Rock. On 10 July, torpedoes from *U 87* destroyed the armed 5,807-ton British steamer *Seang Choon* (1891 – Lim Chin Tsong, Rangoon). This attack was made 10 miles off Fastnet Rock. The ship had been in the last stages of a journey from Sydney, Australia to Liverpool with a general cargo and nineteen crewmen are believed to have perished.

KNOWN FATALITIES OF *SEANG CHOON*, 10.7.17

Bhamgara, K., Surgeon, 38yrs
Dunbar, Robert, 3rd Officer, 23yrs
McGregor, Angus, Snr Wireless Operator, 23yrs
Owen, Arthur, 4th Officer, 20yrs
Phillip, H., Assistant Baker

Next day Schneider pounced upon the armed 6,183-ton SS *Kioto* (1910 – Bucknall SS Lines Ltd, North Shields) an estimated 20 miles off Fastnet Rock at 51°05'N 10°00'W. *Kioto* was transporting a general cargo from New York to Manchester.

Fortunately for the ship's crew, Schneider made his next interception on 12 July under the Prize Regulations. The 2,395-ton ore carrying *Castleton* (1891 – English & Co., Middlesbrough) was captured, shelled and sunk, 60 miles off Bishop Rock. *Castleton* had been en route from La Goulette in Tunisia to Middlesbrough with iron-ore.

Moses Pratt, a Sierra Leonian Fireman, was less fortunate when the steamer *Tamele* (1910 – British & African Steam Navigation Co. Ltd, Liverpool) was torpedoed and sunk on 17 July. Fireman Pratt was the only casualty of the 3,932-ton *Tamele*, which had been steaming between West Africa and Liverpool with a general cargo.

U 87 was returning up the Irish coast when she chanced upon the 1,788-ton full-rigged Norwegian ship *Artensis* (1885 – Skibs-Aktieselskapet Artensis, Drammen) on 19 July. The sailing ship was sunk with charges and happily no lives were lost. Seventy miles off the Butt of Lewis, Schneider sank the armed 3,738-ton *Coniston Water* (1908 – Coniston Water SS Co. Ltd Cardiff) by torpedo. *Coniston Water* had been shipping coal, army stores and foodstuffs from Newport, Wales to Archangelsk when *U 87* attacked. On 24 July *U 87* returned to Wilhelmshaven.

(3) Leaving port on 16 August 1917, *U 87* proceeded to an area between Shetland and Norway to attack allied convoys. The SS *Eika II* (1906 – Aktieselskapet Eika II, Skien), a 1,268-ton Norwegian

steamer, was torpedoed and sunk off Utvaer on 19 August. From her crew of seventeen, Swedish Stoker Anders Herman Anderson died. Schneider next decided to try his luck closer to Lerwick. Convoy had been introduced to the Lerwick/Bergen route as early as 29 April 1917, though the reciprocal organisation of Lerwick-bound convoys from Bergen was not properly devised until June 1917. From Lerwick the convoys were shunted down the Scottish east coast as far as the Forth in convoys coded either HZ (southbound) or OZ (northbound). Although the elderly escorts were stretched to absolute limits in these early stages, the results of convoy were promising. According to the Technical History monograph describing these early convoy efforts, successful U-boat attacks were the results of 'lucky shots'. *Oslo* (1906 – Ellerman's Wilson Line Ltd, Hull) had the misfortune to fall victim to one of these 'lucky shots'. *Oslo*, an armed 2,296-ton steamship was in a southbound HZ convoy on 21 August, bound for Liverpool with copper ore. *Oslo* was carrying a crew of forty-nine and seventy passengers. Fifteen miles from the Outer Skerries at 1400hrs, Schneider unleashed a torpedo. The detonation killed firemen Clarke and Rossiter but the remainder of those on board were able to take to the boats. One female passenger later drowned.

While sailing in convoy could, on occasion, be hazardous, the perils were small compared to those faced by vessels steaming independently. The 1,652-ton Danish *Alexander Shukoff* (1881 – Dansk Russiski Aktieselskabet) was lost with all hands on 28 August, when Schneider discovered the ship inbound from Bergen to Lerwick in ballast. The day previously, *U 87* had destroyed the Danish collier *Anna* (1914 – Dampsk. Selsk. Vesterhavet, Esbjerg) on the same route. The interception of *Anna* took place according to the Prize Rules and there were no fatalities. Schneider torpedoed the 768-ton Danish collier *Aurora* (1905 – Det Forenede Dampskibs Selskab, Copenhagen, sinking her 25 miles off Lerwick. *U 87* arrived back at Wilhelmshaven 1 September 1917.

(4) Departing Helgoland on 2 October 1917, *U 87* sailed for a North Channel billet, sailing via the *norweg*. This was destined to be Schneider's last patrol because fate was about to take an unexpected twist. At 1045on 13 October, *U 87* encountered heavy seas, which washed the unfortunate Schneider overboard. Fortunately one of the crew managed drag him back on board but he died of internal injuries soon afterwards. At 1730 that same day, the crew solemnly buried their commander at sea. *IWO Kplt.* Rudolf Freiherr von Speth-Schülzburg assumed command. *U 87* sank no vessels during this patrol, returning to Wilhelmshaven on 3 November 1917, travelling back via the Isles of Orkney, the Skagerrak, the Baltic Sea and Kiel.

FINAL PATROL

(5) On 8 December 1917, *U 87* departed Wilhelmshaven under the command of von Speth-Schülzburg. The boat, in company with *U 100*, was escorted by a minesweeper, until the two boats parted company that evening and sailed independently: *U 87* for operations at the western end of the English Channel. Von Speth-Schülzburg was given the freedom to transit to his billet via whichever route he chose. Evidence suggests he travelled via the Dover Strait rather than the *norweg*. What is known is that von Speth-Schülzburg sank two small sailing vessels. The 114-ton Fowey-registered *Little Gem* was sunk with gunfire west of the Casquets on 13 December.

FATALITIES OF *LITTLE GEM*, 13.12.17

Fernandez, Cassina, Able Seaman, 46yrs
McLeod, A. T., Boatswain (Bosun), 35yrs
Rundell, William J., Master
De Oliveira, Joaquim, Cook/ Seaman, 58yrs

The 56-ton Bridgwater sailing vessel *Charles* was sunk by gunfire north-west of Guernsey on 18 December: the skipper and two crewmen were taken prisoner, but Mate William Durant was killed.

On Christmas Eve the defensively armed 3,238-ton British steamer *Daybreak* (1911 – Scarisbrick SS Co. Ltd, West Hartlepool/Cardiff) was torpedoed and sunk, 1 mile east of South Rock Light-vessel. *Daybreak* was on passage from Huelva to Glasgow with a cargo of pyrites. All hands were lost.

KNOWN FATALITIES OF *DAYBREAK*, 24.12.17

Barrett, James, Ordinary Seaman, 18yrs
Bianchi, Paolo, Fireman, 37yrs
Collins, W., Able Seaman
Dobson, John, 2nd Mate, 30yrs
Fredericksen, T., Able Seaman, 19yrs
Gomez, Jacine, Able Seaman, 35yrs
Greenway, Thomas, Boatswain (Bosun), 35yrs
Gulwell, Ernest, Mess Room Steward, 17yrs
Harrop-Griffiths, Joseph, 2nd Engineer, 23yrs
Holland, James, Ship's Cook, 45yrs
Kennedy, Joseph, Fireman, 35yrs
Muscat, Michael, Fireman, 39yrs
O'Connor, William, Able Seaman, 39yrs
Owen, William, 1st Mate, 39yrs
Pope, S.F., Master
Postlethwaite, Tom, Steward, 62yrs
Sumner, Frank, Signalman, RNVR, 18yrs
Verney, Samuel, Able Seaman, RNVR, 19yrs
Wilkens, W., Fireman, 27yrs

On Christmas Day 1917, the 4,812-ton British steamer *Agberi* (1905 – African Steamship Co., London) was on passage from Dakar for Liverpool with 3,500 tons of African produce, a crew of fifty-four and nine passengers. She was in convoy and close to home when *U 87* torpedoed her 18 miles from Bardsey Island. The torpedo detonated at 1445hrs, destroying all the portside lifeboats amidships. The passengers and crew escaped in the five remaining boats before the ship sank at 1510hrs but one crewman was injured. Patrol vessels landed them all at Holyhead. One of the escorts, *P56*, was just 150 yards away from the ship at the time and she turned in to ram. What follows is an extract from the log of escort sloop HMS *Buttercup*:

Log of *Buttercup* – 25/12/17:

02.42   SS Agberi torpedoed
03.30   While zig-zagging round Agburi submarine spotted on surface. HMS P56 engaged and rammed it. Buttercup fired and hit conning tower
03.40   SS Agberi sank, Submarine sank
05.00   rejoined convoy

Some accounts claim the crews of both *Buttercup* and *P56* witnessed the enemy boat sliced clean in half and that the bow section remained afloat for ten minutes with men visible within the submarine. It will be noted there is no evidence of this in the log. However, *P56* was left badly damaged suggesting that *U 87* may have been fatally holed in the encounter. The position given in *Buttercup*'s log is 52° 56'N, 5° 7'W.

FATALITIES OF *U 87*, 25.12.17

Adam, Friedrich, BootsmannsMt
Andermann, Fr, MaschinistenMt
Balleer, Max, MaschinistenMt
Brandt, Johann, Ob/Matrose
Collinet, Josef, Heizer
Dahlmann, Friedrich, MaschinistenMt
Dethloff, Otto, Ob/Matrose
Dost, Fritz, F.T.Gast
Fehsel, Herbert, Matrose
Fimpler, Adolf, Ob/Heizer
Gassmann, P., BootsmannsMt

Labahn, Hans, Ob/Matrose
Lehmann, E., BootsmannsMt
Lehmann, Walter, Maschinist
Ludwig, Edwin, Matrose
Mtodzikowski, Ob/Heizer
Paege, Paul, MaschinistenMt der Reserve
Petermann, H., Ob/MaschinistenMt
Preisker, Th, Ob/Matrose
Reuting, Hermann, Ob/Heizer
Schnellke, H., Heizer
Schaaf, Paul, Matrose

Grill, Georg, Ob/BootsmannsMt
Hansen, Robert, MaschinistenMt
Heinrich, Triedrich, Ob/Steuermann
Hilgenberg, Karl (LI)
Hoffmann, W., Heizer
Hummel, Ernst, F.T.Gast
Jörgensen, J., MaschinistenMt
Kloß, Karl, Ob/Lt. zur See (IWO)
Koppehele, Fritz, Heizer
Krimme, Otto, Matrose
Kurth, Jacob, MaschinistenMt

Siebke, Johann, Heizer
Seibel, Johann, Masch.Mt
Speth-Schülzburg, Rudolf, Freiherr von, Kplt.
Tetmeyer, Robert, Ob/BootsmannsMt
Viebranz, R., MaschinistenMt der Reserve
Wandt, K., F.T.Mt
Wille, W., Ob/MaschinistenMt
Willmer, Hubert, Heizer
Wodrig, Franz, Ob/Lt. zur See (WO)
Zander, Paul, Heizer

WRECK SITE

The wreck is orientated in an almost south/north (160/340-degrees) direction and lies on a seabed of coarse sand, shingle, pebbles and shells in a general depth of 97m (318.2ft) (LAT). The wreck is upright, but broken in half and standing 8m high around the conning tower, which is covered in marine life and home to a large shoal of fish. Both propellers are still in place. Two hundred metres to the south, in 95m (311ft) of water lies what may be the bow section of the boat, which stands about 5m high.

ADM 53/36508 ADM 137/2962 ADM 137/2963 NARA T-1022, Roll 38 CWGC

U 1172, KRIEGSMARINE U-BOAT

DATE OF LOSS: 27 January 1945
DEPTH: 86m
REFERENCE: 53° 02'N, 05° 23'W (historical position)
SUGGESTED POSITION: 52 °59.829' N, 05° 17.899'W
LOCATION: 22.64-n.miles WNW of Penrhyn Mawr, Lleyn Peninsular, Wales

Type: VIIC/41 ocean-going attack boat *Builders:* Danziger Werft AG, Danzig, for Kriegsmarine *Ordered:* on 16 July 1942, within the batch of U 1171 – U 1172 *Keel laid:* as Yard No.144 on 7 June 1943 *Launched:* on 3 December 1943 *Commissioned:* by *Oblt.z.s.* Jürgen Kuhlmann on 20 April 1944 *Feldpost No.:* M 02 593

Jürgen Kuhlmann was born in Weissenfels on 3 March 1920 and commenced his naval career in 1938 with an appointment as watch officer on the destroyer *Z 4 – Richard Beitzen.* Kuhlmann displayed promise and was duly promoted to *Oblt.z.s.* on 1 January 1943. On 20 April 1944, *U 1172* was assigned to 8.U-Flottille at Danzig, serving as *Ausbildungsboot* until 30 November 1944. On 1 December 1944, boat and crew formally transferred to 11.U-Flottille at Bergen for frontline service.
    (1) On 7 December 1944 *U 1172* left Kiel and sailed to Horten, arriving on 10 December.

FINAL PATROL

(2) *U 1172* departed Horten on 22 December 1944 sailing for operations in British coastal waters. BdU had been heartened by Thomsen's 6 January situation report. Kuhlmann was ordered to enter the North Channel, then patrol south of Anglesey. *U 1172*'s projected patrol track was: 7/1 AM52, 8/1 AM92, 9/1 AM64, 10/1 AM65, 11/1 AM68, 12/1 AM92, 13/1 AM95, 14/1 AM95, 15/1 AM95 but Kuhlmann was given freedom of action.
    As matters transpired, a large convoy (CU 53 – New York to Liverpool) had recently entered the Irish Sea via St George's Channel. While most of the convoy headed on to the Mersey, a contingent had peeled off for Belfast. By 15 January these ships had left Belfast and were shaping an unescorted course for Greenock. The largest and most distinctive of these ships was the 11,400-ton 'Ruler' Class British Escort Carrier HMS *Thane* (D48 – formerly USS *Sunset*). *Thane* had suffered storm damage during the Atlantic crossing and it was therefore planned to offload her aircraft as soon as practicable.

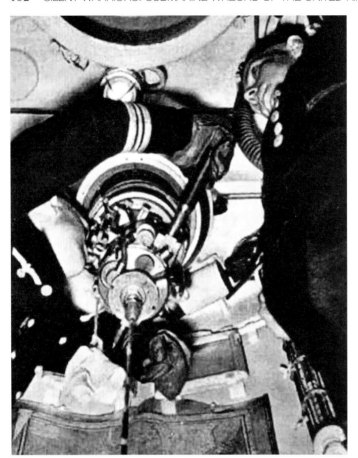

'*Torpedo Lohs!*' The *Kaleun* is perhaps a little too well dressed for this image to be genuine but the cramped conning tower setting, with the *IWO* at hand, is authentic enough. With the exception of 'H' boats, British submarines were designed with the conning tower fitted outside the pressure hull, therefore submerged attacks were always made from the control room. (P. Armstrong)

At 1328hrs the carrier was approaching the swept channel near the Clyde Light-vessel when *U 1172* struck. A single *T5* torpedo detonated against *Thane*'s starboard aft quarter, causing significant damage. One of the 5in guns was blown over the side, taking the sponson with it. The stern aircraft lift was displaced by the force. A huge hole had been blown in the ship, mangling the starboard propeller shaft. The carrier was taken in tow by the frigate *Loring* then moored at No.1 Casualty Buoy at Tail O' the Bank, Greenock. HMS *Thane* was later declared a total loss.

FATALITIES OF HMS *THANE*, 15.1.45

Almon, Ralph, ERA 4th class (RCNVR), 35yrs
Bowler, Wilfred, AB, 22yrs
Clarke, James, AB, 34yrs
Docherty, William, Naval Airman 2nd class, 20yrs
Dunnigan, William, Naval Airman 2nd class, 20yrs
Edwards, Charles M., Act/AB, 18yrs
Fry, James, Act/AB, 19yrs
Latter, Jesse W., Act/L/Seaman, 27yrs
Scobbie, John D., L/ Seaman
Townsend, Mark, Air Mechanic (E) 1st class, 23yrs

Less than half an hour after this attack, Kuhlmann hit the 7,429-ton Norwegian SS *Spinanger* (1927 – Westfal-Larsen & Co. Aktieselskapet, Bergen) in position 55° 08'N, 05° 25'W, about a mile from the Clyde Light-vessel. The *Zaunkonig* detonated on *Spinanger*'s starboard side, aft about 50ft forward of the sternpost. Three crewmen were killed in the engine room and four more were left injured. However, overall the crew was incredibly lucky because the vessel was carrying fuel oil. A doctor from a nearby destroyer came on board to tend the injured, until an RAF Rescue Launch arrived later to take them to port. Gunner Thorsen bravely entered the oil and water-filled engine room to rescue a man who later died of his burns.

FATALITIES OF *SPINANGER*, 15.1.45

Bø, Lars, Engineer
Olsen, Nicolai, Mechanic
Ulriksen, Gunvald, Mechanic
Vestvik, Lars, Mechanic

Spinanger was taken in tow to Rothesay and repaired. *BdU* detected her distress calls, a factor which further emboldened it to order more operations in this sector.

Meanwhile Kuhlmann drew south, skirting the Isle of Man. At 1650hrs on 23 January, *U 1172* torpedoed the 1,599-ton Norwegian SS *Vigneses* (1930 – A/S Kristian Jebsens Rederi). The ship had just left convoy MH 1 (Milford Haven to Holyhead) NNE of Lynas Point, Anglesey. She was steaming from Cardiff for the Mersey with 1,936 tons of coal. The torpedo detonated in the portside forward. So much steam, water and smoke had filled the engine room, it was impossible to re-enter in order to stop the engine. *Vigneses* (Capt Haakon Tronstad) listed to port and started to sink, though she actually lingered until 1700hrs. The ship sank at position 53° 33'N, 04° 17'W. All onboard were evacuated by the lifeboat to safely reach shore at Lynas Point, Anglesey.

Now Admiralty could be in no doubt that a U-boat was running rampant in the Irish Sea; in fact there were two. At noon on 27 January 1945, Stoelker's *U 825* attacked *Solor* and *Ruben Dario* in convoy HX 332, off Cardigan Bay. At 1230 news of these attacks reached warships of the 5th and 6th EGs. The hunters spread out at 3,000-yard intervals, course 180-degrees, then commenced to scour the Irish Sea. At 1955hrs HMS *Keats* (Lt-Cdr N. Israel) obtained an ASDIC contact. The frigates HMS *Bligh* (Lt-Cdr R.F. Blyth), *Keats* and *Tyler* (Lt-Cdr Rankin) latched on to *U 1172*, WNW of Holyhead.

Attack by *Keats*, *Tyler* and *Bligh* (Lt-Cdr Blyth) 5 EG – 52° 24'N, 05° 42'W – 27/29/1/45:

> At 2016 Keats obtained first contact and fired Hedgehog, obtaining two hits five seconds after the projectiles struck the water (suggesting boat was deep)...a large oil patch appeared...Bligh obtained contact and attacked with Hedgehog at 2045 producing more oil identified as diesel. The position was buoyed.

More Hedgehog attacks were made by the group:

> Tyler carried out echo sounder runs, obtaining traces of an object approx. 200' long and 24' high on the bottom: this was attacked with depth-charges at 0020 on the 28th....On instruction from Commander-in-Chief Western Approaches, 5 and 2 EGs detached, leaving Keats and Tyler to continue the hunt. Almost immediately Tyler sighted an oil streak and was ordered to follow it to the source...At 1909 Tyler attacked with Hedgehog producing a volume of oil, which eventually spread over a four mile area. At 2100 wreckage was seen including two inflated rubber dinghies about 4ft by 3ft, plywood and presumably two bundles of clothing, wood and....an onion.

5 EG was fast becoming an experienced submarine hunter, having dispatched *U 1051* just six days earlier.

FATALITIES OF *U 1172*, 29.1.45

Arnold, Manfred, Mech.Mt, 23yrs	Lenz, Gerhard, Ob/Strm, 29yrs
Bauer, Franz, Mtr.Ob/Gfr, 21yrs	Menke, Gustav, Masch.Mt, 24yrs
Bauer, Josef, Ob/Bts.Mt, 26yrs	Mikolaiczyk, Paul, Mtr.Ob/Gfr, 21yrs
Bender, Walter, Masch.Ob/Gfr, 21yrs	Müller, Gert-Rainer, Mech.Gfr, 20yrs
Berg, Heinrich, Masch.Gfr, 20yrs	Neumann, Horst, Masch.Mt, 23yrs
Beyersdorf, Heinz, Masch.Mt, 22yrs	Opitz, Walter, Mtr.H.Gfr, 24yrs
Böckenkröger, Manfred, Fk.Mt, 21yrs	Oskamp, Ludwig, Ob/Bts.Mt, 24yrs

Büttner, Alfons, Masch.Ob/Gfr, 21yrs
Dicks, Wilhelm, Masch.Ob/Gfr, 20yrs
Fischer, Friedrich, Fk.Ob/Gfr, 21yrs
Gehmair, Karl, Ob/Strm, 27yrs
Giesbertz, Josef, Mtr.Ob/Gfr, 20yrs
Glatz, Willi, Mtr.Ob/Gfr, 20yrs
Gollojuch, Karl-Heinz, Masch.Ob/Gfr, 21yrs
Grönhaut, Josef, Masch.Gfr, 24yrs
Hammer, Ernst, Fk.Mt, 23yrs
Heinz, Herbert, Mtr.Ob/Gfr, 21yrs
Helle, Hermann, Mtr.Gfr, 20yrs
Holst, Hugo, Ob/Masch, 25yrs
Jena, Erich, Masch.Mt, 23yrs
Jung, Robert, Mtr.Ob/Gfr, 21yrs
Juraschek, Walter, Mtr.Gfr, 20yrs
Kiefer, Hans, Masch.Mt, 21yrs
Kiefer, Jakob, Ob/Masch, 30yrs
Kuhlmann, Jürgen, Ob/Lt.z.s, 25yrs
Kunz, Anton, Lt. Ing, 23yrs

Osterkamp, Wilhelm, Masch.Ob/Gfr, 24yrs
Ostermann, Heinz, San.Ob/Mt, 25yrs
Ostertag, Karl, Mtr.Gfr, 20yrs
Pfeifer, Josef, Masch.Ob/Gfr, 20yrs
Raeder, Helmut, Lt.z.s., 24yrs
Rambauske, Bruno, Masch.H.Gfr, 24yrs
Riemer, Bruno, Mtr.Ob/Gfr, 20yrs
Rohde, Willi, Fk.Ob/Gfr, 25yrs
Romahn, Willi, Mech.Gfr, 21yrs
Röper, Rudi, Mech.Gfr, 21yrs
Schön, Hermann, Fk.Ob/Gfr, 25yrs
Schwinger, Erich, Masch.Mt, 24yrs
Seiler, Franz, Masch.Ob/Gfr, 21yrs
Sievers, Hans-Heinrich, Masch.Gfr, 21yrs
Tembrink, August, Mtr.Ob/Gfr, 20yrs
Thiebes, Josef, Masch.H.Gfr, 24yrs
Vacha, Felix, Mtr.Ob/Gfr, 21yrs
Völker, Herbert, Bts.Mt, 24yrs
Wartmann, Werner, Masch.Ob/Gfr, 21yrs

WRECK SITE

The wreck, which has not been positively identified, lies on a seabed of sand and shells, in a general depth of 86m (LAT). This wreck stands upright, appears intact and stands 4m high. It is, of course, a war grave. Tidal streams are also very strong in this area.

ADM 199/1786 ADM 1/30267 NARA T-1022, Roll 3900, PG30360-62

RESURGAM

DATE LOST: 24 February 1880
DEPTH: 15m
REFERENCE: 53° 23.78'N, 03°, 33.18'W
LOCATION: North Wales off the River Dee

Builders: Britannia Works, Birkenhead **Launched:** on 26 November 1879 **Dimensions:** 13.71m (45ft) in length x 3.04m (10ft) in diameter **Weight:** 30 tons

While there were many experimental submarine designs during the nineteenth century, very few were actually viable submersible craft. *Resurgam* however must be regarded as one of the first powered submarines, incorporating innovations later capitalised on by the Nordenfelt Submarine Torpedo Boat Company, which was in turn influential on so much of early German design. *Resurgam* was the brainchild of a maverick cleric with a penchant for technology, the Revd George Garrett of Moss Side, Manchester.

Although educated for the Church, Garrett had additionally studied chemistry and general science at Owens College, Manchester. Possessing both mechanical ability and scientific knowledge, Garrett was driven by intellectual curiosity. Garrett's first real invention was a diving suit, which he demonstrated for the French Navy in 1877. His next design was the 'pneumatophore', a pump used to recycle air used in coal mines by extracting carbon dioxide. Modifying this invention to provide breathable air in an underwater craft was a logical extension of this concept, one which introduced Garrett to the science of hydrodynamics. To attract much needed capital, the curate founded the Garrett Sub-Marine Navigation and Pneumatophore Co. Ltd based in Deansgate, Manchester. The Royal Navy expressed an interest in Garrett's experimentation but demanded a prototype on which to base any assessments.

With this in mind, Garrett's first powered experimental submarine design, The Curate's Egg, was drawn up in 1877. The craft was built by Cochrane & Co. and successfully took to the Great Float Dock, Birkenhead in July 1878. It is known that this prototype was cylindrical with conical bow and stern.

Next Garrett refined his earlier design with a second, more ambitious submersible. In 1879 he commissioned the steam propelled *Resurgam* from the Britannia Works in Birkenhead. *Resurgam* was constructed using iron plates fastened over iron frames. The central section was clad with wood retained by iron straps. Propulsion was provided by a steam engine patented by Eugene Lamm in 1872 and designed for installation in locomotives. Garrett witnessed these engines in operation in both the London underground and the Royal Dockyards and commenced to modify the design to power his submersible. The concept was simple. The steam engine was fired on the surface. Once harnessed, the heat produced by the engine could be applied to drive the screw for an estimated four hours. Hydroplanes sited amidships were used to control the dive.

Prior to the launch on 26 November 1879, Garrett, ever the showman, arranged for the peculiar little vessel to be dragged through the streets of Birkenhead towed behind thirty shire horses with a brass band bringing up the rear. By all accounts *Resurgam* successfully dived in Wallasey's East Float Dock, however for the most part the little boat sailed 'conned down' rather than travelling completely submerged. However, she was capable of total submersion, if required.

Resurgam's regular three man crew consisted of Garrett himself, Capt Jackson Birkenhead Master Mariner and Engineer George Price. It is not clear whether these intrepid pioneers were Garrett's friends, business associates or employees but the obvious risks suggest a personal loyalty to Garrett. In an age dominated by health and safety concerns and child protection, it is interesting to note that Garrett's nine-year-old son often came along as an extra hand. His diminutive stature made him an ideal candidate for crawling from fore-ends to stern via the 12in gap above the boiler tubes. In later life he recalled the discomfort caused by the extreme heat of the boiler, coupled with the acute ear pain resulting from changes in pressure. Richard Compton-Hall relates how on one dive in Liverpool Bay, Capt Jackson became disorientated. *Resurgam* surfaced near a passing vessel to enable Jackson to ascertain directions back to port. The master provided the required information, while archly observing that the submariners were 'the three greatest fools he had ever met'.

Garrett was no fool. He realised that success depended upon attracting investors, be they Government or entrepreneur. Either way, he required a platform to demonstrate *Resurgam*'s capabilities and reasoned he would stand a better chance if the boat was put through its paces in Portsmouth. In 1880, Garrett transferred his base from Birkenhead to Rhyl in North Wales in readiness for the journey to the south coast. Moreover Garrett was aware that commercially astute Swedish armaments baron Thorsten Nordenfelt was extremely interested in his experiments. With opportunity knocking, Garrett used what little remained of his money to buy the steam yacht *Elfin* with the intention of towing *Resurgam* to Portsmouth. It would have been possible to send the little craft by rail but Garrett reasoned that a sea voyage would enable him to identify flaws and carry out modifications on passage.

FINAL VOYAGE

Under tow from the steam yacht *Elfin*, *Resurgam* left Rhyl Harbour on 24 February. Off the mouth of the Dee, heavy seas threatened to swamp *Elfin*, forcing the submarine crew to transfer over to assist the yacht. By the following morning the battle to save the yacht had been won, but the tow rope broke. Swamped, the little submarine sank with Garrett looking on helplessly. Nor did *Elfin* make it home to Rhyl, she was accidentally rammed and sunk by a vessel that had come to her assistance as she approached harbour.

The rest is history. The creditors closed in for the kill. Although his business was wound up, Garrett continued designing submarines, becoming a junior partner in Nordenfelt's Submarine Torpedo Boat Company. The remainder of Garrett's life was a depressing downward spiral of poverty, frustration and untimely death. Others profited from his work however. The millionaire Nordenfelt capitalised upon Garrett's steam-driven designs (with the added attraction of torpedo tubes) to produce *Nordenfelts I, II* and *III* sold to the Greek, Turkish and Russian governments. *Nordenfelt II (Abdulhamid)* famously became the first submarine to fire a torpedo.

WRECK SITE

Diver Keith Hurley was clearing fouled fishing boat nets off North Wales in 1995 when he found a cone shaped obstruction in 15m covered in rust and marine growth. Despite having spent 120 years on the seabed, *Resurgam* is in remarkably good condition. The iron plates are in place but the wooden cladding in the central section has predictably rotted away. There is a mystery 'V'-shaped dent in the conning tower, which suggests the little craft may have been accidentally rammed by *Elfin* as the yacht crew fought for control. The submarine lies on her starboard side with bows pointing roughly due west. The conning tower hatch, rudders and port hydroplane are missing. Aspects of the wreck brought Mr Hurley to some interesting conclusions:

> I was very surprised to see that her main hatch had been removed – not ripped off, but clearly taken off. Also, the submarine lies some way from the area where she might have been expected to be. It is my opinion that the Resurgam was deliberately scuttled and that, to save face, George Garrett had headed off for Portsmouth as if all was well – but knowing he had some problem with the sub, made sure that she never arrived...I remember thinking, that day when I first clapped eyes on her, that you'd have to be very brave, or very mad, or both, to put to sea in what was really an enormous boiler which travelled under water! But that's what pioneers do, I suppose. They risk things the rest of us might well avoid. [38]

Scientific research conducted in the course of the *Wreck Detectives* documentary in 2004 not only discounted deliberate scuttling as a cause of loss, it was scientifically proven that Garrett's submarine design was indeed viable. The historical significance of this craft was recognised in the designation of *Resurgam* as Protected Wreck No.42 on 6 July 1996. It is prohibited by statute to dive within a 300m radius of position 53° 23.78'N, 03° 33.18'W. The curious must content themselves with the replica at Woodside Terminal esplanade.

U 1051, KRIEGSMARINE U-BOAT

DATE OF LOSS: 26 January 1945
DEPTH: 75m
REFERENCE: 53° 39.316'N, 005° 19.933'W
LOCATION: 29.48-n.miles SW of Calf of Man and 30.9-n.miles NW of Carmel Head, Anglesey

Type: VIIC ocean-going attack boat *Builders:* F. Krupp Germaniawerft AG, Kiel-Gaarden for the *Kriegsmarine Ordered:* on 5 June 1941, within the batch of U 1051 – U 1058 *Keel laid:* Yard No.685 on 11 December 1943 *Launched:* 3 February 1943 *Commissioned:* by *Oblt.z.s* Heinrich von Holleben 4 March 1944 *Feldpost No.:* M 50 396

Heinrich von Holleben was born in Vina del Mar, Chile on 13 March 1919 and commenced his naval career in 1938. Von Holleben served as an A/S commander in the 17th *UJ Flottille* between January 1942 and March 1943. On 1 April 1943 Holleben was promoted to *Oblt.z.s.*

U 1051 was assigned to 5.U-Flottille in Kiel as *Ausbildungsboot* on 4 March until 31 December 1944.

(1) On 18 December the boat sailed from Kiel and arrived at Horten near Oslo on 23 December. On 1 January 1945, *U 1051* formally transferred to 11.U-Flottille, Bergen, for frontline service.

FINAL PATROL
(2) Leaving Horten on 28 December 1944, *U 1051* sailed for operations in British coastal waters, specifically the Irish Sea. The boat reached her billet by 20 January 1945. Next day von Holleben encountered the 1,152-ton Norwegian steamer *Galatea* (1912 – A/S D/S, Galatea, Bergen) steaming independently between Liverpool and Barry in ballast. A single torpedo was fired with the vessel in position 52° 40'N, 05° 23'W, south-west of Bardsey Island. It was quite sufficient. The torpedo detonated on the starboard side, forward. There was but one survivor, Stoker Harald Hvidtsten who was rescued by the frigate HMS *Tyler* (K576) next day.

FATALITIES OF *GALATEA*, 21.1.45
Bernsten, Kristoffer, Boatswain
Bradley, Percy, DEMS Gunner
Brendsdal, Peder, Master
Halvorsen, Harald, 2nd Mate

Hampshire, Harry, Act/AB (DEMS Gunner)
Hansen, Arthur, Stoker
Hatlø, Hans, 2nd Engineer
Johansen Aune, Cook
Johansen, Johannes, Trimmer
Jørgensen, Odd, Ordinary Seaman
Kasparsen, Sigurd, 1st Engineer
Lilleberg, Albert, Able Seaman
Lund, Jon, 1st Mate
Nilsen, Petter, Steward
Pedersen, Oskar, Able Seaman
Slinning, Leif, Donkeyman
Thomassen, Arne, Stoker
Tøsse, Johannes, Able Seaman
Wassether, Harald, Able Seaman

Now the story digresses slightly. The frigate HMS *Manners* (K568) sailed from Falmouth on 25 January bound for Gladstone Dock, Liverpool, under the command of Lt Dennis Jermain (see Vol.2). U-boats were known to be operating in the Irish Sea and standing orders required the warship to stream foxers, zig-zag at speed and maintain ASDIC watch at all times. Indeed *Manners* was steaming at 18 knots and the consequent vibration rendered the ASDIC set inoperable. By the morning of 26 January, the ship had reached 53° 29.05'N, 05° 09'W, some 21 miles 280° of the Skerries, Isle of Man (and within the protective minefields). At 1042 *Manners* was shattered by an explosion, the epicentre at her stern, just under the crowded canteen. *Manners* had been 'gnatted'. *U 1051* had struck her with a *T5*. German sailors called the *T5* a *Zaunkonig* or wren because of the melodious singing noise it made as powered towards its target but there was nothing sweet about this particular bird. Within moments the flames had spread to *Manners*' depth-charge rack and the secondary explosion which followed caused the already weakened stern to simply shear off and sink, taking forty-three men (including one civilian) down with it to the bed of the Irish Sea. Holyhead-based MTBs raced to the scene to provide assistance to the stricken ship. The wreck of HMS *Manners* was towed to Barrow-in-Furness.

FATALITIES OF HMS *MANNERS*, 26.1.45

Adam, Albert, AB, 22yrs	Hill, Francis, Stoker 1st class, 21yrs
Angold, Herbert, AB, 32yrs	Knott, James, AB, 18yrs
Abbott, Albert C., Stoker 1st class, 27yrs	Ledger, Albert, AB, 18yrs
Attree, Albert, AB, 19yrs	Legget, Robert, AB, RNVR, 27yrs
Banning, Fred, AB	McMillan, Robert, Sig 23yrs
Barsdell, William, PO	Meredith, William, AB (dow), 18yrs
Barnley, Phillip H, O/Tel., 19yrs	Neve, Richard, AB, 20yrs
Blackwell, Sidney, AB, 19yrs	Nickless, David, AB 22yrs

One of the most remarkable images of the Second World War taken from the bridge of HMS *Aylmer*. *U 1051* has just broken surface. *Aylmer* is thundering in to ram at top speed. Seconds after this photograph was taken, *Aylmer* struck the U-boat at 22 knots, momentarily skewering her, then riding over her stern. (P. Armstrong)

Photographed from a circling Hudson, the U-crew has less than a minute left to live. (Dennis Petrie)

Brown, Dennis, AB, 20yrs
Bush, James A., AB, 18yrs
Buckley, Walter, Stoker 1st class
Butcher, John, Stoker, 29yrs
Carter, John, Lt, RNVR
Cheal, William, AB, 18yrs
Collard, Edward, PO Motor Mech, 30yrs
Collins, David, Lt, RNVR, 30yrs
Cranage, Frank, O/Sig, 18yrs
Cross, Harry, Stoker, 18yrs
Delooze, Noel, AB, 19yrs
Glynn, Glyn, Sub-Lt, RNVR, 20yrs
Grubb, Ronald H., Stoker, 18yrs
Hardy, Fred, AB (dow)

Nolan, Thomas, AB
Norris, Tom, ERA 3rd class, 24yrs
Peralta, Pena Guillermo, O/S, 24yrs
Pierrepoint, Arthur, PO, 26yrs
Pickering, Colin, AB, 21yrs
Pym Stanley, AB, 19yrs
Rew, Thomas, L/Seaman, RNVR, 29yrs
Ribchester, William, Canteen Manager, RNCS, 28yrs
Riches, Edward, Lt, RNR, 42yrs
Vallance, Francis, L/Stoker, 25yrs
Waters, F, Stoker 1st class (dow), 21yrs
Wilson, Derek, AB
Wood, Donald Edward, AB

Why von Holleben should have been tempted to attack a strategically unimportant target in such shallow, confined waters must remain speculative. Whatever the reason, the U-boat had compromised her position and nemesis was on its way in the form of six A/S groups racing to the scene. Submarine warfare teaches one immutable rule: make an attack then make an escape. Von Holleben chose to remain in the vicinity. We know this because PO Foster and AB Beeby SD managed to restore power to *Manners'* ASDIC set. As the oscillator was trained, a clear echo was detected at maximum range. This was interpreted to mean that the bottomed U-boat was reloading torpedoes ready to administer the *coup de grace*. Contact was maintained with the U-boat and vital information was relayed to the warships of EG 5 when they reached the scene. At 1230hrs HMS *Bentinck* (Cdr E. Chavasse) was sweeping alongside HMS *Calder* (Lt-Cdr E. Playne) when she gained a contact. A depth-charge attack commenced at 1319hrs. Contact was gained, lost and then regained. This is the official report of what transpired:

> EG 5 in Aylmer (Lt B. Campbell) obtained contact at 1440. Calder closed and gained contact at 253 degrees at 1,700 yards, bearing 004 and made a depth-charge attack at 1525. This was followed by an echo sounder run, the trace giving an object at fourteen fathoms. The target appeared to be coming towards Calder and going right towards Aylmer... Aylmer ran in and delivered a Hedgehog attack. The explosion sounding like two bombs hitting not quite simultaneously...At 1603 the U-boat surfaced bows on, just as I was turning to port with the result that Calder was beam on. I ordered full ahead, port thirty degrees while all guns opened fire. I had to order 'Cease Fire!' as Aylmer went in to ram.
>
> My view of the U-boat was restricted, but she was definitely down by the stern when she surfaced. As far as I could see she was of the 250-300-ton type with no net cutter or gun forward. There was a cut-away portion abaft the bridge with grandstand rails but these and the bridge appeared to be damaged when surfaced. This suggests that one bomb hit the bridge and another the hull, which accounts for the double explosion. Members of the ships company report seeing five aces painted on the conning tower but no number. There was no visible sign of the schnorchel. One of my officers reports that the forward escape hatch was opened before she sank but no-one got out.

A unique series of photographs were taken from the bridge of *Aylmer* in the course of this incident. One photograph shows *U 1051* lying square on the course of the warship as she thunders in to ram at maximum speed. The second photograph shows *U 1051* skewered on the warship's bows. A close examination of this second photograph revealed a shield bearing the figure '7': the bar across the seven, being in the form of a fish. It was this motif which ultimately persuaded the Naval Historical Branch to re-assess the loss of *U 1051.*

FATALITIES OF *U 1051*, 26.1.45

Albern, Otto, MtrO/Gfr, 21yrs
Albert, Günter, FkO/Gfr., 20yrs
Anders, Kurt, O/BtsMt, 23yrs
Anders, Walter O/BtsMt, 23yrs
Antheck, Kurt, Masch.Ob/Gfr, 21yrs
Antweiler, Hans, Mtr.Ob/Gfr, 20yrs
Augustiniack, Alfred, Mtr.Ob/Gfr, 20yrs
Baumann, Franz, Mtr.Ob/Gfr, 20yrs
Bieseke, Hans-Joachim, Fk.Ob/Gfr, 21yrs
Brödling, Karl-Heinz, Mech.Gfr, 20yrs
Clement, Wilhelm, StOb/Strm, 30yrs
Döhler, Walter, Fk.Mt, 26yrs
Eder, Josef, MtrGfr, 20yrs
Egelhof, Heinrich, Masch.Mt, 23yrs
Empte, Heinrich, Masch.Mt, 25yrs
Enke, Kurt-Walter, Lt.z.s, 21yrs
Erfurth, Herhard, Mtr, 20yrs
Gröf, Hans, Masch.Ob/Gfr, 21yrs
Hagenlocher, Karl, Mech.O/Gfr, 23yrs
Henke, Hans, Oblt.z.s, 24yrs

Kiene, Kurt, Ob/Masch, 28yrs
Knothe, Wolfgang, Ltz.S, 23yrs
Koch, Martin, Masch.Gfr, 21yrs
Max, Philipp, Ob/Masch, 28yrs
Noack, Peter, Masch.Mt, 25yrs
Petzoldt, Werner, Masch.H/Gfr, 23yrs
Pszolla, Heinz, Masch.Ob/Gfr, 24yrs
Schmitz, Heinz, Masch.Mt, 24yrs
Schröer, Willi, Ob/Fk.Mt, 27yrs
Schween, Heinrich, Masch.O/Gfr, 21yrs
Sittner, Werner MaschOb/Gfr, 23yrs
Teuner, Heinz, BtsMt, 26yrs
Töpper, Anton, MtrOb/Gfr, 19yrs
Velentin, Erich, Masch.Ob/Gfr, 21yrs
Wald, Heinz, Mtr.Ob/Gfr, 24yrs
Weber, Fritz, Ob/Mech.Mt, 26yrs
Weber, Johannes, Mtr.Ob/Gfr, 23yrs
Weick, Günter, Fk.Ob/Gfr, 21yrs
Weidmann, Karl, Mtr.Ob/Gfr, 24yrs
Weiser, Ernst, Masch.Mt, 26yrs

Hö, Helmut, Masch.H/Gfr, 25yrs
Holleben, von Heinrich, Oblt.z.s., 26yrs
Käfer, Georg Masch.Mt, 25yrs
Kemming, Herbert Mech.Ob/Gfr, 21yrs

Weißer, Willy, Ob/San.Mt, 25yrs
Wieker, Erich Ob/Lt.z.s., 33yrs
Willenberg, Otto, Masch.Ob/Gfr, 24yrs

WRECK SITE

The wreck is orientated in a south to north (175/355-degrees) direction, with her bows facing north. She lies on her port side on a seabed of mud and shingle in a general depth of 75m (246ft), being the lowest astronomical depth. Despite having been rammed by *Aylmer*, the wreck is intact, with the scarcely recognisable conning tower almost level with the seabed. The wreck, which is a war grave, is coated in colourful anemones.

ADM 199/1786 ADM 199/197 NARA T-1022,Roll 4066,PG30841

U 1024, KRIEGSMARINE U-BOAT

DATE OF LOSS: 12 April 1945
DEPTH: 64m
REFERENCE: 53° 44. 016' N, 04° 57.433'W
LOCATION: SW of Calf of Man and NW of Carmel Head, Anglesey

Type: VIIC/41 ocean-going attack boat **Builders:** Blohm & Voss AG at Hamburg for the *Kriegsmarine* **Ordered:** 13 June 1942 within the batch of U 1019 – U 1025 **Keel laid:** as Yard No.224 on 20 May 1943 **Launched:** 3 May 1944 **Commissioned:** by *Kplt*. Hans-Joachim Gutteck on 28 June 1944 **Feldpost No.:** M 39 246

OTHER SPECIFICATIONS OF *U 1024*

Two non-reversible (no *schnorchel* cam-shaft) Germaniawerft (GW) diesel/oil engines and fitted with *Gebläse* (super-chargers), powered the two propellers. Armament consisted of one 37mm (1.46in) gun fully automatic on lower bandstand plus 1,195-rounds and two twin 20mm (0.79in) Flak guns on upper bandstand with 4,380-rounds, plus Type 15 machine guns. She also had five torpedo tubes (one stern and four at the bow) and carried six *LuT* and four *T5 (Zaunkonig)* torpedoes. In July 1944, an experimental steel cover was fitted to the *schnorchel* head at the Schichau Werft, Danzig and in January 1945: the steel caging was replaced at Howaldts, Hamburg by ridged rubber.

Hans-Joachim Gutteck was born in Greifswald on 10 April 1914 and commenced his career with coastal artillery in 1935. He served with 3rd *Sperrbrecher Flottille* between March 1943 and September 1943 before commencing U-boat training. On 1 November 1943 Gutteck was promoted to *Kplt*. (R).

    U 1024 was assigned to 31.U-Flottille at Hamburg as *Ausbildungsboot* on 28 June 1944 until 31 January 1945 with *Kplt*. Gutteck the CO. On 1 February 1945, the boat and crew formally transferred to 11.U-Flottille at Bergen as a frontline boat. *U 1024* made one patrol but was involved in various transfers.

    Sources indicate the following movements:

(1) Leaving Kiel on 30 December 1944 *U 1024* transferred to Horten near Oslo, Norway, arriving on 2 January 1945.

(2) On 28 February 1945, *U 1024* departed Horten for Marviken (the haven slightly east of Kristiansand, now called Marvika) on 1 March

FINAL PATROL

(3) British Naval Intelligence extracted this information from prisoners. Its accuracy cannot be verified:

    U 1024 lay in Marviken until 3 March, when she left with two other VIIC boats and one IXC boat. Her course was between the Faeroes and Iceland, submerged except for when a *Passiermedung* was transmitted shortly after passing Iceland. *U 1024* sailed for British coastal waters via the *norweg*, between the

Færoes and Iceland, and then down the west coast of Ireland, lighthouse plotting providing the crew with navigational fixes. By 1 April the boat had entered St George's Channel but to Gutteck's dismay, the waters were heavily patrolled. Foxer noise was constant and a leak in one of the compensating tanks only added to the crew's discomfort.

On 4 April Gutteck claimed to have fired two *T5* torpedoes, sinking a 'corvette': this audacious claim is not substantiated by British records. Two large hospital ships were apparently allowed to pass unmolested. Off Holyhead on 7 April, at 1731hrs, *U 1024* came to periscope depth amid the inbound transatlantic convoy HX 346. The boat was forced to dive to 20m in a frantic effort to avoid being rammed.

Post-war account of Lt.z.s. Horst–Güther Mueller:

> The captain waited until the large vessels had passed over us before ordering the boat to be brought to peri-scope depth. A spread of two LuT torpedoes was fired, one of which failed to fire, but the other was sent on its way. After an appropriate time lapse we heard a loud explosion followed by horrible noises as the ship's bulkheads collapsed. This was a frightening noise audible throughout the boat…Oblt.Grohman did not realise that one of the torpedoes was still in the tube. You see he compensated for four torpedoes instead of just one. Result: down we went by the bows, 'smack' into the seabed. Everything that could shake loose came tumbling down the boat, including me.

The victim was 7,176-ton Liberty ship *James W. Nesmith* (Master R. Rossiter, McCormick SS Co., San Francisco). Her cargo included such diverse items as tobacco, fertiliser, aircraft parts and eight crated P 47 fighters stowed on deck. The ship was at position 53° 24'N, 04° 48'W when Gutteck's torpedo detonated on the port side aft, destroying the steering gear and causing immediate flooding. As matters transpired the ship was successfully towed into Holyhead by HMCS *Belleville*, only later to be declared a total loss.

Lt Mueller again:

> The captain did not like the idea of bottoming out, he much preferred to keep on the move using the motors. We had an impressive hydrophone operator who really knew his box of tricks. We dodged around those tommies, firing SBT whenever an escort seemed to be running in for an attack, then quickly altering course ninety degrees to starboard. When foxer was loud and clear we ran at half speed, changing to silent running speed when foxer was not audible and the tommies were presumably using their hydrophones. Later we found a hollow and lay low while the escorts thundered away elsewhere. We knew the tommies usually gave up submarine hunts after eight hours, so at 2200 we headed off, back on course again.

On 10 April Gutteck made an abortive attack on a 'frigate', which responded with a Hedgehog attack lasting five hours. Gutteck noting in his log: '1930 Corvette has been shaken off. Good job, she looked practised in the U-boat hunting game'. The hunter was HMCS *Strathadam* and the reason why the pursuit had been broken off was because a Hedgehog pattern had exploded on deck, killing five men.

FATALITIES OF HMCS *STRATHADAM*, 10.4.45

Comish, John, Tel., RCNVR, 21yrs
Friend, James, Tel., RCNVR, 28yrs
Jones, Harold, AB, RCNVR, 23yrs
McEwan, Dennis, L/Tel., RCNVR, 25yrs
Shimmin, Alfred, L/Stores Assistant, RCNVR, 34yrs

Perhaps unwisely, *U 1024* remained off Holyhead. At 1350hrs on 12 April Convoy BB80 hove into view. The convoy, steaming between the Clyde and Bristol, was divided into two columns of five ships, with the trawler *Lancer* at the head. Gutteck brought *U 1024* to periscope depth and waited until the 7,200-ton *Will Rogers* (Master T. Lewis, Merchants and Miners Transportation Co., Baltimore), the leading ship in the starboard column had drawn parallel. The ship was transporting general cargo from New York to Antwerp via Southampton. A spread of three *LuT* torpedoes was fired. Gutteck remained at periscope depth to observe one of his torpedoes detonate on the starboard side of the ship, abaft the forepeak bulkhead. Two more explosions were heard once the periscope had been lowered but these were prob-ably the sound of the torpedoes striking the seabed at the end of their run. This attack took place at 53°

U 995 – the Navigator's table with just enough space to lay out a chart. The torpedo firing panel and TDC were originally affixed over a continuation of this table, immediately to the left. (Kev Belcher)

48'N 04° 46'W. Once again the ship was not fatally damaged although the flooding was serious. She was ultimately beached at Holyhead, earning grim celebrity as the last torpedo casualty in the Irish Sea. Meanwhile *Lancer* radioed news of the attack then commenced an 'observant' course, boxing the location of the attack. What follows is the Report of 2 and 8 EGs, which incorporates material derived from prisoner interrogation:

On intercepting Lancer's report of the torpedoing, EG8 and EG2 closed the position at full speed. The Senior Officer EG2 assumed command, and ordered EG8 to carry out a Square Search of six-mile sides, whilst Wild Goose (of 2nd EG.) searched a square of two-mile sides inside EGs. In order to 'help the U-Boat Commander think along the right lines' single depth-charges were dropped when six to eight miles NNW of the datum. It was hoped to encourage the U-Boat to alter his ideas if he had thought of going north, and to lull him into a false sense of security if he was already going 'the right way'.

2nd EG was then spread in accordance with a Group Scheme known at this time as the 'Rogers Search' later to become the 'Pi' Search. To date the only attack had been by HMT Lancer on a probable 'non-sub', soon after the torpedoing.

EG8 had arrived at 1605 and by 1700 ships were all in position. So were the non-subs, and reports of contacts and the noises of explosions were coming from all directions.

It is not certain which of the many contacts was U 1024, but the boat was badly shaken. The crew maintain that her position was given away by the LI allowing the keel to hit the bottom several times. At least 120 depth-charge explosions had been counted which, although bad enough for morale, had not so far been near enough to put anything out of order.

EG8 detached—Loch Glendhu gains contact:
At 1925 Commander-in-Chief Western Approaches ordered EG 8 to support ON296. The Group had formed up at 2005 inline abreast at 3,000 yards apart on course 265°, at ten knots, when, at 2025 Loch Glendhu (Lt-

Cdr E. Knapton) – starboard wing ship – obtained contact with U 1024 on 345°, range 1,800 yards (unifoxer streamed) and turned towards. The echo was weak but there was high doppler, and by 1,600 yards contact was firmly established. The plot at first suggested a stationary target, but shortly afterwards: a two-knot southerly movement, coinciding with the doppler report, made it look promising. Action Stations were sounded, and although convoys ON296 and OS122/KMS96 were approaching from the northward, it was decided that they were still out of torpedo range and that a deliberate attack was justified.

The action teams took over, but the change-over was not quite in time to allow of accurate lining up. An Echo Sounder run was made with negative results and the range opened for a deliberate attack.

Loch Glendhu's Attack:
The run-in presented no difficulty and everything went according to plan. At 1,200 yards all instruments were lined up correctly and 'steer by ASDIC' ordered. Contact was obtained by 147B at 220ft. The Squid fired at 2041 but owing to a defect in the depth setting gear, two projectiles did not fire until thirteen seconds after the remainder.

The German perspective – *Bootsman* Legat:

An escort headed towards us, firing depth-charges. The explosions sounded just like aircraft bombs. We dived, but the engineer lost trim and she banged her keel off the bottom. The English could not have failed to hear that. They knew where we were and they knew it was shallow water. Of course they gave us hell.

After five hours of this punishment the emergency lighting and both compasses had failed. The boat took on a heavy list when two depth-charges exploded close, causing Gutteck to observe, 'Pretty good aiming'. The same explosion blew one of the propeller shafts out of alignment. The hydroplane operators reported that the controls had become loose in their hands.

The British Report continued – *U 1024 Brought to the Surface:*

The first four projectiles fell uncomfortably close. Lights were broken, the starboard motor was stopped and both compasses went off the board. The boat went to the bottom. Then the two remaining charges went off – 'it was hell!' All the overhead fittings fell down, one motor left its mountings, the switchboard disintegrated, the galley-hatch burst open and water poured in. Gutteck ordered the life-saving gear to be prepared, tanks were blown and at 2045 the U-boat surfaced 500 yards on Loch Glendhu's starboard quarter, 240°, six miles from the datum position of the original Square Search.

Bootsman Legat continued:

As the boat broke surface, the English were firing at us. The captain tried to tell them not to shoot but a shell blew half of his left hand away. The Engineer (Grohmann) was also hit by a shell fragment and fell over the side. Even as men were sliding over the casing into the water the English were firing depth-charges. The IWO was badly injured. The IIWO and a matrose were killed in the water.

The British Report continued – *Away Boarding Parties:*

All ships of the Group opened fire with everything that would bear. Gutteck himself was first through the conning-tower hatch but had his left hand shot away – he then shot himself. There was no more fight left in U 1024 and boarding parties were sent by Loch More and Loch Glendhu. No opposition was encountered and the U-boat's crew were herded on the forecastle.

The boarding parties found that there was practically no water entering the boat except in the engine room, although the damage aft was obviously serious. The air was pure and some lighting was still on. No attempt was made, however, to go further aft than the engine room as the W/T bulkhead seemed intact and it seemed inadvisable to open it, owing to the damage aft.

The U-boat's bridge structure had been badly damaged by gunfire and there was no sign of any Radar aerials. At least two direct hits with four-inch guns had been obtained on the starboard side forward of the bridge, but there had apparently been no penetration of the conning-tower plating.

A safe was found that was locked and attempts to open it failed. All books and papers were collected from the U-boat and passed into whalers or on board the Loch More.

On boarding HMS Loch More, prisoners were searched and segregated. Personal effects such as wallets, etc., were put into sealed envelopes with owners name on outside. No trouble was experienced with the prisoners who seemed to be very subdued.

Gutteck's preference for suicide rather than capture greatly disturbed all who witnessed it and profoundly distressed Lt-Cdr Knapton. Nevertheless, having captured a U-boat, the 8th EG had achieved a *coup*. *Loch More* dispatched a boarding party to enter the boat and prepare her for towing. With the U-boat apparently secured, the strange little convoy set course for Douglas on the Isle of Man:

The British Report continued – *U 1024* Taken in Tow:

Loch More got the U-Boat in tow by 2145 and speed was worked up to 4½ knots when Loch More's rudder jammed at 20° starboard, and at 2336 the tow parted. By this time the initial list on the U-boat of 5° had noticeably increased and she began to settle, and when Loch More again contacted her in the fog she reported that she was sinking. U 1024 was abandoned just as she sank by the stern at 0002 and the boarding parties were successfully recovered, together with some thirty-seven survivors. None of the searches laid on succeeded in finding U 1024 and if she had not repeatedly returned to dangerous waters and finally put herself in the way of an efficient Squid-fitted vessel, she might have escaped.

The U-boat sank 23 miles north-west of Holyhead. Interestingly AB William Alfred Oliver of HMS *Loch Glendhu* was decorated with the DSM for his part in sinking of *U 1024*. His medal is now on display at the RN Submarine Museum at Gosport. AB Oliver transferred to the Submarine Service only to die on HM S/M *Truculent* (see Vol.1).

FATALITIES OF *U 1024*, 12.4.45
Gutteck, Hans-Joachim, Kplt.
Grohmann, Günter, Ob/Lt. Ing
Stocker, Franz, Ob/Masch.Mt

CREWMEN CAPTURED
Barthel, Johannes, Masch.Gfr
Becker, Robert, Masch.Mt
Bouillon, Hannes, Fk.Mt
Brueckler, Alois, Masch.Gfr
Buchwald, Karl, Matr.Gfr
Crecelius, Johann, Masch.Gfr
Forschbach, H., Fk.Ob/Gfr
Gutekunst, Matr.Ob/Gfr
Hamer, Karl, Matr.Ob/Gfr
Hartner, Josef, Matr.Gfr
Heil, Kurt, Matr.Ob/Gfr
Holtrup, Karl, Mech.Ob/Gfr
Junior, Willi, Masch.Ob/Gfr
Kaiser, Hans, Mech.Mt
Kerth, Phillipp, Ob/Bt.Smt
Kleen, Gerhard, Matr.Ob/Gfr
Knoepfler, Johann, Mech.Gfr
Lange, Heinrich, Ob/Strmn
Legat, Karl, Bt.Smt

Loehrl, Johannes, Ob/Bt.Smt
Mantey, Georg, SanFeld
Meissner, Johann, Matr.II
Moritz, Otto, Matr.Ob/Gfr
Mueller, Horst-Günther, Lt.z.s
Mueller, Karl, Ob.Masch
Pietsch, Horat, Masch.Ob/Gfr
Praeger, Arno, Masch.Mt
Preuss, Heinz, Masch.Ob/Gfr
Roeske, Kurt, Masch.Mt
Rosemeyr, F., Matr.Ob/Gfr
Schmidt, J., Matr.Ob/Gfr
Schneider, Franz, Masch.Mt
Schoppman, H., Masch.Mt
Troeger, J., Masch.Ob/Gfr
Van-Huemel, Hans, Masch.Mt
Wagenhofer, Peter, Matr.I
Wege, Heinz, Fk.Mt

WRECK SITE

The wreck has not been positively identified but the position offered above has provided a trace consistent with a Type VIIC U-boat.

ADM 1/17649 ADM 199/2062 ADM 1/17649 ADM1/17666, NND873041, NARA T1022, Roll 399, PG30840

U 246, KRIEGSMARINE U-BOAT

DATE OF LOSS: March 1945
DEPTH: 45m
REFERENCE: 53° 39.979' N,04° 54.292' W
LOCATION: 19.6-n.miles NW of Carmel Head, Anglesey and 23-n.miles SSW of Calf of Man

Type: VIIC ocean-going attack boat *Builders:* J. Krupp Germaniawerft AG, Kiel-Gaarden for the *Kriegsmarine* *Ordered:* on 10 April 1941, within the batch of U 241 – U 246 *Keel laid:* as Yard No.680 on 30 November 1942 *Launched:* on 7 December 1943 *Commissioned:* by *Kplt.* Ernst Raabe on 11 January 1944 *Feldpost No.:* M 53 307

Ernst Raabe was born on 5 February 1907 in Gross-Engelau, East Prussia and commenced his naval career in 1926. Raabe served on the heavy cruiser *Admiral Hipper* between December 1939 and March 1943 before beginning U-boat training. Raabe was promoted to *Kplt.* on 1 April 1943.

U 246 was assigned to 5.U-Flottille in Kiel as *Ausbildungsboot* on 11 January 1944 until 31 July 1944, with Raabe the CO.

On 1 August 1944, U 246 formally transferred to 3.U-Flottille at La Pallice, for frontline operations. The boat remained with the flotilla until 30 September, spending most of the time at her building yard for *schnorchel* fitting.

(1) On 28 September 1944 U 246 sailed from Kiel and arrived at Horten on 30 September.

U 246 was formally transferred to 11.U-Flottille, Bergen for frontline duties on 1 October 1944.

(2) The boat left Horten under Ernst Raabe on 4 October 1944 and was directed to proceed into the English Channel for operations against allied shipping. However, on 23 October the U-boat was located by destroyers of EG 6, south-west of Ireland in BE33. The encounter began when Raabe ordered the *schnorchel* to be lowered following completion of battery charging. Vibration, allied to the smoking *schnorchel* head, had rendered periscope watch near impossible. The boat was deaf as well as blind as the noise made by the *schnorchel* process ruled out hydrophone drill except at very low speeds. The ships of EG 6 detected a suspicious radar contact, tracking it for several minutes. When the contact disappeared, an ASDIC search commenced. Once U 246 returned to motor propulsion, the *funker* heard warship engines as EG 6 turned in to attack. A sustained depth-charge attack ensued. Diving tanks three and five were damaged and the attack periscope standard was thrown out of alignment with its securing runners. Raabe adopted the classic evasion technique of keeping his stern towards the enemy vessels, providing a minimal ASDIC target. In this fashion U 246 was able to creep away at slow speed. Foxer, known in *KTBs* as 'circular saw', was audible throughout. U 246 arrived at Bergen on 12 November.

FINAL PATROL

(3) Following three months of repairs and refit, U 246 left Bergen on 21 February for operations to the south of Ireland and the western end of the English Channel. The writers have been unable to ascertain why Dr Ernst Thurner was on board for this mission. On 6 March U 246 transmitted a *passiermeldung* from AM 4314 (position 56° 20'N 12°50'W, off the west coast of Ireland). On 9 March *BdU* ordered U 246 into the Irish Sea.

It is believed that on 21 March, U 246 and two other U-boats attacked convoys, TBC 102 and BTC 103. By 1 April her estimated track placed the boat off the Welsh coast but there is no evidence U 246 reached this far. The boat was officially listed as '*Vermisst ein Stern*' with her crew on 5 April 1945. Post-war British research assumed she had been destroyed by depth-charges from the British frigate HMS *Duckworth* on 29 March 1945 near Land's End, in position 49° 58'N, 05° 25'W (Vol.2), but it seems

The conning tower hatch. So near yet so far. Like their British counterparts the U-crews used the twill trunk escape method. And in common with British submariners, successful escapes were depressingly rare. (Kev Belcher)

probable that this attack actually sank *U 1169*. Now we must examine the evidence produced by an attack on a U-boat by EG 14 on 30 April:

> Whilst in the vicinity of 55°N and while en route to relieve the 10 EG as 'Force 38' a series of signals were intercepted from Sunderland H/201 indicating that a U-boat had dived in position 58°42 N, 04 °55 W at 0810. *Hesperus* together with *Hotspur* proceeded to the position indicated. When south of Chicken Rock a further contact was received from the same aircraft reporting a positive sonar buoy contact at 56°N 04° 44W including German voices and radio. This was 025 degrees, fifteen miles from the previous sighting. Assuming that the U-boat had bottomed following attack by the aircraft in 53° 42'N, 04° 55'N a square search of ten miles was commenced...At 1504 *Hesperus* obtained contact to starboard classified 'bottomed'. Two Hedgehog attacks were made, the results being inconclusive...a further six attacks were carried out by *Hesperus* and *Havelock*. As a result of these attacks, air bubbles, diesel oil and bubbles broke surface. Oil and debris including foodstuffs, locker lids etc.

Items recovered included a pair of socks bearing the name tag of 'Gunther Schaaf'. Post-war research indicates that *Oberfahnrich (ing)* Schaaf was posted as missing while serving on *U 246*. Now our little tale takes a mysterious twist. *U 246* was expected to have turned for home in early April, therefore the attack of 30 April must have been against the *already destroyed U 246*. Actual cause of loss must therefore remain unknown. True, minefields H1 and H2 had been laid on 10 March as part of 'Operation CH' (this section consisted of 160 Mk XV11s laid at 65ft west of Calf of Man) but there was no minefield in the location where the wreck was ultimately discovered. A loose mine may feasibly have been responsible, equally another cause such as a diving accident or *schnorchel* valve failure cannot be ruled out.

FATALITIES OF *U 246*

Ahrlich, Johann, Ob/Strm, 30yrs

Beyer, Günter, Gfr, 21yrs

Boeker, Ewald, Ob/Mt, 23yrs

Ciuppa, Erich, Ob/Gfr, 21yrs

Cleres, Erich, Gfr, 21yrs

Deisen, Peter, Mt, 24yrs

Dommick, Gerhard, Gfr, 20yrs

Giesers, Heinrich, Ob/Gfr, 21yrs

Glatzel, Hans-Heinrich, Oblt.z.s. 1WO, 23yrs

Glindemann, Albert, Ob/Mt, 23yrs

Goerigk, Heinrich, Mt, 24yrs

Grünmann, Karl, Mt, 23yrs

Heyer, Jakob, Ob/Gfr, 23yrs

Hinneburg, Herbert, Mt, 26yrs

Hofmann, Kurt, Ob/Gfr, 23yrs

Horbach, Günter, Mt, 25yrs

Hübner, Karl-Heinz, Mt, 24yrs

Hüls, Johannes, Ob/Masch, 33yrs

Kemke, Helmut, Ob/Gfr, 21yrs

Körner, Fritz, Mt, 24yrs

Kuckelkorn, Herbert, Oblt Ing, 28yrs

Lange, Gerhard, Mtr, 20yrs

Lony, Herbert, Mt, 24yrs

Lorenz, Heinz, Ob/Gfr, 21yrs

Lüchau, Harald, Mt, 22yrs

Müller, Helmut, Ob/Gfr, 23yrs

Müller, Kurt, Ob/Gfr, 21yrs

Müller, Rudolf, Ob/Gfr, 21yrs

Münchenberg, Hans, Ob/Gfr, 21yrs

Münster, Hans, Ob/Masch, 29yrs

Nettelroth, Horst, Gfr, 23yrs

Neumann, Günter, Ob/Gfr, 21yrs

Obermayr, Franz, Ob/Gfr, 21yrs

Peters, Wilhelm, Ob/Gfr, 21yrs

Raabe, Ernst, Kplt.

Ratsch, Joachim-Hans, Ob/Gfr, 21yrs

Rübke, Gerhard, Ob/Strm, 25yrs

Schaaf, Günter, Ob/Fahnr.Ing, 21yrs

Schreiner, Kurt, Ob/Gfr, 21yrs

Schröder, Ernst, Ob/Gfr, 20yrs

Schröder, Peter, Ob/Gfr, 21yrs

Schuster, Johann, Ob/Gfr, 25yrs

Sommer, Heinrich, Gfr, 21yrs

Staude, Siegfried, Haupt.Gfr, 24yrs

Thurner, Ernst, Dr, 34yrs

Vogt, Paul, Ob/Gfr, 21yrs

Volkmann, Erwin, Ob/Gfr, 21yrs

U 246 has since been discovered midway between the Isle of Anglesey and the Isle of Man.

WRECK SITE

The wreck is orientated in an east to west (090/270-degrees) direction, with her bows facing east. According to the Lindberg identification system, a bow slot pattern of 3-16-2 might be expected for *U 246*. She lies on a seabed of gravel, shell and pebbles, in a general depth of 45m (147.6ft) (LAT). The wreck, which is broken, lies at an angle to starboard. A sand wave has built up against the port side. The hull has been split open in a number of places, exposing machinery, ballast tanks – and live torpedoes. It is not possible to say whether this damage was caused by mining but this seems plausible. Interestingly, both the conning tower hatch and forward hatches are open, suggesting a failed attempt to escape on the part of the crew. Looking aft, propellers and the torpedo tubes are visible. The conning tower is in place and the D/F aerial, *schnorchel* and periscope were clearly visible at the time of writing. Fair numbers of large fish, mostly pollack, pout whiting (bib) and coley, shoal over the conning tower.

ADM 199/1786 ADM 199/1786 NARA T1022, Roll 3900, PG 30224, 31752

CHAPTER TWO

HMS *THETIS* – A REAPPRAISAL

BY PAMELA ARMSTRONG

June 1939 witnessed the most infamous submarine accident in British maritime history, an event closely associated with the area covered by this book. Although the wreck of *Thetis/ Thunderbolt* lies far away off the north coast of Sicily, the story is too compelling to ignore in this, the seventieth anniversary of her original loss. Combining primary documentation with eyewitness testimony, what follows is an attempt to shed some much-needed illumination on the dark events in Liverpool Bay.

THETIS, HM SUBMARINE – 'I BIDE MY TIME'

DATE OF FIRST LOSS: 1 June 1939 SECOND AND FINAL LOSS: 14 March 1943
DEPTH: 60m
REFERENCE: 38° 20.002'N, 015° 20.001' E
LOCATION: Off S. Vito lo Capo in Sicily

Type: 'Triton' Class British patrol submarine of 'T' Group I *Builders:* Cammell Laird & Co. Ltd, Birkenhead for Royal Navy *Pendant No.:* 11.T *Ordered:* 1936 Programme on 10 August 1936 *Keel laid:* as Job No.1027 on 21 December 1936 *Launched:* 29 June 1938 *Commissioned:* 4 March 1939

TECHNICAL SPECIFICATION

Hull: Admiralty saddle-tank type, with a riveted pressure hull of 12.7mm (half-inch) thickness *Compartments:* six watertight *Surface displacement:* 1,325 tons *U/Dt:* 1,573 tons *LBD:* 82.83m × 8.09m × 4.82m *Machinery:* 2 × Sulzer diesels that developed 2,500bhp *Props:* 2-bronze *S/Sp:* 15.2kts *Op/R:* 8,000-n.miles @ 10kts & 42-days duration *Sub/R:* 80-n.miles @ 4kts *U/Power:* 2 × General Electric motors that developed 1,450shp, gave 8.75kts *Batteries:* accumulators of 336-cells, weighing 150 tons *Fuel/Cap:* 132 tons in internal tanks *Armament:* high bulbous bow-casing to enclose the forward external tubes. 10 × 53.34cm (21in) torpedo tubes, 8-bow and 2-amidships and all firing forward *Torpedoes:* 16 × 53.34cm (21in) *Guns:* 1 × 10.16cm (4in /40) Quick Firing Mk XII gun that had a revolving breastwork, which could be mounted about 45.72cm (1.5in) above the casing. (This was to facilitate early manning of the gun when surfacing and also provided protection for the gun-crew against the weather.) Also one Lewis or Vickers 7.69mm (0.303in) machine gun *Diving:* max-op-depth 91.44m (300ft) *Complement:* 6 officers & 50 ratings (peacetime) *Cost:* £350,000

Other equipment: ASDIC Type.129, Type 710B hydrophones and Type.55 W/T.
Nomenclature: One of the *Nereides* or sea nymphs and thirteenth RN vessel of the name: the first being in 1717.

Author's note: the 'e' in *Thetis* should properly be pronounced as the 'e' in 'jet'. Cammell Laird had built eight submarines during the First World War. Forty more[39] were built in the years which followed, among them HMS/M *Thetis*. *Thetis* was the third submarine of her class but the first 'T' class boat to be built on the Mersey.

HMS *Thetis* cap tally. The cap belonged to Norman Longstaff. (P. Armstrong)

JOB NO.1027 – A FOUNDATION OF FACT

Thetis, launched on 29 June 1938, was named by Mrs Anne Power, the wife of the captain of *Ark Royal*, then under construction in the Birkenhead yard. A long period of fitting out (i.e. the phase between launch and final acceptance trials) followed. A knot of experienced submarine officers comprising Lt-Cdr Bolus and Lts Chapman[40] and Glenn[41] had been patiently standing-by the boat since April 1938. The genial 'Sam' Bolus, with fifteen years in submarines, had spent three years in command of HMS/M *Shark* in the Mediterranean, followed by a stint as spare submarine CO on HMS *Lucia*.[42] Lt-Cdr Bolus was delighted to be appointed to *Thetis*, one of the new 'T' class boats, the most powerful submarines in the Royal Navy, but he chafed at the disappointments and frustrations inherent in standing-by a submarine fitting out. The sense of momentum was rekindled when a party of twelve petty officers joined the commissioned officers on 4 January 1939. Suitable accommodation was sought and found in the terraces of Tranmere. Many found lodgings in Park, Moorland, Parkside, Union and Sidney roads, fringing Mersey Park and within convenient walking distance of the Yard. Bolus himself rented a house some distance away in Hooton with his wife, Sybil.

By 28 February, Bolus felt confident enough to request Captain (S) 5 Blockhouse, Harry Oram, to despatch the remaining thirty-four ratings detailed for the boat. Records reveal that the crew was a cross section of inter-war career submariners, ranging from seasoned engineers like CERA Bill Ormes, to twenty-year-old AB Stan Crombleholme of Blackburn, a newcomer to submarines. Most of the ratings were volunteers and each rating possessed at least one good conduct badge. At this juncture the Submarine Service could afford to be selective and these men were the very cream of the Royal Navy. As the crew shaped up, so the boat neared completion, so that by 4 March 1939 HMS *Thetis* was officially entered into the ledger of the 5th Submarine Flotilla[43] at Blockhouse, as 'submarine currently fitting-out'. Once accepted into the Royal Navy, the boat was scheduled to join the 6th Flotilla at Portland.

At this stage HMS *Thetis* was moored against the south wall of the Wet Basin within Cammell Laird's Yard. Much of the remaining work had been sub-contracted, with the result that a variety of unfamiliar faces trooped down Green Lane into the Yard, as the Cammell Laird men looked on with professional interest. Much attention focussed on Mr Arthur Hill, familiar to British shipbuilding circles as the Senior Admiralty Ship Overseer. The forthcoming series of trials would be held under the joint control of Mr Hill and Arthur Robinson, Cammell Laird's Senior Engineer. First came a series of trim dives within the yard basin, designed to test valves and fittings. No torpedoes were carried at this stage, therefore compensation in the form of water ballast was admitted to the tubes. Responsibility for the trimming process lay in the hands of dockyard and Admiralty staff. The figures obtained would later be passed on to the First Lieutenant Chapman and Stoker PO Dillon-Shallard in the form of the 'trim chit'. The conventional, if tedious, method for trimming was to charge the torpedo tubes using clean water from the WRT or 'Water Round Tube'. The short-cut was simply to open the bow-cap and fill up with water from the harbour. It must be stressed that the method used in this case must remain speculative.[44] What is certain is that all work carried out while the boat was fitting out, had been duly signed off by senior Admiralty overseers, Messrs Hill and Bailey.[45] As the contract expressly required, Cammell Laird certified that the vessel was 'in a proper condition to undertake the forthcoming diving trial', the certificate, dated 12 April 1939, was duly countersigned by Lt-Cdr Bolus.

It was therefore surprising that when the boat left for sea and engine trials in the Gairloch on 26 April, the crew and yard staff discovered three days later that the steering gear rods had been assembled in the wrong order by technicians sub-contracted from Vickers Armstrongs. When the fore-hydroplanes jammed at hard-a-dive, the trials were aborted, *Thetis* returning to Cammell Laird's fitting out basin on 1 May 1939. It was not an auspicious start.

Once the steering gear rods had been carefully re-assembled, it was time to carry out torpedo equipment trials and install the complicated hydraulic bow-cap indicator equipment. Meanwhile on behalf of

Cammell Laird advert. In 1938 the Yard was proud of its new 'T' class submarine orders but the name '*Thetis*' would soon be known over the world for very different reasons to those envisaged. (P. Armstrong)

the Royal Navy, torpedo expert Cdr Alfred Maguire had carried out a preliminary inspection on 5 May in which it was discovered that a quantity of rust had built up in the tubes. This was not unusual given the length of time the boat had spent in the basin. Maguire prescribed a two-stage response designed to protect the torpedo tubes in future. Following removal of the rust, the tubes must first be coated with a skin of bitumastic solution, followed by a layer of bitumastic enamel. *There was no instruction to paint the internal face of the tube doors.* At any rate Cammell Laird decided to sub-contract the tube coating to Wailes Dove Bitumastic Ltd of Hebburn, a company specialising in the application of protective coatings to torpedo tubes. This banal process was to have an acute bearing on subsequent events.

The internal painting of the torpedo tubes was carried out between 13 and 17 May[46] by Jack Stimson, later dismissed by the Bucknill Tribunal as a 'humble painter' and absolved from any real responsibility. The reason for Stimson's absolution was because once the painting was completed, both the bitumen coating and the enamelling work were scheduled to have been inspected by Cammell Laird's charge hand painter, Mr William Taylor, followed by a second inspection at the hands of Mr Edward Grundy, the Assistant Admiralty Overseer. This was Edward Grundy's first experience of examining a bitumastic application within a torpedo tube. During the later Tribunal, Taylor and Grundy argued fiercely about the date on which Grundy's inspection of No.5 tube had taken place. This date is crucial because Grundy would later argue that he had merely made an interim examination of the tube on 16 May, *prior to* the application of the bitumen coating. Mr Grundy maintained that he had never inspected the completed rear tube doors 'because he had not been called in to do so'. Taylor countered by claiming that Grundy had inspected the finished work on 17 May. What is abundantly clear is that the internal painting of the tubes had never been properly checked because a fragment of bitumen coating had been inadvertently allowed to seal the test-cock aperture on No.5 tube door. As Justice Wrottesley was later to observe, it constituted 'a slovenly piece of work' by all concerned. The price paid for this shoddy work would transcend comprehension.

No submarine could be commissioned into the Royal Navy until diving trials had been completed. The postponed diving trials for *Thetis* were scheduled to take place on Thursday 1 June, not in Gairloch but in Liverpool Bay instead. The location was carefully selected by Guy Bolus in consultation with Arthur Hill and Mr Crout, Cammell Laird's Ship Manager. In order to ensure a minimum of dangerous interference from merchant vessels, the chosen location was well outside the frequented shipping lanes. On 24 May the Admiralty agreed to the changes. Arrangements were finalised.

Dockyard tradition turned diving trials into celebrations, 'big eats' in naval parlance. City Caterers of Liverpool were hired by Cammell Laird to provide a worthy spread. Two of their staff, Billy Bath and Gilbert Dobells, having been detailed to attend the dive. Meanwhile Lt Glenn drew up the list of guests. Norman Willcox, the twenty-five-year-old Mersey Pilot and a mixed bunch of Cammell Laird technicians enthusiastically put their names forward for the trip. One who did not have a choice was Frank Shaw. Shaw, a charge hand fitter, had worked at Cammell Laird's Yard for nine years. During this time he had worked on three submarines. Shaw's specialism was fitting the engines and the control room auxiliary machinery. Frank Shaw had worked on *Thetis* at every stage of her evolution and he was not to be spared the forthcoming sea trials. Mr Robinson the Engineering Manager had scheduled Fitter Shaw to take charge of the port diesel engine.

It should be understood that the same system of dual control which pertained during the inspections also extended to the trials. The submarine flew the Union Flag on her jack staff rather than the White Ensign because *Thetis* was not yet technically a Royal Navy ship. Although the dive was due to be carried out by naval personnel, Cammell Laird staff officially retained responsibility for main and auxiliary machinery.[47] Among the VIPs was Frank Shaw's boss, Arthur Robinson, the Cammell Laird Engineering Manager. Admiralty was not to be outdone. Arthur Hill, the Admiralty Ship Overseer, brought six members of his staff with him. As two other 'T' class submarines were currently fitting out in Cammell Lairds' basin, Lt-Cdr Garnett of *Taku* and Lt-Cdr Lloyd of *Trident* attended as professional observers and each brought four additional officers along as observers (on what the Submarine Service calls 'makee learn' trips). Among these officers was Pat Ryan, First Lieutenant of *Trident* and Lt Jamison, her Engineer Officer. Joining them on the trial was Capt Harry Oram, destined to be the most senior officer on board HMS *Thetis* on that fateful day. Also making the journey was the rotund Engineer Capt Stanley 'Daddy' Jackson OBE, attached to the staff of Rear Admiral (S). Jackson, the oldest man on the boat, was a master *raconteur* and Submarine Service legend.[48] It was inevitable that a significant number of shipyard personnel would be present for the surface trials but it was anticipated that the majority of civilians would transfer over to a waiting vessel prior to the dive. All told, above and beyond her crew of fifty-three, *Thetis* was due to carry an extra fifty personnel that day. On Tuesday 30 May, Bolus asked Mr Watters, the Assistant Shipyard Manager, to ensure that the escort tug was equipped with a lifeboat to transfer personnel. Mr J. Watters:

Trident leaves Cammell's Wet Dock. The funnel belongs to a hidden tug, not the submarine. (IWM FL_020221)

It was always understood that there would be a tug for the diving trial and no particular orders were issued to me though I discussed arrangements for the tug with Lt-Cdr Bolus. He said he intended to put Lt Coltart on board the tug with a signal rating. Nothing was said about wireless, or salvage gear.[49]

In response Watters hired in the Liverpool Screw and Lighterage Company tug, *Grebe Cock*. Although a relatively new vessel, questions would subsequently be raised about her fitness for purpose. Some last minute work was required within the boat. Once the requisite number of DSEA sets were stowed for crew and guests, the 'trim chit' had to be altered accordingly. An amount of fine-tuning was carried out upon the tubes. When it was completed, Thomas Wolfe, Cammell Laird Assistant Foreman Ship Fitter and Mr Harry Horsman, Admiralty Ship Fitting Overseer, returned the bow-cap operating levers to the 'neutral' position.[50] While preparations for the trials continued in earnest, there was some time for relaxation. Some of the crew visited cinemas off Old Chester Road, while a contingent spent Tuesday night in the Royal Castle Hotel bar, playing darts and enjoying a song with the locals. As the submarine was due to leave Birkenhead for good on the 16 June, the people of Tranmere set about organising a farewell dance to be held on 6 June in the Kingsland Dance Hall, Borough Road, once the trials were over.

'SHE'S GONE DOWN FUNNY, SIR'

At 0940 on Thursday 1 June 1939, *Thetis* left her familiar mooring against the Boiler Shop Wall in the Wet Dock. It was planned to carry out surface trials en route with diesel trials planned for the return journey. This was the schedule:

Leave Basin 09.30 (HW 11.32am-27' 4")
Proceed to about fifteen miles due West of Bar Lightship, carrying out on way:-
After hydroplane trials on secondary power and local control and auxiliary steering trials at full power on ship's telemotor and local control.
Diving trials to commence at about 1330.
After completion of Diving Trials, carry out Diesel Electric Trials on passage back to Works.
Enter basin 2230hrs (HW 2352hrs – 28ft 1in)

It was anticipated that *Thetis* would dive for three hours.

1 June 1939 was a warm day. Excellent visibility and a smooth sea augured well for the trials ahead. As Bolus increased speed to 16 knots, down below, beer and sandwiches set up on trestle tables in the fore-ends compensated somewhat for the discomfort caused by overcrowding and there was a deal of good-natured banter between the sailors and 'mateys'.

Naval personnel often mixed uncomfortably with this boiler suited, cloth-capped craft union aristocracy, structured by a hierarchy as formal and as stratified as their own. Frank Shaw of Ivydale Road epitomised the breed. Frank Shaw was a man of substance in Tranmere. A married man in his early thirties, Shaw took immense pride in his status as highly-skilled Laird's engineer and as any of the civilian workers could have confirmed, Laird's built the best ships and submarines in the world. Nevertheless memories of the hungry thirties were never far from the minds of these men. Security depended upon the Yard being awarded more contracts and everyone from senior manager to caulker was on his toes. There was time for self-indulgence too, thanks to the generosity of his employers. Frank remembered that by the time *Thetis* reached the Bar Lightship, the queue to use the heads stretched half way down the boat. Capt Oram recalled that 'a faint carnival atmosphere' prevailed, although he also noted that even at this stage the ventilation system was struggling to deal with the amount of people on board. Frank Shaw remained at the port engine controls until the order to stop engines and proceed to diving stations was received, then he made his way to the control room to monitor the auxiliary machinery.

Just after 1200hrs, the boat duly rendezvoused off the Mersey Bar Light Ship with the tug, *Grebe Cock* (Master Alf Godfrey). *Grebe Cock* was ordered to follow some distance behind, as *Thetis* carried out her steering tests. It will be recalled that *Grebe Cock* had been hired by Cammell Laird to act as both escort and observer during the trials. It was anticipated that upon arrival in the diving position, the supernumerary personnel on board *Thetis* would transfer over to the vessel prior to the dive. However, the novelty of the situation proved irresistible. Bolus requested that all those wishing to transfer over to the tug should gather in the control room. There were no takers. At 1330hrs Bolus addressed the following

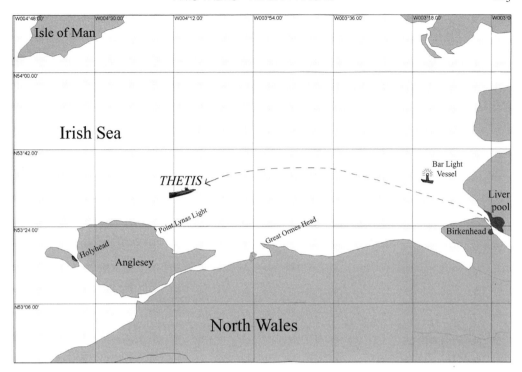

Fig.10: 'Track of *Thetis*.' (R.Young)

message to *Grebe Cock* by megaphone: 'I shall not be disembarking anyone. Take station half a mile on my port quarter. The diving course will be 310-degrees.'

The upshot was that *Thetis*, designed to operate with crew of fifty-three, would make her dive with 103 men onboard. The scenario is not quite complete. Unbeknown to those on board *Thetis*, the bow-cap of No.5 tube was actually *flooded and open to the sea*. The question as to who opened this tube and when it was opened would dog the subsequent inquiry. Was it left open by civilian workers back in Birkenhead? Had the bow-cap been accidentally wedged open by harbour debris? Or did naval personnel open it for some unknown reason just before the dive? Prior to analysing what transpired within the submarine, it is appropriate to examine events as monitored from the deck of *Grebe Cock*.

Thetis duly arrived at her designated diving position north-east of Point Lynas Light and roughly 15 miles north-west of Great Ormes Head. At 1340hrs the following routine signal was relayed via Plymouth wireless station to Blockhouse:

'THETIS TO CAPTAIN S5 AND ADMIRALTY. C IN C PLYMOUTH ASCB.S
IMPORTANT. DIVING IN POSITION 53° 35' N, 04° 00' W FOR 3 HOURS'

The naval wireless station at Plymouth acknowledged *Thetis* at 1356hrs but this message did not actually reach Blockhouse until 1405hrs. As a result there was doubt at Gosport as to the precise time the dive had commenced. *Grebe Cock* dutifully took up position half a mile away as requested. The assigned naval Liaison Officer, submariner Lt Richard Coltart, observed proceedings from her deck. Coltart watched as the submarine's W/T aerial was lowered. At 1400hrs Coltart noted that Bolus had given the order to clear the bridge. Air rushed from the vents as *Thetis* commenced her dive. However, it was soon clear that something was wrong. Tel Victor Crosby, also an experienced submariner, described what he saw:

> She appeared to be light. She got her bow down at a slight angle and remained in that position for approximately twenty minutes. Then she levelled off until the top of her guard rails…were just showing above the water…she later went down until her gun was awash and half her conning tower showing above the water.

The tube space of HMS *Alliance*, similar in dimension and layout to that of *Thetis*. 'A faint carnival atmosphere prevailed. A couple of large tables were piled with fresh sandwiches and soft drinks.' (P. Armstrong)

By 1450hrs the boat remained obdurately on the surface. Finally, at 1458, HMS *Thetis* made her fateful dive. Lt Coltart:

> I watched Thetis submerge slowly until her gun was just awash. She was on an even keel and making about four knots. About 1458, her bow came up, just broke the surface and I saw a splash of air just forward of the bow. Thetis dived horizontally and fairly fast, then completely disappeared at 1459...

Tel Crosby described this dive as being with much the same effect 'as you would get if you pushed a round stick into a deep pond, straight down'. Alf Godfrey turned to Coltart, observing memorably: 'She's gone down funny, Sir!'

Coltart was sufficiently disturbed by what he had seen to request that Godfrey maintain *Grebe Cock* at her present location, rather than proceed towards the estimated surfacing position as originally planned. As the possibility of an emergency situation began to dawn upon the observers, so the shortcomings of the tug were becoming apparent. The depth of water prevented *Grebe Cock* from anchoring immediately. Only by the laborious process of shackling two anchor cables together, was the vessel able to maintain station. By this time *Grebe Cock* had drifted some distance from her original position. None present had sufficient local knowledge to factor the currents of Liverpool Bay into his calculations. It had previously been arranged that *Thetis* would fire smoke candles when a depth of 60ft had been reached. Coltart's fears were further reinforced when no such smoke candles were forthcoming. These anxieties were confirmed when the boat failed to surface in order to make the scheduled trim regulation. Richard Coltart faced a dilemma, Should he raise the alarm and look a fool in the eyes of his peer group when the submarine surfaced, or delay and risk endangering life in the case of a genuine emergency?

Despite convincing evidence that something had gone seriously wrong, Richard Coltart delayed alerting Blockhouse for one hour and forty-five minutes.

'*CAPTAIN S(5) FORT BLOCKHOUSE FROM TUG ATTENDING ON THETIS
WHAT WAS DURATION OF THETIS DIVE?*
Coltart Tod 1645'

Unfortunately *Grebe Cock* was fitted with a short-range transmitter necessitating the relay of this message via the Seaforth wireless station. Due to weak reception, Seaforth did not acknowledge the message until 1656. The transmission failed to arrive in Gosport until 1715. This summarising transmission log was later used as evidence by the Bucknill Tribunal:

1546 – Seaforth alerted by pilot boat that *Grebe Cock* was attempting to call her
1556 – Forth receives *Grebe Cock's* alert
1603 – Seaforth transmits message to Liverpool
1619 – Liverpool retransmits message to London
1638 – Message received at Gosport
1707 – Message leaves Gosport carried by telegram boy
1715 – Message reaches Fort Blockhouse

By 1715hrs Cdr George Fawkes, Duty Staff Officer, Blockhouse and Acting Captain (S) 5, Lancelot Shadwell had already become seriously worried without the benefit of Coltart's signal. Let us retrace what had taken place. The 1340hrs message sent by Bolus outlining a three hour dive had been received by Blockhouse at 1405hrs. It was estimated that all being well, *Thetis* should have resurfaced sometime between 1640hrs and 1705hrs to transmit a routine signal to inform Blockhouse that all was well. As no surfacing message had been received, Shadwell ordered Blockhouse W/T office to send a contact request to *Thetis* every ten minutes. At 1740hrs Commander-in-Chief Portsmouth was notified. At 1820hrs Capt Macintyre, Staff Officer attached to the 5th Flotilla (and duty CO at Blockhouse in the absence of Oram) first alerted the Admiralty Duty Officer, Whitehall then advised the Commander-in-Chief Plymouth to take appropriate action. The dreaded Admiralty Fleet Order 971/35 'Subsmash' was transmitted throughout the Royal Navy:

'SUBSMASH'

AFO 971/35 (incorporating AFOs 568 and 569/34) codified the steps to be taken in the event of a submarine going missing in British coastal waters (see Appendix 2) and it is clear these steps were closely followed by those in authority. At 1822hrs, the nearest unit, ASDIC-equipped destroyer HMS *Brazen* (Lt-Cdr R. Mills) was alerted. *Brazen* was en route between Belfast and Plymouth On receipt of the signal, *Brazen* built up maximum speed and headed for the scene, arriving at 2106 that evening. At 1830 Fawkes rang Cammell Lairds to inform them that *Thetis* had failed to surface. Fawkes made a second call to the shipyard to inquire whether Lt-Cdrs Garnett and Lloyd had embarked on *Thetis*. He was erroneously told they had not. This was followed by a call to the Royal Air Force at 1850hrs requesting reconnaissance aircraft to help in the search. A flight of three Ansons from Abbotsinch near Paisley, duly provided a series of aerial sweeps which continued until nightfall. By 2140hrs, the entire Portland-based 6th Destroyer Flotilla had shaped course for Liverpool Bay. With them went the sweeping experts of the 1st M/S Flotilla and the new minelaying submarine *Narwhal* was also deployed, as it was now rightly assumed that *Thetis* had suffered damage to her ASDIC dome, preventing transmission. *Narwhal* was equipped with crude but potentially useful Fessenden equipment.

While the Royal Navy steamed into action at 2015hrs, Capt Bayne on the staff of Admiral Martin Dunbar-Nasmith VC (Commander-in-Chief Plymouth) telephoned Capt Hubert Hart RNR (ret.), the Mersey Docks and Harbour Board, Surveyor/Bailiff, requesting his assistance. Admiral Dunbar-Nasmith, an old acquaintance, 'knew that he (Hart) possessed salvage vessels and Mersey Docks and Harbour Board Marine facilities always available.'[51] Hart, the highly respected Surveyor with twenty-three years of salvage behind him, was to play a key role in the unfolding drama. Unfortunately none of this wealth of experience involved submarine salvage.

Without a moment to lose, such equipment and personnel that could be found around the harbour was gathered and stowed onboard the Mersey Docks and Harbour Board salvage vessel, *Vigilant*. Those present on *Vigilant* included Capt Hart, Charles Brock, Salvage Plant Supervisor, diver Fred Orton, Mr Watters of Cammell Laird and Lt-Cdr Bittlestone, Naval Liaison Officer and SNO, Liverpool. Hart does not appear to have harboured any doubts that *Vigilant* was the right vessel for the task, nor did he seek any assistance from either the London and Glasgow Salvage Association or Trinity House. At 2145hrs *Vigilant* weighed anchor and steamed for the last known position of HMS *Thetis*.

There was a major setback during these early stages when the deep diving vessel *Tedworth*, moored at Inveraray, reported that she would have to first coal on the Clyde before heading south. *Tedworth* housed the Royal Navy's elite divers, each man experienced in working in depths of 300ft. It will be noted from Appendix 2 that *Subsmash* allocated three flying boats for search purposes but none of those directing the operation saw fit to fly these divers and their equipment down to Speke. The structure of command underlying this rescue bid was confirmed by an Admiralty memo transmitted at 2250 on 1 June:

> Ops under the direction of C in C Plymouth (Martin Dunbar-Nasmith), assisted by RA (S) (Bertram Watson)
> Press informed but news will not be broadcast until next of kin have been informed.

Commander-in-Chief Plymouth's role was largely one of co-ordination. Rear Admiral (S) Watson being ill at home in Hambledon, Capt Macintyre, acting CO at Blockhouse, took his place. Unfortunately Macintyre had spent the day observing exercises at sea and did not return to Blockhouse until 1940. Distrusting aerial communications and anxious to stay in touch with events in Liverpool Bay, Macintyre and his assistant Fred Lipscomb (see *H47*) opted to sail on the old duty destroyer *Winchelsea* rather than fly from Lee on Solent to Speke in a fraction of the time. Macintyre justified this decision on the grounds that at this critical phase, communications on board the vessel were superior to those of an Anson. This is a credible argument but some have diagnosed the malaise of inter-service rivalry underpinning his actions. Macintyre did not arrive until late afternoon on 2 June. The implication being that until Rear Admiral (S) or his Deputy arrived at the scene, control of the situation would simply devolve upon the shoulders of the senior naval officer present. The rescue would lie in the hands of General Service.

An impressive array of vessels now converged in the seas north of Anglesey. Sadly, they were heading for the wrong location. A combination of factors ranging from unpredictable currents to inaccurate reckoning had resulted in *Grebe Cock* drifting some 4 miles to the west of the submarine's actual position. At dusk one of the Ansons spotted *Thetis'* indicator buoy. Flt-Lt Avent offered two fixes. The first suggested a position of 322-degrees and 13 miles from Ormes Head – just 1 mile south-west of the actual position. The second recalculated fix gave a position of 303 degrees, some 10 miles from Ormes Head. The result was an error of twenty degrees in bearing and 7 miles in distance. As if to compound an already appalling catalogue of errors, this second fix was the one the Royal Navy acted upon. Rear Admiral (S) Bertram Watson left his sickbed and headed for the Mersey. He recorded the following entry in his Preliminary Report dated 4 June 1939:[52]

> At 2106 Brazen reported to be in vicinity and searching.
>
> At 0023 general policy signal made by Winchelsea to all ships and aircraft who would take part in the search. Situation at midnight 1 June all ships proceeding to position indicated twelve miles north-west of NW Buoy.
>
> At 0034 Rear Admiral (S) 0021 was received, giving description of a buoy which appeared to be a submarine indicator buoy. Winchelsea then informed Brazen and all authorities. Brazen ordered to search for and locate submarine in this vicinity.
>
> At this point it was considered by Winchelsea that divers and all necessary gear should be got out as soon as possible…observing that Tedworth could not reach the position before dark on Friday. At 0255 information was received from Admiralty that Vigilant had been despatched to the position but no recompression chamber was available.

It is apparent that RA (S), at least, was unaware of just how poorly equipped *Vigilant* was. 'Divers and all necessary gear' were certainly available on the Mersey but as we shall see, not every organisation capable of responding had been alerted.

The extract also suggests that Watson was expecting a salvage operation to unfold, in spite of recently-adopted policy, as we shall see. Early on the morning of 2 June, lookouts on *Brazen* spotted the submarine's stern protruding on a surreal thirty-five degree angle off the ship's starboard bow. At 0754hrs this W/T transmission was sent from *Brazen* to Rear Admiral (S), Admiralty and C in C Plymouth:

'HAVE LOCATED SUBMARINE. TAIL OUT OF WATER. POSITION FOLLOWS: 328 DEGREES DISTANCE 14 MILES GREAT ORME HEAD'

Then at 0807:

'... Have located submarine. Tail out of water...' But with orders to await the expected DSEA escapes, the sleek warships could only stand impotently by and watch.

Camel No.3 at the scene. Sadly this photograph was taken on 3 June when it was all far too late. (P. Armstrong)

'NOSE OF SUBMARINE APPEARS TO BE STUCK IN BOTTOM, TAIL PROJECTING ABOUT 18 feet'

Long before this information was received, as early as 0554hrs, Capt Macintyre on behalf of Rear Admiral (S) made a request to the duty commander at Admiralty to ensure that 'camels' be provided from Liverpool Docks.[53] Salvage camels are large hollow cylinders used to support a vessel. Once flooded they sink to the bottom; filled with air they float. A camel takes position on either beam of a vessel, then hawsers of sufficient strength are passed beneath the wreck in support. The vessel is secured enabling work to take place. Camels would have been essential to any salvage attempt on *Thetis*, yet Admiralty *did not respond* to Macintyre's request. In order to understand why this vital equipment was not already standing by when *Thetis* was located, we must briefly digress and examine Subsmash policy as it was configured in June 1939.

The post-war AFO regarding submarine rescue in British coastal waters is given in Appendix 1. It will readily be seen that the emphasis is upon salvage. DSEA was introduced in 1929. Its introduction stimulated much discussion about submarine rescue policy and in 1931 Capt Phillip Ruck-Keene was appointed to study the future of submarine safety measures following the failure to salvage *M2*. Admiralty Fleet Orders 568/34 and 971/35 emerged directly from his deliberations.[54]

AFO 568/34 (Appendix 2) dictated that following the introduction of DSEA, a submarine crew had the means of salvation within its own hands. Rather than wait for the boat to be salvaged by outside rescuers, as had been the case in the past, the trapped crew should resort to DSEA 'in all circumstances'. The adoption of this policy resulted in the sealing of salvage blows in existing submarines, as this quotation from a memo written by Rear Admiral (S) indicates:

> …in view of the approval of this policy [568/34], it was apparent that the air connections fitted to each compartment in existing submarines as possible aids to rapid salvage, could be dispensed with in the interests of fighting efficiency as the more the pressure hull is pierced by such fittings, the more the vulnerability to depth-charges…

> A/1939/0002 Admiralty Policy Respecting the Salvage and Saving of Life from Submarines

Nor could politicians subsequently feign ignorance. This policy was announced in the Commons by First Lord Sir Bolton Eyres-Monsell in his 6 March 1934 Naval Estimates:

> …The Fleet was therefore being informed that the salvage organisation would be scrapped so far as it was now designed for raising submarines and only that part retained which provided that surface vessels should locate the sunken submarine…

Hansard reveals the Commons dissected the estimates on 12 March 1934 but the new submarine policy bundled amongst them was not discussed. The estimates package sailed through the Commons on a majority of 254 to 35. A fascinating report (M591/33) survives, written by Martin Dunbar-Nasmith to Admiral Raikes and dated 14 June 1939 at a time when the former was gathering information for his internal inquiry and the latter was trying to justify his actions in retrospect. In Section III of this report, Dunbar-Nasmith writes:

> The question of ordering salvage gear to the scene was considered during the evening of 1 June but was treated as a secondary consideration because:
> (A) The immediate need was to locate the submarine
> (B) It was known that Capt Hart RNR (a man with considerable experience and local knowledge in salvage work) with divers, was proceeding to the scene
> (C) The policy laid down in AFOs 568/34 and 971/35

Capt Mills of *Brazen* therefore did not adopt a proactive approach by immediately summoning salvage gear. Subsmash guaranteed a massive search for a missing submarine. The one thing it did not promise was salvage *because salvage was explicitly excluded*. Once the submarine was located, the primary role of the searching vessels was to stand-by and wait for the trapped men to escape. Two vital factors were overlooked by the Subsmash policy: firstly that outside intervention could be highly successful as in the case of *K13*. Although by no means a model of submarine rescue, barges and camels were used to support the boat as soon as located and a high pressure ventilation line connected. Secondly, while DSEA had undoubtedly saved a handful of men from HMS *Poseidon* in 1931, the case of *M2* suggested that DSEA was, at best, of uncertain efficacy as a means of submarine escape. It was one matter to escape from a 15ft-deep exercise tank using a DSEA set, quite another to evacuate a boat lying at an acute angle in 150ft of water.

It is not too difficult to imagine circumstances in which a trapped crew might be rendered unable to escape by its own efforts but imagination was not one of the requisites of the pre-war naval hierarchy. The author contends that as a direct result of this policy, the fate of most of those on board *Thetis* was already sealed by the time the submarine was discovered. Even in the event of Lt-Cdr Mills having disobeyed fleet orders by prescribing salvage equipment for *Thetis*, as soon as the stern had been spotted at 0754hrs, it would have taken at least two to three hours for a suitably equipped vessel to arrive at the scene. Salvage gear was abundantly available 38 miles away on the Mersey. Yet it could have been so different. Prior to sailing on 1 June, Capt Hart had ordered that three of the Mersey Docks and Harbour Board's lifting camels be 'steamed up' ready for departure 'if required'. When *Vigilant* weighed anchor at 2145 and headed for the last known position of *Thetis*, the camels were left behind. They could have sailed at high tide just before midnight but were not ordered to do so. Capt Hart later justified this fatal omission on the grounds that as all concerned expected systematic DSEA escapes to be made: 'If I had put camels alongside while men were endeavouring to come up, I can imagine nothing more likely to interfere with their escape. There was also a considerable swell and the camels would have damaged the sides of the submarine irrevocably.'[55]

In pursuance of the AFOs, Capt Mills ordered that *Brazen's* whaler take up position adjacent to the projecting stern in readiness for DSEA escapes. It was estimated that the stern rescue chamber could only be a mere 20ft below the surface. Next, the requisite twelve charges were dropped in anticipation of imminent escape bids. The passive policy outlined above seemed to have been vindicated when at 0800hrs, to the sound of relieved cheers from the destroyer crew, two men bobbed to the surface. Lt Woods, the Torpedo Officer and Capt (S) 5 Oram were hauled spluttering and retching aboard *Brazen*, alive but suffering from the effects of asphyxia. At 0826hrs *Brazen* transmitted this message to Admiralty:

'IMMEDIATE: CAPTAIN ORAM AND LT. WOODS ARE IN BRAZEN. ALL THE REST OF THE CREW ARE ALIVE AND IN SUBMARINE AND ENDEAVOURING TO ESCAPE BY DSEA'

The men on the ships could only line the rails and wait.

EYE DEEP IN HELL

What had gone wrong with *Thetis?* Both escapees were well placed to provide the answer, or rather they would have been, had they had not been too sick to make adequate reports. To reconstruct what had happened, it is necessary to turn to the later testimony of Capt Oram, who was standing beside Bolus in the control room during the dive.

> Lt Chapman reported, 'Submarine is opened up for diving, Sir!'
> 'Permission to flood Q tank?'
> 'Flood Q', came the order, followed by 'Q tank flooded, Sir!'
> 'Dive the boat, Number One.'
> The motors were put to half-ahead group-up and the hydroplane operators put ten degrees on their wheels. The boat would not dive. Clearly something was wrong with the trim. After a few minutes the captain turned to Mr Bailey and asked, 'Why do you think the boat is so light?'
> Mr Bailey replied, 'Well she shouldn't be. The trim was calculated to account for the lack of torpedoes.'
> Now Bolus turned to Lt Chapman, asking, 'Which tubes should have been filled with water to compensate for the torpedoes?'
> 'Five and Six should be full Sir,' replied Lt Chapman.

It will be recalled that Lt Chapman had received the trim calculations prepared by the Cammell Laird technicians and Admiralty overseers. Lt Woods also viewed this 'trim chit', which clearly indicated that all the bow tubes including Nos 5 and 6 had been flooded prior to the dive. Yet the failure to dive was an obvious indication that the submarine was bow-light. Inevitably doubts were cast over the accuracy of both the 'trim chit' and the condition of the tubes. Capt Oram:

> Bolus again turned to Lt Chapman: 'Ask the tube compartment if Nos 5 and 6 tubes are full of water or not.'
> Lt Chapman telephoned this instruction through to Lt Woods and the men in the fore-ends. We stood around chatting and waiting for a reply. By now it was nearly three in the afternoon and we had spent an hour trying to submerge.

We can reconstruct what took place in the tube space from the testimony of Lt Woods. First, a word on the general arrangements within the fore-ends of *Thetis*. The first bulkhead, a short distance behind the tubes was known as the collision bulkhead. Beyond this bulkhead lay the torpedo stowage space. There were two oval doors in the collision bulkhead. While travelling on the surface both doors were routinely shut and clipped, once dived however, one door was left open for access. On this morning the port door was open and hooked back while the other was closed. Lt Woods responded to Lt Chapman's telephone call by systematically lifting the test-cocks fitted to the rear door of each tube. There was a dribble of water from No.6 indicating that it was partially filled (had it been full, water would have spurted out with force). *No. 5 produced neither air nor water.* At this juncture Woods made his way back to the control room both to report his findings and to question Lt Chapman about the trim status of tubes Nos 5 and 6. Lt Woods:

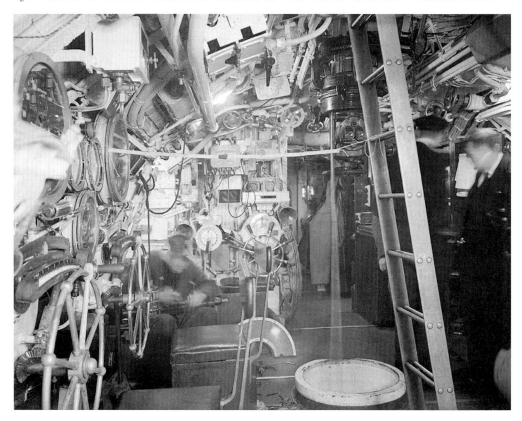

The control room of *Tribune* was identical to that fitted in *Thetis*. Note the hydroplane operators' positions on the left and the helmsman's wheel beyond. Because of the joint control regime, the control room of *Thetis* would have been very crowded indeed. (IWM A_010904)

> After a time I returned to the control room and asked the First Lieutenant if there was a possibility of having to flood a tube to get the submarine down. He said, 'Decidedly yes.' I asked Mr Robinson if the bow-caps were opened up to telemotor pressure and he said, 'No'. I said 'I will get them ready'. I returned to the tube space. PO Mitchell was on the telephone reporting the movements of 'A' vent, so I gave the order to L/S Hambrook to open up pressure to the bow-caps. He did this and reported all correct to me. I asked him if the levers were in the 'Shut' position. He replied 'Yes'.

It is worth highlighting at this juncture that Lt Woods had been interviewed by the Royal Navy as early as 4 June 1939 and the transcript survives in the Submarine Museum archive.[56] In this earlier account Lt Woods clearly states that after Hambrook had reported all levers to be in the 'Shut' position, Woods himself: '…then went between the tubes and made a close visual inspection of each mechanical bow-cap indicator to see that each pointer was to "Shut". This was the case.'

In his later evidence to the Tribunal, Lt Woods was asked whether he had harboured any doubt when Hambrook reported to him that the levers were actually in the 'Shut' position. Woods replied: 'I am not sure of that but it is what I had intended.'

It is pertinent to explain that an inexplicable design anomaly resulted in a situation in which once the bow-caps were shut, the indicator dials did not all point in the same direction. However, as Tony Booth observes, experienced submariners would undoubtedly have risen to the challenge.[57] Frederick Woods had been a torpedo officer since 1936, having spent a year in *Grampus* at the China Station. He returned to Britain in June 1938 and four months later was appointed to stand by *Thetis*. It is known that Woods, Mitchell and Hambrook had closely observed the installation of the tubes.

Woods and Hambrook now re-checked the tubes. The test-cocks were opened with identical results. Only No.6 showed any evidence of water. These results were telephoned through to Lt Chapman in the control room. At this point Woods decided to turn delay to his advantage by carrying out an examination of the tubes, specifically to test the watertight joints in the bow-caps for any signs of leakage resulting from sea pressure. This procedure would require the opening of the rear tube doors. Woods acted according to his own initiative and did not first notify the control room.

Lt Woods:

> I decided to inspect all the tubes to see that they were dry so that the First Lieutenant should have full information of their condition. I then went between the tubes and made close visual inspection of each mechanical bow-cap indicator to see that the pointer was set to 'Shut'. This was the case. I then commenced to open tube rear doors. I opened Nos 1, 2, 3, 4 and found them all dry. No.6 I left as I knew it was half full. I then opened No.5 test-cock. There was no escape of air or water.[58]

L/S Hambrook was then ordered to open the rear tube door. Lt Woods did not first test the aperture with a rimer (pin). Now that fragment of bitumastic paint blocking the test-cock on No.5 tube re-enters the story. Lt Woods:

> It did not occur to me that the hole was choked because surely Cammell Laird's people would have seen that the holes were clear…I did not notice that a rimer was fitted to the test-cock.[59]

Water did not spurt from the test-cock because the aperture was blocked by bitumastic paint but the absence of water convinced Woods that the tube must be dry. We now know that the outer cap of No.5 tube was in fact open to the sea. Woods (who had been joined by Lt Jamison) now ordered Hambrook to open the rear door of No.5 tube. Lt Woods:

> L/S Hambrook under my orders then started to pull up the rear door lever to No.5 tube. It was extremely stiff but I did not worry about this as a number of moving parts in the fore ends were stiff. L/S Hambrook had to kick the lever for about the last six inches of its movement. On the last movement the rear door was swung open by a flood of water.[60]

Lt Woods yelled through to TGM Mitchell and ERA Howells standing at the bulkhead: 'TELL THEM [control room] TO BLOW FOR CHRIST'S SAKE!'

As the boat already assumed a bow-down angle, Mitchell rang through to the control room: 'FLOODING FAST THROUGH NUMBER FIVE TUBE. BLOW MAIN BALLAST!'

Woods immediately assumed that the tube had suffered a fracture: 'I realised there was no hope of shutting the rear door and shouted to Hambrook and AB Crombleholme who was sitting between 1 and 2 tubes watching 'A' vent, to get out of the compartment.'

No attempt was made to close the bow-cap using telemotor pressure. Lt Woods later told the inquiry, 'Had I realised that No.5 bow-cap must have been open, I might possibly have been able to get at the bow-cap operating lever.'

Such was the ingress of water, Hambrook and Woods were forced to abandon all attempts to close the tube door and turned instead to shutting the collision bulkhead door at the rear of the torpedo room. Efforts to pull the door against the slope of the dive were difficult enough but a wing-nut used to secure the bulkhead door dropped out to become wedged between the door and the coaming. Lt Woods:

> Hambrook had great difficulty in getting out of the compartment as he had been thrown all over the place by the force of water coming in. After he had got through, Lt Jamison and ERA Powell attempted to shut the door but the lower butterfly clips hung below the lower position of the door coaming and prevented it closing onto its rubber seating correctly. They endeavoured to lift these clips up but before they could do so, water had commenced to come through rapidly. The water level in the tube compartment must have risen from the level of the lower tubes to the level of the middle of 1 and 2 tubes in ten seconds. Lt Jamison shouted to us to evacuate the compartment. The submarine had taken on a steep angle and we began climbing aft. PO Mitchell and I were the last two in the compartment. We had great difficulty in getting out due to the increasing angle of the boat and in my case, wet leather shoes on the corticene and also because the tables and stools for the Cammell Laird's men feeding in the fore-ends, kept falling on top of us. The lights went out when I was half way up. After sliding backwards several times, I succeeded in hauling myself up along the embarking rail. I got past No.40 bulkhead and the water tight door was then shut behind me.[61]

This door was successfully clipped but as Capt Oram was later to observe, the enemy was now within – all 170 tons of it. Working in the engine room, Frank Shaw experienced the flooding as:

> ...a rush of air coming aft, and the ship began to develop a list and she went down very fast. I felt a bump and was flung against the watertight door of 69-bulkhead. I heard an order given to 'blow tanks' followed by an order to close all watertight doors.

'Mac' Arnold was standing just aft of 40 bulkhead:

> There was a terrible rush of air from the foremost compartments and I heard people shouting from forward to the control room to surface. I realised that it was a torpedo tube open. A few seconds afterwards by the time the water had started rushing in, the men were trying to shut No.25 bulkhead door.

As the last of Wood's men made their escape from the torpedo stowage area, the water surged down the boat. It was just about to lap over the coaming (and onto the batteries in the compartment below) when the men succeeded in closing and clipping the door. Bolus and Chapman had instinctively realised that the sharp rise in pressure signified flooding in the fore-ends.

Bolus immediately gave orders to 'Blow Tanks', while simultaneously attempting to drive the submarine astern on her motors, with hydroplanes set at hard-a-rise. It soon became clear that *Thetis* had shipped too much water to surface under her own power. Bolus judiciously allowed the submarine to sink to 160ft, having conserved sufficient reserves of compressed air and battery power to carry out a salvage blow once conditions allowed. Bolus now gathered information, questioning Woods and the others to determine what had happened. Then, accompanied by Oram, he went for'rard to look for himself. There was bad news. Although the impact with the seabed had not been violent, it had nevertheless been sufficient to crush the ASDIC dome, with the result that *Thetis* was unable to transmit. Hopes of effecting a salvage blow were also dashed. The torpedo loading hatch fitted to *Thetis* had been designed to withstand external rather than internal pressure. A salvage blow would surely force the hatch to lift. The only remedy was to secure this hatch by strongbacks applied by divers. Now that it was apparent that the submarine could only regain the surface with outside help, it was imperative that rescue vessels should find the submarine without delay. With this in mind, a red smoke candle and two marker buoys were ejected at 1545hrs. Unfortunately one of the buoys became entangled with the stern, while the cable securing the second buoy snapped and the marker was whipped away by the strong current.

Bolus, Capt Oram, Messrs Robinson, Bailey and the assorted submarine officers now withdrew to the wardroom to digest the reports and consider a rapidly narrowing range of options. Right from the outset the calculations did not look good. Basically there were far too many people and too little air. Normally a 'T' class boat could expect to survive for thirty-six hours submerged. Once the extra men on board *Thetis* were factored into the equation, there was only sufficient air for eighteen hours. Aided by Messrs Bailey and Robinson, Oram calculated that sufficient air remained in the submarine to sustain life until 1500hrs on the following afternoon, 2 June.

Bolus was acutely aware that AFO 568/34 ordered all trapped submariners to escape by DSEA rather than wait for outside help. Assuming that both escape chambers could be brought into operation, it would take an estimated thirty minutes to flood up, drain down and then prepare each chamber for the next escape. At this stage it was assumed that only two men could escape from each chamber at any one time. While DSEA escape was feasible, it would take at least twelve hours to complete. Those left behind would suffer increasingly from oxygen starvation and carbon dioxide poisoning (asphyxia) to an unknowable degree. Moreover a significant proportion of those onboard were civilians who, although they had received some instruction, had never handled a DSEA set. There was considerable dismay when it was discovered that many of the DSEA lockers were within the flooded fore-ends.

AFO 971/35 recommended that a crew should wait for signs that rescue vessels were present before resorting to DSEA escape because without the rescue vessels in attendance overhead, there was an excellent chance that escapees would be dispersed by the currents to drown or die of exposure.[62] Given that rescue ships were unlikely to close the position until darkness had fallen, Guy Bolus reasoned that it might be wiser to delay escape until dawn. As air was running out fast, it may seem that Bolus was taking a gamble. In reality he had little option.

In the meantime there would be one last attempt to save the submarine without relying upon outside assistance. *Thetis* had suffered a very serious accident but this was not yet a disaster. It could be argued that

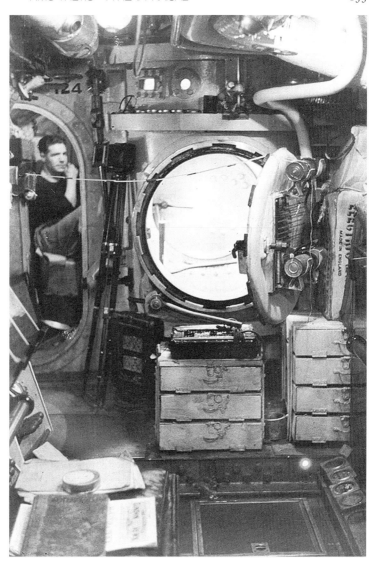

Stern escape chamber
fitted in *Tribune*. Although a
modification of the chamber
installed in *Thetis*, the
principle was the same. Note
the claustrophobic space,
dual control and dual access
with the escape chamber
door opening into both
steerage and engine rooms.
(IWM 010930)

rather than opt for a series of individual escapes, the best hope for saving all on *Thetis* lay in driving the
boat back to the surface. Providing that No.5 bow-cap could be closed from *within* the torpedo room,
it was perfectly possible that water could be pumped out of the two flooded forward compartments. In
order to close the bow-cap the flooded compartments would first have to be re-entered via the escape
chamber, a highly dangerous and demanding task. Lt Harold Chapman, aged twenty-nine, volunteered
for the job. He donned a DSEA prior to taking up position in the forward escape chamber. Lt Woods:

> I volunteered to go with Lt Chapman but he seemed to think he would be better alone. He was equipped
> with a wheel spanner and heavy belt strapped round his waist. As the chamber was flooded up, he was unable
> to stand the pressure on his ears and signalled to Mr Glenn who was operating the chamber, to drain down
> again. The drains from both escape chambers had no leads to the bilge and in this case the drained water had
> to be collected in buckets and chain of hands aft, where it was poured into the coxswain's store to avoid it
> getting on top of the battery boards. As I knew the position in the torpedo compartment I said I could try
> to get through but said I would like an assistant. PO Mitchell immediately volunteered. Our plan was still to
> reach No.5 rear door. We prepared ourselves in the same way as Lt Chapman and entered the chamber. When
> the water was up to our eyes, PO Mitchell indicated that his ears were in great pain. I gave the signal to drain
> down again. We got out and after I had recovered from the cold, about an hour later, I entered the DSEA

chamber with volunteer PO Smithers. We flooded up but PO Smithers showed signs of distress and I again gave the signal to drain down. After this no more attempts were made to get through. The whole thing seemed impossible to me as the torpedo compartment was pitch black and odd deck boards and furniture were floating about there.

It was now 1900hrs on 1 June. The officers and civilian experts held a second somewhat downbeat meeting in the wardroom. With the help of outside divers securing the torpedo loading hatch, Bolus was still planning on saving his boat by means of a salvage blow. Providing a high pressure air hose could be fitted to either the whistle valve on the conning tower or the recuperator on the gun mechanism, it ought to have been possible to force the water out of the boat. Reasoning along the same lines as Lt-Cdr Herbert of *K13* before him, Bolus recognised that General Service rescuers would possess no in-depth knowledge of submarines. In order to ensure they understood the condition of *Thetis* and precisely what was required, would mean sending a volunteer to the surface. A message plus sketches was drawn up by Roy Glenn then placed in a watertight package. Glenn's message survives in the National Archive:

ON BOTTOM. DEPTH 140ft. TUBE SPACE AND FORE ENDS FLOODED. NO.5 BOW-CAP AND REAR DOOR OPEN. COMPARTMENTS EVACUATED. HP AIR REQUIRED TO CHARGE SUBMARINE THROUGH GUN RECUPERATOR CONNECTION OR WHISTLE CONNECTION ON BRIDGE. DIVER REQUIRED TO TIGHTEN DOWN FORE HATCH SO THAT BLOW CAN BE PUT ON FOR'RARD COMPARTMENTS WITHOUT LIFTING HATCH. STRONGBACK REQUIRED ON HATCH AS SOON AS POSSIBLE. KEEP CONSTANT WATCH FOR MEN ESCAPING THROUGH AFTER ESCAPE CHAMBER.

There were three implications to this strategy. Firstly, appropriate joints would have to be fashioned by the rescuers and this would take time; secondly this scheme presupposed the active participation of those within the submarine. In this aspect, Bolus seriously underestimated the toll carbon dioxide was taking on the trapped men. Thirdly, to give the volunteer a fighting chance, the stern escape chamber would have to be raised closer to the surface. It was calculated that an inclination of fifteen degrees would force the stern above water, thus bringing the escape chamber within 20ft of the surface. Meanwhile the Cammell Laird and Admiralty experts set about conjoining the water and oil systems required to force out the fuel and lighten the stern. This work required the technicians to fashion valves and pipes. The men, and Frank Shaw was in the vanguard, worked tirelessly. At midnight the sound of hissing air signified that the first fuel tanks had been emptied. Robinson and Bolus moved through the crowded submarine, informing the men of the plan and reassuring them that outside help would soon be with them. Walter Arnold was optimistic he would soon taste freedom and fresh air. According to Frank Shaw, the prevailing mood remained one of quiet optimism amongst the Cammell Laird men but he recalled one ERA's response when questioned as to how long it would take to get the boat back to the surface: 'Don't hold your breath chum. This boat is hell and we're eye-deep in it.'

Ominously, conditions within the boat were deteriorating fast as Capt Oram relates:

…there was no sign of chlorine though the battery boards had a good deal of water over them at one time or another. The general temperature was warm, the pressure increased to 3.5. As luck would have it all food was in the torpedo compartment. This did not matter as one felt no hunger. The air was getting rather foul by midnight and it was noticeable that men needed several minutes of rest and deep breathing after exertion.

Lt Woods: 'There were no blankets, no food (our last meal was at lunch) and I laid down the whole night. Breathing got noticeably fast as the night went on and people began to get headaches. The older men suffered far more than the younger.'

The volunteer was initially scheduled to make his ascent at dawn, 0500hrs, but this was delayed. Capt Oram again:

…pumping the tanks took longer than expected and it was after 0700 on 2 June when we had pumped out another fifty tons of fuel, released the drop keel, blown No.3 main tank and 'Z' auxiliary tank that the ship was inclined to thirty-four degrees and I felt that it was now time to take the next step and I offered to make an attempt to reach the surface…

It may surprise the reader that the senior officer on board should have been the first to leave the submarine but it should be borne in mind that as Capt (S) 5, Oram had experience of both submarines and General Service. In short, he was regarded as gold braid with the power get things done. The case of *K13* demonstrates how such individuals can play a key role when lives are at stake. Moreover, given the fate of Lt-Cdr Goodhart in that incident, Oram was volunteering for a near suicidal mission.

Oram again:

As no sign had come from surface vessels, we presumed that we had not been found and I therefore secured the salvage instructions in a watertight cover on my arm in the hope that if I did not arrive, the message would be found. As a precautionary measure I called for a volunteer to go with me so that there was a chance for someone with inside knowledge to be found on the surface, if I failed. Lt Woods and two seamen immediately volunteered. I chose the former because of his greater knowledge of the submarine…With difficulty owing to the inclination of the submarine and laboured breathing we reached the after compartment. The situation in the submarine was now acute. The air had become very foul and it was necessary to take deep and distressing breaths even when quiescent – many men were retching and yawning and watering from the eyes was continuous. One also felt lassitude and required a distinct mental effort to co-ordinate mind with action…on my slow passage through the submarine I found the men physically distressed but cheerful and willingly lending a hand to help us climb aft. On arrival it took fifteen minutes before we had sufficient breath to enter the escape chamber…I wish to make known the very gallant behaviour of the men on board Thetis. I saw no sign of panic at any time and without a single exception men showed quiet courage. Whenever anything had to be done, men sprang to help. Even when breathing became distressing, men worked unceasingly and cheerfully. Men talked and joked until the foul air forced them to remain quiet. Right up to the time when I left I heard no word of complaint and I saw in no man any sign of the fear which I knew to be in our minds.

Oram realised that time was fast running out:

Before leaving the control room I told the Commanding Officer that on reaching the surface, if the luck of the tide permitted, I would try to reach the indicator buoy or tail of the submarine and hold on until found…I advised him to then take steps and get men out of the after escape chamber as rapidly as possible. I also suggested that men should escape in pairs, one naval rating with one Cammell Laird's man…Lt Woods and I entered the escape chamber and were flooded up by Lt Chapman. Just before we opened the top hatch I heard three charges fired and knew that the submarine had been located. Escape was not difficult owing to the shallow depth of the chamber – about twenty feet – but I had found considerable difficulty in concentrating on the DSEA drill while flooding up…

'Mac' Arnold later recalled how, when the hatch was opened, a shaft of diffused light danced on the chamber walls. These patterns of hope were visible to men peering through the observation window, observers who could only pray for deliverance themselves. At 0800hrs Woods and Oram made their successful escape to be picked up by *Brazen*'s whaler. Capt Oram had played a controversial role in the loss of *H47*, now 'Lucky Joe' was one of the few to leave HMS *Thetis* alive. However, Oram was unable to play the role Guy Bolus had envisaged for him. Exhausted and suffering from asphyxia, he was wrapped in a blanket and taken below decks. In *The Rogues Yarn*, Oram maintained that Lt Glenn's salvage instructions had been duly passed to Lt Coltart but one hour elapsed before the rescuers realised the importance of this message. Despite his desperate state, at 0943hrs Oram had apparently recovered sufficiently to transmit the following message to Admiral Dunbar-Nasmith, Rear Admiral (S) Bertram Watson and Cammell Laird:

Immediate Intercept. Thetis is flooded to 40-bulkhead. No.5 tube bow-cap and rear door presumed open. Port door of 25-bulkhead is believed to have only one clip on both compartments therefore flooding being common. S/M lying with bows on bottom in 130 feet and by pumping fuel the stern has now been raised above water. Air is urgently needed and crew are expecting diver to connect armoured hose to whistle or gun recuperator when they will endeavour to lighten bow with salvage blow on 40-bulkhead. Before this can be done, fore-hatch must be strengthened with strongback as it is feared any pressure in torpedo compartment will lift hatch off its seating. All on board are alive and endeavouring to escape by after DSEA which is near the surface but air in submarine is getting very foul.[63]

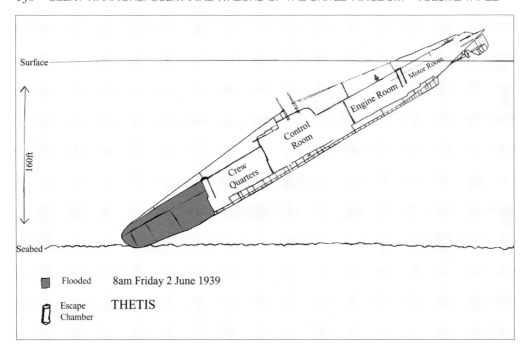

Fig.11:'*Thetis* bows-down, 0800, 2 June.' (R.Young)

Now that had *Vigilant* had arrived, a guideline was attached to the submarine's stern. Unfortunately *Vigilant* proved as inappropriately equipped as *Grebe Cock* had been before her. Her diver, Frederick Orton, although an experienced diver, had never been deeper than 90ft. The short length of high pressure hose carried by *Vigilant* could never hope to reach the submarine. The ship had no compressor, relying instead upon a hand pump. Crucially she held no cutting gear because none had been available at such short notice. If those trapped could not escape by DSEA, deliverance would not be coming from the direction of *Vigilant*.

Meanwhile, the escape of Woods and Oram had galvanised the crew of HMS *Brazen*, who scrutinised the sea looking for the slightest disturbance on the water that might signify the next batch of escapees was on its way – but they waited in vain. To understand why, we must turn to the recollections of L/ Stoker Walter Arnold:

> The effects of carbon dioxide poisoning were all too apparent when the escape chamber door was opened prematurely following the ascent of Lt Woods and Captain Oram. Water ran in over the escape chamber coaming and into the main motors. The short circuit which resulted sent an acrid white cloud through the submarine. This smoke was thick and choking but it was not chlorine. All we could do was put on DSEA sets or grab gas masks. This must have used up quite a lot of our air. Things were looking desperate.

Breathing became painful as men neared the absolute limits of both mental and physical endurance. A growing number lapsed into a torpid indifference to the events around them. 'Mac' Arnold noted that Bolus himself could no longer stand without help. Management of the next escape bid passed to Lt Chapman. Conditions were now so desperate that Harold Chapman saw little option but send four men up at a time from an escape chamber designed to hold just two. Walter Arnold:

> Lt Chapman now suggested that four of us should go in the escape chamber and make an escape. They decided to send two with experience of DSEA and two without, so four got in, two of each. L/Stoker Kenney, Stoker Hole and two of the Cammell Lairds people. We went through the procedure of flooding the chamber up and we gave them plenty of time, fifteen minutes, quarter of an hour…nothing…
>
> We could not see what was happening in the chamber because our torches had just about run out. We drained down again and carefully opened the door. Three of the men were dead, Kenney, Hole and one other.

The fourth was still alive but could not have lasted much longer. All but the one who was still alive had their sets torn off them. They were all very weak when they had entered the chamber but had not shown any nervousness. The one who was still alive could not give any explanation of what had happened. He was talking but you could not understand him.

But Frank Shaw, one of those who rushed over to support the man, clearly understood what 'Neal' Smith had said. He gasped: 'We couldn't get the hatch open… just couldn't get it open.' Then 'Smithy' fell back and died.

'BE SEEING YOU BLOKES SOON'

The hatch had not jammed. The men had attempted to open it before pressure had equalised. Now the plan reverted back to two escapees at a time. At 0953hrs Glenn surveyed the unspoken despair around him and approached Stoker Arnold, directing him to make the next escape attempt, *'only take someone with you who looks as though he might make it'*. Arnold looked for a resilient-looking civilian to partner him. Catching the words of Bolus, Frank Shaw immediately stepped forward. By this stage the submarine had been submerged for twenty hours.
   Walter Arnold:

> Just before I left the boat the air was getting a bit better, though it was still very thick. It may have been because the smoke was spreading through the boat or it may be that air was coming in through the 'Z' vents. The lights were still on when we entered the chamber.

Frank Shaw: 'By this time the air was so very thick, I could hardly speak. I had a choking sensation around the throat.'
   Bolus had one last word with his Stoker: 'For God's sake, Arnold, do it right and give these chaps some hope.' Arnold turned to Lt Harold Chapman and the knot of men gathered around the escape chamber: 'So long Sir, be seeing you blokes soon.' Chapman smiled back: 'Good luck and thanks.'
   The escape chamber door was shut and clipped. The operation of this chamber was surprisingly complex (see Fig.12). First, Arnold reached up to unscrew the hatch clips (1) while the men outside the chamber disconnected the hatch operating clutch gear (2). All that now secured the hatch in place was the device known as the 'toe clip' (3). Arnold turned the flood valve (4) and freezing water surged into the chamber. This escape chamber method did not rely on the creation of an air lock. Once the chamber was sufficiently flooded, Arnold turned the handle to release the toe clip (5). Frank Shaw would later relive the experience of flooding-up in the evidence he gave to the Bucknill Tribunal:

> When you put on the [DSEA] mouthpiece for the first time and the water covers your head, you can barely see. You have the feeling of being trapped and you put your hand up to shove the hatch. If you do that straight away it will not open. It is simply terrifying.

Initially Arnold and Shaw had the same problem as the previous would-be escapees, the hatch would not budge. Arnold realised that pressure had not yet equalised:

> I had a bit of difficulty in opening the outboard vent but I eventually succeeded and the next thing Frank Shaw was shot out of the chamber…he hit the wires as he headed for the surface. I got caught up on the hatch clips as I came out in consequence of the angle of the boat. I kicked myself out, hit the [jumping] wires then went on up. The first thing I saw was Vigilant's motor boat and they picked me up.

Dr Stark's evidence indicates that Arnold was not suffering unduly from carbon dioxide poisoning, yet the resilient Stoker was neither asked, nor given the opportunity to provide a verbal situation report. Instead, the rating immediately was rushed below *Brazen's* decks and sedated. None of the other escapees were treated in this fashion and no explanation was ever provided to Arnold. Even allowing for the grotesquely paternalistic attitude of the pre-war navy, the treatment meted out to Arnold remains one of the most controversial aspects of this harrowing affair.

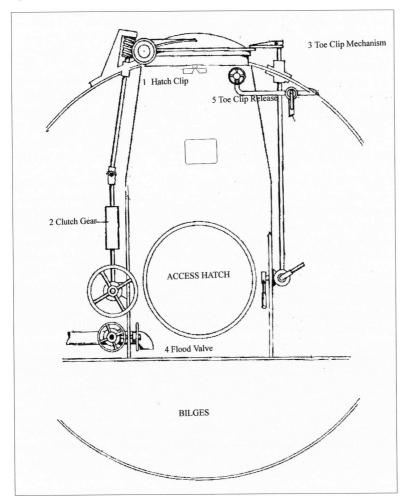

Fig. 12: 'Escape chamber arrangements as installed in *Thetis.*' (P. Armstrong)

Surely more men would emerge now. The desperate vigil continued but no more escapees appeared. Diver Orton regularly tapped out the message, 'C-O-M-E O-U-T' on the stern with his spanner but to no avail. At this juncture, one hour after the stern had first been located, it began to slowly dawn on those in authority that the expected continuous DSEA escapes were not taking place and some alternative strategy may be required.

Capt Hubert Hart:

> We were told most definitely that everyone onboard was quite happy and that they were all expecting to escape by Davis equipment. There was no immediate thought of all or any of the crew being lost, in view of the message that they were coming out.
>
> As an additional precaution and as a possible eventual necessity in the salvage of the submarine, I sent for burning gear. [64]

At 0855hrs Hart sent this message to the Mersey Docks and Harbour Board: 'SEND BURNERS AND BURNING GEAR OUT AT ONCE WITH TUG.'

At 0936hrs Capt Hart followed up with a second message. At last word was sent to the Liverpool and Glasgow Salvage Association:

PLEASE SEND OUT WITH A TUG FOR URGENT DISPATCH, PORTABLE MOTOR AIR COMPRESSOR CONNECTIONS FOR AIR PIPE TO COMPRESSOR, BURNERS AND BURNING GEAR, FOREMAN FITTER AND FROM CAMMELL LAIRDS 400' OF AIR PIPE

FOR AIR COMPRESSOR WITH SUITABLE CONNECTIONS TO ATTACH TO THE HOSE
CONNECTIONS ON GUN RECUPERATOR. SEND FOREMAN FITTER BLACK ALSO SEND
DIVER AND TENDER FROM THE LIVERPOOL AND GLASGOW SALVAGE ASSOCIATION BUT
DO NOT DELAY IF DIVER AND TENDER ARE NOT READY.

Meanwhile at 1040hrs Capt (D) 6 Randolph Nicholson[65] had arrived with his sleek destroyers to take
over command of the operation from Lt-Cdr Mills of *Brazen*. His first step was to call those heading the
rescue to a meeting on *Somali*.

At 1130hrs the tide allowed *Vigilant*'s diver Fred Orton to at last be able to make an exploratory
descent but it was already late in the slack water period. Orton succeeded in attaching guidelines to the
fore-hatch but at 1145hrs he was ordered back to the surface because both Hart and Brock had been
summoned to the meeting with the recently arrived Nicholson and recoiled at the safety implications,
should Orton descend in their absence. By the time Orton surfaced, it was becoming obvious that the
trapped men could not escape by DSEA. Worse still, time was rapidly running out to implement Bolus'
salvage blow. While the strong back was reported to be ready for collection by 1200hrs, because of the
distance involved, the estimated time of arrival was 1500hrs. High water was due soon and Hart could
not expect his diver to work in such dangerous conditions.[66] With the tide about to turn (see Appendix
4) there would be no opportunity to connect the air hose until low water at 1730hrs. The trapped men
could not wait that long. One further factor entered the equation. All that morning, the two and a half
knot flood tide which had repeatedly forced the postponement of Orton's dive, had nevertheless supported the stern of *Thetis*. Once the tide turned, without adequate support it would surely force the
stern back under. Rear Admiral (S) Watson appreciated the dangers as his preliminary report reveals:

> It was quite evident by this time that either the DSEA escape arrangements were inoperable or the personnel
> were incapable of escaping…it was realised that the grave risk of total flooding was being accepted but judged
> by conditions of survivors at the time of their escape…it was obvious that desperate measures were essential
> to meet a desperate situation.

Dr Stark and Lt Woods now implored Nicholson to act immediately and Capt D did not disappoint. In
effect he abandoned all attempts to put the Bolus plan into operation in favour of more direct means.
Nicholson ordered his ships to send all the air hose they possessed to *Somali*, where the CERAs stood ready
to fashion joints and connect it. First, Nicholson reasoned, the stern must be supported then lifted as clear
as possible; next a hole could be burned or drilled through the exposed stern. This was a sound proposition with echoes of the *K13* rescue of 1917. Securing an airline would inevitably depend upon the active
participation of the trapped men and it remained to be seen how far they would be capable of responding.
Charlie Brock and his men succeeded in attaching a 3.5in securing wire around the stern. At 1310hrs
Vigilant manoeuvred alongside the stern of *Thetis* and began to heave. A couple of tugs took up position on
either beam and proceeded to haul the stern towards the vertical. *Thetis* was raised from a position at which
her hydroplanes were flush with the water to an angle at which her propellers were visible.

Capt Nicholson:

> What was the idea behind it? To try at all costs to get into the submarine and save lives. At the back of our
> minds at this time was to drill a hole in the submarine and to do this it was necessary to lift the stern out of
> the water.

Drilling or cutting a hole in the stern of a submarine may sound simple enough but the reality was
far more challenging. Working from a precarious perch, in constant danger from the water lapping
about him, the welder would be required to first cut through the casing. Next he would have to burn
through the potentially flooded 'Z' tank, work his way past the maze of tubing to cut a sizeable manhole through the bulkhead beyond. This work would take an estimated two hours. With the 1500hrs
deadline fast approaching, the cutting gear urgently requested from Liverpool had not yet arrived.
Nobody knew whether the ill-secured stern would stand up to *Somali*'s drill. Only forty-five minutes
of slack-tide remained.

Brock recognised he was locked into a race against time and so far, he was losing. He must reach
the trapped men before they suffocated. Given the desperate situation, it was decided to try a different approach. At 1330hrs Wreckmaster Brock took up position astride the stern where he attempted to

DSEA escapee: 'You have the feeling of being trapped.' (P. Armstrong)

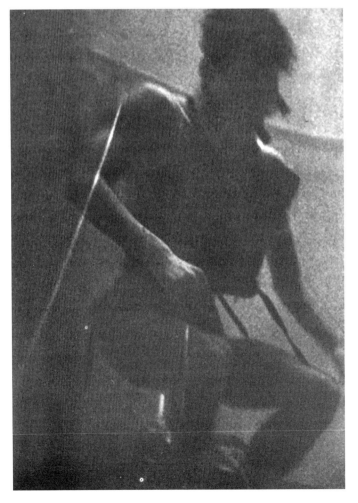

The DSEA escapee is holding out the skirt attached to the apparatus in order to slow his ascent to the surface and avoid bursting his lungs or preventing the onset of a bend. (P. Armstrong)

unscrew the manhole cover used for accessing the rudder head in 'Z' tank, armed with only the vaguest information as to what lay beneath. The nuts were loosened, the outer cover was prised off, revealing a second manhole plate beneath. Beyond Z tank lay No.46 Bulkhead and the steering compartment where many of the men now huddled in anticipation of imminent rescue. As the pins securing this second manhole cover were carefully removed, there was a sudden unnerving hiss of compressed air. The stern began to pivot and shudder alarmingly. The cable began to strain. Hart decreed that this potentially promising avenue could not be safely explored. In retrospect it can be observed that drilling alone would not have sufficed. Brock would not have progressed far though 'Z' tank without the benefit of cutting gear. At 1350hrs divers reported renewed knocking from within the submarine. As the ebb-tide battered *Thetis*, the more the stern began to cant and shudder. At 1440hrs the despondent Charles Brock was finally ordered off the stern for his own safety. The ERAs on *Somali* were preparing their electric drill for action when *Crosby*, bearing the cutting gear, finally hove into view.

CLOSE ENOUGH TO TOUCH?

What of the world outside? Rumours of a submarine accident had already begun to permeate outwards from Blockhouse and Portland on the evening of 1 June. As we have seen, the BBC withheld the news until the following terse telegrams had been sent at 2240hrs:

> Submarine Thetis has failed to return to surface after diving trial off Liverpool. XXX is believed to be on board.
> – Submarines Gosport

At 2300hrs that night, the BBC first informed the world of the predicament of HMS *Thetis*:

> 'The Admiralty regrets to announce that His Majesty's Submarine Thetis has failed to surface following trials in Liverpool Bay.'

A subdued crowd numbering 2,000 gathered outside the Cammell Laird gates on Green Lane. The London press caught the night train to Liverpool. Newspaper barons competed to hire aircraft from Speke to obtain aerial photographs of the exposed stern. Next morning all over the English-speaking world newspaper placards shrieked, 'SUBMARINE DISASTER. THETIS SINKS'. Anxious knots of people discussed it on street corners, they talked about it in pubs and in their homes they huddled close to wireless sets for the latest news. The release of this news was (perhaps understandably) carefully managed. To cheers, at 2045hrs Mr Woodward of Lairds confirmed the rumour to the people gathered at the gates that the boat had been found.

The following *communiqué* was released to the media on 2 June, but it was actually held back by mutual agreement until 2200hrs, when the BBC announced:

> HM S/M THETIS HAS BEEN LOCATED IN POSITION 328 DEGREES 14 MILES FROM GREAT ORMES HEAD. HER BOW IS IN 130' OF WATER AND HER STERN IS ON THE SURFACE. CAPTAIN ORAM, LT WOODS, STOKER ARNOLD AND MR FRANK SHAW OF CAMMELL LAIRDS HAVE ESCAPED BY DAVIS ESCAPE APPARATUS. CAPTAIN ORAM ESCAPED TO DIRECT SALVAGE OPERATIONS AND TO MAKE A FULL REPORT ON THE STATE OF THE SUBMARINE. THE COMMANDING OFFICER AND THE REMAINDER OF THE CREW WERE ALIVE AT 10AM AND SALVAGE EQUIPMENT IS BEING RUSHED TO THE SPOT.

Admiralty and Cammell Laird otherwise remained tight-lipped. The BBC wisely adhered to the driblets of information dispensed at Admiralty briefings, not so the newspapers. Starved of information, the press made some investigations of its own. Newspapers reported, quite rightly, that a 'T' class submarine could remain dived for thirty-six hours. In response Admiralty personally contacted leading Fleet Street editors to inform them that *Thetis* was actually carrying far more personnel than her quota of crew but the press did not see fit to modify its earlier optimistic reporting. The world expected a massive rescue operation to unfold in Liverpool Bay and news of a massive rescue operation was duly delivered. In reality, this operation existed only in the fertile minds of journalists.

'A subdued crowd gathered outside the gates of Cammell Laird.' The woman with the baby is believed to be Mrs Caroline Hole. (Graf Alexander, SOS Thetis)

Perhaps one of the most dispiriting aspects of the saga was the emergence of a *laager* mentality on the part of the rescuers. Ranks closed against even credible offers of help. Despite inefficiencies, delays and mistakes, those trapped in *K13* had survived because the boat had been supported by barges and an oxygen line successfully attached to the boat. Above all they had survived because two maverick commanders had effectively sacrificed their own careers to ensure that the operation was masterminded by submariners. There was a prevailing belief that General Service lacked the knowledge to deal with submarine rescue but would never lose face by admitting it. In this instance the obvious advisors, Lt-Cdrs Garnett and Lloyd were trapped in *Thetis* but a pool of experienced submariners sat around kicking their heels in frustration at Birkenhead and Barrow. These men were warrant officers and CERAs standing by *Taku* and *Trident*: men like Robert Ostler. Warren and Benson describe how CERA Ostler[67] had earlier devised a two-way ventilation feed system for submarines, one that could be rigged quickly and with minimum effort on the part of those trapped. Moreover, Ostler had constructed his air line with the 'T' class specification in mind. Ostler's telephone calls to the Mersey Docks and Harbour Board and Cammell Laird were not even returned. When he arrived at the Reporting Office at Cammell Laird on the morning of 2 June, pleading to be taken out to Liverpool Bay to offer his air line directly to the rescuers, his request was refused. When the remaining CPOs offered their expertise to the RN Reporting Office at the Yard, the response from the duty officer was, 'Sorry, the best brains are already out there'. Posterity may offer a different judgement.

Stoker Arnold, had he been asked, could have told the 'best brains' that all that could possibly save the men on *Thetis* now was an immediate transfusion of air. The only submarine officers present at the scene were Capt Oram, Lt Woods and Lt Coltart. As we have seen, both Woods and Oram were debilitated by carbon dioxide poisoning. Lt Coltart was already *persona non grata*. Stoker Arnold, a mere rating, had been sedated and bundled away. Watson and Macintyre were still in transit. The hard fact was that Nicholson, Hart and Mills possessed a wealth of good intention but negligible knowledge of submarines.

The actions of Cammell Laird (and the Mersey Docks and Harbour Board) deserve scrutiny. The mantra drilled into Cammell Laird personnel and later repeated *ad nauseam* at the Bucknill Tribunal was, '*We were not responsible for the salvage which was undertaken under the orders of the Admiralty and the Mersey Docks and Harbour Board*'. Given the all-too-obvious inadequacies of their own vessels, why did the Mersey Docks and Harbour Board not request urgent support from other organisations? Trinity House had lifting vessels at Holyhead but the Liverpool and Glasgow Salvage Association was the company with the track record in submarine salvage, *Ranger* having participated in the *K13* rescue. The Liverpool and Glasgow Salvage Association did not possess camels. The camels on the Mersey belonged to the Mersey Docks and Harbour Board. Records reveal that in this instance the London and Glasgow Salvage Association was first made aware of the accident at 0400hrs on 2 June when it was asked only to provide a recompression chamber.

It will be recalled that Capt Hart had first sent out a request for cutting gear at 0855hrs. At 1440hrs this plant finally arrived at *Vigilant*.

ADMIRALTY, C IN C HOME FLEET – 1440hrs 2/6/39

BURNING GEAR HAS ARRIVED FROM LIVERPOOL BUT CAPTAIN HART REPORTS THAT
NOTHING CAN BE DONE UNTIL THE TIDE SLACKENS AT 1800 AS IT IS NOT POSSIBLE TO
BRING SUFFICIENT OF THE TAIL OF THE SUBMARINE ABOVE THE SURFACE TO CUT A
HOLE. UP TILL NOW ABOUT 15' OF THE TAIL HAS BEEN HELD CLEAR OF THE WATER BUT
THE STRENGTH OF TIDE HAS NOW PUSHED THIS UNDER.
Captain D (6)

It is impossible not to feel sympathy for Nicholson, who now found himself in nominal command of a desperate situation, rapidly spiralling out of anybody's control. Nicholson knew little about submarines. Hampered by angry tides and lacking basic equipment, he found himself directing an operation requiring the active co-operation of opinionated civilians who had no intention of unquestioningly following orders. Tensions bubbling under the surface between Capts Nicholson and Hart now burst into the open. Capt Nicholson:

The plan discussed in the charthouse of Vigilant was that further wires should be passed around the stern of the submarine by two tugs, with a view to lifting her further out of the water. Captain Hart agreed to do this while at the same time explaining the small likelihood of the attempt being successful. In view of the desperate situation and the necessity for keeping the stern out of the water, it was generally agreed to carry on with this operation.

Capt Hart:

After consulting his staff, Captain Nicholson suggested that we should raise her higher and cut the hole while pulling the submarine into the tide. I told him I disapproved of it and would not agree to it but that if he insisted I would carry out his desire to the best of my ability but he must assume all responsibility as I considered that the chances were one hundred to one against success. Captain Nicholson agreed to take full responsibility so we set about putting his plan into action.[68]

In the years that followed, many theories were offered as to how those trapped could have been saved. It is highly debatable whether lashing the submarine to a couple of Tribal Class destroyers, prior to racing her towards a beaching location would have resulted in a different outcome. If a precedent exists for affixing a tapering, hopelessly unstable submarine stern to a destroyer (or for that matter any other vessel other than a barge), the author has been unable to find it. It defies logic to suggest that, with the destroyers steaming at high speed through the currents of Liverpool Bay, the stern would not have slipped away. Others have opined that explosive charges could have been used to blow the submarine open. Given that *Thetis* was literally hanging by a thread, the prospects of success can be roundly dismissed. On 4 July 1939 the celebrated salvor Ernest Cox wrote an oft-quoted letter to the Bucknill Tribunal, describing how the salvage of *Thetis* ought to have been a straightforward task, 'a gift', in his parlance: 'All that was required was some-one with salvage experience to take charge and direct operations. The first thing was to get out on the spot with compressors and tools and drill a hole in the stern of the submarine.'

When he wrote this letter, Ernest Cox clearly did not appreciate that adequate cutting gear had not been available until *Crosby* appeared at 1440hrs. Nor did he realise that no camels were present at the scene. It must be understood that the stern of *Thetis* had never been secured at any stage. Nevertheless Cox did not hold back: 'This would be child's play as we have done similar jobs hundreds of times in worse conditions and my divers have done the job under water. The time at the very outside should be 15/20 minutes.'

Mr Cox was unfamiliar with the vicious tides of Liverpool Bay. Any reader harbouring doubts as to their ferocity should examine the *Thetis* salvage papers in the National Archive. It is unclear to the writer how much experience Cox and Danks had of saving lives from submarines[69] but in retrospect it seems injudicious for the (otherwise admirable) Ernest Cox to openly pontificate over an immensely difficult operation carried out in circumstances he evidently had so little knowledge of. As the Metal Industries men, the *Tedworth* and Liverpool and Glasgow Salvage Association divers and the dependants of PO

The engine room of HMS *Alliance*, of similar dimensions to the engine room of *Thetis*. Sixty-seven men crammed into a space no bigger than this, awaiting what they prayed was an imminent rescue. (P. Armstrong)

Perdue all discovered, *Thetis* was a lot of things but she was not, never had been, and never would be, a 'gift' to salvors.

Capt D (6) insisted that an additional reinforcing cable be run out to secure *Thetis* to *Vigilant*. This done, the tugs took up position on either beam. Rather than secure them to the submarine's increasingly unstable stern, wires were run from the tugs into the bows of *Vigilant*. The stern was slowly hauled to a near vertical position, from forty to sixty degrees. Capt Hart continued to protest that the strain would prove too great for the cable. That said, the only alternative Hart could offer was to lash *Thetis* to *Vigilant* then wait until 1800hrs when favourable tide was expected. With Dr Stark emphasising that survival beyond 1800hrs was extremely unlikely, Nicholson recognised that delay was no longer an option.

Above the surface, it was a balmy June day. Below, in the submarine the air was sickly and fetid, the silence broken only by the occasional murmur. Less than 20ft separated these two worlds. It might as well have been 20,000 miles. What happened within the boat must remain speculation. The Bucknill Tribunal heard forensic evidence suggesting that a third, abortive escape attempt was made shortly after Shaw and Arnold left the boat. When examined by salvors, it was found that the clutch mechanism used to close the hatch had not been properly re-wound. The implication being that the subtleties of the hatch mechanism were lost on minds poisoned by carbon dioxide. With the toe-clip still in place, the hatch would not open. This failed escape bid possibly ended with the death of young Lt Poland.[70] His DSEA-clad body was found reverentially stowed in the aft machinery space, alongside those of the predecessors who had died in the earlier escape bid.

There was evidence of one literally last-gasp but equally doomed escape, involving Lt Glenn, Stoker Matthews and another unknown. Once again the hatch could not be raised but this time the door between the escape chamber and the steering compartment was left open, allowing the sea to flood in. The bodies of these two men were swept out of the escape chamber by the torrent of water. Salvagers found Stoker Matthews, hanging by his entangled clothing from the escape chamber door latch. Not only did the extra weight burden caused by this sudden inundation cause the fragile wire supporting the stern to snap, the sudden, sharp rise in carbon dioxide levels may well have killed those who remained alive within the steering compartment. The body of Lt Glenn was found with, his hands still holding the flooding valve open.

On the other hand it has been argued by Surgeon Rear Admiral S.G. Rainsford[71] that shortly after Arnold and Shaw made their exit, the remainder decided to attempt an escape from the engine room and the steerage compartment by using the stern escape compartment as a twill trunk. Because of the angle of the boat, this would have necessitated flooding first the engine room then the steerage compartment. As the engine room sea-cocks were tucked behind the diesels and therefore difficult to access, it was decided to flood-up using the escape chamber. This theory would explain why the door between the control and engine rooms was closed, thus reducing available air capacity by half. It would also justify the closure of the stern escape chamber valves. There is further evidence in support of this version of events.

It is known for certain that the men abandoned the control room and made their way to the rear compartments, against the angle of the boat. No fewer than sixty-seven crammed into the engine room with a further thirty-two huddled in the steering compartment beyond. Not all were wearing DSEA sets and not everyone wearing a set was breathing from it. While the oxygen supply in the set worn by Bolus was exhausted, Hambrook's was full and unused. The forward door of the escape chamber was open, not the result of impaired judgement, according to this version, but in a deliberate attempt to flood the compartments. As this chamber was open to the sea, water could have been admitted into the steering compartment and providing the door was left open, into the engine room beyond. Unfortunately it was too late. It would have taken two hours to flood the engine room alone. Those not wearing DSEA sets would have been killed by carbon dioxide long before the compartments had flooded sufficiently. According to this view, the two men swept out of the escape chamber were overcome while attempting to set the hatch mechanism to 'Free' to 'Open'.

Within minutes of this photograph having been taken, the stern slipped beneath the surface. Note the figures of Oram and Coltart in *Vigilant's* bows and the group of naval officers crammed into *Somali's* launch. Observe the state of the sea. (P. Armstrong)

Unaware of events within *Thetis* and following Nicholson's general directions (but under Hart's initiative) *Crosby* and *Storm Cock* took up position ahead of *Vigilant*. The tugs hauled away at *Vigilant* which in turn commenced to tow the stern of *Thetis* against the tide, in the hope of providing greater lift in readiness for burning the hole. Had camels borne this weight none of this would have mattered, but as we know, camels were not present. Water flooded in to the ballast tanks through the Kingston valves while the air supply, built up with such effort during the night, hissed out from the main vents. Critical buoyancy was lost. At 1510hrs the strain on the suspension wire, caused by this combination of inundation and tidal force, proved too great for the securing wire. The cable supporting *Thetis* snapped with a resounding crack. The stern slipped away beneath the surface and there was nothing anyone could do. Capt D (6) sent the following despairing transmission:

ADMIRALTY, C IN C HOME FLEET – 1649 – 2/6/39

FURTHER TO MY 1440 NO ESCAPES HAVE BEEN MADE SINCE THOSE OF STOKER ARNOLD AND MR SHAW AT 0950. THESE TWO SURVIVORS REPORTED THAT THE CREW WERE ABOUT TO USE DSEA BUT IT APPEARS THAT ESCAPE DRILL MAY HAVE BEEN IMPROPERLY CARRIED OUT AND THAT THE ESCAPE COMPARTMENT MAY HAVE BECOME FLOODED. ATTEMPTS HAVE BEEN MADE TO CUT A HOLE IN THE STERN BUT THIS HAS HAD TO BE ABANDONED TILL THE TIDE SLACKENS AT ABOUT 1800. STRONG TIDE HAS AT PRESENT CAUSED SUBMARINE TO CANT AND STERN TO GO UNDERWATER. I CONSIDER THAT THERE IS VERY LITTLE HOPE OF THE MEN ON BOARD BEING RESCUED ALIVE
Captain D (6)

At 1720hrs Capt Macintyre in HMS *Winchelsea* arrived at the scene to take over command, then at 1745hrs the first camel steamed into view.

Following his arrival at 1900hrs Bertram Watson was handed overall command of operations. Bertram Watson's diary records that the submarine was relocated by sweeping at 2300hrs. It was civilians who took the initiative when Metal Industries salvage expert Mr Tom McKenzie arrived from the Orkneys with four of his volunteer divers but no equipment. These tough, resolute men routinely pushed against the boundaries of what was considered to be safe diving. It had been assumed that all life on *Thetis* had been extinguished by 1500hrs on 2 June but this extract from the preliminary report of Rear Admiral (S) provides evidence that at least one wretched soul survived for much longer. This passage also contradicts the pervasive assertion which has dogged *Thetis*, namely that preserving the integrity of the pressure hull was prioritised over saving the trapped men:

At 0000 a Metal Industries Diver (Sinclair McKenzie) was put down and found himself in the vicinity of the bridge. As he had no telephonic communication he came up direct to the surface to report that his taps had been answered from the control room. Having made this report he immediately went down to carry out his decompression… All authorities were unanimous that air should be admitted direct to the control room by drilling through the pressure hull. All necessary appliances to ensure this operation being carried out were made ready.

The divers returned at 0630hrs. Afterwards, Bertram Watson made the following valedictory entry in his diary:

During this dive, the conditions for drilling and the short working period available caused Captain Hart to increase his estimate for the job to 3 or 4 tides… In view of this and the fact that no reply had been made to the tappings, it was agreed that the operation should not be continued because it was considered that the personnel in the submarine would not have a chance of survival for the length of time involved…

Watson later sent this message:

ADMIRALTY, C IN C HOME FLEET – 1144 – 3/6/39
AT 0500 DIVERS HEARD NO TAPPING WITHIN THE SUBMARINE. REGRET HOPES OF SAVING LIVES NOW NEGLIGIBLE AND QUESTION OF SALVAGE WILL REQUIRE DECISION…
Rear Admiral (S) Bertram Watson

At midday the blinds were drawn down in the Cammell Laird offices. The press knew the signs. Mr Woodward, the Company Secretary, emerged to read a statement to the wretched women and children lining Green Lane. It was followed by the posting of an Admiralty telegram on the gates which stated that hope of saving lives in *Thetis* must now be abandoned.[72] Having earlier digested the optimistic reports served up by the press, they were stunned. Dependants of service personnel received the shattering news by telegram. It was now time to tell the rest of the world. As the nation settled down for tea on Saturday 3 June, the BBC made the following announcement:

> THE ADMIRALTY ANNOUNCED AT FOUR-THIRTY THIS AFTERNOON THAT THERE WAS NO LONGER ANY JUSTIFICATION FOR HOPE THAT ANY FURTHER LIVES COULD BE SAVED FROM THE SUBMARINE *THETIS*. SALVAGE WORK IS TAKING PLACE AND IT IS UNDERSTOOD THAT THE SUBMARINE WILL EITHER BE TOWED TO THE NEAREST SHORE OR BROUGHT BACK TO BIRKENHEAD.

Misled by the press, fed a diet of hopelessly optimistic opinions, this news devastated all who heard it. It seemed incredible that with the submarine located and welders already working on the stern, a rescue mission carried by the world's greatest navy could possibly have ended in such abject failure. For many, the impact reached far beyond the loss of single a submarine. Nearly sixty years after the event, submariner Capt George Phillips DSO, GM was still seared by the *Thetis* affair:

> Every time I see that photograph it makes me feel physically sick. Not just because they were my friends dying in there but because of the wider implications. You can't just write it off as bad luck. It should not have happened. It need not have happened. Could there have been a more eloquent, more damning comment on the ways of the peace-time Royal Navy than that stern projecting above Liverpool Bay and nobody able to do anything about it?[73]

At a time of rising international tensions, the inadequacies of the Royal Navy had been exposed and by implication, Britain herself had been left tarnished. There would be a time to ask questions in the future but now was a time for grief.

At 1000hrs on Tuesday 6 June, the HMS *Hebe* embarked 200 dependants and set course for the green buoy marking the position of *Thetis*. On arrival at 1400hrs a service commenced. While this was going on, a fleet of lorries arrived in Birkenhead to remove the personal effects of the dead men. They were driven down to Blockhouse for auctioning-off in the time-honoured custom of the Submarine Service. There was the usual chorus of condolences. Even Hitler sent a sympathy telegram.[74] The dance due to take place that night at the Kingsland Hall was cancelled. The sea had claimed HMS/M *Thetis* and the ninety-nine men on board but the world had not seen the last of her. *Thetis* would bide her time and rise again.

THE THEATRE OF THE WORLD

An 8 June Mersey Docks and Harbour Board memo described the vessel as 'lying sunk upright on an even keel in 155ft of water…two compartments – the torpedo stowage and torpedo tube chambers – are completely flooded with 160 tons of water.' The engine room was also partially flooded as a result of the final escape attempt but the salvors did not know this. On 13 June Diver Dicky Oliver reported that the shutter on No.5 Tube was open.

Salvage operations were belatedly placed in the hands of the London and Glasgow Salvage Association. HMS/M *Thetis* infamously claimed her hundredth victim when PO Perdue, one of the *Tedworth* divers, caught a bend while diving and died on 23 August 1939. The boat was run ashore on the north side of Traeth Bychan, the bight-like beach on the east side of Anglesey where the *denouement* was played out. Bad weather constantly delayed the 'evacuation' of *Thetis*. On 7 September the stern was entered via the escape chamber. Within a couple of hours of having been removed, two of the least decomposed bodies of the crew were taken to Stanley Hospital for post-mortem examination carried out by Dr Woods, Consultant Pathologist for the Royal Navy and Surgeon Cdr Rainsford. The bodies of PO Mitchell and an unknown stoker were carefully examined for evidence of cause of death. The surgeons concluded that both men had died from asphyxia. Because the bodies were deteriorating fast, it was decided that further post-mortem examinations would serve no useful purpose.

It was planned that each one of the remaining bodies should be extricated by a mines rescue team brought in from Gornall Colliery in Staffordshire, reinforced by a party of volunteers from HMS *Drake* under Lt J Western. It was felt unwise to expose naval volunteers to the horrors within *Thetis*. Most bodies in the engine room were removed by seven Holyhead policemen. The names of these stoic men deserve to be recorded: Sgt. Glyn Evans was aided by constables Roberts, Hughes, Owen, Shaw, Williams and probationer John Hughes. Sufficient to add that these volunteers carried out their appalling task with as much dignity and reverence as conditions would allow. Mr Forcer Evans, the Coroner, sent a bottle of whisky to the team. As PC John Hughes recalls, it was required:

> Our task was to remove the bodies from Thetis to a temporary mortuary on Turkey Shore, then try to identify them…Looking back on it, as a policeman I have seen some dreadful sights but nothing ever came close to Thetis. You could not imagine the conditions inside that submarine in your very worst nightmare. We worked in an oily black soup up to our thighs. There was all sorts floating around in it, clothing, personal belongings, lumps of decomposing flesh and hair, lots of hair lying in clumps on the engine room plating… At first I did not realise that the obscene, slimy things that my colleagues were attempting to lever out of the engine room had once been people. These were not men, they were gas-bloated hulks with no distinguishable facial features whatsoever. In places the skin had sloughed away exposing the bones beneath. I just kept telling myself that each was some mother's son. When we attempted to lift them on stretchers the guts would explode, showering us with entrails. Often they would grunt and jerk as it [the gas] released. Some were so tight packed we had to cut them apart with hacksaws to get them out.. The stench hung around us like an aura. Even though we washed thoroughly before leaving the scene, that aura hung around us for weeks, clinging to our clothes and hair. I walked into my digs one day and my landlady was violently sick.

Locals still recall the charnel-house stench which lingered over the Turkey Shore road for weeks afterwards as vehicles drove the victims to the now-demolished Old Pontoon House in Holyhead Docks. The hard-pressed local police tried to dissuade the long procession of dependants from viewing the bodies, diverting them instead towards identification by means of personal belongings. Stoker Arnold, previously excluded from the rescue operation by authority, was now urged to help identify former shipmates who scarcely resembled human beings at all. It was possible to identify some thanks to personal effects or tattoos. Several Cammell Laird workers were named by their numbered overalls. The officers were identified via their uniforms and possessions. Guy Bolus was found some distance from one of the youngest ratings, twenty-two-year-old Glaswegian rating Billy Orrock. In circumstances which will never be explained, Stoker Orrock was found to be wearing his skipper's uniform jacket. One man was recognised via a tattoo which read, 'In Memory of My Dear Mother'. Two bodies of ratings removed from the stern could not be named in spite of distinctive markings. One bore a tattoo of a bird with the name 'Jean'. On each of the forearms was a sailing ship and the words, 'In the days of command'. As a symbolic gesture, it was initially planned to bury one of these bodies at sea but rough weather prevented this.

While fifty-five were buried privately ('Sam' Bolus and 'Daddy' Jackson were both buried at sea in Holyhead Bay on 28 September) forty-four zinc-lined coffins were interred in a brick-lined mass grave in Maeshyfryd Cemetery, Anglesey. The White Ensigns draped over each of the naval victims masked the necessarily grotesque size of the coffins. All told, there were three funerals at Maeshfryd. The final ceremony took place on 16 November 1939, conducted by Canon Hughes of Holyhead and Archdeacon Morgan of Bangor. The general public was excluded. The naval contingent included the representative of Commander-in-Chief (Western Approaches) Capt Kitson. Understandably, Rear Admiral (S) Bertram Watson remained at his war HQ at Aberdour in Scotland, leaving Commander Shadwell to attend in his place. Mr J. Watters had the unenviable task of representing Messrs Cammell Laird at the funeral. Many within the Submarine Service archly observed that a greater degree of competence and organisation was demonstrated during the funeral obsequies than had been witnessed at any stage during the rescue.

On 11 November *Thetis*, now under the control of NOIC Holyhead, Cdr Roe, was towed to the LMS Dock at Holyhead. The last victim was removed from the engine room on the following afternoon. The body was that of twenty-nine-year-old L/S Walter Hambrook who had been with Lt Woods in the fore-ends when tube No.5 flooded.

That evening PC Hughes[75] watched as one of the submariners attached to the salvage team clambered onto the fore-ends casing. The sailor was obviously drunk. He glanced down the open hatch, jabbed an

The *Thetis* mass grave, Holyhead.
(Reproduced by kind permission of
Donna and Mark Jones)

accusing finger into the void, loudly yelling, '*Bugger You!*' John Hughes heard the sailor's voice reverberate through the empty, partially flooded compartments before echoing back with equal force, 'Bugger *You*'. *Thetis* had enjoyed the last word after all.

BLAME GAME

Immediately following the accident, Commander-in-Chief Portsmouth ordered the highly respected submariner, Rear Admiral RH Raikes to carry out an internal inquiry into the loss of *Thetis*. Aware that Chamberlain had promised a public inquiry, Raikes focussed upon avenues of potential Service criticism in order for the Treasury Solicitor to prepare arguments in defence.[76] Raikes commenced his evidence gathering assisted by Capt Barry and Rear Admiral Wake-Walker. *Thetis* was still on the bottom at this stage so the investigation could not draw upon forensic evidence of the boat. The Raikes Board report was delivered on 29 June.

The actions of the late Lt-Cdr Bolus came under question because of his failure to transfer the civilians to *Grebe Cock* before the dive. Additionally the Raikes Board found it inexplicable that Bolus did not blow Nos 5 and 6 main ballast tanks at the time of the accident to keep the stern above the surface. It seems likely that Bolus was keeping a reserve of air in reserve for later use but when that critical time came, he was too disorientated by carbon dioxide poisoning to bring it into effect.

Oram and Woods were closely questioned. Raikes held that in failing to use the rimer, Woods had not followed procedure. However the inquiry conceded that Lt Woods had possibly never been trained in its use.[77] There was more:

...there was no adequate reason for Lt Woods opening the rear tube doors and he was not justified in doing so without instruction.[78]

Woods was additionally criticised for failing to close the tube door immediately after the accident at a time when this ought to have been possible using telemotor pressure. Conversely there was no hard evidence that telemotor pressure had ever been applied in the first place. Capts Nicholson and Hart were rebuked for the decision to tow the stern of *Thetis* against the tide:

> …we cannot find anyone directing the operation at this time who had any clear idea with what object they were employing this rather drastic method of lifting the stern. There was a general impression that a hole was to be cut but where exactly it was to be cut was not decided and the burning gear had not yet arrived…to try and tow the tail up was unsound and certain to fail and the alternative of a vertical lift should have been tried.[79]

Yet with hindsight, we can see that buoyancy would have been lost just as surely in the course of a vertical lift. Air would have escaped and water would have flooded in with every probability that the securing wire would have proved just as unequal to the strain. The solution did not lie in a vertical lift any more than it lay in towing against the tide, because without adequate support and cutting gear to hand, there simply had been no answer to the crisis. And Rear Admiral Raikes knew it.

All told, the internal inquiry deflected scrutiny away from procedures, directing it instead upon the individuals concerned, but the promised public inquiry was likely to be more wide ranging. Raikes now drew up a memo, anticipating five potential lines of criticism. This document, circulated within closed Admiralty circles, is the key to unlocking the disaster. Raikes was a perceptive man who knew his trade. Without directly criticising Subsmash, he nevertheless highlighted aspects closely related to the operative AFOs:

'Why were camels not sent to the approx. location of Thetis rather than waiting for her to be found?'
'Why were deep sea divers not sent earlier and why was no equipment provided?'
'Why were so many extra people on board the boat?'
'Why had the reporting of the marker buoy been so inaccurate?'
'Had reliance upon DSEA rather than salvage been misplaced?'

On 15 November, an impressive array of naval gold braid gathered at the LMS Dock to formally inspect the wreck. With them went Mr Watters and Foreman Black of Cammell Laird and Mr Rolland of the AEU. They confirmed that the bow-cap of No.5 Tube was wide open. Had Rear Admiral Raikes known about it, he would doubtless have added another question to his list: *Who* had been responsible for opening the tube and *when* was it opened?

In November 1939 a salvo of memos ricocheted between Admiralty and Whitehall. Admiralty urged that in wartime the future inquiry should hear evidence in private. It should be stressed that Admiralty was motivated by pragmatism, a desire to expedite the affair, rather than some conspiratorial instinct to hide the truth. With Britain fighting for its very survival, the Royal Navy felt it had better things to do than deliberate in a court room. The First Sea Lord took a different view; after all there was cross-party political support that an open inquiry was in the public interest. Acting on behalf of civilian dependants, the trade unions had already signalled an intention to sue Cammell Laird and, if possible, Lt Woods. It was not difficult to anticipate the howls of moral indignation that would arise from Fleet Street at any suggestion that the hearing be suppressed. In the words of the senior Admiralty lawyer Mr Synnott: 'the onus of proof is on the Admiralty: this department has little to gain and something to lose by continuing but on the other side there is a great deal to lose by discontinuing.'[80]

The Tribunal commenced on 3 July 1939 under Mr Justice Bucknill and the examination of witnesses was fully reported in the press. Bucknill was aware of the Raikes Inquiry findings but decided to follow his own interpretations. Bucknill identified six factors contributing to the loss of *Thetis*:

- The blocking of the test-cock on No.5 tube door
- Opening the rear door to No.5 tube when this tube was itself open to the sea
- Inability to secure the watertight bulkhead door in the fore-ends
- Failure to surface the submarine
- Failure to provide outside assistance
- Failure of those trapped within the submarine to escape

From the outset it became clear that Bucknill's civilian Tribunal was following a very different tangent from the lines of criticism identified by Raikes, the naval insider. While the examination of witnesses was fully reported in the press, Bucknill kept a firm grip on counsels' line of questioning. Nevertheless the dubious standards of civilian and Admiralty dockyard inspection regimes were laid wide open to public scrutiny. While the Royal Navy as an organisation enjoyed the privilege of crown immunity, Cammell Laird and its sub-contractors were exposed to legal action from civilian dependents, as were certain individuals – providing negligence or dereliction of duty could be established.

Bucknill sought to address the questions relating to torpedo tube No.5, specifically *when* had it been opened and *who* had been responsible for opening it? Either the cap had been opened by civilian workers back in the Wet Dock or, alternatively, it had been opened by the fore-ends personnel while at sea. Here the testimony of the embattled Lt Woods swayed Bucknill. Lt Woods gave evidence that shortly after ordering L/S Hambrook to open up pressure on the bow-caps, he had personally examined the bow-cap indicator dials situated between the tubes. All had been in the 'Shut' position. The implication being that No.5 bow-cap could not have been opened before this point. In Bucknill's words: 'The answer therefore to the question: When was the bow-cap opened? is that it was opened after the power was turned on not many minutes before the accident but that there is no reliable evidence establishing the time more precisely than that.'

L/S Hambrook was the last man known to have operated the bow-cap operating levers. Weighing up the balance of probability, Bucknill offered this scenario:

> It is possible … that the bow-cap crept open: that the creep started when the power was turned on at the request of Lt Woods and continued until the bow-cap was wide open and that the lever was then put into the 'Neutral' position in which it was found when Thetis was raised…Possibly during the morning No.5 lever was moved towards the 'Open' position sufficiently for the bow-cap to start creeping open as soon as the power was turned on…This explanation involves the conclusion that L/S Hambrook did not put the lever effectively to 'Shut' or find it at 'Shut' after the power was turned on to it, and that he must have put it from the creeping position to the 'Neutral' position in which it was found.

Now Hambrook's widowed mother, Matilda, as legal *executorix* of her dead son's meagre estate, joined Sybil Bolus and Lt Woods as the targets for legal action. Bucknill however added a caveat for anyone tempted to blame the dead Torpedoman:

> To decide that he [Hambrook] pushed the lever to 'Open' and thereby opened the bow-cap solely because he was, according to evidence, the last man to have attended the lever, would be to guess and to guess in so grave a matter and in his absence, would be unjust…it may be this theory is not the right one. The truth may lie in some fact which has escaped all those who have tried to solve the problem.

One flaw in Bucknill's reasoning is that as Warren and Benson pointed out, the opening of the bow-cap would have been clearly audible and instantly recognisable to the men in the fore-ends for several minutes as the ram went through its motions. It defies credibility to suggest that L/S Hambrook, ERA Howells and PO Mitchell would not have been alerted. Bucknill was unaware of the highly irregular but depressingly common practice described by Capt Shelford, author of 'Subsunk', of filling tubes directly from the docks rather than via the time-consuming filtered WRT system. Once flooded in this fashion, the tube operating levers may have been returned directly to the 'Neutral' position without having first been taken through the 'Shut' gate. In these circumstances the bow-cap would have been open from this point onwards. Shelford argued that flotsam may have become lodged under the cap. In these circumstances the tube controls would have indicated that the cap was safely closed when it was actually wedged open. The civilian workers (and their trades union outriders) blamed the submariners and the submariners (reinforced by their own establishment supporters) blamed the dockyard workers. All that can be said is that the mystery of No.5 bow-cap remains.

Bucknill was astonishingly restrained when it came to institutional criticism, in particular with regard to the systemic failure to provide outside assistance to the stricken *Thetis*. Capt Ruck-Keene, architect of AFO 568/34, was briefly called to explain the grounds for adopting the Subsmash policy. Ruck-Keene recounted that the fruitless attempts to raise *M2* had demonstrated 'that salvage could not be accomplished in time to save life was reinforced by the views held by the American authorities.'

This was quite correct; the Americans had indeed downgraded salvage. What Phillip Ruck-Keene did not mention was that, unlike the British, the Americans had additionally invested in the McCann Diving

Bell, thus offering their submariners a fighting chance in circumstances when the Momsen Lung escape set could not be used. Moreover, as the entire world knew, a diving bell had been used to save most of the crew of the USS *Squalus* a mere week before the *Thetis* disaster.[81]

Although fully briefed on the potential of DSEA and its role in shaping Fleet Order 568/34, Bucknill's summing up made no reference whatsoever to the successful proactive *K13* rescue of 1917. There was no censure of the Royal Navy's passive submarine rescue policy, nor were there any directives regarding future submarine diving trials, though Bucknill's deliberations would ultimately lead to the establishment of the Nasmith Committee. The fact remained that Cammell Laird, the Mersey Docks and Harbour Board and the Royal Navy had escaped any real criticism. In fairness, Britain was at war and with national survival at stake, Bucknill was at pains to ensure that his Tribunal should not apportion blame to any individual. The hearing ended in December 1939. The case on *Thetis* was now closed. It was time to get on with the war. The findings of the Tribunal were presented to First Sea Lord Winston Churchill in February 1940, eliciting the following response:

FIRST SEA LORD'S PERSONAL MINUTE SERIAL NO.194
All interest in this tragedy has now been submerged by the war. I should deprecate any disciplinary action [being taken] unless some definite act be traced to an individual. Indeed I should be glad if Lt Wood's mind could be set at rest. I think the Second, Fourth and Fifth Sea Lords should look into this matter and advise what the Admiralty should say and do. They should also advise on publication. WSC.
First Sea Lord 12.2.40

Until this point the *Thetis* dependants, civilian and naval, had remained nobly united in dignified grief. Following the Tribunal, consensus broke down as civilian bereaved seized upon his findings as the basis of compensation test cases and a rather distasteful new chapter began. It is impossible not to feel profound sympathy for these dependants. Their men had been snatched away by a faceless authority. They believed that someone must be responsible and ought to be brought to account, even if in practice this meant directing legal action against naval widows and mothers as impoverished as themselves. It is profoundly unedifying to read of the appalling treatment meted out to the *Thetis* dependants in the years that followed. Whether this treatment was any different to the shabby attitude displayed towards other armed service or civilian dependants who found themselves caught up in an inter-war catastrophe, is rather more open to question. Aided by the engineering unions, Rose Duncan and Mabel Craven brought actions against Matilda Hambrook, Sybil Bolus and Lt Woods. In October 1943 Justice Wrottesley dismissed the negligence cases against the individuals but issued a reserved judgement against Cammell Laird. A welter of appeals and cross-appeals followed. The Court of Appeal reversed the Wrottesley judgement by dismissing the claim against Cammell Laird, while conversely upholding the actions against Woods and Hambrook. Finally, on 27 February 1946 the law lords overturned this judgement by ruling that the *Thetis* disaster had been a non-negligent accident. No individual liability could be established. Once and for all, nobody was to blame.

The later history of *Thetis* lies largely outside the remit of these pages and a brief outline must suffice. Once rebuilt as HMS *Thunderbolt*, she was handed over to the command of the no-nonsense Cecil Crouch, who proceeded to assemble an equally hard-headed crew, all volunteers. In November 1940 *Thunderbolt* joined the 3rd Flotilla at Holy Loch for operations in the Biscay sector. Crouch set a blistering pace, torpedoing the Italian submarine *Tarentini* on *Thunderbolt*'s first patrol. The boat spent several months escorting convoys in and out of Halifax NS but on 8 July 1941 *Thunderbolt* was ordered to the Mediterranean theatre. The boat, based successively in Alexandria and Malta, enjoyed a successful commission as her Jolly Roger preserved at the Submarine Museum testifies. On 27 March 1942 the boat arrived back on the Clyde as prelude to a refit at Blyth which lasted until May.[82] By December 1942 *Thunderbolt* was back in the thick of the action at Malta.

On 2/3 January 1943 the boat participated in the ill-fated chariot carrying mission named 'Operation Principal' against Italian battleships in Palermo. On 9 March *Thunderbolt* left Malta for her new base in Algiers, with orders to patrol the Straits of Messina en route. Hunting between Marittimo and Cape San Vito, she accounted for *Estorel* on 12 March but Italian escorts were in hot pursuit, the corvettes *Libra* and *Cicogna* claiming to have gained, lost then regained contact with *Thunderbolt* over a three day period. *Cicogna* allegedly spotted the periscope of *Thunderbolt* at 0854 on 14 March, responding with a barrage of twenty-four depth-charges in position 38.15'N, 1515'E. For the second time in her story, that infamous stern was seen to momentarily break surface at a sharp angle before disappearing forever, taking Lt-Cdr

Cecil Crouch DSO★ and sixty-one men with her.[83] In 1991 divers found her remains lying at a depth of 60m. They were able to identify her from a plate bearing her works number.[84]

Thetis cast an intense shadow over all involved, though in some cases, not a long one. Richard Coltart, roundly criticised for his tardy response in raising the alarm, died in 1940 when his command H49 was destroyed by German warships. L/Tel Victor Crosby, who had been present with Coltart on Grebe Cock, was lost in the submarine Saracen in 1943. For the remainder of his life Wreckmaster Charles Brock was dogged by the belief that far more could and should have been done to save the men trapped in Thetis. Capt Oram returned to General Service, joining the cruiser Hawkins. As we know Oram had made his escape with the very best of intentions but at face value it does not look good when the first man to leave a stricken vessel is the senior officer and Oram was stigmatised. In mid-1943 Oram left Hawkins for appointment to a training role at a time when the Royal Navy was undergoing unprecedented expansion in preparation for the Normandy landings. It was largely due to Oram's training regimes taught at HMS King Alfred and other establishments that the Royal Navy was able to respond to the challenges forced upon it by massive expansion. He never did receive the kind of recognition that a senior officer with his achievements might expect. In his ninetieth year and shortly before his death in 1986, Oram finally broke his silence with his autobiography The Rogues Yarn. It contains little evidence of bitterness.

Despite his experiences, Walter Arnold opted to remain within the Submarine Service and found himself drafted to the much depth-charged Spearfish at Blyth, but a subsequent change of heart resulted in a draft back to General Service and the cruiser HMS Fiji. Walter Arnold survived both the sinking of Fiji and the Second World War to die in 1974. The books of David Roberts are recommended for those who wish to know more about the later life of this extraordinary man. Frank Shaw returned to a life of middle class anonymity in Tranmere. He continued to work for Cammell Laird. Frank may have preferred to forget about the Thetis disaster and rarely spoke about his experiences but for many years attended the annual commemoration at Holyhead. Frank Shaw died on 14 January 1981 at the age of seventy-three.

Of the Thetis survivors, none suffered more than Lt Woods. He too returned to General Service, first to HMS Norfolk then to the destroyer HMS Worcester, where he soon found himself the object of speculation and contempt. The prejudice against Woods had a sinister edge. A letter in the Submarine Museum Archive indicates that the captain of Worcester would not even speak to Lt Woods directly. Yet if brother officers ostracised him, evidence collected by Gus Britton suggests that Woods was a caring officer, empathetic with, and respected by, the lower deck. Nor did he lack courage, for he was awarded a DSC for his work at the Dunkirk evacuations. At the end of the war, Woods was appointed to the staff of the Commander-in-Chief (Mediterranean), just three months after learning of his total exoneration at the hands of the law lords. Lt Frederick Woods died in May 1946, following a car crash near Toulon. He was buried at sea. Lt Woods could accurately be described as the last victim of HMS Thetis.

As a direct consequence of the Bucknill Tribunal, Thetis once again entered the life of Admiral (S) Martin Dunbar-Nasmith when the latter agreed to head a committee appointed to look into improving underwater escape. Dunbar-Nasmith re-affirmed that the policy of reliance upon DSEA rather than salvage, must continue. Despite the lessons of Thetis, salvage and DSEA would not co-exist.[85] Dunbar-Nasmith additionally recommended that a safety clip be fitted to all torpedo tube doors to prevent such a disaster ever happening again. This was a single clip which prevented the tube door opening more than a fraction when the lever moved from 'Shut' to 'Open'. It was called the 'Thetis Clip' and remained in use for many decades. The Nasmith Committee also pointed out the inadequacies of the 15ft-deep tank at Blockhouse and advised that a much deeper tank be built (this was not carried out until 1953). There was one further consequence. Claustrophobic escape chambers were phased out in favour of a return to the collapsible twill trunk system. The twill trunk remained the standard escape method used in British submarines throughout the war. Not until 1946, with the formation of a second panel (with what some might regard as delicious irony) chaired by Phillip Ruck-Keene, were the broader implications of the Thetis disaster upon submarine escape strategy fully considered. Its recommendations were to shape British submarine safety policy and practice throughout much of the twentieth century but they lie outside the scope of this account.

THE ADMIRALTY REGRETS…

Bucknill was a decent and humane man. The reader might like to reflect on the fact that a wider web of secrecy surrounded the losses of HMS/Ms *Vandal* and *Untamed* than ever encompassed *Thetis*. However, Bucknill was constrained by fact of wartime expediency coupled with his own innate sense of patriotic duty. The points raised by Admiral Raikes following his report were never publicly examined. It is now time for a reappraisal:

Why were so many extra people on board the boat?

There is abundant anecdotal evidence of a common, if unofficial, tradition in commercial yards for civilians to remain on board during submarine trial dives. 'The Story of our Submarines' by 'Klaxon' (Lt-Cdr J Bower) provides description of a similar trial from Barrow in 1916. The term 'supernumerary' is misleading. Most civilians were only present because of the dual control arrangements agreed by Yard and Navy. The only real civilian supernumeraries present on *Thetis* were the two caterers and Norman Willcox, the Mersey Pilot. The decision to permit these people to remain on board was made by Bolus alone. Hence the targeting of Sybil Bolus as *executorix* in the civil actions following the Tribunal. The large number of extra Service personnel carried that day was present because as Admiralty knew full well naval protocol demanded they be invited. A second group of officers from *Taku* and *Trident* was there for training purposes. With the benefit of hindsight, we may doubt the wisdom of Bolus in allowing so many extra personnel to participate in the dive but it was a widespread practice condoned by Admiralty.

Why had the reporting of the marker buoy been so inaccurate?

A submarine marker buoy of the period looked much like the buoys carried by fishing boats – especially when observed from an aircraft flying at 200mph from a height of 8,000ft. The first aircraft fix was reasonably accurate, the last was to send *Brazen* off in the wrong direction. It was just bad luck. If only the navigator had stuck with his first fix. To paraphrase Warren and Benson, in the final analysis the *Thetis* story constitutes a distressing series of 'if onlys'. If only the ASDIC dome had not been damaged. If only Coltart had acted sooner, if only Cammell Laird or the Mersey Harbour Board had requested the use of *Ranger* on 1 June. If only Liverpool Bay had not been subject to tidal surges. If only Hart had ordered his camels to the scene on 1 June. If only the Admiralty had developed a submarine rescue strategy worthy of the name… The events leading up to the discovery of *Thetis* constitute a series of mishaps which on their own need not have been fatal, but in this instance fell into a deadly alignment. Above all, it must be understood that the *Thetis* disaster was a freak accident. This does not mean her predicament could not have been foreseen and contingency plans laid for such an eventuality.

Why were deep sea divers not sent earlier and why was no equipment provided?

It is an incontrovertible fact that the stern remained exposed from the time of its discovery at 0800hrs to 1510hrs on 2 June 1939. AFO 569/34.6 (d) stipulated that *'HMS Tedworth is to embark six divers and necessary diving stores and remain at immediate notice'* but as we know, the imperative to coal forced *Tedworth* to divert to the Clyde before proceeding to the Mersey. Had the *Tedworth* divers and their equipment been flown to Speke as soon as Subsmash was transmitted, it is possible that armed with their knowledge of submarines, they could have succeeded in fixing a high pressure air line to the boat. With this air line in place and the fore-hatch secured, the planned salvage blow could have taken place. None of those in command of the operation requested that the divers be flown to the scene. Warren and Benson argued that the absence of RN divers was a major setback. Despite their undoubted skill and tenacity, it must be doubted whether these men could have defied the Liverpool Bay tides to achieve what others could not. Surviving logs reveal that the Metal Industries divers were constantly hampered by the tides during the later salvage operations. The *Tedworth* divers would have been equally constrained. The fact remains that whatever organisation the diver was from and whatever his level of experience, diving was only possible for a maximum of sixty minutes during slack tides. We will never know whether the *Tedworth* divers could have fixed an airline in the small time available. It is obvious that all concerned, including Bolus and Oram, underestimated the impact of the tides on diving operations. With this in mind it seems unlikely that the Bolus plan could have been made to work on 2 June.

It will be recalled that shortly after his arrival, Capt (D) Nicholson had given instructions for the *Somali* crew to conjoin destroyer air lines. The absence of a stable platform rendered drilling a hole in the stern, a dangerous prospect but preparations were well underway when the cutting gear finally arrived. In 1917 the men trapped in *K13* had been able to secure an air line fed in by rescuers. It remains highly debatable whether men who were by this stage incapable of responding to the frantic rapping of Messrs Brock and Orton, would have been sufficiently *compos mentis* to handle a high pressure line after the Arnold/Shaw escape, beyond 1000hrs. The window of opportunity for fixing a ventilation feed was a very narrow one, restricted between 1045hrs when the 6th Flotilla destroyers arrived and 1300hrs[86] when the tide began to turn. Fixing a ventilation feed during this phase was not merely the best hope of saving the trapped men, it was their *only* hope.

We must pose the question as to whether or not the absence of submarine expertise among those directing operations contributed to the outcome? Certainly an experienced submariner would have quickly recognised on the morning of 2 June that the absence of continuous escapes could only signify that something was preventing DSEA escape. Whether submariners could have persuaded those in command of the operation to disregard AFO 568/34 in favour of direct intervention at the earliest instance, is arguable. A ventilation feed would not have been available until 1130hrs when the *Somali* ERAs had produced an air hose of appropriate length.[87] Submariners could have directed Mr Brock in his heroic efforts to remove the manholes covering 'Z' tank. An experienced submariner would have recognised that the stern angle signified 'Z' tank had already been blown, thus posing no danger. If Charles Brock could not have ventured further without cutting gear, it may have been possible to create a hole using *Somali*'s drill, prior to introducing a dual ventilation feed. Submariners of any rank would doubtless have warned Capt Nicholson that hauling *Thetis* ever further out of the water was to invite disaster, by allowing the cushion of air keeping the boat afloat to escape. The lack of submarine expertise surely undermined rescue efforts and it is impossible not to draw parallels with the successful *K13* salvage. Unlike *K13*, however, there was none of the calibre or experience of Kenneth Michell or Godfrey Herbert to bully, cajole, plead and direct rescue operations.

Why were camels not sent to the approx. location of Thetis rather than waiting for her to be found?

Admiral Raikes ranked this as the most damning criticism that could be levelled against the Royal Navy (judging from the notes and comments in the file, Synnott evidently agreed) with good reason. The reader will recall that at 0554hrs on 2 June, Capt Macintyre on behalf of Rear Admiral (S) had requested that Admiralty send camels to the scene. It would have taken three hours for these salvage pontoons to reach *Thetis* but as we now know, Admiralty did not respond to this request because AFO 568/34 made no allowance for salvage. On first being alerted of the accident on 1 June, Capt Hart, acting quite independently of the Royal Navy ordered that camels be brought to readiness. Tragically he did not order them to sail. The Mersey Docks and Harbour Board camels rocked idly in Canning Dock. In fact the first camel did not arrive at the scene until 1800hrs on 2 June as a direct result of Capt Hart's 0855hrs request to the Mersey Docks and Harbour Board. Similarly the Liverpool and Glasgow Salvage Association's vessel *Ranger* equipped with powerful cutting gear remained in the Mersey.

Herein lies one of the most disturbing facets of this terrible story. Correspondence reproduced in Appendix 3 provides evidence that the Liverpool and Glasgow Salvage Association was only alerted to the crisis at 0400hrs on 2 June, when it was asked to provide a recompression chamber. Despite assertions to the contrary made by Admiralty to the Raikes Inquiry, George Critchley affirms that at no stage had the London and Glasgow Salvage Association been contacted by Admiralty on 1 June.

This is of crucial importance because as the letter between Critchley and Raikes makes clear, had the Liverpool and Glasgow Salvage Association been informed of the situation once *Thetis* was declared missing, *Ranger* could have been at the scene by 0600hrs on 2 June. Memos in the Raikes Board file indicate that Synnott and his team of Admiralty lawyers greatly feared the consequences should George Critchley offer this evidence to the Bucknill Tribunal and the latter's failure to testify must rank as one of the greatest mysteries of this appalling affair.

The author contends that had salvage vessels, camels and cutting gear been standing by in the vicinity of the last known position of *Thetis*, immediately Subsmash was transmitted, it is not unreasonable to suggest that welders could have worked on the supported stern from daybreak on 2 June. Had salvage been an option from the outset, Wreckmaster Brock could have breached 'Z' tank to reach the steering compartment beyond. Crucially, this ought to have been achievable within two hours. Under these circumstances, a ventilation feed could have been established between rescuers and trapped at an early juncture. With these factors in mind, the author believes that the *Thetis* disaster could and should have had a very different outcome.

Had reliance upon DSEA rather than salvage been misplaced?

If one single factor can be said to have doomed the trapped men, that factor was the non-interventionist Subsmash policy as adopted in 1932. Subsmash had failed dismally. Why? The reader is invited to contrast the documents in Appendices 1 and 2. AFO 568/34 dispensed with salvage simply because Admiralty believed DSEA offered the best chance of escape. Rather than adopt a twin track salvage and DSEA approach, Admiralty had placed all its eggs in one basket; a trapped crew must escape by DSEA or die. Admiralty had overlooked what now seems obvious to us and, in the light of *K13* and *M2*, should have been obvious to them, namely that trapped men cannot always escape by their own efforts. A series of freakish incidents had delayed discovery of *Thetis* and there were sound reasons why DSEA escape from the submarine had been delayed: the absence of rescue vessels in the vicinity, the imperative to drive the stern closer to the surface and the inability to bring the forward escape chamber into operation. Had Bolus permitted DSEA escape from the outset, he would have been sending men to certain death from drowning and exposure.

By waiting for the trapped men to escape by DSEA rather than opting for a more proactive approach, the rescuers inadvertently exacerbated the earlier delays. Yet, as we have seen, the rescuers were merely following the terms of AFO 568/34. Capt Oram and the other escapees had erroneously reinforced the belief that further DSEA escapes were imminent. The reader can surely only conclude that reliance in DSEA rather than salvage had, in this particular instance, been severely misplaced and as a result turned a serious accident into the worst submarine disaster in British history. The author believes that the rescuers did everything that could have been required of them. They were working within the confines of what transpired to be a profoundly flawed policy. By the time this passive policy was abandoned in favour of intervention, without supportive camels, the tide had turned decisively against a salvage operation. In short, the AFO in Appendix 1 would have saved the men, the AFO in Appendix 2 killed them. Interestingly, Admiralty did not rush to abandon AFO 568/34. On the contrary, it remained in force throughout the war and its impact upon the *Untamed* disaster is open to analysis.

Much has been made of the suggestion that efforts to cut into the stern of *Thetis* were curtailed because Admiralty, on the cusp of war, opted to preserve the integrity of the pressure hull rather than save the men within. The authors hope that material in this book will lay this allegation for good. The reader is invited to examine the extent of the rebuilding work carried out on *Thetis*. The post salvage transformation of *Thetis* to *Thunderbolt* can be traced through an examination of plans in the Cammell Laird collection and in the National Archive. Following salvage significant alterations were made to the pressure hull, including the rebuilding of the fore-ends. So much for prioritising the intact pressure hull. There is a more fundamental flaw in this save-the-pressure-hull-at-all-costs theory. In wartime a trained and experienced submarine crew is infinitely more valuable than the submarine they man, a fact appreciated by even the most Machiavellian Admiralty strategist. Those who persist in a belief in this theory might also reflect on the numbers of people who would have had to be involved in such a conspiracy. None of these institutions could be described as monolithic and how credible it is that none would have broken silence in the years that followed? However, the evasive behaviour of some of the organisations involved merely added to the sense that they had something to hide.

Cammell Laird sought to erase the shadow of *Thetis*. Managing Director Robert Johnson refused to allow the Royal Navy to return the boat to remove the bodies in the Laird Yard. The Company felt 'unable to assist' authors Warren and Benson in their research for 'The Admiralty Regrets' in 1956. The author is in possession of an authoritative booklet produced in 1960 entitled 'Cammell Laird and the Royal Navy', detailing the Yard's naval output between 1840 and 1960. It is perhaps telling that in this otherwise well-researched book, no mention whatsoever is made of *Thetis*.

The black mythology surrounding *Thetis* can be traced to one source in particular, Graf Michael Alexander's *SOS Thetis* of 1944 – a book published in Germany and bearing the heavy hand of Goebbels' propaganda ministry. Among a welter of unsubstantiated claims, Michael Alexander added a twist to the current rumour that Admiralty had prioritised saving the submarine above rescuing the crew, by outlining an insurance fraud allegedly hatched between the British Government and Cammell Laird. These conspiracy tales have one thing in common. They pre-suppose that events were controlled by a venal establishment but as we have seen, nobody was in control of events, not Nicholson, not Hart, not Oram, not Robert Johnston, not the Royal Navy, not the politicians, not Cammell Laird, not the civil service, not Neville Chamberlain, not even Jock Colville, whose throwaway observation has been given much weight by Tony Booth. The real explanation was far more prosaic. Events in Liverpool Bay unfolded according to their own fumbling logic. The only element truly in control was the tide. Be that as it may, the seed of conspiracy was sown and it fell on fertile ground in the post-war years, particularly in Merseyside, where the failure of the compensation test case encouraged a deeply rooted belief that the trapped men had been betrayed by the establishment. In a sense, they *had* been betrayed but in a more subtle manner than the conspiracy theories proposed. The reader may reflect on the reasoning behind AFO 568/34:

> The conference laid emphasis upon the psychological reasons against providing means to salve submarines for saving life and recommended emphatically that no provision should be made to salve submarines for the purposes of saving life, the DSEA being relied upon to fulfil this duty and that this should be the accepted policy. This recommendation was approved and the policy promulgated in AFO 568/34.

> Statement concerning the policy of submarine Salvage and Rescue Adopted and Promulgated in AFO 568/34 dated 19 June 1939.

The men who devised this policy were the products of a class-based caste system. They were myopic, certainly. Unimaginative, undoubtedly, but they were not monsters. For conspiracy theorists to maintain that officers with the calibre of Nasmith, Nicholson and Watson would have placed their own careers ahead of rescuing the trapped men and that, by extension, Admiral Raikes and Justice Bucknill were subsequently prepared to participate in such a travesty of justice, is as offensive as it is ludicrous.

The policy in question was drawn up with the very best of intentions. Subsmash, as it existed in 1939, was framed in the light of tragic experience. Salvage had worked for *K13* but it had emphatically failed the rest as this series testifies. The adoption of this AFO must be viewed within the framework of preceding submarine accidents. In the final analysis the author believes the courts broadly arrived at the correct conclusion, no *individuals* were to blame for this freak accident. All told, the tragedy exposed abundant evidence of institutional and systemic failure at all levels of both naval and civilian organisations. The rescuers stuck doggedly to the only guideline they had – AFO 568/34. By the time it became obvious that further DSEA escape was not going to happen and that it was time to 'think outside the box', it was far too late. In conclusion, the victims of *Thetis* were not murdered by a ruthless Admiralty intent on sacrificing the men to save the submarine, rather they died as a result of their lives having been entrusted to complacent naval and civilian hierarchies, operating an inadequate system of submarine rescue.

What of *Thetis* today? *Thetis* memorials of one sort or another are scattered throughout the country. These range from a plaque within the little chapel in Fort Blockhouse, to the Garnett Memorial Window in Clitheroe. *Thetis*-related material can be found in the Submarine Museum, while Fort Perch Rock and the Holyhead Maritime Museum both mount fascinating exhibitions. On 7 November 1947 an impressive memorial incorporating slate tablets bearing the names of the victims, surmounted by a cross and fouled anchor stele, was added to the mass grave in Holyhead. Each year, on the anniversary the loss of *Thetis*, the Submariners Association holds a memorial service here. But it is perhaps on the Mersey where the *Thetis* disaster is most keenly felt.

The bell removed from *Thetis* during salvage operations could, until recently, be found in the foyer of Derby House, Liverpool, while on the other side of the Mersey a fine memorial tablet has been placed within Birkenhead's Williamson Art Gallery and Museum. Cammell Laird has also passed into history now. The last vessel, HMS/M *Unicorn*, was launched in 1993 and the site is given over to mixed use. The giant Ship Construction Hall is still now and the slipways lead only to oblivion but echoes of Merseyside's proud shipbuilding heritage seem to haunt the very fabric of this place. The Engine Shop was torn down in 2006 but the adjacent Wet Dock where so much of this story took shape, is still very much in use and has been absorbed into Lairdside Marine Technology Park. No longer do hordes of overall-clad workers from 'over the water' disgorge at Green Lane Station, racing to clock on before the 0725 buzzer sounds. For much of its length, Green Lane has been renamed Campbeltown Road. The Royal Castle Hotel where civilian and submariner enjoyed an eve-of-trial celebration, is still there. The adjacent New Chester Road roundabout passes the site of the old Green Lane gatehouse block. Should you ever pass this way, spare a thought for Caroline Hole, Mary Gisborne, Sybil Bolus and all the other dependants who kept vigil at these gates throughout those terrible June nights so long ago.

'…Jack and dockyard matey, side by side.' Memorial within the tower of St Mary's, Birkenhead. (P. Armstrong)

Not all reminders of *Thetis* have been obliterated. If you mount the stairs within the tower of Birkenhead Priory, St Mary's Gate, set into the handrail above each step is a small metal plaque bearing the name of every man lost, Jack and dockyard matey, side by side. The views encompass Oxton Ridge, Bidston Hill and the much of the Wirral, but the keen eyed will see that the tower overlooks the site of No.1 slipway where HMS *Thetis* was conceived, born and strangely reforged.

It is not known who decided upon this memorial, but whoever chose, has chosen well.

FATALITIES OF HMS *THETIS*, 2/3.6.39

THE CREW

Allen, William, L/Tel., 26yrs	Jackson, Peter, ERA
Bambrick, Thomas, Stoker, 23yrs	Kendrick, Edward, AB
Batten, Francis, L/Sig, 24yrs	Kenney, Thomas, L/Stoker
Bolus, Guy, Lt-Cdr, 37yrs	Longstaff, Norman, AB
Brooke, Robert, L/Stoker, 26yrs	Luck, Walter, L/Seaman
Byrne, Alan, ERA, 31yrs	Matthews, William, Stoker
Chapman, Harold, Lt, 29yrs	Mitchell, Ernest, PO, 33yrs
Cornish, George, CPO	Morgan, James, AB
Costly, James, AB	Mortimer, Thomas, Tel.
Craig, James, Stoker	Ormes, William, CERA
Creasey, Jack, ERA	Orrock, William, Stoker
Crombleholme, Stanley, AB	Poland, William, Lt
Cunningham, David, L/Stoker	Read, John, L/Smn
Dillon-Shallard, H., Ch/Stoker	Rogers, Frank, AB
Dunn, Alfred, Stoker	Smith, Alfred, L/Smn

Feeney, James, L/Stoker
French, Howard, ERA
Glenn, Roy, Cdr (E), 40yrs
Goad, Theo, P O
Graham, Charles, Tel., 27yrs
Green, Sto, 25yrs
Hambrook, Wr, Act L/Smn, 29yrs
Harwood, George, PO
Hills, Albert George, Stoker
Hole, Wilfred, Stoker
Hope, John, PO Tel
Howell, Harold, ERA
Hughes, Joseph, PO Cook

Smithers, Cecil, TGM, 27yrs
Stevens, Stanley, AB
Stock, Francis, L/Steward
Turner, John, L/ Smn, 24 yrs
Wells, James, PO Stoker
Wilson, Thomas, AB
Yates, Albert, Stoker
Youles, Edward, L/Stoker

OFFICERS OF SUBMARINES BUILDING AT CAMMELL LAIRD
Garnett, R., Lt Cdr (Holyhead)
Lloyd, Thomas, Lt-Cdr, 33yrs
Ryan, Patrick, Lt (Holyhead), 28yrs
Jamison, Anthony, Lt (E) (Holyhead), 29yrs

NAVAL OFFICERS
Hayter, Reginald, Cdr (Holyhead), 38yrs
Pennington, Lionel, Cdr (E), (Holyhead)
Jackson, Stanley, Engineer-Capt, OBE
Henderson, Colin, Lt (E) (Holyhead), 25yrs

ADMIRALTY AND OVERSEEING OFFICERS
Aslett, W., 44yrs
Bailey, F. (Holyhead), 43yrs
Gisborne, E. (Holyhead)
Hill, A. (Holyhead)
Horsman, H. (Bebington), 47yrs
Hunn, L. (Holyhead)
Hillhorne, C.

EMPLOYEES OF CAMMELL LAIRD & CO. LTD, MANAGERS AND FOREMEN
Armstrong, J., 50yrs
Crout, R., 48yrs
Kipling, R., 38yrs
Owen, W., 32yrs
Robinson, A., (Landican), 46yrs
Rogerson, R., 27yrs
Watkinson, A., 50yrs
Beattie, W., (Bebbington), 45yrs

ELECTRICIANS
Broad, S., (Bebington), 38yrs
Chinn, A., 25yrs
Hamilton, C., 36yrs
Lewis, E., (Holyhead), 29yrs
Smith, W., (Holyhead), 18yrs
Summers, G., (Flaybrick), 33yrs

ENGINE FITTERS
Bresner, F., (Bebington), 55yrs
Brown, W., 32yrs

Eccleston, H., (Bebington), 38yrs
Griffiths, J., (Rake Lane), 39yrs
Homer, R., (Overpool), 33yrs
Page, J., 41yrs
Quinn, P., 36yrs
Smith, C., (Rake Lane), 27yrs

SHIP FITTERS
Craven, A., (Flaybrick), 39yrs
Scarth, G., 37yrs
Watterson, W., (Holyhead), 35yrs

EMPLOYEES OF VICKERS-ARMSTRONG LTD
Ankers, T.
Cragg, H.
Tyler, D., (Holyhead), 42yrs
Young, J.

EMPLOYEE OF BROWN BROS & CO. LTD
Duncan, D., 27yrs

MERSEY PILOT
Willcox, N., (Woodchurch) Carlaw Road, Trenton, 25yrs

EMPLOYEES OF CITY CATERERS (LIVERPOOL) LTD
Bath, W., 47yrs
Dobells, G., 63yrs

WRECK SITE

Today *Thetis-Thunderbolt* lies on a sandy-gravel seabed, in a general lowest astronomical depth of 56m, off St Vito lo Capo in Sicily. She is upright, but listing to port with the top of the boat standing 5m high. The casing has largely gone but the boat shows obvious evidence of depth-charge damage in both the control and engine rooms. It is clear from the shattered condition of the wreck that, at least on this occasion, those within died instantly.

SOURCES

ADM 1/8774/112 Change in Admiralty Salvage Policy
ADM 53/107837
Internal Inquiry into loss of HMS *Thetis* ADM/116/3817
Bucknill Inquiry
ADM 116/4115 No.194, ADM 116/4311, ADM 116/4429, ADM 116/4115, ADM 116/319-22, ADM 116/3817-3820 Treasury Solicitors File TS 32/166
The Times, Hansard
Thetis Down, Tony Booth, Pen and Sword, 2009
Thetis – Secrets and Scandal, David Roberts, Avid Publications, 1999
The Admiralty Regrets, C. Warren and J. Benson, Harrap, 1958
'Close Enough to Touch', BBC Radio 4, 1997

CHAPTER THREE

U-BOAT CREW RANKS/RATES 1914–1945

'As boys they dreamed of being heroes, as men they prayed they'd survive' – so ran the billing for the 1982 film *Das Boot*. The doomed *U 96* slipped out of La Rochelle and into immortality with 'Herr Kaleu' Prochnow and propaganda journalist Herbert Gronemeyer on her bridge. Historians may take issue with aspects of the Petersen film (and the Buchheim novel) but a non-German audience was confronted with a somewhat challenging and unfamiliar notion. Here the U-boat men were not portrayed as mindless Nazi automatons but rather as decent, flesh and blood individuals caught up in a tragic maelstrom of events, one they were scarcely able to comprehend, let alone influence.[88] Fiction aside, who were the real U-crews? Where did they come from? Historians Jak Mallman-Showell and Timothy Mulligan have brilliantly analysed the background and ideology of Second World War *U-boot Fahrer* and the reader seeking to learn more is urged to read their work. Here there is scope to make only a few broad points about these men.

There is a fascinating elliptical pattern common to both wars. At the outset of hostilities the *U-bootwaffe* is a small professional elite, the cream of the German Navy. German naval planners in both wars were confronted with an identical dilemma in their efforts to balance quality of manpower against the overwhelming demand to provide sufficient numbers of trained U-crews to prevail against Britain. As the *U-bootwaffe* expanded so the character and organisation of U-crews changed over time. The ratio of conscripts to regulars reached its tipping points in 1917 and 1941 respectively. Thereafter the service became dominated by men who may not have chosen to become U-boatmen, yet nevertheless felt compelled to do their duty in the highest traditions of the service. Let us start by considering the men who served in the *Waffe* at the outbreak of the First World War.

Rossler tells us that at the start of the First World War the *U-bootwaffe* had forty-five boats and a strength of 1,400 men (but only 747 of these were classified as operational crew). The first *U-boot-Fahrer* were skilled pioneers drawn mainly from the *Waffe*'s erstwhile parent, the Torpedo Divison. All had spent varying amounts of time training in the *U-Schule* at Kiel, run under the auspices of the U-boat Inspectorate. Recruitment had always been problematical for the authorities because U-boats demanded a higher ratio of skilled *unteroffiziere* (NCOs) to *mannschaften* (ratings) than did General Service. Following the creation of an independent *U-bootwaffe* in 1913, the service was free to attract key personnel by offering payments and perks such as the *Raumbeschrankungszulage* (hard lying allowance) and the *Tauchzulage* (diving allowance). By 1914 there was no shortage of volunteers and General Service wrung an agreement from the U-boat Inspectorate that all officers and *unteroffiziere* were to be returned to the surface fleet after a period of three to four years, lest the *U-bootwaffe* evolve into a service within a service. The pre-war *U-bootwaffe* was therefore an attractive and financially rewarding proposition for the man with the right skills.

As Germany expanded its armed forces, so the military authorities began to rely increasingly upon conscription as a source of manpower. All males between the ages of seventeen and forty-five were liable for conscription. The *KDM* had grown at a rapid rate. In 1897 there had been 26,000 men; by August 1914 this figure had risen to 80,000. Where did these men come from?

Rolf Guth's analysis of the 1913 naval intake denotes that 51 per cent of the conscripts were apprentice metal workers or '*schlosser*'; 21 per cent of the conscripts were from the traditional coastal recruitment areas fringing the North Sea and Baltic. These coastal areas were traditionally exempt from army conscription simply because the *KDM* regarded them as its own recruiting back yard, particularly for its *Seemanner* branch. Fishermen, boatmen and all others involved in maritime trades were fair game. As likely as not, these men would be absorbed into the seaman branch. All naval conscripts were expected to train and serve for two years prior to signing on as reservists. Ernst Hashagen recorded that Paulsen and Bening, successive *Oberbootsmen* in his boats, had both been the sons of Friesian fishermen. Only 28 per cent of the 1913 naval intake had been volunteers in the accepted sense.

We can reasonably expect that in 1914 *U-bootwaffe* manpower reflected these statistics. In both wars the German Navy had a seemingly insatiable demand for metal workers or 'schlosser'. The *KDM* was forced to cast a broader geographic net to catch these prized men. Evidence suggests that these apprentice electricians, mechanics, plumbers and engineers were often conscripted from the cities and industrial areas far away from the coast. However it is important to bear in mind that while a significant proportion of these men may have been conscripted into the *KDM* in the first instance, most if not all, volunteering for the *U-bootwaffe* from this pool of manpower would have been volunteers and rigorously selected at that. Thus the picture that emerges of the First World War U-boat crew profile is that of a *Seamanner* branch drawn from coastal states contrasting with the *Techniker* branch recruited from a much broader geographic area. In order to understand how these branches interconnected to forge a U-boat crew, it is necessary to understand organisation and function.

Figs 13-14 depict various U-crew profiles 1918–45. Each crew is divided into three categories based on function, namely *Offiziere* (Officers), *Techniker* (Technical Staff) and *Seemanne*r (Seamen). The Royal Navy operated a similar model, in its case divided between officers, seamen and engine room staff. The profiles can be further sub-divided into specific *laufbahn* or career tracks such as *Mechaniker* (Torpedo mate), *Matrose* (Seaman), *Heizer* (Stoker), *Funker* (Telegraphist), *Maschinist* (Artificer). In turn it is possible to examine these *laufbahn* vertically according to rate and seniority. For instance the lowest rate of the seaman's *Laufbahn* was the *Matrose* (AB), the highest being the *Oberbootsman* (CPO). Now let us examine the components starting with the commissioned officer.

There were traditionally two kinds of officers within the *KDM* – *Seeoffizier* and *Ingenieur*. The commanding officer of a U-boat usually held the rank of either *Kapitänleutnant* or *Oberleutnant zur See*, the suffix indicating his status as a *Seeoffizier* or 'line officer'. An officer *kadet* committed himself to the navy for twenty-five years. There was one annual intake of 200 *kadets* at Murwik, referred to as a 'crew'. For example all *kadets* accepted into the *Reichsmarine* in 1909 were titled 'Crew 09'. Mulligan quotes a survey carried out in 1907 indicating that 46 per cent of all naval cadets in the survey had fathers in academic professions, 26 per cent came from naval families with just 11 per cent originating from an aristocratic background. Despite the incidence of 'vons' in our crew lists, the patrician outnumbers the aristocrat. We can say with certainty that naval *kadets* largely came from all areas of the country, i.e., Prussia, Bavaria, Saxonia... and were mainly Protestant (the Prussian-dominated *KDM* having a lingering aversion to Catholic officers). Furbringer (Vol.1) was a naval brat with a brother, Gerhardt, who was also serving in U-boats. Hashagen (Vol.2) originated from an old Schleswig-Holstein whaling dynasty. Both Furbringer and Hashagen joined U-boats to see action with the intention of achieving command at an early age, something that may have proved difficult in the faction-ridden wardrooms of General Service. Klaus 'Lala' Lafrenz also came from a military family. Lafrenz felt stultified by the petty discipline and pointless regulations in General Service. His response was to seek an appointment to U-boats. 'In U-boats,' he later told his British captors, 'nobody looks too closely at your mess bill or your gambling debts because they really don't think you'll be coming back'. The officer training course at Murwik remained the standard education establishment for naval officers in both wars and the course is worth looking at in detail.

An officer candidate faced a few weeks of basic training similar to that endured by all recruits. This training was designed to teach how to wear the uniform, the correct way to salute, how to march, basic shooting/cleaning of weaponry, handling of grenades and digging of trenches. Once this ordeal was over, training began in earnest and usually commenced with three months spent learning seamanship the hard way on one of the *KDM*'s training vessels. The curriculum included knot tying, sail mending, elementary navigation, small boat handling, watch-keeping, rigging of hammocks and scrubbing of decks. Successful completion saw the candidate return to that sprawling red brick *alma mater* of the German Navy, the Murwik *Marineschule* near Flensburg for a year or more of study. Instruction in weapon technology and propulsion systems was intense, amounting to over forty-six hours per week of classroom study followed by examinations. There was time to inculcate the *esprit de corps* of the *KDM*. The curriculum included team sports, fencing and horse riding along with lessons in grooming and etiquette. The *KDM* officer was a gentleman of considerable social standing with values to uphold. The service retained the right to veto the officer's choice of wife should she fail to reach accepted moral standards.

Theoretical training was followed by the 'world cruise' as the *kadets* embarked on a cruiser or large warship, leaving Germany for nine months to a year, visiting foreign ports ranging from Shanghai to Boston with a view to broadening their experience of the world. *Kadets* received practical training in their chosen *laufbahn*, engineers in the engine room, line officers on deck or in the wheelhouse. Voyage over, the *kadets* returned to Murwik for further instruction, evaluation and interminable examinations. The successful *kadets* dispersed for more specialised training followed by appointment to a warship. Theoretic instruction over, the *Fahnrich* was appointed to a warship for further practical experience. Unlike the British cadet, the *Fahnrich* was classed as an *unteroffizier*. Denied the wardroom, the *Fahnrich* was quartered among the petty officers. This was probably the most insightful training in man-management any prospective submarine officer could receive. Evaluated and probed at every step, the promising *kadet* was rewarded with increasing levels of responsibility until the happy day when the other line officers voted on his election to *Leutnant zur See* (Sub- Lt.).

A new *Leutnant zur See* opting for U-boats would face up to six further months, part sea-training, part theoretical instruction, at the Kiel *U-Schule* where hydrodynamics, propulsion systems, weapons training and *Drager* instruction was taught. One important departure from the British model should be noted at this point. While British cadets were required to select a specialism from gunnery, signalling, torpedoes or navigation, the German *kadet* received intensive training (and was expected to be proficient) in *all* these areas. This functional flexibility enabled the relatively seamless transfer of personnel from General Service to submarines as the *U-bootwaffe* expanded and training regimes became ever shorter.

Typically drawn from a *Mittelstander* (middle class) background, the *Ingenieur* was a gentleman who habitually got his hands dirty. *Ingenieur kadets* often dispensed with sail training and received theoretical instruction instead. In consequence neither the *KDM* (nor the *Kriegsmarine*) fully afforded commissioned engineers the status of line officers, and the cadets knew it. Comparatively few of these technicians secured positions of influence within the naval hierarchy; opportunities for advancement were equally limited. 'Papa' Thedsen, Dönitz's engineer officer in the Second World War being an obvious exception. The prejudice against engineering officers was to contribute to a dire shortage at the very time they were most needed, when the *Waffe* expanded in both 1917 and 1941.

The backbone of any U-crew was its knot of *unteroffiziere*. The U-boat inspectorate demanded that men moving from General Service to submarines be:

> … of good character and physique. They must be capable of enduring physical as well as mental strain. They must be free of cardiac or pulmonary disease. Men with complaints such as syphilis, rheumatism, fits, defective vision, skin diseases, arterial degeneration, oral sepsis, varicose veins or hernia, are to be rejected from the outset. Neither will the service suffer any officer or man with a history of alcohol abuse.

Any failure would result in a rapid draft back to General Service. Each of the trade branches (Figs 12-14) had its own sub-divisions, known as *laufbahn* or career tracks. Generally speaking (with the notable exception of the *Obersteuermann laufbahn* as *Obersteuermanner* tended to be selected from highly suitable *Oberbootsmanner*, i.e. men who had already been through *Laufbahn* I) once a man committed to his *laufbahn*, he would remain in that division for the remainder of his career. For instance it was not possible for a man to train as a *Maschinist* then decide he wanted to learn the art of the *Mechaniker* (Torpedo Mate) instead. *Laufbahn* I was the seaman's career track. After one year a humble *Matrose* could expect promotion to *Gefreiter* (Second World War). With the passing of a further year he would be eligible for rating as an *Obergefreiter*. Initial selection for *unteroffiziere* training required written recommendation from a commissioned officer. Candidates for *unteroffizier* status might spend up to three years serving as ratings, followed by study in a specialised trade school which might take up to a year. Career progression and the opportunities such gradation advancement brought varied with the *laufbahn* concerned but promotion to *unteroffizier* status invariably required a combination of theoretical and practical training combined with examination success. It would take four years to be rated as a *Maat*, with a further three years service to make *Obermaat*. Many *unteroffiziere* passed through the portals of the *Marineschule* at Friedrichsort. Here specialised training took place alongside classroom theory, nautical studies, drill and team sports. Prior to 1914 the *U-bootwaffe* would only consider men who were highly experienced in their trade. The course at the Kiel *U-schule* concentrated upon familiarising *unteroffizier* with the difficult technical operating conditions they could expect upon transferring to U-boats.

Marine colleges in Wilhelmshaven and Kiel turned *schlosser* or apprentice metalworkers into *Techniker*, the course culminating in an eventual draft to the engine room of a warship where a carefully structured career track modelled on that of the Royal Navy artificer followed. *Techniker* volunteering for U-boat instruction were skilled in the art of improvisation. The ideal *Techniker* was perhaps personified by *Maschinistmaat* Niklaus Jaud of *U 24* who specialised in casting minute, flawless engine parts at sea by pouring molten metal into moulds made of bread and asbestos packing. We can conclude that the forty-five U-crews who took to the seas under the *aegis* of the High Seas Fleet in August 1914 were an elite band of volunteer specialists, trained in relative peacetime leisure by the Kiel *U-schule*. Everything was to change with the coming of war.

The German U-boat campaign of the First World War is generally divided into four distinct phases; the initial purely naval phase lasting from the outbreak of war until February 1915; the first phase of unrestricted submarine warfare stretching from 4 February 1915 to 18 September 1915; the so-called 'lost opportunity' of 1916 followed by the second phase of unrestricted submarine warfare lasting from 1650hrs on 31 January 1917, to the end of the war. The early strikes of Weddigen, Hersing *et al* fired the imagination of the German public and numbers of young men felt sufficiently inspired to volunteer specifically for U-boats. Some like Karl Detlef Blunck originated from the sort of backgrounds in which volunteering for the navy would have previously seemed unthinkable. Blunck held the *Mittlere Reife* certificate and was destined for the civil service. Disgusted by the British naval blockade – 'a war against civilians' – Karl volunteered for submarines. Although he could easily have chosen a more rewarding *laufbahn*, Karl Blunck opted to train as a *Matrose* (seaman) because it offered the shortest route to active service.

Maschinist Karl Wiedemann had served in torpedo boats before the war but volunteered to join U-boats once hostilities commenced. He later recalled how in August 1914 the volunteers had been herded into the U-boat depot ship *Meteor* at Kiel. During the mornings they took part in 'day running' on *U 19*. From eighty skilled volunteers only Wiedemann was selected for U-boats. He was told to pack his kit and handed a manual on U-boat diesel management. This was the only specialised training for U-boats Karl Wiedemann was ever to receive. Not all volunteers were given the postings they expected. At the outbreak of war, Anton Seidel was an underaged boy sailor undergoing instruction on a training ship in Flensburg Harbour. The boys aged between fifteen and seventeen were presented with the option of returning home or remaining in the ship (providing parental assent was given). Seidel recalls that most opted to remain. Initially detailed for airships, Siedel found himself drafted to U-boats, observing that if he was unable to fight the enemy from above, at least he could attack him from below.

If the German people thrilled to the deeds of the U-boat crews, the string of early successes equally heightened awareness of the U-boat's potential amongst naval strategists. As the prospects of Germany mounting a U-boat blockade of her own around the British coast began to receive serious consideration, so attention became focussed on the numbers of submarines needed to mount such a blockade (pre-war analyst Lt Blum had famously calculated that 220 U-boats would be required for this enterprise). From 1915 the *U-bootwaffe* underwent expansion from twenty-six boats in August 1914 to 120 boats by September 1916, growing to 180 boats by October 1918 (with significant numbers under construction). Once Germany had decisively determined on a course of unrestricted submarine warfare in 1917, the implication was clear, an expanded *U-bootwaffe* was going to require a massive injection of manpower. One further factor entered the equation in mid-1916 as it now became clear that Jutland was unlikely to be repeated. There was to be no decisive North Sea battle fleet action. The High Seas Fleet was redundant but possessed one saving grace in that it could usefully provide a pool of trained personnel for the U-boats. In direct consequence, 1917 is usually cited as the year in which the balance tipped away from a pre-war trained U-boat elite in favour of a force dominated by conscripts and reservists.

The complements of warships laid up in the Jade Basin were scoured for potential U-boat personnel, among them twenty-eight-year-old *Obersteuermann* Fritz Marsal who was serving on a destroyer. Marsal, who had been present at both the Helgoland Bight Battle in 1914 and Jutland, was one of a tranche of seamen *unteroffiziere* transferred *en masse* to the *U-bootwaffe* in early 1917. Marsal would be captured by the British while serving on *UC 63* in November 1917 (see Vol.1). Naval intelligence observed that while he was not the most imaginative German sailor they had encountered, he was nevertheless 'highly proficient', his Admiralty intelligence interrogator noting, 'I hope there are not too many like him over there'. Actually there were quite a few. Notes on the interrogation of *maschinisten* captured from *UC 39* indicate they were well above average intelligence.

As reservists, many officers and men serving with the German shipping lines were duly absorbed by the *U-bootwaffe* expansion plans. Germany's small but elite merchant navy tapped personnel possessing advanced navigational and wireless skills. Bernard Haack, aged twenty-six, was acting *Obersteuermann* of the minelayer *UC 30*. Haack was a *Handelschiffsoffizier* (HSO) who had served on Hamburg tramps importing coal from the Tyne, the Wear and the Tees since the age of fourteen. Having first earned his navigator's ticket on a cargo vessel, Haack passed as *Maat* in 1910. Haack commenced a year-long stint of national service with the *KDM* in 1913, on the battleship *Hannover* as a *Matrose*. Following the outbreak of war, the *KDM* retained his services, rating Haack as *Obermatrose* in 1915. By the autumn all merchant seamen under forty possessing a *Maat* certificate were summoned to Kiel for further training in navigation and pilotage. Because of his knowledge of the North East, Haack was rated as a *Kriegslotse* or 'war pilot' for that sector. In April 1916 he allegedly took part in an instructional patrol in the Helgoland-based *U 76* to lay mines off the Farnes. Next came a bout of track-copying on the Wilhelmshaven depot ship, *Lenne*.

In August 1916 Bernard Haack was drafted (the term 'appointed' seems too delicate) to the *U-bootwaffe*, initially to *UB 35* operating off the Forth. Haack found himself cycled backwards and forwards between minelayers *UC 32* (Breyer) and *UC 31* (Stenzler) which regularly fouled Tyne and Wear. Haack would later tell his British captors that he had served in four different minelayers within the space of a year – evidence of a high level of *unteroffiziere* mobility. Haack (now rated as *Steuermannsmaat*) soon found that *KDM* line officers regarded even highly skilled reservists as children of a distinctly lesser god. On 25 January 1917, with the prize rules still in force, *UC 31* encountered a number of fishing vessels 45 miles east of the Farne Islands. The line officers handed Haack the unwelcome task of rowing alone to the British vessels with a view to blowing them up. The arrival of a patrol vessel forced *UC 31* to dive, leaving the unfortunate German in vengeful British hands. During interrogation Haack lied to his captors on several counts and he was certainly prejudiced against the *seeoffiziere* of *UC 31* but evidence gleaned from other sources reinforces the view that reservists faired comparatively badly in the *KDM* (as they often did in the Royal Navy).

The rate of *Obersteuermann* marks a fascinating departure from the Royal Navy model. Although it was possible for warrant officers to study for a 'navigation ticket' (King's Regulations 1913, Part XIII), in practice the Royal Navy would have it considered unthinkable to hand responsibility for submarine navigation over to an *unteroffiziere* but the *KDM* had no such qualms. Navigation, the calculation of an interception course and maintenance of trim calculations for the stowage of provisions were the responsibility of the most senior *unteroffizier* on the boat, the *Obersteuermann*. An *Obersteuermann* traditionally took third bridge watch, otherwise he spent his time in the control room bent over charts. Like Haack, many minelayer *Obersteuermanner* had formerly been merchant marine reservists. As previously mentioned, others were highly experienced *Oberbootsmanner* with a penchant for maths. This was the highest rank a seaman could aspire to. Although some of these valuable *unteroffiziere* were commissioned and rose to their own commands in the Second World War, rather ironically the only *Obersteuermanner* given this responsibility in the First World War were the men charged with sailing their boats over to Harwich for surrender in 1918.

At the beginning of 1918, largely through conscription, the *U-bootwaffe* was estimated to have an active strength of 11,400 men. By continuously cycling an estimated 15 per cent of *unteroffiziere* within each submarine crew, the *Waffe* was able to simultaneously expand while managing to retain a hard core of experienced personnel. The British first became aware of the widespread use of conscription in the *U-bootwaffe* following interrogation of the *U 48* crew in 1917 (Vol.1). As we have seen, veterans might be drafted to a boat for as little as three patrols, just enough time to pass on experience to a fledgling crew. Submarine training, particularly sea training, was cut alarmingly from three months to nil for seamen drafted from General Service.

A salient point perhaps ought to be made at this juncture which is true of both world wars. While there is abundant evidence of men being conscripted to U-boats after 1917 and 1941, there is no evidence that these men were compelled to serve against their will. The absolute interdependence of submariners means that a man who is serving in a boat against his will is a liability for all concerned. Mechanisms existed for drafting reluctant men from submarines back into General Service but these were rarely triggered. We can conclude that howsoever the men who fought the undersea war came to be serving in submarines in the first place, they remained because they wanted to remain.

Michelsen in *U-bootskrieg* estimated that 20 per cent of all non-commissioned personnel had received no submarine training whatsoever by 1918. Conscription, training cuts and the recycling of key personnel all played their part in enabling the *waffe* to cope with manpower dilution resulting from unparalleled expansion. Profile diagrams enable a useful insight into the organisation and composition of submarine crews. The U-boats profiled in Figs 13 to 15 have been selected at random from boats lost

FIG.13 DIAGRAM OF A UB III CREW (*UB 115*) *c*.1918			
Oberleutnant z.S.			
2 *Lts zur S* (Sub-Lts)		1 *MN ING* (Engineering Officer)	
(Seemanner)		*(Techniker)*	
1 *OB/STEUERMANN* (Navigator)		1 *OB/MASCH.ANW* (Engineering trainee)	
	1 *OB/BOOTSMANN* (CPO)	1 *MASCH.ANW* (Engineering trainee)	
1 *OB/* *MECHANIKERSMAAT* (TI)	1 *OB/MAAT* (PO)	1 *FT MT* (Tel) 1 *FT*	
	2 *OB/MATROSEN* (L/Seaman)	2 *OB/MASCHINISTMAATEN* (ERAs 2nd class)	
	8 *MATROSEN* (ABs)	4 *MASCHINISTMAATEN* (ERAs 3/4th class)	
		1 *OB/HEIZEN* (L/Stoker)	
		7 *HEIZEN* Stokers	

around the British coast as representative of typical cross sections of UB III and UC II crews in the final year of the war. *UB 115*, commissioned in May 1918 (see Vol.1), was a new boat lost on her first patrol while *UC 49* was a veteran minelayer commissioned in March 1917 (Vol.2). In both profiles crew members have been organised according to their status as Officers, Seamen or Technical specialists. Within the main divisions between *Seemanner* and *Techniker* the crews have been further sub-divided according to *laufbahn*. Officers are sub-divided into *Seeoffiziere* and *Ingenieur*. With regard to the rest of the crew, several *laufbahn* are evident: *Mechaniker, Matrose, Maschinist, Funker* and *Heizer*. The British equivalents of these career tracks are given in brackets. Sadly it has not been possible to ascertain the ages of the men concerned.

Warrant officers were given a special status within the *KDM*, known as *unteroffizier mit portepee* (sword knot). These senior POs can be distinguished by the prefix 'Ober' such as *Obermaschinist* within the *Techniker* category. It will thus be seen that the highly skilled warrant officers belonged to both *Seemanner* and *Techniker* divisions. Note: *Obermatrosen* and *Oberheizen* did not belong to this exalted group, rather they were leading rates, classed as *mannschaften* or ratings. The role of the *Oberbootsmann* can be compared to that enjoyed by a Royal Navy coxswain. One important difference was that during an attack the *Oberbootsmann* did not oversee the hydroplane controls, rather his place was in the conning tower alongside the commander. Nor was the *Oberbootsmann* the most senior *unteroffizier* on the boat, as mentioned previously, that title belonged to the *Obersteuermann*.

Each boat would have its quota of *unteroffizier ohne Portepee* or junior POs. These might range from *Obermaat, Bootsmannmaat* (seamen POs), *Funkmaaten* (Telegraphists) to *Mechaniker* (Torpedo Mates) through to *Machinisten* (ERAs). In the Royal Navy, Torpedo POs and Telegraphists tended to be grouped under the seaman branch but in the *U-bootwaffe*, all specialists came under the *Techniker* umbrella. The various differences between *Seemanner* and *Machinisten* could be expressed in subtle ways. The seaman wore a star badge on his trade shoulder while engine room personnel sported a cogwheel motif.

What do our case studies tell us? *UB 115* was reasonably well officered for a U-boat at this late stage in the war. *Oberleutnant zur See* Thomsen had the support of two line officers; the senior would

FIG.14 DIAGRAM OF A UC II CREW (*UC 49*) *c.*1918	
Oberleutnant z.S.	
Lt z S der RESERVE	*1 MARINE INGENIEUR ASP*
(Seemanner)	**(Techniker)**
OB/STEUERMANN/KRIEGSLOTSE (Navigator Reservist Officer)	*2 OB/MASCHINISTMAATEN* (ERAs 2nd class)
1 OB/ *BOOTSMANNSMAAT* (PO)	*5 MASCHINISTMAATEN* (ERAs 3/4th class) *1 FT MT* (Tel) *1 FT*
4 OB/MATROSEN (L/Seaman)	*3 OB/HEIZEN* (L/Stokers)
6 MATROSEN (ABs)	*4 HEIZEN* Stokers

be designated as IWO. *UB 115* (Fig.13) was fortunate in also having had a qualified Engineering Officer appointed to the crew. Readers familiar with the crew lists given in these volumes will recognise that more often than not, by 1918 a U-boat engine room was likely to be in the hands of a capable *Obermaschinist* or an as-yet-unqualified *Aspirant* rather than a commissioned *Ingenieur*. It will be observed that the officer in charge of the engine room of *UC 49* in Fig.14 was an *Aspirant*. *UC 49* was also in the hands of an *Oberleutnant zur See*, but the minelayer was a much smaller boat and notably deficient in commissioned officers. There are two reservist officers, one classed as a *Kriegslotse* or 'war pilot' because he possessed specialist navigational knowledge of the roads to be mined. As there was no third commissioned officer on board *UC 49*, the third watch would have presumably been taken by the *Oberbootsman*.

It was usual to find four trained gunners amongst the *Matrosen*. It is not clear whether the adoption of unrestricted submarine warfare led to a decrease in gunnery skills by 1918 but evidence contained in this book suggests not. *UC 49* had certainly destroyed vessels with her gun in previous patrols and *UB 115* may have sunk *Staithes* with shells. Torpedoes were the primary armament for *UB 115*, with the *Matrosen* working under instruction from the *Obermechanikersmaat*. *UC 49* carried no identified *Mechaniker* at the time of her loss but as this boat had accounted for *Warhilda* on her last patrol (and several more ships on previous patrols) presumably some of her *Obermatrosen* had received torpedo training.

Two *Funker* (Telegraphists) per crew was the norm for U-boats of the period and both case studies conform to this model. The usual arrangement was for a qualified *unteroffizier* to be assisted by a rating. Radio and wireless was in its infancy. Hydrophone technology was making rapid advances and the *Waffe* would doubtless have wished to equip the boats with more men but faced a shortage of trained and qualified *Funker* in both wars.

Engines like the hydrophones needed constant attention. The more routine, mechanical tasks were carried out by the *Heizer* or stokers usually under *Maschinist* supervision. Boats usually carried seven to eight stokers but three *Oberheizen* present in *UC 49* testifies to the boat's primary role as a minelayer, the maintenance, preparation and laying of mines being the responsibility of the *Heizer laufbahn*, a practice later emulated in the 'E' class British submarines.

Differing work patterns evolved over time. While the engine room staff and most *Techniker* worked a shift of six hours on, six hours off, the *Seemanner* branch and some of the *Techniker* worked a rota of eight hours of sleep, followed by eight hours of work plus a further eight hours of routine tasks which might range from torpedo maintenance to bridge watch. Bridge watch duty lasted four hours and would usually involve one watch officer and four lookouts. At least one of the lookouts would be an experienced *unteroffizier*. It was a hard life, particularly on watch in a North Sea storm, as *Obermatrose* Willi Schlichting describes:

Time to relieve the watch. Complete with oilskins and tarred cape, with a sou'wester on my head, I stand ready for the moment to clamber up from the control room up to the bridge. She is rolling from side to side like an old sea cow. My mate Hein is certain that my oilskins will not hold out for long, but we shall see. Now, in a brief moment between two oncoming waves I am through the hatch, greeted by grunts from the relieved watch, 'About sodding time too!'

I am met by spray from a breaking wave which bursts over me the moment I steady myself on the bridge. 'Damnably cold weather,' murmurs the officer. Day is turning into night and we are caught in a North Sea hissing, swirling witches cauldron. Down she goes. Up she rises like some berserk whale. We have to clutch the conning tower rail so as not to be washed overboard. Hailstones bombard us like artillery, stinging our faces and somehow penetrating our oilskins. Hein was right. I was frozen to the bone and frankly did not care whether I lived or died. Everyone else threw up but me. I was determined that Neptune would have no tribute from this sailor.

Even the longest watch comes to an end. My relief appeared and I stumbled blindly down the hatch and onto the back of the officer of the watch who was standing below. I lurched along to my bunk. A pallid face peeped out from one of the bunks and retched and retched. At this sight my own stomach began to turn again and I could barely contain myself. The atmosphere below was beyond description. The damp, warm, stifling air made me feel more nauseous than ever. Before I lay down I swallowed a little tea and glanced into the engine room. An appalling burst of heat flung me backwards. The thermometer read 45 degrees Celsius. The men were standing over their engines in the minimum of clothing and their drawn, gaunt faces smeared with oil looked like skulls. The air was unbelievable. The thudding diesel engines had exhausted such air as could be pumped in through the ventilators. Hot eddies of vapour hovered over the engines and gradually drifted to the other compartments; the men were continually mopping their foreheads and now and again one of them would sip the revolting lukewarm tea which, like all the food and drink on the boat, tasted strongly of oil.

I fled from this oil-reeking domain and tried to get some sleep in my bunk. Earlier the cold had been the cause of my discomfort. Now it was the foul air that made breathing a torture and would not let me sleep. Sweat broke from all my pores. I had tried to wedge myself in every conceivable position so as not to be hurled out by a sudden heave of the boat. Those five hours of 'rest' seemed more like eternal torment. The summons to 'Stand By to relieve the watch' came almost as a relief. Exhausted, shattered, without a wink of sleep, I hoisted myself from the bunk. As I made my way through to my post in the control room, I passed one of the old hands heartily tucking in to a plate of beans and bacon. To my poor sea sick belly, this was like a red rag to a bull. I couldn't help myself. I spewed up all over him.

Germany started the First World War with twenty-eight commissioned submarines and ended it with 180 U-boats. Dilution arising from such unparalleled expansion was inevitable. The evidence of service expansion can be found in the two case studies outlined above, one crew inexperienced, the other veteran, both pared down to their manpower limits. In conclusion we can never be certain what contribution, if any, the relative inexperience of many of the late war U-boat crews may have had to operational losses; there does not appear to have been any serious effect upon either morale – or performance. Despite sustaining a 51 per cent casualty rate by 1918 (5,132 died, 729 were captured) unlike the rest of the *KDM*, the *U-bootwaffe* remained a viable fighting force by November 1918. Moreover it had evolved into a distinct organisation animated by its own identity and inspired by its peculiar mythology, the flavour of which can be found in these post-war reminiscences:

Oberbootsmaan Oscar Wehner:

Only a sense of duty kept us going for love of our people, helping overcome our very real fears, and only the thought that we could help Germany in those desperate years gave us strength for the ordeal. Above all it was mateship that kept us going out on patrols. Never mind what those corrupt politicians and military idiots did, we kept going for each other.

Karl Neureuther summed up the 'U-boat spirit' with this address to a gathering of old submarine comrades in Munich in 1921:

What kept us going when all seemed lost? The profound sense of loyalty within a small group of men bound together by a common purpose. It was this community of labour, this absolute interdependence which fused all sections of a U-crew into an indivisible whole. It wasn't just me, the commander, who held the destiny of the crew in my keeping. No, even the most humble seaman or stoker held the fate of the entire crew in his own hands. Submariners of all nations know that moment when a man's life means nothing; we know those seconds when life hangs by a thread and survival is nothing more than a dubious 'maybe'. We know what it means when a man puts his life into the hands of his superiors, or those under his command, his brothers in arms – a little band of men isolated in enemy waters, far away from home. Looking back on it now, the experience taught us one thing which we should never forget, that in future men ought only to sacrifice themselves for what is worthy of that sacrifice.

On the last count he was to be very disappointed.

A famous *Kriegsmarine* recruiting poster *c*.1942 depicts a decorated U-boat officer in his best uniform standing before a U-boat under the legend, '*Freiwillig zur Kriegsmarine!*' (Volunteer for the Navy!). The story of U-boat recruitment in the Second World War is however far more complex than the image peddled by propagandists.

The Versailles Treaty forbad Germany from building U-boats and her remaining flotillas were surrendered to the allies. Germany was, however, allowed to retain a rump of a navy, now styled the *Reichsmarine*. Changes were made to the officer training regime that was to have implications for the generation who fought in the Second World War. Possession of the *Abitur* qualification was made a de rigeur pre-requisite for *kadets* but the *Abitur* rule was waived for otherwise qualified and experienced merchant marine officers, particularly those with an engineering background. Interestingly, several men who later became commanders, such as Prien and Bleichrodt, entered the *Waffe*, having earlier served in the merchant marine. The emphasis was now upon merit rather than social standing. Mulligan provides evidence from his Second World War statistics that although boys from patrician backgrounds still formed the majority of *Kriegsmarine* officers, they had been joined by increasing numbers from middle-class backgrounds. The ratio of middle class to patrician boys undergoing officer training would increase during the Nazi years but this was a revolution which began with the Weimar Republic, not with Hitler.

Under Admiral Raeder, who became commander of the *Reichsmarine* in 1928, the German Navy attempted to follow a strictly apolitical course. This did not mean that Raeder believed in following the dictates of the Versailles Treaty to the letter, particularly when it came to submarines. In 1932 a school for anti-submarine training opened within the grounds of Murwik (or, as the Nazis later renamed it, the *Marinekriegschule*). It was a front for submarine training where selected volunteers from General Service were schooled in hydrodynamics, hydrophone drill, propulsion systems and escape techniques. Sea training required submarines and Raeder proposed building sixteen small U-boats. A combination of German subterfuge and *entente* naivety enabled the Admiral's strategy to come to fruition before Hitler came to power. In 1935 Raeder selected his *protégé*, Karl Dönitz, to spearhead this U-boat revolution. Hitler was elected Chancellor in January 1933. Hitler's power base was largely in the army and the *Reichsmarine* (now styled the more belligerent-sounding *Kriegsmarine*) admirals regarded the Nazis with thinly veiled contempt. Nevertheless, Hitler held out the promise of social stability and as long as naval and Nazi objectives coincided in the form of a greatly enlarged fleet, the German Navy was content to overlook their extremism and do business with the new Chancellor and his boorish followers.

The foundations were now in place for a U-boat training infrastructure far superior to that which had existed during the First World War. The *Unterseebootsabwehrschule* was opened at Kiel in October 1933 with a second training establishment later founded at Neustadt in 1937. In 1940 the Neustadt school (1 *ULD* or *Unterseebootslehrdivision*) moved to Pillau and a third training establishment (2 *ULD*) opened at Gotenhafen. In 1935 the Weddigen Flotilla was formed at Kiel, consisting of the *Einbaum* (canoes) *U 7-U 12*. Meanwhile *U 1-U 6* were attached to Neustadt as training boats. Similarly, *unteroffiziere* training expanded with the founding of a new *Marineschule* at Wesermunde in 1935 followed by a third school at Plon in 1938. Dönitz himself devised the Kiel training programme, introducing interminable day and night simulated mock torpedo attacks.

Following the introduction of conscription laws in 1935, some form of military service became compulsory in Germany, where an annual intake of 12-14,000 men took place. From December 1936 participation in the *Hitler Jugend* or *Hitler Marine Jugend* became mandatory. Once six months' service in the *Reichs arbeitsdienst* had been completed, a German youth was compelled to register for military service.

Rather than be conscripted into the army, at this point many boys, faced with the inevitable, volunteered for the *Kriegsmarine*. To youth already indoctrinated in values of courage, adversity, nationalism and self-sacrifice, the prestigious *U-bootwaffe* had a ready appeal. Nevertheless, in the first instance the

FIG 15 DIAGRAM OF A TYPE VII CREW (*U 33*) *c.* 1940			
KAPLT.			
1 *OBLT z.S*		*OBLT ING* (Senior Engineering Officer)	
1 *LT.z.S*		1 *LT. ING.* (Engineering officer)	
(Seemanner)		*(Techniker)*	
1 *STABSOB/STEUERMANN* (CPO)		1 *STABSOB/MASCHINIST* (CERA)	
	1 *BOOTSMANN* (CPO)	5 *OB/MASCH* (ERAs 1)	
1 *MECH MT* (LTO)	2 *BOOTSMANNSMAAT* (POs)	1 *MASCH MT* (ERA 2)	
		1 *MASCH MT* (ERA 3)	
		1 *MASCH H/GFR* (L/Stoker PO)	
	1 *MTR H/GFR* (PO)	6 *MASCH OB/GFR* (L/Stokers)	
	4 *MATROSEN OB/GFR* (L/Seamen)	6 *MASCH GFR* (Stokers)	
	4 *MATROSENGEFR* (ABs)	1 *FK MAAT* (PO Tel)	
	1 *MATROSE* (Ord Sea)	1 *FK O/GFR* (Tel)	

recruit joined the navy and once accepted volunteered for U-boats. The *Kriegsmarine* could afford to be selective.

Naval recruits were required to be between the ages of seventeen and twenty-three and must be in possession of a *volksschule* certificate and provide details of any technical qualifications, linguistic skills or sporting achievements. A declaration of Aryan racial purity was now essential. Recruits from naval families or from a *schlosser* background were particularly prized but it was now the service, rather than the individual concerned, which selected the *laufbahn* each recruit would enter, based upon an assessment of his abilities. *Matrosengefreiten* signed on for a minimum of twelve years but men wishing to follow the *unteroffizier* career track were expected to commit themselves to a twelve-year minimum term. The statistics for naval recruitment in 1937 are interesting. Thirteen thousand men applied to join the *Kriegsmarine*. From this figure, only 33 per cent of those who later volunteered for U-boats were considered suitable.

Analysis carried out by Timothy Mulligan indicates that the typical U-boat volunteer of the late 1930s came from central Germany (Saxony having the largest number of volunteers among German states), was likely to be Protestant and more often than not came from a skilled blue collar background. The parallels between 1939 and 1914 are striking in that the *U-bootwaffe* consisted of a small, highly professional volunteer elite. The profile diagram in Fig.15 illustrates the crew organisation of *U 33*, one of the twenty-seven U-boats which started the Second World War in September 1939. Here we are concerned with the organisational structure of this Type VIIC crew at the time of its loss in 1940. First some name changes.

It will be seen that the *Marine Ingenieur* of 1918 has been replaced by an *Oberleutnant Ing* or *LI*. The changes extend to the lower deck where the simple *Matrose* has been replaced by the more aggressive sounding *Matrosengefreiter*. *Matrose* is now reserved for the most junior of the seaman branch. The old name *Heizer* has slipped into history; engines are now tended by *Maschinengefreiter*.

Hans-Wilhelm von Dresky (Crew 29) had earlier served as Watch Officer on *U 20* between February 1936 to September 1937, prior to promotion as *Kapitänleutnant* on 1 August 1938. Von Dresky (aged thirty-two) had the assistance of four officers, including two *Seeoffiziere*: *I IWO* Vietor (twenty-eight) and *IIWO* Becker (twenty-eight). In charge of the *Techniker* were *Oberleutnant Ing* Rottman (thirty-nine) and *Kplt.* Schilling, the *LI* (thirty-five). The *unteroffiziere* include a *Stabsobersteuermann* Anger (thirty-five) and *Stabsobermaschinist* Kumpf (thirty-three). There were no fewer than five *obermaschinisten* to oversee valves, engines and motors and direct the work of the thirteen stokers (who would also have attended to the mine cargo). The presence of four *matrosenobergefreiten* and three *matrosengefreiten* points to an equally veteran lower deck. These men had been amongst the first to volunteer for U-boats from General Service, following Raeder's decision to defy the Versailles and London Naval treaties.

Each *Matrosenobergefreiter* had trained for six months at Kiel, with further additional courses on torpedoes and gunnery. For a boat otherwise well supplied with specialist *unteroffiziere*, surprisingly there was just one *Mechanikermaat*, Friedrich Braun (twenty-three) to oversee torpedo maintenance. Radar was not introduced widely until 1943 and we see a continuation of the First World War pattern with one qualified *funker unteroffiziere* aided by a rating. While there is little doubt that Dönitz and his staff underestimated the capacity of ASDIC to evolve, we should also be mindful that the *Kriegsmarine* was dogged by a shortage of qualified *funker* in both wars.

The average date of birth for this crew was 1914, in line with larger samples which indicate the average age for U-boat crew in 1939/40 was twenty-five to twenty-six. The average age of line officers was twenty-nine, a figure corroborated by our crew profile. The youngest man on board was twenty-one-year-old *Matrosengefreiter* Winterhoff. By whatever measurement is applied, *U 33* was manned by pre-war trained personnel with an abundance of technical expertise, just some of the 3,000 *U-boot-Fahrer* who commenced the war. It is not unreasonable to conclude that the twenty-six U-boats which began hostilities with *U 33* were similarly crewed by highly experienced men, in short, a very special breed. In common with the crew of *U 33*, 40 per cent of this elite was destined to fall in the first year of the war.

Dönitz estimated that 300 U-boats would be needed to prevail against Britain's Atlantic lifeline. By 1944 Dönitz aimed to have 881 U-boats at his disposal. As early as November 1939 he proposed a vast rolling programme of recruitment and training. Dönitz planned that 4,000 men would enter the *Waffe* by the end of 1940, rising to 26,000 during the years 1943/44. The breakdown of this ambitious plan was 3,538 *unteroffiziere*, 6,220 *maschinisten*, 3,900 *funker*, and 3,000 *mechaniker*. U-boat manpower reached its peak in 1944 with a strength of 810,000, but they were quite different from the first 3,000 who had started hostilities. 1941 is usually cited as the watershed, the date at which the balance tipped from a volunteer-based *U-bootwaffe* in favour of a service consisting primarily of conscripts and reservists. However conscription from General Service had been an element in the maintenance of manning levels since the outbreak of war. For instance, following the loss of German destroyers at Narvik in 1940, numbers of otherwise redundant *Mechaniker* and *Maschinisten* had been pressed into U-boats. Nevertheless Dönitz faced the dilemma his predecessors had confronted in 1917, namely how to massively expand an elite force without sacrificing quality? Mulligan claims the balance tipped decisively towards the conscript element in mid-1941 (identical to the time when Horton made conscription to submarines routine practice in Royal Navy).

By July 1941 the pressing of trained men from General Service into the *U-bootwaffe* was to become systematic. For example until this point every *Kriegsmarine* destroyer had carried three engineering officers. From this juncture every third officer was removed and appointed to the *U-bootwaffe* for training. Commissioned officers operating light surface units or coastal artillery positions, or naval pilots, were creamed off and, providing they passed the medical, dispatched for submarine training. One further method of addressing the officer shortage was by increasing the number of officer intakes. Thus the second 'Crew 40' intake was labelled 'Crew 40B'.

The officer shortfall was partly addressed by creating *volksoffiziere*, commissioning able *unteroffiziere*. This extended not just to engine room personnel; suitably experienced *Obersteuermanner* were also commissioned. No fewer than thirty-five went on to command U-boats.

Unteroffiziere were likewise persuaded to 'volunteer'. One method was to make it known to *Techniker* under training that despite qualification they would not be rated in their specialised fields until they signed up for U-boats. For reservists, the definition of just what constituted 'seafaring classes' became ever more elastic. *Marine Hitler Jugend* trainees were to be turned over to U-boat training *en masse* as the authorities turned to conscription. In terms of civilian conscription *Kriegsmarine* was forced to compete with the other services but in 1942 the navy's percentage was fixed at 30,000, with the overwhelming majority pressed into U-boats. Thus there was a greater truth in that '*Freiwillig zur Kriegsmarine!*' recruitment poster than the authorities had ever intended – only the '*Freiwilliger*' element was absent.

Post-1941 demand for personnel resulted in a more streamlined approach to training individuals. Each training *ULD* could cater for up to 4,000 students, divided into *laufbahn* and rank. Each establishment possessed an 8m (26ft) deep tank. In theory every student was supposed to be capable of making a simulated escape using the *Dräger* set but in practice this test was often waived. Although each *ULD* had a number of training boats at its disposal, such was the pressure to produce personnel mid-1941 that only the five highest scoring *seemanner* students were permitted sea-training prior to being drafted to an operational U-boat. The remainder simply had to make do with visits to berthed submarines or day trips in 'E' boats. By early 1942 the *seemanner* training regime had been cut from six to three months. By 1944 a *Matrosengefreiter* would be lucky if he had received eight weeks' training. The classroom training of *Maschinengefreiten* was reduced to six weeks in late 1944. More time was devoted to *Techniker* but their specialist courses were steadily reduced from six months to five weeks. Courses for *Mechaniker* were just four weeks long by 1945. Comparison with the British training regime is interesting. The British kept their pools of 'Spare crew' at the submarine flotilla base itself but the Germans maintained their *Unterseebootausbildungsabteilung* near to each training establishment. Grouped according to rate and *laufbahn*, all personnel in these *UAA* establishments had to remain in readiness for a draft to an operational U-boat at a moment's notice. Here it must be stated that a general introduction of conscription did not equate with a falling away of standards. As late as 1944–45, the *U-bootwaffe* was rejecting 60 per cent of recruits.

Line officers generally received three months of U-boat training, including time spent on various simulators. Fifteen successful convoy attacks using models and bridge mock-ups must be achieved before the trainee could progress. By 1944 training had been reduced to eight weeks. There is no evidence that the *Kommandantenlehrgang*, the German equivalent of the 'Perisher', was reduced. First, would-be commanders received four months' specialised training in torpedoes and communications followed by the six week long *Kommandantenlehrgang* either with the 24th Flotilla at Memel or the 23rd Flotilla at Danzig. Each intake, averaging between eighteen to twenty candidates, was under the tutelage of former U-boat skippers, making endless simulated attacks and just as importantly, learning how to evade ADSIC, radar and, increasingly, aircraft. There can be little doubt that this was submarine training at its very best dispensed by real U-boat skippers who had been masters of their art. However the realities of 1944/45 were very different from the conditions faced by the 'Tonnage Kings' of 1939–42 and it is debatable whether any available training in this late period could ever prepare crews for the ordeal ahead. Fig. 16 is a crew profile of *U 1302*, just one of the late war boats which never came home. The boat was destined to fall victim to a Hedgehog mortar in March 1945.

Wolfgang Herwartz was born in Hildesheim in 1917 and commenced his naval career in 1937 (Crew 37a). Intriguingly Herwartz was seconded to the *Luftwaffe* from October 1939 until June 1943 prior to commencing U-boat training. On 1 August 1944 Herwartz was promoted to *Kapitänleutnant* and given command of *U 1302*. If the reader contrasts this boat with *U 33* it will be apparent that there was only one executive officer on *U 1302*, second and third watches presumably being taken by the two *Obersteuermänner*. From August 1944 to May 1945, 30 per cent of the Type VIIC frontline boats carried two *Obersteuermänner*. As late war patrols involved negotiating coastal minefields, one of these men would concentrate on navigational issues while the other assumed watch duties. *U 1302* carried an *Obermaschinist* assisted by a *Maat*, plus six *Maschinistmaat*. In comparison with *U 33* the boat was deficient in senior *maschinisten*, though LI Zembsch and his team were doubtless proficient in the science of *schnorchel* operation and deployment, it is clear that the boat's complement has been reduced to the bare minimum.

There are a couple of areas where skills have been reinforced. It will be noted that *U 1302* had retained thirteen sailors, *U 33* had nine. The primary role of the sailors was to assist the *mechaniker* in the maintenance and loading of torpedoes but most of these men would have also been trained in gunnery skills, the late Type VII being armed with a dual *flak* platform to deter aircraft. Now that the boats spent most of their time submerged, gunnery was considered less important; there was a tendency at this late stage of the war to sharply reduce the numbers of sailors in order to make living conditions more tolerable. *U 1302* carried four *mechaniker* of varying rate, reflective of the introduction of acoustic weapons and the use of decoy devices. Late Type VIIC/41s carried an array of radar and listening devices and it will be noted that the old quota of *Funker* has been doubled with two qualified *unteroffiziere* aided by two ratings. At this stage of the war, medical orderlies were routinely assigned to U-boats, largely to help deal with injuries sustained in aircraft attacks.

FIG 16 DIAGRAM OF A TYPE VIIC CREW (*U 1302*) *c.*1945		
KAPLT.		
1 *Lt zur See* (Sub-Lt)		*Lt ING* (Engineering officer)
(Seemanner)		*(Techniker)*
OB/STEUERMANN		
1 OB/ *STEUERMANNSMAAT* (CPO)	1 OB/ *BOOTSMANNSMAAT* (CPO)	1 *OB/MASCH* (ERA 1)
		1 *OB/MASCH MT* (ERA)
1 OB/*MECH MT* (TI)	1 *BOOTSMANNSMAAT* (PO)	5 *MASCH MT* (ERAs 3–4)
2 OB/*MECH GFR* (PO)		1 *OB/SAN MT*
1 *MECH GFR* (PO)		
	2 *MTR H/GFR* (L/S)	6 *MASCH OB/GFR* (L/Stokers)
	8 *MTR OB/GFR* (ABs)	5 *MASCH OB/GFR* (Stokers)
	1 *MTR GFR* (ABs)	2 *FK MAAT* (PO Tels) 2 *FK OB/GFR* (Tels)
	2 *MATROSEN* (Ord Sea)	

This was a young crew in comparison to the men of *U 33*. Wolfgang Herwartz the Commander was twenty-eight years old, his *IWO* Hans Groniger was just twenty-one. *LI* Hans Zembsh was an equally youthful twenty-two. As regards *unteroffiziere*, the two *obersteuermanner* Wackerbarth and Frankenstein were twenty-nine and twenty-five respectively. The thirty-year-old medic was the oldest man in the boat. Twelve of the crew were twenty years old, while one *Obergefreiter* was just nineteen. Of course youth does not necessarily equate with inexperience or inability. As previously indicated, *U 1302* was lost on her first patrol, what has not been mentioned is the fact that she sank three ships by torpedo prior to her loss.

By June 1944 young conscripts like these faced the resurgent allies, now superior in terms of numbers and technology. Instead of reducing the pressure on his crews, Dönitz returned to the policy he had adopted at the start of hostilities, namely attacks on allied shipping pressed home in shallow British coastal waters. Only now, these waters were littered with mines and closely patrolled by hunter-killer groups. True, there were isolated incidents (for instance one of the *U 1302 unteroffiziere* shot himself on 17 September 1944 in Gotenhafen) but in the main, young predominantly conscript crews like these rose to the challenge. There were few serious problems of insubordination, desertion or indiscipline – factors usually associated with declining morale. The question as to why the *U-boot Fahrer* kept going out on patrol in such adverse conditions has absorbed many historians. Dönitz himself offered this view as to why his U-crews kept faith:

> Morale remained high to the end because of the leadership we gave them. They understood that the orders were necessary and ones we would be willing to sacrifice our own relations – don't forget my two sons also fell. They understood that although the Battle of the Atlantic had been lost, every time they put to sea they were tying down enemy planes that would otherwise have been bombing the fatherland.

Of course historians point out that this generation of U-boat men had been indoctrinated with Nazi ideology from an early age and were consequently unlikely to question orders. In the 1941-set *Das Boot*, two veteran U-boat commanders, both holders of the Knight's Cross, stand at a La Rochelle bar and lament the boorish behaviour of the 'new men', their courage fuelled by a combination of drink, bravado and Nazi slogans. True, with the possible exceptions of Luth and Schepke, few of the 1939–41 aces had overt Nazi sympathies. As for the post-1941 influx, the authorities maintained a ruthless control. The price of dissent in a totalitarian state was death, as the unfortunate *Oberleutnant* Oskar-Heinz Kusch discovered. Kusch, denounced by his *IWO*, was shot by firing squad for openly making seditious observations. Dönitz himself was forced to save Werner Henke from the attentions of the *SS* following a dispute. Some of the U-crews were undoubtedly rabid Nazis but evidence indicates that the overwhelming majority merely paid lip service, followed orders and hoped for the best. Few had the nerve of the incomparable *Kapitänleutnant* Reinhard 'Teddy' Suhren. Returning to harbour from a long patrol, Suhren called out to some nearby dockers to enquire whether the Nazis were still in control. When answered in the affirmative, to general hilarity, Suhren manoeuvred as if to take his boat out to sea again.

The new generation of U-crews was shackled to the past as its sole route guide to present and future, in that it readily identified with the mythology of duty and heroic sacrifice that had characterised the earlier generation of *U-boot Fahrer*. The most prevalent manifestation of this identification was in stoic acceptance, a sense of ordinary men battling against seemingly insurmountable forces, both natural and man-made. There was genuine pride in a war well-fought. Whatever allied propagandists might claim, for the most part U-boat men in both wars fought as honourably and as chivalrously as the undersea war had allowed.

All told, the principal factor motivating *U-boot Fahrer* in the closing months of the war was not National Socialism, nor was it fear or unthinking loyalty or deference to past achievement. Rather it was rather a transcendent *esprit de corps* common to submariners in both wars. Psychologists know this phenomenon as 'primary group cohesion'. Others call it mateship. It is found in varying degrees among all the armed services but assumes an almost reverential quality among submariners and it arises from the absolute interdependence and shared privation noted above by Karl Neureuther and Oscar Wehner. This group loyalty might extend laterally between, say, men within the same *laufbahn*, or departmentally between 'lords' in the fore-ends, who would in turn be acutely aware of just how reliant they were upon the men in the engine and control rooms. Group cohesion operated vertically through rank, irrespective of social milieu. U-boat crews famously revered '*Der Lowe*' (The Lion) as they called Dönitz, even though he ordered them to their deaths. Successful commanders such as Saltzzwedel or Hundius or Prien were near worshipped by their crews and the skippers reciprocated. The relationship between a submarine commander and his crew, which transcends mere paternalism, has never been more movingly described than by *Kplt*. Werner Furbringer. Exhausted and ill, Furbringer had just brought his ailing boat home:

My crew was given leave but remained at the disposition of the Flotilla because the repairs to the boat would be fairly major…Meanwhile I reported to the military hospital in Harzburg for a course of treatment. It was 18th February 1918…it came as a hammer blow on the tenth day of my recuperation to be informed in a letter from the U-Flotilla staff officer that UB 58 had been sent on a Channel patrol without me, under a new commander. All of the requisite repairs having been postponed till their return… After reading this I sank down, feeling sick in the pit of my stomach. I felt that someone had stolen my boat and kidnapped my crew. I knew each man-jack of them like a brother. I had brought at least half of them with me from the previous boats I had commanded and felt a sense of personal responsibility for each man. It seemed an act of crass betrayal that they should have been turned over to strange hands simply because I was sick. I was appalled by the decision of the U-Flotilla because I would have returned to Bruges at once to resume command, had I been informed. And I had lost my steward, the most loyal friend I had ever known, Matrose Theide, whom I had dragged with me from boat to boat. Theide who had become engaged, then married on the same day as me, and who always had a ready grin no matter what. I had always forced from my mind the thought I could lose all these people at a stroke …Inwardly I knew for certain the moment I read the letter from the U-Flotilla that UB 58 would not return from this patrol. Three weeks later U-Flotilla wrote to tell me that UB 58 was missing, believed lost with all hands.

And that day, a big part of me died with them.

Werner Furbringer, 'Alarm, Tauchen!'

Cicero observed, *'Silent leges inter arma'* – war elicits the worst on both sides. He might have added that sometimes it brings out the best.

A – Z OF RATES IN VARIOUS U-BOATS BETWEEN 1914 AND 1945

S = *Seamanner* branch

T = *Techniker* branch

Bt.Mn. = *Bootsmann* **(S)** – Petty Officer 1st class. The *Bootsmann*, who wore a fouled anchor and a star on his trade arm, was primarily concerned with maintaining discipline and order among the seamen. Other tasks might include the storage and issue of crew clothing, overseeing the daily cleaning of the boat. Traditionally the *Bootsmann* was allocated to the first watch.

During the Second World War crew dilution often required the *Bootsmann* to carry out tasks that had previously been the lot of the *Oberbootsmann*. In this fashion, during an attack the *Bootsmann* took up position in the conning tower to input information into the torpedo computer. In some cases the *Bootsmann* was assisted by a *Bootsmannsmaat*.

D.Ob.Masch = *Diesel Obermaschinist* **(T)** – Chief diesel mechanic and CPO. The nearest British equivalent would be a CERA. The *Diesel Obermaschinist* ran the engine room, reporting directly to the *LI* (who was likely to spend most of his time in the control room). The *Ob.maschinist* was assisted by three to four *Maschinenmaat* roughly equivalent to the Royal Navy's ERAs. Highly skilled, much prized engineers, usually the most senior man within the engine room, the *Ob.Maschinst* wore a trade badge of an anchor superimposed on a cogwheel with two or more chevrons below.

El.Ob.Masch – *Elektro Obermaschinist* **(T)** – Chief electrical mechanic and CPO. The *Elektro Obermaschinist* was in charge of the motor room, aft of the engine room. This dual *Obermaschinist* regime held authority over the *Techniker* branch, maintaining discipline and drawing up the *Techniker* watchbill.

F.T. Gast or Fk.Ob.Gfr. = *Funkobergefreiter* **(T)**. Because of the imperative to maintain round the clock watch, the *Kriegsmarine* tended to pair ratings with specialist Telegraphists. These ratings were known as F.T. Gast.

Fh.z.S. = *Fähnrich zur See* – The rank of *Fähnrich* was a title between *Unteroffizier* and *Offizier*. During both wars an officer *kadet* or *Fahnrich* was assigned to a U-boat as part of his officer education, it was the practical or on the job training, under the beady eye of an experienced Watch Officer. The more experienced *Fähnrich* might supervise the third bridge watch and assume an officer's duties. Once rated as a *Leutnant zur See*, he could thus commence service with some practical experience behind him. The *Fahnrich* was rated as a senior PO and paid the same rate, much to the displeasure of the *unteroffiziere*, who, in the words of veteran U-boatman Eric Mohr, 'resented having to nursemaid such human ballast'.

Fk.Mt. = *Funkmaat/ F.T.Maat* **(T)** – Radio operator. Each *Funkmaat* worked a four hour shift, primarily concerned with receiving and transmitting radio messages. The rating of a U-boat Telegraphist largely depended upon the amount and accuracy of the messages he was capable of transcribing within an hour. The *Funkmaat* was distinguished by a lightning bolt badge on his trade arm.

Gftr. = *Gefreiter* **(S)** – AB, 3rd class. During the Second World War the old term for a sailor – *Matrose* – was dropped in favour of the more belligerent-sounding *Matrosengefreiter*. The next rate up was that of *Matrosenobergefreiter* or seaman second class. Each Type VIIC contained about ten of these sailors, who lived and worked in the *Bugraum* or Tube Space. The *Matrosengefreiter* operated under instruction from the *Mechaniker* in the maintenance, loading and firing of torpedoes. Ratings acted as lookouts, while one unfortunate would be detailed to act as *smutje* or cook. *Grefreiter* often referred to themselves as *deckbullen* – 'deck apes' – while dismissing the *Techniker* as 'grease monkeys'. Apart from routine tasks, the ratings took their place on the hydroplanes as *ruderganger* under the ever-watchful eye of the *LI*. Those showing a special aptitude might be classified as *gefechtsruderganger* and called upon to operate the planes during an attack. In the later stages of the second World War, increasing aircraft attacks led to the addition of specially trained flak gunners drawn from the *seemännische laufbahn*. The *Matrosengefreiter* wore a five-pointed star badge on his trade arm.

Heizer (T) – First World War term for a Stoker.

K.Kptn. = *Korvettenkapitän* – Lieutenant Commander; generally referred to as 'Herr Kapitän'.

Kap. = *Kapitän zur See* – Captain.

Kplt. = *Kapitänleutnant* – Lieutenant, usually the submarine captain/commander.

KgLt.s = *Kriegslotse* **(S)** – War pilot. A First World War term. As often as not a conscripted merchant navigator 'loaned' by one of the German shipping lines to the KDM. The *Kriegslotse* often had useful personal experience of an enemy port or roadstead, intelligence that was particularly useful for the UC mining boats.

Lt.Ing. = Leitender Ingenieur. Generally a *Leutnant* or *Oberleutnant zur See* (on boats where the commander was an *Oberleutnant*), this key officer was known as the *LI* (pronounced 'ell ee'). A crucial figure, second in importance only to the commander, the *LI* ran all propulsion and diving systems on the boat, though much routine was delegated to those of *unteroffizier* rate. The *LI* was accountable for maintaining trim, overseeing helmsmen and hydroplane operators. Engineer Officers ate in the wardroom with the line officers but the German Navy tended not to afford them the same level of respect as other commissioned officers.

Lt.z.s. = Leutnant zur See – Sub-Lieutenant. The *Leutnant* often functioned as the *zweiter wach offizier*, or *IIWO* commanded the deck and *Flak* guns in the Second World War. The *zweiter wach offizier* was also responsible for the use and maintenance of the *Enigma* machine, encrypting and decrypting all classified radio messages. As his title suggests, he supervised the second bridge watch.

Maschinengefreiter (T) – Stokers 2nd/3rd class, successors to the *Heizen* of the First World War.

Maschinenmaat/Maschinist (T) – unteroffizier – Engineer. The nearest Royal Navy rank was that of the ERA. The *Maschinenmaat* ensured the smooth running of propulsion systems including electrics within the *zentrale*. Experts in improvisation, they repaired diesel engines often in desperate conditions under depth charge attack. In the course of a dive, the *Maschinenmaat* oversaw the actions of the *Maschinengefreiter* during the crucial change-over in propulsion system from the diesel engines to the electric motors. A less exalted role might be supervision of the high-pressure toilet mechanism. The *Maschinenmaat* was answerable to the *Obermaschinist*. The *Maschinenmaat's* trade badge took the form of a cogwheel superimposed on an anchor.

Masch.Anw = Maschinist Anwärter (T) – An unqualified ERA, usually present to gain practical experience of maintaining propulsion systems in wartime conditions.

Masch.Mt = Maschinenmaat (T) – Engine room *unteroffizier*, equivalent to the Royal Navy ERA 2nd/3rd class.

Masch.Stn = Maschinisten (T) – An ERA responsible for overseeing activity in either Engine or Motor Rooms.

Mech.Gfr = Mechanikergefreiter (S) – Specialised torpedo leading rate, usually operating under the instructions of an *Obermechaniker*. *Mechanikergefreiter* wore the trade badge of a torpedo superimposed on a cogwheel.

Mech.Mt = Mechanikermaat (S) – Torpedo room *unteroffizier*.

Mech.Ob.Gfr = Mechanikerobergefreiter (S) – Senior *unteroffizier* in charge of the maintenance and loading of torpedoes. The *Mechanikerobergefreiter* saw to any last minute setting adjustments of the torpedoes prior to an attack. Traditionally the *Mechanikerobergefreiter* was not quartered in the *Oberfeldwebelraum* with others of his rank. Instead he had his own bunk in the crowded *Bugraum*, surrounded by junior rates (but conveniently close to the focus of his work).

Mn.Ob.Ing = Marine–Oberingeneiur – First World War engineering officer, equivalent to *Oblt.z.s.* rank.

Mn.Ing.Asp = Marine Ingenieur Aspirant – Unqualified Marine Engineer.

Mt.B.Ftr. = Matrosenobergefreiter (S) – Leading Seaman.

Mt. = Maat – *unteroffizier* 3rd class.

Mt. = Matrose (S) – Seaman (First World War). Prior to the Second World War, the *Matrose* was re-styled '*Matrosengefreiter*'. '*Matrose*' now became the term for an Ordinary Seaman in the Second World War.

Mtr.Ob.Gfr. = Matrosenobergefreiter (S) – Leading Seaman. It is often possible to determine the relative experience of a U-boat crew via the number of *Matrosenobergefreiter*.

Ob.Btn. = OberBootsmann (S) – Bosun/Coxswain. The *Oberbootsmann* was the senior *unteroffizier* on the boat, holding responsibility for maintaining discipline in the seamen's branch, often served as fourth watch officer. During an attack the *Oberbootsmann* took up position in the *Turm* alongside his commander. In the First World War he made any alterations to the periscope bearing indicator at the word of his commander. In the Second World War he fed data into the *Torpedovorhaltrechner* or torpedo computer. As both wars unfolded and dilution took its toll, the work of *Oberbootsmann* was increasingly carried out by a more junior *unteroffizier*, generally a *Maat* or a *Bootsmann*. The *oberbootsmann's* combined trade/rank patch consisted of a chevron topped by a fouled anchor.

Ob.Fk.Mt. = Oberfunkmaat (T) – *Unteroffizier* Telegraphist. An *Oberfunkmaat* sported the trade badge of a lightning bolt superimposed on an anchor. An *Oberfunkmaat* qualified as an *Unterwasserhorcher* (hydrophone operator) additionally wore a red specialist patch (on the left sleeve below the rank patch) in the form of two chevrons topped by an arrow.

Ob.Fk.Tel.Mt. = Oberfunkentelegraphiemaat (T) – First World War Radio and Telegraph *Unteroffizier.*

Ob.Hzr = Oberheizer (T) – Leading Stoker.

Ob.Ing.Asp. = Ober-Ingenieur-Aspirant – Engineer Officer candidate.

Ob.Masch.Gfr. = Maschinengefreiten (T) – Leading Stoker.

Ob.Masch.Mt. = Obermaschinistmaat (T) – ERA 1st/2nd class. An *unteroffizier* of this rate might be responsible for servicing and maintaining the batteries.

Ob.Mech.Mt. = Obermechanikersmaat (S) – Torpedo room *unteroffizier.* An important duty of the *Obermechanikersmaat* was to record which torpedo tubes had been flooded prior to a dive and report this figure to the *LI.*

Ob.Mt = Obermaat – *Unteroffizier* 1st class.

Ob.Stm.Mt. = Obersteurmannsmaat (S) – Senior navigator's mate and *unteroffizier* 2nd class.

Ob.Mtn.Mt. = Oberbootsmannmaat (S) – Often referred to as *Nummer Zwo* – Chief Petty Officer (Number Two), assistant to the *Bootsmann.*

Ob.Mts = Obermatrose. (S) – Leading Seaman, next rank would be a *Bootsmannsmaat* (i.e. *unteroffizier*).

Ob.Strm = Obersteuermann (S) – The *Obersteurmann* functioned as quartermaster and was also responsible for navigation, conning the boat and controlling the helmsmen. The *Obersteurmann* helped the commander determine how and when to make attacks. Interestingly the *Ob.Strm* could also serve as third watch officer. On the command '*UZO zum brucke!*' the *Ob.Strm* would race out to fit the *UZO* into the clamp on the pedestal. The *Obersteurmann* was distinguished by his trade badge of two crossed anchors.

Oblt.z.s. = Oberleutnant zur See – Lieutenant. On boats where the commander was an *Oblt.z.s.*, the *Lt.z.s.* would function as the *IWO* ('*Erster wach-Offizier*' or *Eins-WO*). The *IWO* organised the bridge watches and personally supervised the first bridge watch. The RN equivalent would be the first lieutenant. The *IWO* was responsible for the torpedoes and the systems which aimed and fired them. Interestingly it was the *IWO* rather than the commander who conducted surfaced torpedo attacks. An experienced *IWO* could ultimately expect his own command in the fullness of time.

Snt.Mt (S). = Sanitatsmaat – *Unteroffizier*/medical orderly introduced to U-boat crews in later stages of the Second World War, when injury from aircraft weaponry was a real possibility. Just as likely, following the introduction of the *schnorchel*, was the indisposition of engine room staff due to carbon monoxide fumes. The trade badge of the *Sanitatsmaat* bore an anchor with a serpent coiled around the shank.

St.Mn = Steurmann (S) – Helmsman. Graduates of the *Steurmann Laufbahn* wore the crossed anchors trade badge.

Stb.Ftr. = Stabsgefreiter (S) – Seaman 1st class.

Z.Mt. = Zentralemaat (T) – *Unteroffizier* usually a specialised *maschinist* detailed to oversee trim and ballast tank systems. The *Zentralemaat* constantly updated and maintained records detailing the amount of water held in the tanks *and* logs containing data on the weight and distribution of fuel, foodstuffs, ammunition and other materials on board. Additionally the *Zentralemaat* monitored, temperature, oxygen/carbon dioxide levels, serviced the periscopes and air blow valves. This was a highly responsible position and the *Zentralemaat* (often assisted by a couple of seamen) reported directly to the *LI.* The nearest Royal Navy equivalent was that of an Outside ERA.

FIG.17 TYPICAL U-BOAT CREW ROTA 1914-45		
Time	*Seamanner*	*Techniker*
0000	First Bridge Watch	Starboard engine duty Watch
0400	Second Bridge Watch	
0545		Off-duty Port engine duty watch have breakfast
0600	'Lash up and stow' (hammocks) Off duty seamen awake	Port engine duty Watch
0630	Off duty seamen have breakfast	
0700	Cleaning duties for off duty seamen	
0800	Third Bridge Watch. Second Watch now off duty has breakfast	
0845	Off duty watches assigned tasks	
1200	First Bridge Watch Dinner for off duty seamen	Starboard engine Watch. Dinner for off duty *Techniker*
1300	Off duty watches assigned work	
1600	Second Bridge Watch	
1715	'Big Eats' for off duty seamen	'Big Eats' for off duty *Techniker*
1800		Port engine Watch
2000	Third Bridge Watch	
2100	'Lights Out' for off duty watches	'Lights Out' for off-duty watches
2340	First Bridge Watch awakens, ready to take over from Third Watch at 0000	Starboard engine Watch awakes, ready to take over from Port watch at 0000

Sources:
Führer durch Heer und Flotte 1914 by B. Friedag
Ehrenrangliste der Kaiserlich Deutschen Marine
Von Revolution zu Revolution by R. Guth
Bestimmungen für den Dienst an Bord, Heft III (Cuxhaven Archiv)
Neither Sharks not Wolves by T. Mulligan

CHAPTER FOUR

BRITISH SUBMARINE PERSONNEL 1914–1945

INTRODUCTION

In the 1920s veteran officer William Carr looked back with pride when he observed that half of all candidates for the wartime Submarine Service had been rejected. Carr memorably described the submarine crew as 'one big happy undersea family'. The Submarine Service William Carr knew had survived every obstacle placed in its course by enemy and Admiralty 'salt horse' alike, to forge its own unique identity within its parent, the Royal Navy. The man who perhaps did most to shape the distinctive character of the Service was the first Inspector of Submarines (1901–04), Capt Reginald Bacon. Contrary to popular belief, the Submarine Service Bacon did so much to mould, was not (and never would be) an organisation entirely comprised of volunteers.

The first recruitment drive for the 'submarine section' met with a rather disappointing response. Of the thirteen lieutenants who volunteered, only one was a qualified torpedo officer. By 1902 there were insufficient ratings and officers to crew all five Holland submarines on Admiralty books. Men from the battleship *Jupiter* were pressed to crew *Hollands* 4 and 5. Submarines were always uncomfortable and all too often unreliable. In recognition of the dangerous and difficult nature of the service, from 1903 Admiralty offered extra financial enhancements to recruit and retain submarine volunteers. Notably 'hard lying' money was paid to tempt appropriately experienced and qualified men from General Service. In addition officers in command of submarine could draw an additional allowance known as 'command pay' which could have the effect of doubling their wages. Admiralty did not like these increments and reacted with some justification against the creation of 'a service within a service'. Capt Bacon steadfastly fought his corner and the allowances remained.

There was one problem that Capt Bacon could not address on his own. Every sailor from AB to admiral knew that progress up the promotional ladder depended upon 'sea time' spent in big ships. Unless circumstances changed, the Submarine Service would inevitably face problems in retaining ambitious and capable personnel. Because of their allotted role as 'clockwork mice' in anti-submarine exercises, officially submariners were not classed as part of the seagoing fleet. According to regulations they were attached to Portsmouth command as part of the reserve. To qualify for promotion, all ranks must serve minimum periods of service in seagoing warships and this did not include time spent on the reserve list. In 1904 Bacon's modifications to these regulations were reluctantly accepted by Admiralty. Service in submarines now counted as experience in seagoing ships. The Inspecting Captain of Submarines was empowered to promote ratings to full pay without them first having attended a training course. It was a question of compromise; the result was 'the General Service rule'. All officers and men who had spent five years in submarines would be required to return to General Service for at least two years. Only then could they return to submarines for a maximum of three years. The 'General Service rule' was aimed at preventing the Submarine Service from becoming too independent of its parent, but from the outset pragmatism forced the rule to be waived in the case of key ratings. War and a shortage of trained personnel witnessed this policy unravel further.

ADM 1/7644 Inspecting Captain of Submarines memo to C in C Portsmouth

Capt Bacon had a clear idea of the kind of officers required by his fledgling service:

The captains of boats:
1) should be young
2) be good rough navigators
3) hard-headed and careful
4) have a good general electric and Whitehead knowledge.

Memo on the Training of Officers and men for Submarines 'Naval Necessities' April 1903.

Bacon urgently needed specialist level-headed torpedo and engine room ratings, men like the redoubt-able PO William Waller, one of the first intake of volunteers. In the course of his long career, Waller was destined to be blown up, half drowned, electrocuted and crushed (see *A8*) but he still kept returning to his beloved submarines.

Some idea of the relative attractions of the early Submarine Service can be obtained from the table in Fig.17, yet Bacon and his successors sought to develop an *esprit de corps* within the fledgling Submarine Service that went far beyond mere financial inducements.

Commander Robert Turner DSO, who served on *A6*, captures these heady days in his memoirs:

It always surprises me, looking back, how we managed. We were all a lot of amateurs but being young and full of confidence, learned as we went along. Petrol engines were little known and the engine room staff were as ignorant as most of us. However we all got motor bikes and learned the fundamentals without killing our-selves. Electrics were very much the same, the care of two large storage batteries of 120 volts and the various main and auxiliary motors was in our hands, assisted by young leading torpedo ratings. In spite of it all, the submarines functioned and we learned all the time. Little was known about submarines in the general Navy and they were considered more toys than offensive weapons…Submarine crews were provided with divers' sweaters and stockings also leather sea boots. Understandably we were looked upon by the main services as pirates (and dirty at that). Senior officers were horrified at our appearance.

ADM 1/7291 Memo from Inspecting Captain of Submarines to C in C Portsmouth 5/2/07 (Note: the spe-cialist Telegraphist branch had not yet been formed)

In any one year, a big warship would see a turnover of at least 20 per cent of its complement. In sub-marines, turnover was comparatively rare. While they did not disappear altogether, class barriers dividing officers and ratings wilted under the shared privations endured by 'The Trade'. Some of the more extreme conventions of the senior service were abandoned. Ratings living in the Portsmouth area were even allowed to go home after 1600hrs! The work was predictably demanding and the Submarine Service sought a greater level of intelligence and competence among its recruits than that required by General Service. Volunteers were expected to be over twenty-one with at least one good conduct badge. It should be pointed out that the age limit was often waived in the case of Boy Telegraphists, who were always under eighteen years ('Mens time' commenced at the age of eighteen and rating as Ordinary Telegraphist followed). Boy Tel Denison who died in *E4* aged sixteen during the First World War (see Vol.1) was the youngest Boy Telegraphist casualty. Ordinary Telegraphist Walter Hayter joined subma-rines in 1910 because he hated the deck-swabbing culture of General Service:

Blockhouse was heaven! Discipline was quite comfortable and when you were off duty you could lie on the ramparts and sunbathe. It was a different navy altogether and when we got into submarines, you were so near to the officers. In fact everyone was so close to each other and there was no red tape and no falling in and out. Bliss.

With Capt Bacon at the helm and the Machiavellian 'Jacky' Fisher scheming behind the scenes (first as Commander-in-Chief Portsmouth 1903–04 then as First Sea Lord 1904–10) the Submarine Service gradually developed a character and an ethos quite distinctive from that of its parent. Most in Admiralty disliked the division. If Fisher had nurtured the trend, his successor as First Lord (1910–11), Sir Arthur Wilson, was determined to prevent the development of a 'service within a service' by attempting to remove 'hard lying' money (on the grounds that submarines were no longer as uncomfortable as they had formerly been). Ratings responded by leaving the Service in droves (a fact lamented in Admiralty memo AWS/MD18/1913). Roger Keyes, Inspecting Captain of Submarines (1910–15) successfully argued not just for the retention of the perk but also for wider changes within the Submarine Service:

> In view of the present serious shortage of ratings available for entry into the Submarine Service…I submit that the present system of discharging ratings to General Service on the completion of five years in the Submarine Service and of re-entering them two years later for a further period of three years might be abolished and that in future ratings might be allowed to remain in the Submarine Service for so long as they give satisfaction…

> ADM 116/1122 letter from Keyes to Admiralty concerning conditions of service within the Submarine Service 7/2/13

Faced with impending war, Admiralty had no option but to agree with Keyes' recommendations. The 'General Service rule' was allowed to lapse (although until recent times submarine officers were required to return to General Service for a two-year period). One aspect of the 'General Service rule' did linger beyond its time however. Not until after the Second World War were British submariners allowed to wear their own distinctive insignia in the form of paired gold dolphins.

As far as can be ascertained, all known ratings who served in submarines during the Great War were volunteers. Brian Head has uncovered that while there are very few RNR ratings listed in submarines during the First World War, 261 RNR officers are listed with a further six serving RNVR officers. Some of these men had been compelled to join the Submarine Service.

It appears to the authors that RNVR officers were not always treated fairly, the argument being made that the technical and navigational skills of the RNVR officer were not on a par with those of his RN counterparts. On the other hand, the Submarine Service was perfectly content to harness the specialist skills and knowledge of the RNVR when conditions dictated. For instance Lt Palmer of *E15* not only spoke Turkish, his expert knowledge of the Dardanelles minefields proved highly valuable. Lt Palmer became the first RNVR to win the DSC 'for services in submarines'. Similarly, the Service was keen to access the latest RNVR skills and knowledge in navigation and wireless technology. RNVR W/T specialists were routinely seconded to submarines (though generally only on a short term basis). A Canadian, Lt William Thompson RNVR, remained in the Submarine Service longer than most. Admiralty would not appoint him to a submarine following his arrival in *H5*. Thompson became 'spare First Lieutenant' in the depot ship *Alecto* and ultimately did carry out patrols from Great Yarmouth in *H5*. The only RNVR officer to be appointed to command a submarine during the First World War was another Canadian, Lt Bernard 'Barney' Johnson. He transferred from the RCNVR to command *H8*, then building at Montreal. On arrival in Britain, rather than an immediate appointment to a boat, Johnson was 'persuaded' to join the RNR. This done, his command of *H8* was confirmed. Faced with a vastly expanded Submarine Service crying out for officers, old prejudices relaxed towards the end of hostilities and five RNR officers are known to have been given commands before the war ended. There is one further point to make here (and if it is a rather disturbing one, it is an issue well known in naval circles). Whenever events took a serious turn for the worse and a court martial resulted, there is evidence to suggest that RNVR officers suffered more harshly at the hands of the court than their RN colleagues.

Fig 18 RATINGS DAILY PAY IN SHILLINGS (GROSS) 1908			
Rank	Basic pay	Submarine pay	Total gen. service pay
CPO	2/8	5/2	3/2
PO 2	2/2	4/8	2/8
CERA 2	7/0	10/6	8/6
ERA 4	5/6	8/0	6/0
Stoker	2/0	4/0	2/4
AB	1/7	3/7	1/11d

Fig 19 DIAGRAM OF A C-BOAT'S COMPANY *c.*1907			
CAPTAIN (Lieutenant or Lt Commander)			
First Lieutentant (Sub-Lieut. or Lieut.)		NAVIGATOR (Lieut.)	
EXECUTIVE DEPARTMENT (SEAMEN)		ENGINE ROOM DEPARTMENT	
1 SUBMARINE COXSWAIN (Petty Officer)		1 CERA	
1 SIGNALMAN	1 LEADING SEAMAN (LTO)	1 ENGINE ROOM ARTIFICER	
	5 ABLE SEAMEN	1 STOKER PETTY OFFICER	
		3 STOKERS	

All told, the contribution of the RNVR and the RNR to the Submarine Service during the First World War may be unsung but it was undoubtedly significant.

Of course crew compositions varied with the type of boat. Fig.20 illustrates the crew profile of a typical small submarine of early 1918, in this case *H5.* This is just one example but the essence of this crew structure survived into the Second World War (see Fig.21) and beyond.

Note: the diagram reflects the development of an increasingly specialist Telegraphist branch in keeping with the growth in communications/detection technology.

The number of officers and ratings applying for the Submarine Service declined during the inter-war years. As applicants diminished, so Admiralty resorted to compulsion in order to maintain adequate manning levels. The 1930s brought some fluctuation. The stream of volunteers generally flowed healthily in spite of the *M1, L24* and *M2* disasters but suffered predictable drought following the *Thetis* disaster of 1939.

Note: the number of Telegraphists carried indicates the importance of maintaining ASDIC watch. The introduction of radar into submarines from 1943 onwards would witness a further specialisation within the Telegraphist branch.

During the Second World War, Vice Admiral (S) Max Horton faced severe shortages of trained personnel. The statistics tell their own stark tale. The Submarine Service had started the war with fifty boats and a paper strength of 3,502 men. By January 1941, twenty-six boats had been lost along with 1,300 highly trained submariners. The steady stream of volunteers could not keep pace with these losses. Horton sought (and obtained) permission to press trained torpedomen, ASDIC operators and ERAs from General Service. Young men who had been conscripted into the RN as stokers or seamen could find themselves presented with a non-negotiable draft to Blyth for submarine sea training. British submarine crews in the later years of the war tended to be a combination of experienced 'old soaks', new volunteers and 'HO' or pressed 'Hostilities Only' men. Dilution did not bring evidence of any perceptible decline in standards. Statistics suggest that 'HOs' rapidly adapted to life in the Submarine Service and only a relative handful sought a return to 'General Service'.

In the post-war years the boats changed and titles changed with them. For instance by 1950 the wartime stoker had become the 'ME' or Marine Engineer Mechanic, though the nature of his work had not substantially changed. The submarine crew of 1950 was much the same as it had been back in 1905 – 'One big happy undersea family'.

Let us now examine the individual members of this peculiar family in detail.

THE OFFICERS

LT-CDR – 'SKIPPER'

A high percentage of submarine officers emerged from old established military families with a tradition of sending a son into the Royal Navy. The backgrounds of British submarine officers tended to be more homogenous that those of the men they commanded, though a sprinkling of RNR and RNVR men added a touch of variety. The overwhelming majority had been educated at Dartmouth Naval College or a similar establishment geared to preparing cadets for the responsibilities of office. Fees tended to deter all but service or patrician families, therefore social class as well as technological merit was reflected in the submarine officer's uniform. There were notable exceptions, particularly during the First World War, of remarkable men who had succeeded in 'dragging themselves up through the hawser' but they were rare. As has already been stated, with the exception of 'Barney' Johnson, no RNVR men were appointed to submarine command in the First World War; both RNR and RNVR men were given commands in the later stages of the Second World War.

On leaving college a 'Dart' was expected to serve out a term as midshipman in General Service. In time he would acquire sufficient 'seniority' to earn a lieutenancy. Officer volunteers for the Submarine Service were required to have obtained experience in and have studied the disciplines of navigation, weapons, telegraphy and wireless. Most officer candidates had gained the rate of sub-lieutenant before they volunteered for the Submarine Service. Volunteering for submarines appealed to tough, assertive, technologically-minded young men with a healthy contempt for General Service 'bull'. These men were gamblers; just volunteering for submarines would constitute the greatest risk most had ever taken. Failure at any stage would see a promising career in tatters (though exceptions were made in a few rare cases). Conversely, success would bring responsibilities unthinkable elsewhere for so young an officer.

Appointment to a submarine as a navigator or weapons officer would follow. An average of three years of study combined with practical experience was required before the lieutenant could expect an appointment as first lieutenant to a submarine. In peacetime an officer could expect to spend up to four years as a first lieutenant before he could apply to sit the Commanding Officer Qualifying Course (COQC or 'Perisher'). Each candidate was put through a series of simulated attack exercises at Fort Blockhouse. The first submarine officers training course was held in 1915. The periscope course was established in October 1917. Failure resulted in immediate return to General Service. It follows that most peacetime British submarine commanders were in their early thirties but there were exceptions in wartime. Lt Anthony Troup took over command of *H32* in 1943 aged twenty-one. In peacetime it

Fig 20 DIAGRAM OF AN H-BOAT'S COMPANY *c*.1918 (*H5*)			
CAPTAIN (Lieutenant or Lt Commander)			
First Lieutenant (Sub-Lieut. or Lieut.)		NAVIGATOR (Lieut. RNR)	
EXECUTIVE DEPARTMENT (SEAMEN)		ENGINE ROOM DEPARTMENT	
SUBMARINE COXSWAIN (Petty Officer)		CHIEF ERA	
SIGNALMAN	TGM (PO)	ENGINE ROOM ARTIFICER	
TELEGRAPHIST	PO LTO	ENGINE ROOM ARTIFICER	
(BOY) TELEGRAPHIST	LEADING SEAMAN (LTO)	STOKER PETTY OFFICER	
	LEADING SEAMAN 2ND COX'N	LEADING STOKER	
	LEADING SEAMAN	LEADING STOKER	
	3 ABLE SEAMEN	3 STOKERS	

Fig 21 DIAGRAM OF AN S-BOAT'S COMPANY c.1940 (*Swordfish*)			
CAPTAIN (Lt)			
FIRST LIEUTENANT (Lt.)		'THIRD HAND' (Lt) NAVIGATOR (RNR)	
EXECUTIVE DEPARTMENT (Seamen)		**ENGINE ROOM DEPARTMENT**	
1 SUBMARINE COXSWAIN (CPO)		1 WARRANT ENGINEER	
1 L/SIGNALMAN	1 TGM (PO)	1 ERA	
1 PO TEL	1 PO LTO	2 ERAs 2 2 ERAs 3 1 ERA 4	
2 L/TELs	1 L/S LTO	2 SPOs	
2 TELs	5 L/SEAMEN	2 L/STOKERS	
	8 ABs	7 STOKERS 1st	
	1 O/S		

would have taken five to six years' experience in submarines for an officer to attain his first command. During the wars this process was accelerated considerably but even so, by the time he was given an operational boat, the new captain was more often than not a confident, technically competent officer at the apex of his career. As for remuneration, a newly promoted lieutenant commander could expect the highest rate of lieutenants' pay, enhanced by increments in recognition of the increased strains imposed by submarine command. Married men could apply for a dependants allowance together with a sum to cover board and lodgings.

The submarine skipper was the eyes and mind of his crew. He alone co-ordinated their actions and he alone took the key decisions. The success of the mission and the survival of the crew depended upon the skills of the skipper, arguably the most demanding job in the RN. The prestige compensated for the lack of financial reward. Successful skippers were revered by their crews. Some became legends. The skipper embodied the crew's corporate identity, he personified them. The collectivist outlook of the RN Submarine Service was embodied in the convention that medals were held by the captain in proxy for his entire crew. Collectively they faced danger and collectively, in theory, they reaped the rewards.

THE FIRST LIEUTENANT (FL) – 'NUMBER ONE', 'FIRST HAND', 'JIMMY' OR 'JIMMY THE ONE'

In addition to being the ship's executive officer, first lieutenant also performed the duties of electrical, torpedo and training officer. As such he was responsible for the carrying out of all drills and for ensuring that the men handled the submarine according to the requirements of the captain. The first lieutenant calculated trim using data collected by the stoker PO. The first lieutenant ordered which tank was to be blown and which valves were to be opened or closed. He dispensed orders and received reports in the control room. Most skippers were content to leave the everyday running of the boat in the hands of the highly experienced first lieutenant. A four-year stint as first lieutenant was considered the norm in the RN. The equivalent German rank was the *IWO*. On paper the first lieutenant was also the engineer but during the war these duties were often delegated to the chief ERAs while many of the larger boats carried warrant officer engineers.

Successful 'Number Ones' quickly established a good rapport with their senior rates, delegated responsibility to them and relied on their expertise. In handling personnel administration the first lieutenant acted as divisional officer for the entire crew and, through the captain, recommended men for promotions, courses and awards, controlled leave and dealt with all but the most serious misdemeanours. Because of the control he exercised over their lives the sailors always accorded him a subtle extra measure of deference which, in most cases, was well deserved. A good first lieutenant resulted in an efficient and content lower deck.

LIEUTENANT OR SUB-LIEUTENANT – 'SECOND HAND'

This officer was responsible for the maintenance and operation of all weapons systems on board the boat. The Second Hand worked closely with the TI. Upon passing the medical (and from 1932 the tank exercise) the typical sub-lieutenant spent three months training at Blockhouse. The course was semi-theoretical and partly based on sea-training. It was highly desirable that an officer entrant to the Submarine Service be proficient in hydraulics, engineering and electrics. However, these subjects were not introduced to the Blockhouse training course until 1919. General Service tended to regard these areas of expertise as the preserve of the NCO. The result was that many young submarine officers were unprepared for the demands of active service during the First World War.

NAVIGATOR – 'THIRD HAND'

Normally the navigator, a relic of the old days when there was a first captain, second captain and third officer, was a junior regular officer and sometimes a warrant officer or a qualified Mate, an officer commissioned from the ranks through the Mates system. During the war, however, there was a shortage of suitable officers and those of the Royal Naval Reserve were often substituted in their stead. These Merchant Navy officers held at least foreign-going first mates' papers and some had passed the qualifications for Master Mariner. Whether he was RN or RNR the navigator would have been under training for eventual promotion to first lieutenant and assessed to determine his suitability as a future commanding officer. During the First World War, RNR navigators were only considered as potential first lieutenants until late in hostilities. The first RNR officers to take the submarine officers course did so in May 1917 and the first to take the 'Perisher' course did so in March 1918. In later years the Third Hand's role encompassed operation the attack computer (irreverently known as the 'fruit machine'). The navigator in a British submarine was always a commissioned officer unlike the *Kriegsmarine obersteuermann* (a CPO rate).

THE RATINGS

It should be borne in mind that there were two levels of classification, a man's rating, or 'substantive rate', which was based on his rank, and his sub-rating, or 'non-substantive rate' which was his naval occupation or 'trade'. In broad terms, the Engine Room Department was responsible for propulsion and engineering aspects, while the Executive or Seaman's Branch was concerned with weapons systems and communications. The coxswain and chief ERA, the most senior crewmen aboard, occupied positions of considerable importance in the ship's company. Both reported directly to the first lieutenant.

CPO (COXSWAIN)

Coxswains, who were always accorded the status of senior non-commissioned officer aboard, emerged from the Torpedo Branch and qualified in either of two ways. The most common method was to qualify as a 'Submarine Coxswain' (SC). This could be attained by relatively junior petty officers and it was common for them to qualify at the first opportunity in the hopes of filling a vacancy when one occurred. There was also the formal non-substantive Branch qualification of Torpedo Coxswain, which was a qualification with fleet-wide acceptability. Submarine coxswains generally started out as petty officer (submarine) coxswains then acquired higher qualifications and promotions later in their careers.

The coxswain was the first lieutenant's non-technical right hand man and as such was responsible for discipline, messing, maintaining leave records and to a large extent the physical welfare of the men. The coxswain was responsible for maintaining the first aid box and on occasion acting as sick berth attendant. His duties also included the ordering, stowing and issuing of provisions, tobacco, rum, beer, and 'war comforts'. It was the coxswain, with the first lieutenant's approval, who made up the 'watchbill', a rota detailing which duties the men carried out when on watch and at diving or action stations. He ensured the men were properly dressed while on deck. While entering and leaving harbour and at action stations the coxswain traditionally closed-up on the helm and when dived on patrol or when called to diving stations he manned the after hydroplanes. When on watch on the surface he supervised the seamen on watch and assisted the officer of the watch. Respected by all rates, a competent and proficient coxswain was key to maintaining morale and efficiency on the boat. Several Submarine coxswains have passed into Service legend. The nearest German rate was that of *oberbootsmann*.

THE EXECUTIVE DEPARTMENT (SEAMEN)

TORPEDOMEN

The Torpedo Branch during the First World War encompassed not only torpedoes, their tubes and handling gear, but also electrical systems and everything concerned with seamanship generally. In addition to the coxswain, three men from the Torpedo Branch held key positions in the ship's company. They were usually petty officers, although it was not unusual that some were leading seamen, particularly in smaller submarines.

TGM

A seaman chief petty officer or senior petty officer performed the duties of Torpedo Gunner's Mate, or TGM. In the smaller boats he was often a less qualified petty officer (as experienced TGMs were in short supply and most were required on the larger, more complex, submarines). His range of responsibilities included supervision of both the electrical and torpedo departments. The 'TI' was answerable to the weapons officer. He was authorised to deal with the embarkation and disembarkation of torpedoes, the flooding up and draining down of the torpedo tubes during an attack. The TI routinely subjected torpedoes to sectional examinations, air tests and the application of 'torp oil', assisted by a number of petty officers, leading seamen and ABs. The main motors, main batteries, switchboards, Sperry gyro and all other electrical equipment came under his care. The comparable German rate was *obermechaniker* or *mechaniker*.

LTO

A TGM was usually assisted by at least one leading seaman holding an 'LTO' (non-substantive) rate to assist him and to stand the opposite watch. On watch he took charge of the main motor and auxiliary switchboards, regulating speed with the rheostats.

SECOND COXSWAIN

The third, usually a leading seaman in smaller boats but often a petty officer in larger submarines, was the second coxswain, known colloquially as 'scratcher'. He was primarily concerned with the use and maintenance of the upper deck equipment including the anchors, berthing lines and torpedo embarking gear. On the surface he stood watch on the bridge and when dived manned the forward hydroplanes. His action station was in the fore-ends supervising the torpedo loading crew.

SIGNALMAN

For decades the Royal Navy had scoured the annual intakes of *Ganges* and *Impregnable* for the very brightest of boys. These starred youngsters would be trained as signal boys in specialised signal schools at Portsmouth, Chatham or Devonport. The signalman, in addition to his usual duties, acted as the captain's clerk and stood lookout upon surfacing and whenever the captain stood watch on the bridge. Signalmen were proficient in all forms of visual signalling including signal flags, semaphore and flashing light. As only one signalman was carried per boat, it was his misfortune to be constantly on call to perform his duties on the bridge.

WIRELESS TELEGRAPHISTS – 'SPARKERS'

Training and all underwater sound detection equipment remained the responsibility of HMS *Vernon*. As the First World War continued, wireless operation became a key aspect of submarine operations. To keep watch on the sets, two wireless Telegraphists were carried, often one of these was a Boy. When dived, the Telegraphists manned the underwater listening hydrophones within the wireless office. They were also responsible for operating the transmitter, coding and decoding signals and looking after the aerials. They were charged with maintaining this delicate and temperamental equipment.

In 1916 the Admiralty created the Anti-Submarine Division. A specialised hydrophone development section was established at Hawkcraig in Scotland. In 1917 the Royal Navy opened its 'Listening School' ashore at Portland which concentrated on the training of W/T personnel in hydrophone procedure. Further re-organisation took place in 1924 with the founding of HMS *Osprey* in Portland. Osprey became synonymous with A/S training and development, particularly with regard to ASDIC 'Sparkers' doubled as hydrophone operators. In September 1919 the new (non-substantive) rating of 'Sound Detector' was introduced for Portland graduates. An authorised trade badge did not appear until 1930, mirroring the evolution of ASDIC (see glossary). By the outbreak of the Second World War, all British submarines carried a telegraphist rated as either Higher Submarine Detector (HSD) or a Submarine Detector (SD). The growth of this specialised communications branch can be seen in Fig.4. In 1918 *H5* required two telegraphists but in 1940 *Swordfish* carried six.

LEADING SEAMEN

Rated as possessing a greater degree of skill and competence than the AB, leading seamen were frequently entrusted with high responsibilities on British submarines. Leading seamen were allocated duties in the electrical and torpedo departments. When on watch they stood lookout, manned the helm and forward hydroplanes while two shared watches in the forward compartment when dived. At least one leading seaman was responsible for manning the gun, known colloquially as a 'killick' or 'hooky'. The leading seaman's enhanced status was denoted by his fouled anchor badge. The nearest German equivalent was the *mechanikers-maat* (though the latter held petty officer status and the leading seaman did not).

THE AB OR SEAMAN

Volunteers were usually attracted to submarines by the financial inducements referred to above, combined with the generally more relaxed attitude to authority within the Submarine Service, that *enfant terrible* of the Royal Navy. First World War volunteers might be attracted by the benefits of 'prize money' payments made to a successful crew. During the First World War, an AB might expect to earn £30 per year in General Service but this would rise to £67 in submarines. By 1939 the AB in General Service could earn 2 shillings per day but 'hard lying' and 'proficiency' increments in submarines could see this rise to 7 shillings per day. The volunteer would be drafted to Fort Blockhouse, Gosport for a course in basic hydrodynamics. From 1932 the induction course would be followed by simulated escape exercise in the 'tank'. Men who failed would be immediately drafted back to General Service, though in 1941 men could be drafted into boats without the benefit of passing the tank test. Sea training in submarines was negligible during wartime. Most skills were learned 'on the job' during the First World War. In the Second World War, the sea-training course at Blyth lasted just six weeks. The German equivalent to the seaman was the *matrose* or *matrosengefreiter*.

Submarine ABs were required to be highly versatile, depending upon the watchbill. Large boats such as the 'M', 'K' or later the 'T' class carried cooks (whose primary role was the preparation and serving of food). In the smaller boats however these tasks were undertaken by the seamen, the role of cook being allocated to one of the ABs, while the job of steward was performed by a volunteer who received a small stipend from the officers. These domestic tasks were carried out in addition to normal watch-keeping duties. All seamen were encouraged to take their turn as helmsman, following closely the instructions of the coxswain and first lieutenant. During diving stations the coxswain himself would take over the aft 'plane, leaving the other to one of the most experienced leading seamen or petty officers. With the exceptions of the ballast pump operator and the telegraphist, the helmsmen were usually the only men in the submarine provided with seats at their working stations.

THE ENGINE ROOM DEPARTMENT

The engine room was the domain of the CERA (or Engineer Officer in larger boats). Under the CERA were two or three ERAs whose main duties were the running and care of the engines and at least one stoker petty officer who was responsible for the operation and maintenance of the auxiliary machinery and miscellaneous mechanical gear. A couple of leading stokers and three or four ordinary stokers usually completed the engineering complement, depending upon the boat involved.

The Chief ERA was the highest ranked NCO on the boat (however, seniority rested with the Coxswain). The CERA was the mechanical supremo and a good chief possessed an intimate knowledge of his boat and its systems. The diesels, pumps, compressors and all mechanical equipment were in his charge. Larger boats carried an engineer officer, more often than not a highly experienced warrant engineer like Roy Glenn of *Thetis*.

ENGINE ROOM ARTIFICER

Prior to the First World War, ERAs received their training at HMS *Fisgard*. Admiralty generally recruited young civilians by means of a competitive examination for an apprenticeship. As a qualified and experienced ERA could earn substantially more in industry than in the Royal Navy, the Senior Service had to fight hard to retain its artificers.

From 1932 the Boy Artificer School in Chatham (also known as The Mechanics Training Establishment) assumed the role of teaching the four-year apprenticeship. The apprentice would be required to sit the Higher Educational Test, considered essential for anyone seeking to gain warrant officer status within the Royal Navy. Watch-keeping experience would be gained in the engine room of a General Service warship. Next the apprentice ERA would be required to study for the 'auxiliary ticket', qualifying him to '*run, start and stop all auxiliary machinery on a warship*'. Upon passing this exam, the apprentice was able to discard the 'square rig' of an AB for the 'fore and aft rig' (blue reefer jacket, trousers and peaked cap) of a petty officer (ERA 5th Class). The next step up the ladder of marine engineering was to obtain a 'boiler room ticket', a qualification confirming the candidate's ability to 'flash up a boiler room, keep a watch and shut down when required'. Upon passing this examination, the candidate held the status of a qualified ERA 4th class. This was expressed in subtle changes to the uniform. Black buttons were replaced with a brass variety and the ERA now sported the coveted gold laurel leaf on his cap. It should be noted that ERAs 4th to 1st class were awarded the status of CPO *but not the authority*.

Some ambitious young men might continue with their studies for ERA 3rd class status immediately but a significant proportion of candidates volunteered for the Submarine Service at this stage in their careers. Progress up the promotional ladder between ERA 4th class and ERA 1st class would be governed by a similar combination of hands-on experience and theoretical study, until the goal of ERA 1st class was achieved. Parallels can be drawn with the career progression of civilian marine engineers. The Royal Navy was keen to recruit civilians with expertise in diesel engines to become ERAs during the war years, provoking outrage from mercantile shipowners who subsidised marine technical colleges. The technological complexity of the submarine demanded a higher ratio of ERAs and senior rates than General Service, though the actual number carried depended upon the class of submarine.

OUTSIDE ERA (ALSO KNOWN AS 'OUTSIDE TIFFY' OR 'OUTSIDE WRECKER')

Highly experienced ERA (but occasionally a stoker petty officer) responsible for the efficient functioning of all machinery outside the engine room, i.e. in the control room. The Outside ERA serviced systems, including the periscope mechanism, in the control room. At diving stations the 'Outside Wrecker' operated the vents, blowing valves and trim pump, while his staff attended to the blowers and the high pressure air feeds.

THE STOKER

With the exception of 'K' class boats there were no furnaces on submarines. Stokers carried out watch-keeping over the diesels and motors, carrying out routine maintenance and general labouring tasks within the engine and motor rooms, according to the instructions of the ERAs. Whenever diving stations was called, the stokers obeyed the internal telegraph system. First they stopped the main diesels then manually wound out both engine clutches (thus isolating the engines from the screws). Next the muffler valves were shut off to keep exhaust emissions free from tell-tale smoke. Upon surfacing, it fell to the stokers to open the outboard drains to prevent any sea water from entering the engine cylinders.

The throttles on the main engines were manned by ERAs assisted by a couple of stokers detailed to take readings and monitor hydraulic machinery dials and compressed air feeds. Keeping watch over the 'six valve chest' in the engine room was another crucially important job. Working under direct instruction from the first lieutenant, these valves were used in conjunction with a large electric pump to force seawater in or out of the trim tanks.

Not all stokers worked in the engine room. A leading stoker charged with operating auxiliary machinery was often stationed in the fore-ends. A second leading stoker would work with the Outside ERA in the operation and maintenance of the periscope hydraulics. At least one experienced stoker might be detailed to take up position in the motor room, between the two screw shafts. Should the steering motor fail or a problem arise with the maintenance of telemotor pressure at diving stations, the stoker was on hand to manually deal with the problem. A leading stoker known as a 'Fresh Water Tanky' was responsible for providing water for both galley and general sanitation. One of his secondary duties was to weight disposal bags and organise an unpopular 'gash dump' when it was safe to do so. It was a dirty, noisy job. The stokers' mess was known as 'hell's kitchen' for good reason.

As has already been mentioned, relations between officers and men were far less formal than in General Service. While it should be emphasised that it was always imperative to retain discipline, the fraternal bonding within the service was genuine. This extract from Lt-Cdr Godfrey Herbert's account of the mining of *D5* off Harwich in 1914 illustrates the point:

> I now found myself surrounded by a dozen members of my crew. Most were beginning to feel the strain of keeping afloat. First one then another would throw up his hands and go down. For some minutes I held onto one of the stokers who was close to me, urging him to keep going but he got heavier and heavier until seeing that we should both go under I had to release my hold of him...to have been shipmates with these men, to have known them all so well and now to see them die one by one, was terrible beyond words...It would be impossible to describe the loss I felt at the deaths of such a wonderful crew: they were the finest who ever manned a submarine...

In a similar vein, Jim Allaway has written in *Hero of the Upholder* that Second World War submarine ace Malcolm Wanklyn VC, DSO★★ was more at ease with the lower deck than with his brother officers. In common with its German counterpart, the British Submarine Service was an interdependent mechanism (perhaps better described as an organism) bound and animated by a very special *esprit de corps* – what Dönitz perceptively described as a *schicksalsgemeinschaft* – a community bound by fate. Heed the words of Capt Michael Lumby DSO, DSC:

> Your life depends upon good drill and automatic reaction. At sea you relax formality but reaction must be as sharp as ever. I cannot stress this enough. You have to strike a balance – somewhere between being a martinet and a liberal and it's not easy... A submarine is a very close community and anyone can listen into conversations within the wardroom or senior rates mess. Only a curtain separates them from the gangway. One works at very close quarters. You get to know your men, their strengths and weaknesses – and they get to know yours. You might catch a whisper from the senior rates, 'Lumby's got the wind up' or something like it and you know you have to redeem yourself. Officers, seniors and junior rates are rubbing shoulders on a submarine all the time and there is simply nowhere to hide. A close relationship develops between all on board and you really can't improve upon this. You feel immense pride in a good crew, not a pompous kind of pride but something quite extraordinary, even spiritual.

This was William Carr's big happy undersea family.

APPENDIX 1

FLEET ORDER IN OPERATION PRIOR TO 1932

AFO 1803 – PROCEDURE FOR SALVAGE OF SUBMARINES IN HOME WATERS (M.2556/30-11.7.1930)

In the event of the loss or sinking of a submarine in home waters, the senior officer on the spot is to report immediately the name or number of the submarine and the position in which she sank.

1. *The message is to be addressed to the Admiralty, Rear Admiral (S), Captain or Commander (S) concerned. Commanders-in-Chief Atlantic Fleet and home ports, Captain in Charge, Portland, Captain, Fishery Protection and Minesweeping and Captain A/S. It is to be transmitted by the quickest possible route to all addressees. The information contained in this message is to be supplemented by the depth of water obtained by sounding as soon as this is available.*

2. *On receipt of the message of sinking, Rear Admiral (S) will signal to all concerned, stating whether he will proceed to the scene of operations.*

3. *The senior officer on the spot will take charge of salvage operations and is to communicate all his requirements which are not available on the spot or provided for hereafter to the authority concerned (See paragraph 5) and to the Admiralty if necessary.*

4. *The Captain (S) or Commander (S) concerned is to arrange for two submarines to be available on the scene of the sinking for underwater signalling purposes and to provide compressed air if required.*

5. *The following procedure is to be put into operation forthwith by the Commander-in-Chief of the home port in whose area the sinking takes place or Commander-in-Chief, Atlantic Fleet, if the accident occurs during exercises with the Atlantic Fleet: and all necessary arrangements should be made with authorities concerned accordingly.*

    a) 1st Minesweeping Flotilla, Portland to proceed to the area in readiness to sweep

    b) 1st A/S Flotilla, Portland or 6th Destroyer Flotilla, Atlantic Fleet, whichever is most quickly available, to proceed to the area in readiness to search.

    c) The RAF station nearest to the area, to be requested by message repeated to … Air Officer Commanding, Coastal Area to send aircraft to search for oil and air bubbles, subject to the provision that the scope of the operation should be left to the discretion of the Commanding Officer of the RAF station concerned. It should be requested that reports of progress of search should be addressed to the officer in charge of salvage operations. If, however, an aircraft carrier is available this duty is to be carried out by her machines.

    d) Two lifting lighters, together with tugs to tow them to the scene of operations to be provided by Admiral Superintendent Portsmouth, or Captain in Charge, Portland, whichever place is nearer to the position where the submarine sank.

    e) Salvage party and divers to be sent to the scene of operations by the Admiral Superintendent of the nearest dock-yard port, transport to be arranged in conjunction with the Commander-in-Chief.

    f) Self-propelled lifting lighter of the 'Moor' Class to be sent to the scene of operations by the Admiral Superintendent, Portsmouth or Captain Superintendent, Sheerness, whichever port is nearest.

    Note – 'Moor' Class lifting lighters are attached to Sheerness are frequently employed during summer months at Rosyth, Invergordon and the Humber. This procedure may subsequently be modified as necessary by the senior officer in charge of the operations as soon as the requirements of the situation are known. Attention is drawn to Admiralty letter C.P32161/27 of 27 May, 1928 in which authority is given to obtain salvage plant from authorities and commercial firms in the UK for use in cases of emergency to raise a sunken submarine sufficiently to enable life to be saved if it is known or there is reason to suppose that the crew of the sunken vessel are still alive. This letter together with particulars of the plant available as supplied by the salvage firms, corrected periodically, is sent to the following: Commanders in Chief, The Nore, Portsmouth, Plymouth and Atlantic Fleet,

Commanding Officer Coast of Scotland, Rear Admiral (S), Admiral Commanding Battle Cruiser Squadron, Admiral Commanding 2nd Cruiser Squadron, Rear Admiral 2nd Battle Squadron and Captain in Charge, Portland.

a), b) and c) can be countermanded when the exact location of the vessel has been established.

d), e) and f) can be delayed or cancelled if the depth of water or other circumstances render immediate salvage out of the question.

6. *The Admiralty is to be kept informed of the situation and Admiralty sanction must be obtained before all salvage operations are finally abandoned.*

7. *From the time that the original message reporting the sinking of a submarine has been received, too much importance cannot be attached to keeping lines of communication clear to and from Rear Admiral (S) or the senior officer conducting the operations, more especially as he will probably be afloat in a destroyer or small vessel with limited W/T resources. To ensure this:*

i) The correct use of the prefix 'Immediate' must be rigidly adhered to; it should seldom be necessary on any message which does not directly affect the decisions to be made or action to be taken by the officer conducting the operations.

ii) Should any difficulty be experienced by authorities afloat in communicating multiple address messages direct to all addresses such messages should be passed through the nearest Naval shore W/T station with instructions to retransmit them by L/T to as many addressees as possible. Messages may also be passed to the Admiralty for retransmission by Group A when it is not known if addressees afloat have received the messages by W/T direct.

APPENDIX 2

FLEET ORDERS IN OPERATION AT THE TIME OF THE *THETIS* DISASTER

AFO 568/34 SUBMARINE SALVAGE AND RESCUE PROCEDURE TO BE ADOPTED IN THE EVENT OF THE SINKING OF A SUBMARINE IN HOME WATERS

The board have recently had under review the question of the steps necessary for saving life in the event of the sinking of a submarine.

Experience has shown that except in very special circumstances salvage of a submarine in time to save life is impracticable. Even in special circumstances such as a submarine sinking in sheltered water, escape by DSEA would probably be the most efficacious. It has been decided therefore that this apparatus with which all submarines are equipped, is to be relied upon for the escape of the crew in all circumstances.

Local organisation should accordingly be directed to vessels proceeding with the utmost dispatch to the scene of a disaster to locate the submarine and pick up any men who have made, or may be about to make their escape and subsequently be provided medical attention as necessary. As soon as the submarine has been located, or when, in the opinion of the Senior Officer, her position is sufficiently accurately known, twelve half pound charges are to be fired in the vicinity. This is to signal to any men imprisoned in the submarine that surface vessels have arrived and that escape by means of DSEA can be attempted with every prospect of rescue. The charges should be fired at least two and a half cables from the position of the submarine in case men are making their escape at the time.

From the time that the original message reporting the sinking of a submarine has been received, too much importance cannot be attached to keeping lines of communication clear to and from Rear Admiral (S). The correct use of the prefix 'immediate' must be rigidly adhered to.

(AFO 1803/30 is cancelled)
CMF 07066/33 – 15.3.1934

AFO 971/35 PROCEDURE TO BE ADOPTED IN THE EVENT OF THE SINKING OF A SUBMARINE IN HOME WATERS (MF 4391/35-18.4.35)

1 *In the event of the loss or sinking of a submarine in Home Waters, the Senior Officer on the spot is to report immediately the name or number of the submarine and the position in which she sank. The message should be addressed to the Admiralty, Rear Admiral (S), Captain or Commander (S) concerned, Commanders in Chief Home Fleet and Home Ports, Commanding Officer, Coast of Scotland, Captain A/S, Senior Officer 1st Minesweeping Flotilla and Senior Officer 1st A/S Flotilla. It is to be transmitted by the quickest possible route to all adressees. The depth of water should be signalled as convenient.*

2 *On receipt of the message of sinking, Rear Admiral (S) will signal to all concerned stating whether he will proceed to the scene of operations.*

3 *The Senior Officer on the spot will take charge of rescue operations.*

4 *The Captain (S) or Commander (S) concerned is to arrange for two submarines to be available on the scene for underwater signalling purposes.*

5 *The following procedure is to be put into operation forthwith by the Commander-in-Chief of the Home Port or the Commanding Officer, Coast of Scotland, in whose area the sinking takes place, or Commander-in-Chief Home Fleet, if the accident occurs during exercises with the Home Fleet and all necessary arrangements should be made with the authorities concerned accordingly:*

a) 1st Minesweeping Flotilla, Portland, is to proceed to the area in readiness to sweep.

b) An A/S flotilla from Portland or an A/S destroyer flotilla, Home Fleet, whichever is most quickly available, is to proceed to the area in readiness to search.

c) (i) The Air Officer Commanding Coastal Area, is to be requested by message to send aircraft to search for indicator buoys, oil and air bubbles. The Air Officer Commanding will thereupon detail the most suitable units in his command to carry out the search. He will also communicate with any other Royal Air Force units which, by reason of their geographical position, are able to assist in the search, but such units are usually equipped with aircraft unsuitable for prolonged search operations at a distance from land.

(ii) The Air Officer Commanding Coastal Area will co-ordinate the operations of shore-based aircraft from the outset. He should be requested to supply reports of the search to the officer in charge of rescue operations and is to be informed of the call-sign of the latter and the wave frequency to be employed.

(iii) If an aircraft carrier is available the foregoing duties are to be undertaken by her aircraft, but if necessary the Air Officer Commanding Coastal area should be asked to assist as well.

d) HMS Tedworth is to embark six divers and necessary diving stores and remain at immediate notice.

6 *As soon as the submarine has been located, or when, in the opinion of the Senior Officer, her position is sufficiently accurately known, twelve half pound charges are to be fired in the vicinity. This is to signal to any men imprisoned in the submarine that surface vessels have arrived and that escape by means of DSEA can be attempted with every prospect of rescue.*

   The charges should be fired at least 2 and a half cables from the position of the submarine in case men are making their escape at the time.

7 *The Admiralty is to be kept informed of the situation.*

8 *From the time that the original message reporting the sinking of the submarine has been received, too much importance cannot be attached to keeping lines of communication clear, to and from Rear Admiral (S).*

Correct use of the prefix 'Immediate' must be rigidly adhered to.

APPENDIX 3

CORRESPONDENCE BETWEEN ADMIRAL RAIKES AND GEORGE CRITCHLEY OF THE LIVERPOOL AND GLASGOW SALVAGE ASSOCIATION FOLLOWING THE *THETIS* DISASTER

Letter from Rear Admiral Raikes to George Critchley:

22nd June 1939

Dear Sir

With reference to your evidence given to the Board of Enquiry during their recent visit to Birkenhead, I have been in communication with the Admiralty and they affirm that Commander Cross rang up Liverpool Central 0143 at about 11.30p.m. on 1st June and that he was answered; and that a message was given to the effect that the Liverpool and Glasgow Salvage Association would probably be required.

I shall be grateful if you will endeavour to trace this message and inform me of any further details that may be ascertained.

Yours sincerely

RHT Raikes

Letter from Rear Admiral Raikes to the Secretary of the Admiralty:

22nd June 1939

Sir

With reference to the narrative of events in regard to the loss of HMS Thetis which was forwarded to me on 7th June by the Deputy Chief of Naval Staff, it is stated therein that at 2300 on 1st June the 'Admiralty got through to the Liverpool and Glasgow Salvage Company on the telephone, after several unsuccessful attempts and warned them they would probably be required'
*   During the recent visit of the Board of Enquiry to Birkenhead, the evidence of Mr G Critchley, the Joint Manager of the Liverpool and Glasgow Salvage Company was heard. He stated that the Association have no record of such a message being received at that time but that had they done so they would have immediately sent out their salvage vessel Ranger with all necessary equipment, in which case she would have arrived on the scene about 0600 on 2nd of June 1939.*
*   In view of this seeming discrepancy it is requested that the Admiralty message be traced [handwritten] and any other details given which may help to clear up the matter.*

I am your obedient servant

(sd) RHT Raikes
Vice Admiral

A19/22 Exchange Buildings
23rd June 1939

Dear Sir

I received your letter of yesterday and what I now write can be treated as if evidence given in front of a board of enquiry.

I say that an answer by telephone from the Number Liverpool Central 0143 at about 11.30p.m. on 1st of June was impossible because that is the telephone number of our General Office, which was closed at about 7pm on that day. After that time no communication whatever with that number was possible 1) because no one was present in the office and 2) because the telephones are cut off at a general switch box.

I further say that I was at my home during the whole of that evening and throughout the night and I received no message of any kind whatever from the Admiralty or from any other source and was completely unaware of the casualty until 4am on the 2nd of June when I received an enquiry from a representative of the Mersey Docks and Harbour Board for a decompression chamber.

In accordance with you request when I appeared before you on the morning of the 20th instant, I have made enquiries concerning the possibility of the reported message having been communicated to any other official of this Association whose name and telephone number appear in the directory... I wonder whether the Trunk Telephone Authorities can trace precisely the number to which Commander Cross call was connected and whether Commander Cross can state the name of the person to which he spoke? If you can suggest any further enquiries you think I can make, I would be glad to do everything possible.

Yours faithfully

George Critchley

MANAGER

Admiralty Minute 7.7.39

The Naval Board of Enquiry considered this conflict of evidence but came to no conclusion.

It is likely that Mr Critchley in his evidence before the Tribunal will draw attention to this matter, possibly in such a manner as to reflect upon the action taken by the Naval Authorities.

The answer to such criticism would be to draw attention to the Admiralty policy which is not to attempt salvage of submarines. In any case the duty of calling in assistance would rest with the Commander-in-Chief, Plymouth rather than upon the Duty Commander at the Admiralty.

Nevertheless the question will still arise as to whether it would not in fact have been better not only to warn but to call upon the Salvage Co. at an early stage and if so, whether salvage ships could have been sent to the approximate position before the submarine was located...

Mr Synnott

But the question never did arise, because for reasons that remain unclear to this day, Mr Critchley never did give his evidence to the Bucknill Tribunal.

APPENDIX 4

TIDAL CONDITIONS IN LIVERPOOL BAY, 1–2 JUNE 1939

1 JUNE LW 0500
1 JUNE HW 1105
1 JUNE LW 1715
1 JUNE HW 2325

2 JUNE LW 0538
2 JUNE HW 1148
2 JUNE LW 1746
2 JUNE HW 0003

APPENDIX 5

TECHNICAL DETAILS OF THE *KRIEGSMARINE* VIIC & VIIC/41 U-BOATS

COURTESY AND COPYRIGHT OF DR AXEL NIESTLÉ

DIMENSIONS

The VIIC boat became the 'workhorse' submarine of the *Kriegsmarine* during the Second World War. The official tonnage of the original design as per 22 March 1941 was 761.89 tons on the surface and 864.69 tons submerged. However, the figure changed to a very small degree with later modifications. Usually 769 tons and 871 tons are given as the standard official figures throughout the war. Boats from different yards may also have varied to a certain degree due to small design variations. The overall general dimensions measured 67.1m in length overall, 6.22m in beam, 4.8m draught and 9.60m in height around the conning tower.

MACHINERY

Two diesel/oil engines powered the two propellers, originally designed in bronze, but a shortage of non-ferrous metals led to the use of steel propellers during the war. Boats already ordered before the war were fitted either with engines manufactured by Maschinefabrik-Augsburg-Nürnberg (MAN) or by the Germaniawerft (GW). After the start of the war, other companies or yards manufactured these two diesel types under licence. Front-line experience soon showed the more rigid GW construction being superior and new constructions were gradually fitted with GW-type diesels only. Both types were fitted with *Gebläse* (super-chargers) and developed 1,400ps each at 475 revolutions per minute continuous power, or 495 revolutions maximum power for 30 minutes developed 1600ps, which give a maximum surface speed of 17 knots. The boat had a calculated operational range of 9,700-nautical miles at 10 knots, or 6,500-n.miles at 12 knots and carried a maximum fuel/oil capacity of 113 tons.

    For running submerged, two 62-cell lead/acid batter/accumulators usually manufactured by Accumulatoren-Fabrik-Aktiengesellschaft (AFA) powered the two electric motors that developed 375ps at 295 revolutions and gave her a maximum speed of 7.6 knots. The four electric motors manufacturers were:

AEG (Allgemeine Elektricittäts-Gesellschaft)
BBC (Brown, Boveri & Cie.)
GL u. Co. (Garbe, Lohmeyer & Co.)
SSW (Siemens-Schuckert-Werke)

These companies all produced more or less very similar designed motors and sometimes under licence (GL). Using battery power the boat had a calculated operational range underwater of 80-n.miles at a steady 4 knots.

ARMAMENT

TORPEDOES

The VIIC boat was designed with five torpedo tubes, four at the bow and one at the stern.

    Initially fourteen torpedoes were carried until summer 1943, with two of them in the upper-deck reserve containers. These were later then removed to save weight and because it became too dangerous to reload them in North Atlantic waters. In 1944 the number was reduced to ten to increase living conditions in the tube space for prolonged submersion. From autumn 1944 onward, on boats operating in the Atlantic, or British coastal waters, the ten torpedoes usually consisted of five *T5* and five *LuT*, often stowed as follows:

T5: one in forward tube, three in forward bilges and one in aft tube. Five *LuT* stowed: three in forward tube, one in forward bilges and one in the aft bilges.

MINES

Mines were only carried on special order and in exchange for torpedoes and not in addition.

The figures for mines offered in reference books are theoretical numbers and have nothing really to do with operational realities.

There were three different types of U-boat mines, which were called *Torpedominen* and these were delivered through the torpedo tubes:

TMA – moored floating mines, designed for, but never actually used on U-boats.
TMB – small ground mines with various fuses and an explosive charge of 1,276lb (578.7kg).
TMC – large ground mines with an explosive charge of 2,200lb (997.9kg).

The exchange ratios of mines / torpedo were:
One torpedo – three TMB
One torpedo – two TMC

GUNS

Initially, the VIIC gun specifications consisted of: one 88mm (3.46in) deck gun, plus 220-rounds and one 20mm (0.79in) AA Flak gun, plus 4,380-rounds of ammunition. On Atlantic boats the deck gun was removed in summer 1943. The single gun bandstand aft of the bridge (model 0) was modified in early 1943 by adding a second, lower bandstand with another single 20mm gun (this was then called conning tower modification II). The Type I modification (two 13.2mm twin machine-gun mounts on upper bandstand, single 20mm on lower bandstand) was abandoned when test showed that the machine guns were not powerful enough. From May 1943, modification IV was introduced, fitted initially with two single 20mm mounts on the widened upper bandstand and a quadruple 20mm mount on the enlarged, lower bandstand. After 20mm twin mounts became available in July 1943, twin mounts replaced the single mounts. From October 1943 onward, the 37mm mount replaced the quadruple mounts. This represented the final variation of the Type IV conning tower modification. Later in the war 37mm twin mounts were tested experimentally on a few boats, but the *schnorchel* had already reduced the threat from aircraft, by then. This was a summary of standard AA-modifications on Atlantic boats.

Other experimental modifications were carried on some boats, however, but they never became a standard form. Modifications were done to all front-line or working-up boats regardless of their date of commission and boats were continuously upgraded to the latest version, during refits.

DIVING DEPTHS

The operational diving depth of a VIIC boat was 100m (328ft), with a maximum depth 165m (541.33ft) and a crush depth of 200m (656ft). A crash-dive to 20m took 30 seconds on average.

The VIIC/41 boat was almost the same in all respects as the VIIC, but was designed with a stronger pressure hull, which gave the boat an operational diving depth of 120m (394ft) and a crush depth of 250m (820ft).

COMPLEMENT

Both VIIC and VIIC/41 boats carried between forty-four and fifty-two crewmen. With increased AA-armament in 1943/44, crew numbers were at their highest. Following the introduction of the *schnorchel* the crews were often reduced to between forty-six and fifty crewmen (see crew profiles).

Each Type VII U-boat carried thirty-six *unteroffiziere* and ratings, generally two *unteroffiziere* to every three ratings. Apart from the officers, the crew of a U-boat was divided between technical personnel and seamen. The technical division comprised of specialist personnel: diesel machinists, electricians, radio operators and torpedo mechanics. There were four senior NCOs. (Copyright Dr Axel Niestlé)

END NOTES

1 The Prize Rules were generally observed in interceptions prior to 1917 but the sinking of Drumcree, 18 May 1915 off Trevose Head, indicated that when conditions dictated, the U-boats could and would attack without warning.

2 The figures for the spring of 1917 speak for themselves; February: 86 ships sunk, 402 lives lost. March: 127 ships sunk, 699 lives lost. April: 155 ships sunk, 1,125 lives lost.

3 The other victims being: *Oldfield Grange*, *Hare* and *Coningberg*. *Coningberg*, like *Formby* was owned by the Clyde Shipping Co. Both ships sank with all hands.

4 Two inbound convoys sailed for Liverpool every eight days from Hampton Roads (HH). One convoy sailed from Sydney, Canada every eight days (HS) while a further convoy made the 3,050 mile journey from New York to Liverpool (HX). Outbound convoys from Liverpool were coded OLB, OLX and OL, with a sailing from Milford Haven every four days (OM).

5 John Winton 'Convoy', Ch.6.

6 Hashagen devoted a chapter of *U-boot Westwarts* to the dangers of stalking convoys, while Werner Furbringer, author of *Alarm Tauchen!*, ultimately lost his submarine while manoeuvring to attack an east coast convoy (see Vol.1).

7 The MHDB vessel was mined off Black Can Gas Buoy at 0700. Only two men survived. It is unclear why so many were onboard. The mines had been laid by *UC 75* on Boxing Night. A memorial to these men can be found in the foyer of the MHDB Building at Pier Head, Liverpool. There are interesting parallels with the loss of Protector on the Tyne on New Year's Eve 1916.

8 BdU Diary entry 16.9.39, PG50.266 NID, RNHB.

9 By 12 January 1940 the *Kriegsmarine* gradually lifted these restrictions on U-boat operations, firstly in the Bristol Channel, and by the end of the month restrictions were also lifted in the Irish Sea.

10. Ironically *Inverdargle*, a 9,456-ton motor tanker, had been built by Deutsche Werft A.G., Bet. Finkenwerder, Hamburg and launched on 18 May 1938 for Inver Tankers Ltd, Glasgow. The vessel had only recently arrived in Britain on 13 January via convoy HXF15 which had sailed on 4 January. Fore and aft sections of the vessel remain some distance apart on the bed of the Bristol Channel, such was the force of the explosion.

11 '...Das Boot legt sich auf Position AM 6892 auf Grund um die Nacht abzuwarten. Am späten Abend um 23.00 Uhr legt U-30 vor der Hafeneinfahrt von Liverpool seine 12 TMB-Minen im AM 9324' KTB of U30, 4 January 1940. The SS *El Oso* (7,267 tons), from convoy HX 14B, was sunk on 11 January; the SS *Gracia* (5,642 tons), from convoy OB 71, was damaged on 15 January; the SS *Cairnross*, 5,494 tons, from convoy OB 74, was sunk on 17 January; the MV *Munster* (4,305 tons) was sunk on 7 February and the SS *Chagres* (5,406 tons) on 9 February.

12 By the end of May 1943 the Battle of the Atlantic was effectively over. A couple of statistics serve to illustrate the turning point: March 1943: ninety-seven merchants sunk for sixteen U-boats destroyed. May 1943: fifty merchants sunk for forty-one U-boats destroyed. By the end of the Second World War, the loss of 4,786 merchant ships had cost a total of 32,000 lives. An estimated 2,765 of these ships had been sunk in the Battle of the Atlantic.

13 The Declared Minefield lay between these points 52°10' N, 06°15' W and 52°00' N, 07°35' W through 51°35' N, 06°15' W and 51°00'N, 07°15'W to 51°01' N, 04°31' W and 50°33' N, 05°01' W.

14 The story of *U 1202*, including vivid crew recollections, is given in Jens Rohde's *The Lion's Claw* (Die Spur des Lowen).

15 BdU Diary, p358, S14 summary.

16 In the 1950s Admiralty attributed the loss of *U 325* to the depth-charge attack made by *Hesperus* and *Havelock* in position 53°42'N, 04°53'W. However, it is now accepted that this action resulted in the demise of *U 242*.

17 The boat sunk in the Minches has now been identified as *U 965* by Dr Niestlé.

18 Admiralty later requisitioned this vessel as a Q-ship.

19 Hurd, *The Merchant Navy Vol. 3*, p26.

20 Fireman Garthshore and Engineer Martin were lost in the sinking.

21 This was not *Batoum's* first encounter with a U-boat. On 18 July 1915 the ship had been torpedoed by *UB 17* (Ralph Wenninger) a couple of miles off Southwold Lighthouse. Five men died in the explosion. The ship had been beached and subsequently refloated but there was to be no escape for *Batoum* this time.

22 In August 1917, the vessel, which was launched as the *Rosedale* in 1905, was requisitioned by the Admiralty, who operated her as a Q-ship. The vessel operated under the names of: *Alastair, Bendish, Balfame, Dorinda* and *Girdler*. In November 1917 the Admiralty purchased the ship and transferred her to the US Navy as the Q-ship *Santee*.

23 The North Channel was not mined until 13 April and work did not start on the Great Northern Barrage until the autumn. The British did not mine the Irish Sea in fear of damaging international trade and the possibility remains that *U 61* was lost on a loose German mine.

24 *San Zeferino* had previously detonated a mine laid by *UC 6* off Goodwin Light-vessel on 18 September 1915. Two crewmen were killed in this explosion.

25 Lt Getting grew up in Manly, New South Wales and became the first Australian submarine officer to pass the Submarine Commanding Course. He was rewarded with his first boat, *H47*, remaining in command for three months before returning in November to Dolphin as spare CO. Getting was promoted to Commander and returned to Australia in April 1935. Cdr Getting died from wounds received at Guadalcanal whilst in command of HMAS *Canberra* on 9 August 1942.

26 This knot of submarines formed the nucleus of the 6th Flotilla in 1924.

27 Sub-Lt Anthony 'Gamp' Miers went on to command HMS/M *Torbay* in the Second World War, winning the Victoria Cross in the course of his highly controversial career.

28 ADM 137/645.

29 *UC 42* was lost with all hands on 10 September in the Cork roads but the wreck was not discovered until 31 October. The foremost mine chute was empty and the force of the explosion had blown the boat in half. Hatches opened from within pointed to escape attempts but no trace of survivors was found.

30 *Canada's Navy*, Marc Milner, Ch.8, p153.

31 Lt-Cdr Gregory of HMS *Sturgeon* famously transgressed orders to enter the Kattegat and sink a German troop carrier, following a lean spell.

32 Berehaven was one of the Irish Treaty ports held by the British until 1938.

33 Admiralty Technical History No.1, p7.

34 Martin Eric Nasmith 1883–1965. The celebrated submariner had been court-martialled following an accident to *A4* when she was swamped in Stokes Bay in October 1905. Aquitted of negligence, Lt-Cdr Nasmith went on to command the Harwich-based *E11*. On 16 December 1914 (and in common with Godfrey Herbert) a torpedo malfunction robbed Lt-Cdr Nasmith of success against elements of the High Seas Fleet. Nasmith was famously awarded the VC for his exploits in *E11* in 1915. The 'Dunbar' element of his name was a 1920 addition following his marriage. Charming, erudite and tremendously popular with the lower deck, Martin Dunbar-Nasmith went on to successively command HMS *Iron Duke* and the Royal College, Dartmouth. In 1928 he became the first submariner appointed to the role of Rear Admiral (S) and received a knighthood in 1932. As Admiral Martin Dunbar-Nasmith VC, KCB, KCMG he served as Commander-in-Chief, Plymouth in 1939 during the Thetis disaster. By September of that year, he was appointed Commander-in-Chief, Western Approaches. A submariner to his bones, one of the lesser-known aspects of his illustrious career was his work in developing the torpedo data calculator known irreverently as the 'Is-Was' or 'Fruit Machine'.

35 ADM 137/1977.

36 ADM 137/2071.

37 This was but a temporary reprieve as *Bernisse* was mined and sunk on 6 November 1918. The vessel was later raised and returned to service in 1919.

38 From an interview published in April 1996.
39 Including *Sealion*.
40 A South African, Chapman volunteered for submarines in 1933. He went on to serve in *L54* in the 5th Flotilla, Portsmouth and in Parthian in the 4th China Flotilla. Chapman had also served as First Lieutenant of Seahorse, serving with the 2nd Flotilla.
41 Roy Glenn (40) had 'dragged himself up through the hawser', having reached the rank of Commissioned Engineer in 1937. He had volunteered for submarines in 1928 having served on *L52* and *L53* at Portsmouth and Proteus in the 4th Flotilla in China.
42 Having been born in 1902, Guy Bolus was slightly older than the average pre-war submarine commander (35). Educated at Dartmouth and Osborne College, he was rated as Sub-Lt in 1922. Bolus had volunteered for submarines in 1924, serving an apprenticeship on *L53*, *L54* and *Otus*. Passing his Perisher in 1930, he went on to command *H24* in the 6th Flotilla, then successively *L18* and *L69* in the 2nd Flotilla. It was a significant accolade for 'Sam' Bolus to be given command of one of the powerful new 'T' boats.
43 *The Times*, 3 March 1938.
44 Capt Shelford devotes a chapter to *Thetis* in 'Subsunk' in which he posits the theory that a foreign body may have become wedged in the bow-cap.
45 Frank Bailey had been appointed Principle Ship Overseer for Vickers from 1933–36 when he was promoted to Admiralty Constructor in charge of the Submarine Design Section of the Department of Naval Construction.
46 The Tribunal determined that the tubes had been painted on 13 May, in broad agreement with Taylor's version of events. Bucknill, S27 and Part V, S92.
47 Codified in Clause 8, Schedule 'B' of the *Thetis* contract.
48 Stanley Jackson was a pre-war submarine engineer a product of Keyham College. Jackson was commissioned in 1907 and promoted to Engineer Lieutenant in 1909. He was awarded the OBE in 1919 for his work with the Maidstone flotilla. He was in charge of the Baltic submarine flotilla's engines till their destruction at Helsingfors. In 1923 he was assigned to Portsmouth Dockyard where he worked on the design of torpedo tubes. In 1924 he was made Engineer Commander followed by Engineer Captain in 1934.
49 Testimony of Mr J. Watters.
50 Testimony of Thomas Wolfe, Bucknill, S33.
51 Evidence given by Capt Hart to Bucknill Tribunal, 17 July 1939.
52 ADM 116/3818.
53 Rear Admiral (S) Preliminary Report S11, P2. The timing of this request is confirmed in Raikes' avenues of criticism summary No.1 in ADM 116/3817. No camels left the Mersey until 1150 on 2 June, despite Hart's request
54 See papers D.3475/32 and MF. 10379/33 Naval Historical Branch.
55 Ibid.
56 'Story by Lt F.G. Woods, Royal Southern Hospital, Sunday 4 June' P2, recorded by Cdr J. Brown.
57 Procedure was governed by Instruction booklet OU5441 'Care and Maintenance of Torpedo Tubes'. The 1939 version in the author's possession does not mention use of the rimer.
58 Ibid.
59 Lt Woods' evidence to Bucknill Tribunal.
60 'Story-by Lt F.G. Woods RS Hospital, 4 June', p2.
61 Ibid p3.
62 The later experience of the *Umpire* and *Truculent* escapees (Vol.1) would appear to support this reasoning.
63 Dr Ramsay Stark examined the escapees that afternoon. In a letter to Admiral Raikes dated 26 June 1939, Dr Stark describes how Oram and Woods were suffering far more from the effects of asphyxia than either Shaw or Arnold. It is known that Oram transferred to HMS *Somali* and stood alongside Capt Nicholson on the bridge. *The Rogue's Yarn* is silent on his contribution (if any) to the unfolding rescue attempt. Capt Oram felt unable to assist with Warren and Benson's book *The Admiralty Regrets*. While the part he played in the later rescue activities remains uncertain, on the balance of evidence, it is unlikely that Oram was well enough to advise Capt Nicholson.
64 Hart evidence given to Bucknill Tribunal. This upbeat assessment was undoubtedly encouraged by Oram's 0943hrs message to Watson and Nasmith.

65 Randolph Nicholson was a destroyer man to his very marrow, having seen intense wartime service with the 10th (Harwich) Flotilla in HMSs *Loyal*, *Tempest* and *Shakespeare*. Nicholson commenced his career as a sub-lieutenant in July 1914. By September 1917 he had reached the rank of commodore (T). An officer of immense personal courage, Randolph Nicholson had participated in actions against the German battle cruiser raid on Lowestoft and in the April 1918 Ostend raid, which culminated in the award of a DSO for carrying out duties with 'unremitting zeal and devotion'.

66 Warren and Benson made much of Orton's inexperience as a diver. Orton may have been unfamiliar with submarines but he later told the Bucknill Tribunal that he: 'would have had no difficulty in securing an air hose to the gun recuperator valve according to the diagram which Capt Oram brought up and that he would have been able to find and attach strongback screws to the torpedo loading hatch'.

67 CERA Ostler, later Lt (E) Ostler who was standing-by Taku at this time, had carefully analysed the *K13* rescue. Ostler's authority in the sphere of ventilation apparatus was later acknowledged by his involvement with the Nasmith Committee.

68 Hart evidence to Tribunal 18 July 1939.

69 Attempts by Cox and Danks to salvage *M2* had not ended in success.

70 Lt Poland had commenced his submarine career in 1937, spending one year in *Narwhal* prior to his appointment to *Thetis* on 17 December 1938.

71 Rear Admiral Rainsford, 'Some afterthoughts on a Submarine Disaster', ADM 298/499 1956. Rainsford carried out two post-mortems on *Thetis* victims.

72 As reported in *The Times*, 5 June 1939.

73 Interview with author, 1990.

74 *The Times*, 5 June 1939, quotes Hitler's condolences in full.

75 John Hughes' interview with Jim Warren 1971.

76 The intention to hold a full public inquiry had been announced in the House of Commons by Prime Minister Chamberlain on 5 June.

77 Prior to the *Thetis* disaster, instruction in the use of the rimer was provided on a decidedly ad hoc basis and most 'Third Hands' were content to delegate the job to the TGM. Interview with Capt J.S. Stevens.

78 'Finding of the Board of Enquiry into the loss of HMS *Thetis*', 29 June 1939.

79 Ibid.

80 The inquiry was held under the powers of the Tribunals of Inquiry Act 1921 which meant it had full powers vested in a High Court for hearing evidence in public. The public could only be excluded if it was held to be in the public interest.

81 It is doubtful whether a diving bell could have saved the *Thetis* men. The McCann Diving Bell could not be used in tides of more than 3 knots. Additionally the bell could only hold nine men per trip therefore an estimated twelve hours from the point of discovery would be required to rescue ninety nine men. Those attending the *Thetis* rescue simply did not have this generous timescale to work in.

82 While *Thunderbolt* was at Blyth, her cynically enterprising crew capitalised on the notoriety of the 'Death Boat' by throwing her open to the public – in return for an appropriate entrance fee. Scores of credulous dockyard workers and trainee submariners were escorted through her compartments. The highlight of the tour was the tell-tale rust stain which insisted on showing through the engine room walls, no matter how many coats of paint were applied. A dead cat was allegedly secreted under deck boards to enhance the atmosphere. Naturally the boat was haunted. Frank Palmer, ex-*Tribune*, interview with author, 1990.

83 Six of these men held the DSM, and seven had been Mentioned in Dispatches.

84 Cristina Freghireri, 'Thunderbolt -Vissuto e Morto due Volto', Magenes, February 2009.

85 Whether this decision to confirm the policy of total reliance upon DSEA had any later bearing on subsequent submarine disasters, in home waters, notably *Untamed*, is open to debate. DSEA was abandoned following the *Truculent* disaster (Vol.1).

86 The air line, which Capt Hart had ordered at 0936hrs, played no further role in the *Thetis* disaster. It was brought to the scene far too late to be of service in saving life. It was delivered to HMS *Bedouin* at 1700hrs on 2 June but did not arrive at the scene of the accident until 1900hrs, thus fuelling accusations that Cammell Laird personnel had acted in a dilatory manner. Evidence of Shipwright John Rowe, Bucknill, 10 July 1939.

87 The 1957 Robert Mitchum vehicle *The Enemy Below*, based on the Denys Rayner novel, was the first film to offer a more sympathetic image of the U-boatman other than the staple 'heel clicking Hun'.

88 *Stosch, Charlotte, Stein, Moltke, Freya, Hansa, Hertha,* and *Victoria Louise* served as training vessels. The barques *Niobe* and *Gorch Foch* were used by both *Reichs* and *Kriegsmarine*.

SELECT GLOSSARY OF TERMS

A/S	Anti-submarine. ASW being the American term for such warfare.
AA	Anti-aircraft.
Aal	German slang for torpedo (eel).
AEG	Allgemeine Elektricittäts-Gesellschaft – German electric motor manufacturer.
AF = Accumlatoren Fabrik	U-boat battery and parts manufacturers.
AFA = Accumlatoren-Fabrik-Aktiengesellshcaft	German battery manufacturers.
Agrufront = Ausbildungsgruppe für Front-U-Boote	Training group for Front U-boats, or unit for training submarines to be used operationally.
AK = Ausserste Kraft	Highest speed available.
Alberich	2 x 2mm-thick layers of a black rubbery anti-sonar substance called *Alberich*, which was named after the malign dwarf of 'Wagner's Ring Circle'. The dwarf wore a helmet of invisibility and the substance was meant to do the same for the submarine. As the boat travelled through the water, the material oscillated slightly and was thought capable of shielding the boat against ASDIC, by confusing the sound beams.
Artichoke Search	AS search technique introduced in 1944 to combat daylight attacks on convoys. Immediately following a torpedo attack, the escorts in the van turn on a reciprocal course and search back through the convoy lines. Once astern of the rearmost escort, the warships once again alter course to sweep back up the convoy lines. The warship occupying 'Position S', some 6,000 yards astern of the convoy, was given the role of establishing the datum. The torpedoed ship was to be closed and foxers streamed. This warship then commenced a Box Search around the wreck until a contact was found. Reinforcements in the form of aircraft and other EGs would be summoned to execute outer Box Searches until an area of 6 square miles was being combed for suspicious contacts.
ASDIC	Anti-Submarine Detection Investigation Committee – a British term for underwater-acoustic detection equipment. In effect an instrument which transmits an acoustic pulse in water and measures distances in terms of the time for the echo of the pulse to return, used to detect submarines. The American term is SONAR. The overwhelming majority of Second World War U-boats featured in the book were first detected by ASDIC sets. Basically ADSIC was a submarine detection device housed in a dome under the hull of an A/S vessel or submarine. In active mode it transmitted a narrow beam of sound in the form of a series of impulses, which produced a 'ping' or echo from any solid object detected within a maximum range of 3,000-yards from the transmitter. The signal thus produced could enable a skilled

operator to deduce the accurate range and bearing of a U-boat. ASDIC could be used passively in hydrophone mode to detect propeller noise. In this mode it could detect bearing but not range.

ASDIC could be baffled by the sound of rushing water (if the hunting ship steamed at more than 18 knots), differing water densities, by wrecks, a rocky seabed and by shrimps/prawns making their habitual clicking noise.

From August 1944 British warships were fitted with two ASDIC sets: '144-5Q' and '147B'

Set *144-5Q* consisted of:

A range recorder, providing an echo plot (including a bearing recorder) plus details of speed and course to be followed. Control was largely automatic – both the helmsman's gear and the captain's bearing instrument were connected to the ASDIC sets. In effect the hunting warship was steered automatically by the ASDIC gear.

147B consisted of:

A depth oscillator.

A depth recorder aligned to an automatic depth plotter.

144-5 Q was basically used for obtaining initial contact, determining course to steer then time to fire. 147B detected the depth of the target. The Depth Charge Pattern Control System delivered the *coup de grace* by means of automatic firing of projectiles.

ASV   Air to surface radar installed in allied aircraft from 1942. From 1942 the Germans began fitting *FuMB Metox* R600 radar detector sets in the boats, to warn of approaching aircraft.

AUDs   Deliberations of the Anti Submarine Assessment Committee which can be found in the National Archive, Kew, London. The AUD Committee would judge the submarine sinking claim on basis the evidence provided.

Ausbildungsboot   Training boat.

Auxiliary Patrol   In 1914 the commitments faced by the Royal Navy saw it stretched as never before and on 4 August 1914 British trawlers were barred from the fishing grounds, in order to be made available for naval service in auxiliary duties. The Auxiliary patrol bore the brunt of anti-submarine patrols in British coastal waters, thus freeing the RN for more specialised tasks. Five thousand trawlers and drifters were actively engaged, one quarter of them in dangerous minesweeping duties. Trawlers were fitted with surplus naval 6- or 3-pounder guns, but often these guns could not be properly elevated or depressed; the training given to the crews was also as rudimentary as their armament. Nevertheless what the auxiliary patrolmen lacked in skill they made up for in enthusiasm, although discipline was a problem; fishermen did not take too kindly to the King's Regulations.

The primary function of the auxiliary anti-submarine patrol was to keep U-boats submerged, driving them into minefields, or alerting escorts or minesweepers to their presence. At the outbreak of war the British coast was divided into twenty-one patrol areas. The essential unit of each patrol was the trawler section, typically four trawlers serving under the command of a retired RN officer on a steam yacht. The yacht officers would be drawn from the RNR, their expertise was often augmented by a sprinkling of trained RN gunners. Unless involved in a special operation, the trawlers tended to retain their peacetime crews. By the summer of 1918, Jellicoe's training regime, the availability of potent depth-charges, serviceable hydrophones and fast motor-boats all added to the efficiency of the auxiliary patrols. By the end of hostilities, 39,000 British fishermen (49 per cent) were engaged in naval patrols and 2,000 auxiliary patrolmen had died on active service.

BBC	Brown, Boveri & Cie – German electric motor manufacturer.
B-Dienst = Beobachtungsdienst	The German wireless observation service.
BdU = Befehlshaber der U-Boote	Commander-in-Chief of Submarines – being Karl Dönitz from 19 September 1939.
Beam	The greatest width of the vessel.
Billet	British submarine patrol zone.
Binnacle	Compass housing.
Blowers	Precious compressed air was used sparingly. Once ballast tanks had been blown and the boat had reached a state of neutral buoyancy, the compressed air was turned off and fans known as blowers were used to rid the boat of excess water.
Bold	An ASDIC decoy ejected by U-boats and known to the British as SBT – Submarine Bubble Target. Each *Bold* canister contained a mixture of calcium and zinc. The round canister was ejected from a re-loadable mechanism adjacent to the stern torpedo (known officially as *Rohr 6*, or more irreverently by the crew as the *Pillenwerfer* or pill-chucker). A hydrostatic valve on the canister controlled the entry of salt water. Five to ten minutes after ejection, a mass of hydrogen bubbles would be produced. To the ASDIC operator on a British A/S vessel, this mass bore every resemblance to a dived U-boat travelling on a steady course. Thus the hunters would be duped into attacking a mass of bubbles, while their real prey made its escape, see 'Doppler'.
Boot = boat	The submarine. Submariners of all nations tend to regard calling a submarine a 'ship' or a 'sub' to be deeply offensive. A submarine has one deck. It is therefore a boat.
Bridge	The location from which a vessel is steered and its speed controlled.
Bugtorpedoraum or '*Bugraum*'	The tube space of a U-boat.
Camel	Hawser equipped lifting vessel used in salvage operations.
Can Opener	Rather tasteless Royal Navy slang describing a routine practice carried out following a submarine 'kill'. Admiralty demanded incontrovertible proof of the destruction of a U-boat. General service responded by targeting a suspected U-boat wreck with a barrage of depth-charges sufficiently to shatter the casing with a view to 'liberating' human remains.
Casing	The outer protective skin of a submarine, free flooding in many places.
Coaming	The vertical piece around the edge of a hatch, bulkhead etc. to prevent water on deck from running below.
Control Room	The nerve centre of a submarine corresponding to the German *zentrale*.
cyl.	Cylinder.
DEMS	Defence Equipped Merchant Ship – army or navy gunners attached to merchant ships, DAMS being the First World War equivalent.
DSEA	Davis Submerged Escape Apparatus – closed circuit breathing (based on the Fleuss-Davis breathing set) set patented in 1929. The set was standard British escape apparatus from 1932 to 1951.
DC	In the Second World War the British initially relied on the old Mark VII depth-charge fitted with a pistol to guard against pre-

mature detonation. Each canister contained 300lb of amatol. In the early stages of the war, six depth settings were provided between 50ft and 500ft.

The depth-charge was normally discharged in patterns of five, three from rails at the stern at a spacing of 150ft and two charges being thrown from the beam, to produce this pattern:

$$X$$
$$X \qquad X \qquad X$$
$$X$$

The Mark VII depth-charge sank at a rate of 10ft per second in order to allow the hunting vessel to draw clear before detonation. Early in the war it was decided that a faster sinking rate was required to provide a second, deeper layer to the depth-charge pattern. A ballast weight of 140lb was added to one end of the Mark VII depth-charge, which gave it a sinking weight of 16ft per second. This was known as the Mark VII heavy. The pattern was altered to provide for the ejection of one heavy depth-charge along with every standard Mark VII. The heavy was provided with depth settings between 140ft to 550ft. Some vessels were fitted to fire depth-charges in intermediate positions within the pattern shown above to ensure greater coverage. From January 1943 minol replaced amatol as the depth-charge explosive of choice. By the end of the war, depth-charges were capable of detonating at 1,500ft. Four patterns could be discharged successively with two-minute reloading delays. Ultimately the Depth Charge Pattern Control System was introduced. Connected to the ASDIC sets, this system introduced the automatic release of depth charges or Hedgehog projectiles in a Star of David pattern at the most appropriate times.

Allied experiments carried out after the war suggested that a depth-charge containing 320lb of minol would have to detonate within 25ft of a U-boat to rupture the pressure hull. A depth-charge exploding within 50ft could cause sufficient damage to force the U-boat to surface. Cumulative damage was therefore always a better bet than a direct hit. The allies estimated that 158 U-boats had been destroyed by depth-charge (42.8 per cent), although this figure is now open to question.

DF	Direction Finding.
Displacement	The weight of water displaced by a floating vessel, or the vessel's weight.
Doppler effect	The change in frequency of a radio/sound wave, as observer and source shift away or towards each other. *Bold* frustrated many RN A/S hunts. From the late summer of 1944 Royal Navy ships were equipped with ASDIC sets capable of registering 'doppler' effect. Now the hunters could determine the range, bearing and movement of an underwater contact *relative to the ASDIC equipped vessel.* In other words the Royal Navy could discriminate between a stationary *Bold* canister and the impulse produced by a real U-boat.
Drager **set**	Breathing set based, like the British DSEA, upon the Fleuss-Davis closed circuit principle. The *KDM* ordered the first sets in 1912 and the design remained in use until 1945.
Datum	The last known position of a U-boat. It was essential for hunters to establish a U-boat's datum point as quickly as possible from a combination of data derived from ASDIC, HE, visual sightings and survivors able to tell which side of a ship had been struck in

a torpedo attack. The introduction of *FaT* and *LuT* torpedoes made establishing the the the datum something of a challenge.

Drop keel   A retractable keel usually positioned in the centre of a boat's hull.

Druckkörper   German for pressure hull.

DSM   Distinguished Service Medal.

DSO   Distinguished Service Order.

DT-Gerat = Dezimeter Telegraphie   Early series of German radars using 80cm band.
or *Teknik*

eB-Dienst   German Navy Signals Intelligence Service.

EG   British escort group – usually comprising destroyers, corvettes or frigates.

Electra-Sonne   A crude predecessor of the American Loran A (and later C) and the British Decca Radio Navigation System. A master transmitter in Thuringia supported by several slave transmitters as far apart as Spain and Norway sent timed signals, which could be received by *schnorchelling* U-boats at periscope depth. Interpolation of the relative bearing lines enabled navigators to obtain a reasonably accurate fix. U-boats operating submerged for extended periods arrived at the rendezvous points off their Norwegian ports with navigational errors of less than 5 miles by relaying solely on the *Elektra Sonne* system.

Evasion techniques   These varied significantly but U-boat skippers were able to take advantage of the 'blind time' between depth charges rolling off the deck of a ship and the subsequent explosion. During this time the hunting vessel would inevitably lose ASDIC contact. The U-boat skipper would order *ausserste kraft* accompanied by a dramatic alteration in course and depth in the hope of shaking off the hunter at this critical moment.

Methods of foiling an ASDIC hunt varied but one technique commonly used was to remain at periscope depth, keeping the stern directed towards the hunting vessel thus providing the smallest possible target. The escaping U-boat would attempt to keep to a straight course wherever possible rather than adopt a zig-zagging course. If certain of having been observed, the U-boat would dive deep but not on its original course. Many U-boat commanders preferred to dive under convoy's track in order to baffle ASDIC operators. The most skilled submarine commanders, British and German were able to use prevailing conditions to their advantage such as the varying densities of water or the presence of a rocky seabed, all of which would interfere with the acoustic transmissions of hunters.

FaT   *Federapparat Torpedo*, German torpedo designed to adopt a wandering course, with regular 180-degree turns. Most useful against convoy lines.

Fathom   Measure of distance – 6ft (1.82m).

FdU   *Führer der U-Boote* – Commander-of-U-boats.

Flak = Flieger-Abwehr-Kanone   Anti aircraft gun.

Fessenden equipment   A somewhat primitive device enabling submarines to communicate underwater using morse code. A steel plate was affixed via a tightly coiled spring to the casing of the submarine. When the telegraphist pressed his morse code keys, an electric current caused the plate to vibrate, thus making the transmission audible to other vessels, including the enemy.

Fliege (fly)   Replaced *Naxos* radar detection sets in April 1944. The *Fliege* system covered a wavelength between 8cm and 20cm. A cross fertilisation between *FuMB Mucke* (gnat) and *Fliege* was known

	as *Tunis* or *FuMB 26*. This arrangement became standard U-boat radar detection equipment in the last two years of the war.
Flottille	Flotilla.
Fore-ends	The bow section of a submarine.
Foxer	Anti-acoustic gear used by the allies to combat the 'gnat'.
Fuel/Cap	Fuel Capacity.
FuMb = Funkmessbeobachter	Radar detector set. It was the responsibility of the radio operator to tune his set into a variety of wavelengths by manually turning a dial on the *Metox* set. Approaching aircraft were indicated by interruptions on a line displayed on the cathode ray tube oscilloscope. From August 1943 the *Wanz* sets replaced *Metox*.
FuMo = Funkmessortungs Geracht	Radar. Known as GSR to the British. From March 1944 U-boats were fitted with *FuMo 61 Hohentweil*-U (Owl), a large 'mattress' radar antenna, which fitted in an extension built into the port side of the conning tower. This radar operated at fifty-four cms. It was effective against aircraft between fifteen and twenty km. The set was unreliable in detecting low-flying aircraft because the low station of the antenna resulted in the sea causing interference.
Funkpeilrahmen	The circular loop found on the conning tower of U-boats primarily used for taking directional bearings but also for receiving *Goliath* VLF transmissions. This D/F loop was used to receive medium-wave transmissions and to determine the direction of their origins. This loop reinforced the powerful *Telefunken E381 S* all-band receiver. Local communication between U-boats was carried out on the medium-range band. When not in use the loop retracted into a convenient slot built into the conning tower fairing.
Funkraum	Radio room.
Gamma patrol **or Gamma search**	A Gamma search was carried out when an EG was confident of the probable track of a U-boat, usually following a torpedo attack. The escorts would first establish a datum, then carry out a zig-zag sweep in line abreast (3 miles apart) at right-angles to the U-boat's projected course. The objective was to obtain an ASDIC response from the side of a U-boat, a beam echo being far more powerful than a bow or stern echo. The usual practice was to 'guesstimate' the furthest point at which the U-boat could possibly have travelled underwater from the datum point (i.e. if the U-boat had been sailing at maximum underwater speed, then work backwards to the 'furthest in' point – i.e. the point reached if the U-boat had been transiting at slowest possible speed).
Gebläse	Super-chargers fitted to some U-boat diesel engines.
Gens	General Service – submariners' term for the surface Royal Navy.
GHG = Gruppen Horch Gerät	Underwater sound detector.
GL u. Co.	Garbe, Lohmeyer & Co. – German electric motor manufacturer
Goliath	German scientists discovered that VLF (very low frequency) transmissions could be received by a dived U-boat. Messages sent by the massive *Goliath* transmitter built at Kalbe were capable of being received by the U-boats *Telefunken* all-band receiver. Crews described these messages as having been 'sent by Goliath'.
GRT	Gross registered tonnage
GSR	German Search Receiver for RDF transmissions. British term for *FuMo* radar.
GW	Germaniawerft – German U-boat shipyard & diesel manufacturers.
Handelskrieg mit U–Booten	Submarine warfare against merchant shipping, or literally 'trade war with submarines'.

HE

Hydrophone Effect – the sound produced by cavitation of a propeller cutting through water as detected by the hydrophone operator. Fixed shore-based hydrophones designed to monitor minefields were first developed in 1916. Ship-borne hydrophones were introduced in 1915 – the PGS or portable General Service hydrophone. The PGS was suspended by a crane over the side of a vessel to a depth of 30ft. The PGS could only be used if the ship's machinery was shut down, otherwise the operator could not distinguish between the sound of the intruder HE and the ship's own background noise. The hydrophone operator rotated a wheel until the sound of intruder screws was heard with equal strength in both ears then the bearing was read off the dial attached to the wheel and plotted. A problem arose with the '180-degree error', in other words the operator was unable to determine from which side of the head the noise was coming. The Mark I and Mark II portable directional hydrophone (PDH) was introduced in 1917 and largely removed the 180-degree error. In addition it was possible to use the set with the vessel travelling at low speed.

Passive ASDIC transmissions largely fulfilled the same functions during the Second World War.

Hedgehog

The A/S Experimental Establishment at Portland had long given consideration to attacking a submerged submarine by means of charges thrown ahead of the ship (see evasion techniques). The 'blind time' between losing ASDIC contact, the charges sinking to firing depth and the ultimate explosion, was appreciated by both the British and their German U-boat opponents alike. In February 1942 Hedgehog – an ahead-thrown contact weapon – was developed in earnest. British warships were equipped with two Hedgehog mortar guns. It had a sinking rate of 42ft per second, which cut down significantly on the 'blind time' associated with depth charge attacks. Hedgehog projectiles were fired fixed elevation, twenty-four spigot mortars, possessing an average range of 275 yards. The missiles produced a circular pattern ahead of the attacking ship. The fuse was armed after travelling 10ft through the water at high speed. A Hedgehog attack was normally carried out with the hunting vessel steaming slowly in such a way that the target bore straight ahead. The hunter would fire at the moment the correct range was reached. Hedgehog was not considered to be effective against deep targets.

HF/DF

High Frequency Direction Finding. U-boats made wireless transmissions when sighting or shadowing convoys, reporting weather conditions etc. In this the Germans took a calculated risk. They realised that allied shore stations would detect these transmissions and that just two shore stations taking cross bearings were capable of locating a U-boat. The dominant assumption in *Kriegsmarine* circles was that these 'fixes' were inaccurate. By late 1942 the allies had produced a high-frequency ship-borne direction finder (HF/DF or 'huff duff'). Now U-boats could be located with great accuracy. In short, any U-boat transmitting near an allied convoy could be 'fixed' in more ways than one. Indeed *Staff Kapitan* Hans Meckel (the staff officer responsible for U-boat signals) warned German Intelligence late in 1942 that the allies had such a device in their armoury, however, no action was taken on his report.

HMCS

His/Her Majesty's Canadian Ship.

Hohentwiel

A radar device (see *FuMo*).

Horchpeilung	Direction finding or taking a bearing by listening (sound location).
hp	Horse power.
HSD	Higher submarine detector – an operative's role not a machine.
KDB = Kristalldrehbasis Great	Rotating 'T'-shaped hydrophone mechanism found just after the foremost bollards on the bow casing of a U-boat. *KDB* produced far superior direction finding bearings than *GHG*, particularly when the quarry was off the bows; however the operation of KDB required the U-boat to travel at low speeds.
KDM = Kaiserliche Deutsche Marine	Imperial German Navy (1871–1919).
kt	Knot, a measure of speed equal to one nautical mile (6,076ft) per hour.
Körting	U-boat paraffin (kerosene) fuelled engine manufacturer.
Kriegsmarine	German Navy of the Second World War.
KTB	*Kriegstagebuch* – German war diary, or ship's log.
LBD	Length/Beam/Draught.
LBDH	Length/Beam/Draught/Height.
Leitmotif	Recurring theme.
LuT = Lagenunabhängiger Torpedo	A type of German torpedo with a 280-kilo warhead, more sophisticated than the *FaT* and capable of being shot in any position and bearing. The torpedo was designed to steer an interception course programmed by the torpedo computer. BdU initially calculated the probability of hits on targets longer than 60m was 95 per cent but this proved overly optimistic.
MAD	Magnetic Airborne Detector. The presence of a U-boat caused variations to the earth's magnetic field. MAD equipped aircraft at 100ft could detect a submarine up to 300ft below the surface. It was in effect a flying indicator loop. MAD was installed in Liberators, Catalinas, Lockeed Hudsons and Short Sunderlands. In tracking a submerged U-boat the MAD aircraft flew in circles on each side of the probable course of the submarine, dropping a marker during each circle when a contact was detected. Towards the completion of the fourth circle, the aircraft would automatically (or manually) release a 'retro bomb' rather like a rocket-propelled Hedgehog.
Magnetometer	An instrument for measuring the magnitude and direction of a magnetic field and an instrument used for finding metal/wreckage underwater, by means of a electronic 'fish' towed behind a boat/ship.
MAN	Maschinefabrik-Augsburg-Nürnberg – U-boat diesel engines manufacturer.
max-op-depth	Maximum operational depth.
MiD	Mentioned in Dispatches.
ML	Motor launch.
MN	Marine Nationale – French navy.
Mowt	Ministry of War Transport.
MTB	Motor Torpedo Boat.
Mucke	Gnat or *Fu Mb 25* radar detector set (not to be confused with the Gnat torpedo).
MWM = Motoren-Werke-Mannheim	U-boat diesel engine manufacturer.
n.m. = nautical mile	1 sea mile = is approximately 6,076ft or 1,851.96m.
Naxos	German radar detector introduced from November 1943 to guard against aircraft equipped with the ASV III radar introduced by the allies with its 9.7cm wavelength. *Naxos* aka *Timor* was capable of operating on a handy 8–12cm wavelength.

Norweg	Long-haul route – the route north around Scotland, sometimes via the Fair Isle gap, but the safer route was north of the Shetlands. This route made for longer travelling time but the longer route was far safer that the shorter, but infinitely more dangerous, run through the Channel.
NID	Naval Intelligence Division.
Norweg	Long-haul route north around Scotland.
Op/R	Operational Range.
Port	The left side of a boat when looking forward.
Pour le Mérite	Blue Max – Supreme German award of the First World War.
Pressure hull	The vital inner protective membrane of a submarine. A submarine with a leaking pressure hull was in dire straits.
Props	Propellers.
PS = Pferdestärke	German standard for horsepower.
RAMC	Royal Army Medical Corps
RDF = Radio Direction Finder	Better known as Radar. Type 286 M sets were installed in British warships as early as 1941, having previously been used in aircraft. The sets were introduced to submarines in 1942–43. The early British sets transmitted at 214 megahertz or megacycles. At this frequency the transmit/receive aerial was a cumbersome affair which had to be trained by hand. Not only was there a 'blind' area astern, for instance a target travelling across the stern would involve frantic rotation to recapture it. Coastlines appeared as arcs rather than as detailed profiles. Small targets did not even register. Centrimetric radar sets known as SJ were gradually introduced in allied ships from 1943 onwards. Power driven, they gave an all round scan and produced superior target definition. Radar operatives, often known as 'wireless mechanics', were highly regarded. Only 50 per cent of entrants passed the initial exams. Training took place at Holyhead, Ardrossan, Campbeltown and Glasgow. Submarines temporarily stationed in Loch Foyle performed the role of intruder U-boats for the radar ops to practise upon. Should a crew be taken prisoner, the identity of the radar man was always kept a close secret.
Rev/min	Revolutions per minute.
RFR	Royal Fleet Reserve – ratings equivalent to RNR.
RNPS	Royal Navy Patrol Service
RNR	Royal Naval Reserve. War diluted the resources of the Royal Navy. The RN had long relied on RNR as a source of personnel in time of war, particularly experienced officers. Many merchant navy officers had served one year in the RN in peacetime and were granted an RNR commission in wartime. Prior to the Second World War, RNR officers were paid an annual retainer of £25 per year. Warships battled with the sea far more often than they confronted U-boats. The skills of RNR personnel were essential.
RNVR	Royal Naval Volunteer Reserve – This force consisted mainly of younger men with shore-based professions but with a love of the sea. A significant percentage were experienced yachtsmen. Many of the ratings were highly educated potential officers and a commission within the RNVR was highly prized. During the First World War it was said that RNR personnel were sailors trying to become gentlemen and that RNVRs were gentlemen trying to become officers. What is certain is that in the last two years of the Second World War, the RNVR produced most of the junior officers who were required to specialise in gunnery, navigation,

communications and radar. By 1943 RNVR officers began to be awarded their own commands as the escort forces expanded.

Room 40

A top-secret department within Admiralty set up under electronics expert Sir Alfred Ewing (responsibility later passed to Cdr M. James of British Naval Intelligence). The staff of Room 40 comprised of naval technology experts and senior academics. The Naval Intelligence Division established a series of wireless direction finding stations along the British coast, designed to take cross bearings on wireless transmissions from both merchants and U-boats. Lt Hope ran the deciphering section within Room 40. W/T traffic in the Heligoland Bight was particularly useful as the deciphering team could tell very quickly when the High Seas Fleet had put out from the Jade basin because of the warnings given out to civilian maritime traffic to keep away. Room 40 was thus able to visualise enemy movements at any given time. British movements preceding the encounters at Dogger Bank in 1914 and indeed Jutland in 1916 were both pre-empted by Room 40 intelligence gathering. As files in the National Archive demonstrate, Lt Tiark of Room 40 had a very accurate picture of where Bauer's U-boat flotillas were at any given time. Tiark routinely tracked U-boats from departure to return and could anticipate a likely operational zone. The Germans responded by changing cypher codes and signals on a regular basis but by studying the wavelengths, the length of signals and the Direction Finding bearing of the senders, Hope and his people were able to send a steady and accurate flow of intelligence to Commander-in-Chief Grand Fleet and the Operations Division of Admiralty. Jellicoe's 1916 reforms greatly facilitated information sharing between Room 40 and Royal Navy departments.

Runddipol

Permanent radar detector antenna used by the *Wanz* radar detector sets installed in U-boats after 1943. The *Kriegsmarine* feared that the allies were able to home in on radiation emissions; *Wanz* was believed to radiate less than other versions.

SBT

Submarine Bubble Target. The German device to create false U-boat echoes.

Scabbard

A/S technique introduced in late 1944 to combat daylight attacks on ships. Once an attack had been made, a U-boat would bottom, keeping her bow to the tide. First an EG established a datum. Next the warships would take up position 5,000 yards from the torpedoed ship then sweep across the probability area, hoping to detect the boat's beam. Reinforcements from other EGs would describe an outer Box Search.

Schnorchel

Snorkel – a tube device enabling the operation of a dived submarine powered by a fuel-powered engine, using air supplied from the surface. This Dutch design was further developed by the Germans and came into service in February 1944. *Schnorchel*-equipped boats could travel at speeds of up to 8 knots. Higher speeds were often achieved, but a dangerous wake (accompanied by unwelcome vibrations) often resulted. Three hours of *schnorchelling* could charge the batteries of a Type VII U-boat for a whole day. The standard procedure was to drive the boat on one diesel engine running at 3-4 knots, while the other was used to power the batteries. Hydrophone checks were made every twenty minutes or so. Three hours of *schnorchelling* could charge the batteries of a Type VIIC U-boat for a whole day. *Schnorchelling* removed the imperative to surface and charge batteries at night, a necessity that had dominated submarine operation up to this point. This was a vital advantage post D-Day. Two types of *schnorchel* heads were fitted, the ball-float type or *kugelschwimmer* and the uncommon cylindrical ring float or *ringschwimmer*. This is no mere technical detail; the *schnorchel* head provides a useful means of identifying wrecks. A *schnorchelling* school was established in Horten, Norway to train crews in the handling of this useful device. The *schnorchel* mast was designed to work with the exhaust mast 0.5m underwater. If this depth increased or trim was lost, there was every possibility that the counter pressure would force the diesels to discharge exhaust gases including carbon monoxide back into the boat. The head of the mast was often covered with an anti-radar coating known as *Tarnmatte*. This coating, a combination of synthetic rubber and iron oxide powder, was capable of masking the presence of a raised *schnorchel* head from the allied H2S radar.

S/M U-boat = *Seiner Majestät U-Boot* His Majesty's Submarine – First World War German submarine.

SNO Senior Naval Officer (Royal Navy).

Square Search When an EG was oblivious to the track of a suspected U-boat, the standard procedure was to adopt 'Observant' or square search. This involved equally-spaced warships, sailing in line ahead, describing a square around a datum until contact was restored and depth charging could begin. The Box Search was a variation which required more than one EG usually organised into an inner and outer Box Search. The procedure was designed to render it extremely difficult for a U-boat to escape from the perimeter of a box without being detected by ASDIC.

Search Scheme No.2 was a variation of the Square Search, requiring EGs to make two box sweeps in line abreast, 2-3000 yards apart, through a U-boat probability area. It was calculated that in order to escape, a U-boat would have to cross the perimeter of the box at a speed of 3-4 knots, which under normal conditions, ought to be audible as HE.

Squid Destroying U-boats became increasingly mechanised and by the closing stages of the war, the process was largely automatic (see ASDIC). From August 1944 Hedgehog firing mechanisms were connected to the ASDIC gear enabling the depth to be pre-set at the last possible moment before discharge. In fact the firing process became increasingly automatic. The result was the Squid system, which was fitted to new ships. The weapon consisted of two three-barrelled mortars, fitted into a frame, which could be rotated through 90 degrees for loading (which was automatic). The time-fuse gave detonation settings from 20-900ft. HMS *Loch Killin* is credited with one of the earliest Squid 'kills', using this system in 1944. Squid was arguably the deadliest A/S weapon in the armoury.

Spare Crew British submarine flotillas maintained a pool of specialist personnel, e.g. there were spare crew ERAs, spare crew torpedomen and spare crew officers. Should any crewman fail to turn up on patrol, an appropriate member of the spare crew pool would be given a 'pier head jump' and ordered to join the submarine at harbour stations.

S/Sp Submerged Speed.

SSW Siemens Schuckert Werke – electric motor manufacturer.

Starboard The right side of a boat when looking forward.

Sub/R Submerged Range.

Subsmash	Code name for submarine lost/sunk.
Sur/Sp	Surface Speed.
T5	A German acoustic torpedo, or *Zaunköning,* with a warhead weighing 274 kilos, intended to be used as escort killer, designed to lock onto the loudest noise after a run of 400m from its launch. Foxer was introduced to thwart the 'gnat' as it was known to the allies.
Tauchretter	See *Drager set*
TMA	Torpedo-Mine-A – moored German mines, designed for, but never actually used on U-boats.
TMB	Torpedo-Mine-B – small German ground mines with various fuses and an explosive charge of 578.7kg (1,276lb).
TMC	Torpedo-Mine-C – large German ground mines with an explosive charge of 997.9kg (2,200lb).
Trim	Fore and aft balance of a boat. If a submarine was in perfect longitudinal and lateral balance it was said to be 'in trim'. Obviously trim changed as torpedoes were fired, stores were loaded or even when personnel moved around the boat. A badly trimmed boat might show its periscope or even its stern to an enemy. Maintenance of trim was of crucial importance and (RN) was the responsibility of the first lieutenant and the stoker petty officer. Using graphs and tables, these men calculated the amount of water to be admitted, or expelled from the tanks, in order to maintain correct trim.
Trimmed down	State in which a submarine's tanks were flooded until a state of neutral buoyancy was reached. The advantages of a low profile could be combined with the obvious ones of diesel propulsion. Only the conning tower would show above the surface, thus hiding the submarine from view. However, the submarine was vulnerable should it suddenly enter a patch of denser water.
Trot	Manoeuvre carried out by RN submarine usually in harbour, when coming alongside or leaving for patrol or exercise.
Tunis	The *Tunis* system of radar detection (a combination of *FuMB 24 Fliege* and *FuMB 25 Mucke*) required two antennae added to the conning tower. Firstly a forward-facing *Mucke* cone and secondly the aft-facing parabolic antenna of the *Fliege* system. By late 1944 a U-boat conning tower was becoming quite crowded.
Turm	Conning tower of U-boat. One important distinction between the British submarine and the U-boat was that a U-boat commander conventionally made a dived attack from the cramped chamber within the conning tower of his boat. British submarine skippers preferred to make their torpedo attacks from the control room. The design of German conning towers evolved between 1939 and 1945 from the plain cylindrical *Turm 0* to the elaborate *Turm 4* with its dual flak gun platforms known to crews as the *wintergarten.*
Twill Trunk	The favoured British and German submarine escape method during the Second World War. Following the Nasmith committee recommendations, escape chambers were removed from submarines as it was felt that their claustrophobic nature had hindered the *Thetis* escape.
	Instead of a dedicated escape chamber, new submarines were fitted with a Twill Trunk mechanism under designated escape hatches. The Twill Trunk was a rubberised cotton concertina, strengthened with metal hoops. When stored, the Trunk was designed to collapse under the hatch. When required the Trunk

could be extended and tethered to the floor of the chamber. In the highest part of the chamber the flood valve was fitted, backed up by a flap valve. These were used to flood the chamber once the skirt was in place and securely tethered. Water entered the chamber via a bore pipe discharging into the bilges near the floor, thus ensuring that the point of ingress would never be higher than the hatch, so enabling the formation of an airlock. A gauge was fitted near the hatch giving pressure reading both inside and without the submarine. Once pressure had equalised, the escape hatch could be opened. The resultant air lock formed within the Twill Trunk enabled a trapped crew to escape to the surface. This method was successfully used by the crews of *Umpire* and *Truculent* to evacuate their boats (Vol.1), but sadly failed the crew of *Untamed*.

U-boat = *Unterseeboot*	Submarine.
U/Dt	Underwater Displacement.
U/Power	Underwater Power.
Uzo = *Uberwasserzieloptik*	The U-boat torpedo-aiming device mounted on front of conning tower.
VC	Victoria Cross.
Verschollen	German meaning for missing or lost.
W/T	Wireless Transmission.
Wabo/Wasserbomb	Water bomb – German term for depth-charge.
Wanz	German radar detector set replacement for *Metox*. *Wanz* was considered to be more sensitive than *Metox*. Better still, *Wanz* introduced automatic frequency search but manual fine-tuning was possible. The *Wanz* set required a permanent antenna known as the *Runddipol*.
Wintergarten	By mid-1944 most Type VII U-boats were armed with one big 3.7cm AA gun on the lower platform and twin C/38 guns mounted on the upper platform. Ready ammunition lockers were built into the *wintergarten* to aid supply of shells. In late 1944 this model was replaced by, either a 1-2cm quadruple 38/43U with armoured shield, or a 1-3cm twin M42.
Zentrale	German term for the central compartment known as the control room in an allied submarine.

SOURCES OF INFORMATION

A SELECT LIST OF FIRST WORLD WAR PRIMARY SOURCES

The only real means of researching this subject is to critically examine primary sources, particularly ships' logs and patrol reports which are at least largely free of the malicious embroidery of propaganda. Admiralty files held at Kew are separately referenced in the text. German KTBs within the PG Series are held at both NARA (Records of the German Navy T-1022), National Archives, Washington; and The RN Historical Branch Library, Portsmouth (however, at the time of writing, the latter is not always easily accessed).

FIRST WORLD WAR U-BOATS AND THEIR CREWS

ADM 137/3060, ADM 137/3872, ADM 137/3874, ADM 137 /3897 and ADM 137/4126, Interrogations of German submarine survivors 1917-1918
ADM 137/3888-3898, Admiralty notes on the UC class
ADM 137/3899-3917, Admiralty notes on the UB class
ADM 137/4698, *U-Flotille* organisation 1914-1918
ADM 116/, Salvage operations series

ADMIRALTY ASSESSMENTS OF FIRST WORLD WAR U-BOAT ATTACKS 1914-1918

ADM 137/4137-4150, Particulars of U-boat attacks including Board of Trade returns 1916-18
ADM 137/3965

AUXILIARY PATROL REPORTS

ADM 137/2653, ADM 131/75-76
Bristol Channel ADM 137/800-801
Holyhead ADM 137/120, ADM 137/942
Liverpool ADM 137/272-
Milford ADM 137/ 897-898
Queenstown ADM 137/453-534
The Admiralty Technical History Section series (Naval Staff Monographs 1922-1929) are excellent sources of information, particularly Vol.7: *The Anti-Submarine Division*, with the formation of the convoy system in 1917
The Auxiliary Patrol Red Book, Caird Library, Greenwich
War Instructions for British Merchant Ships, August 1917, CB No.415, Trade Division, Naval Staff

A/S DIVISION MONTHLY REPORTS

The following can be useful but must be treated with *extreme* scepticism as they have been sieved through the Admiralty Intelligence propaganda machine and designed for newspaper consumption. They make interesting comparison with the unadorned ships' logs cited in the text:
ADM 186/394, ADM 186/408

History of British Minefields 1914-1918, Lockhart Leith (Naval Staff Monograph *c*.1920)
Records of Messrs.Cammell Laird, Birkenhead
Records of Messrs.Vickers, Barrow Archive

A SELECT LIST OF FIRST WORLD WAR SECONDARY SOURCES

The best overview from the German perspective is Konteradmiral Arno Spindler's epic 1932 *Handelskrieg mit U-Booten*. The English translations of vols 4 and 5 in the Caird Library have been extensively used. *Der Krieg in der Nordsee* by Otto Groos, 1922, vols 1-7, Mittler, Berlin 1932. The charts alone are priceless.

The most authoritative British book is Gibson and Prendergast's *The German Submarine War 1914-1918*. It is a reliable source with regard to British material but it is untrustworthy when dealing with German information.

The Merchant Navy, Vols 1-3, A Hurd – draws on useful Board of Trade sources but tends to be marred by a shrill propagandist tone.

Beating the U-boats, E. Keble Chatterton, Hurst & Blackett
British Warships 1914-1918, Dittmar and Colledge
The Crisis of the Naval War, Lord Jellicoe, Cassell, 1920
Die UB Boote der Kaiserlichen Marine 1914-1918, Harald Bendert
Die UC Boote der Kaiserlichen Marine 1914-1918, Harald Bendert
Fighting the U-boats, E. Keble Chatterton, Hurst & Blackett
Find and Destroy, D. Messimer, Naval Institute Press
From Dreadnought to Scapa Flow, Vols 1-5, A. Marder
History of the Great War: Naval Operations, Vols 1-5, Sir Julian Corbett and Sir Henry Newbolt, Longmans
Room 40, Patrick Beesley
Seaborne Trade, Vols 1-3, C. Fayle
The Auxiliary Patrol, E. Keble Chatterton, Lauriat & Co.
The U-boat, E Rössler, Cassell & Co.
U-boat Hunters, Robert M. Grant, Periscope Publishing
U-boat Intelligence, Robert M. Grant, Periscope Publishing
U-boats Destroyed, Robert M. Grant, Periscope Publishing
Verschollen, D Messimer, Naval Institute Press
The Wonders of Salvage, D. Masters, 1924

MEMOIRS
Als Fuhrer der U-Boote im Weltkrieg, H. Bauer, Koehler, 1930
Memoirs of a Swedish Seafaring Family, E. Ternstrom-Lidbetter-Sessions, Ebor Press
U-Boote Westwarts!, E. Hashagen, Mittler, 1931

A SELECT LIST OF SECOND WORLD WAR PRIMARY SOURCES

There are two outstanding complementary sources of information relating to the subject of U-boat losses and their causes. The first is the body of research carried out by Dr Axel Niestlé published in his *German U-Boat losses of World War II*, Greenhill Books. The second is the set of unpublished U-boat loss analyses undertaken by Mr Bob Coppock, formerly of the Foreign Documents Section, Naval Historical Branch, Portsmouth Dockyard.
A source extensively drawn upon was the BdU Diary, *Befehlshaber der Unterseeboote*, NID, PG50.266, held in the RN Library, Portsmouth. This document runs until January 1945
SKL War Diary 1945 (PG31752, PG34425, PG34426, PG31739, PG31740) which runs from January until 20 April 1945, albeit in much less detail than the BdU Diary
Anti-U-Boat Operations 1945 ADM 199/139
Anti-U-Boat Reports ADM 199/197-245
ADM 199/502 U-Boat operations and assessments 1944-1945

ADM 199/1786 AUD Committee Reports 1944-1945
ADM 199/1925 Attacks on Allied submarines, RN ship and submarine losses
ADM 239/415-6 Defeat of the Enemy Attack on Shipping, CB 3304
Monthly S/M Incidents 1945, ADM 199/2056, ADM 199/2062
The Monthly Anti-Submarine Reports
The Shipbuilder

COASTAL CONVOYS
ADM 199/2130-2148 MN Survivor Reports

GENERAL NAVAL SUBJECTS
ADM 199/2062

MINEFIELDS
British Mining Operations 1939-45, Vols 1 and 2, BR 1736 (BR) (1)
The Staff History: British Submarine Operations 1939-45 (Home Waters)

ULTRA DECRYPTS
ADM 223/21 (Issued on a weekly basis)

A SELECT LIST OF SECOND WORLD WAR SECONDARY SOURCES

Allied Submarine Attacks of World War Two, J. Rowher, Greenhill Books
Axis Successes of World War Two, J. Rowher, Greenhill Books
Beneath the Waves, A.S. Evans, William Kimber
Birkenhead Priory and After, W. Bushell
British and Commonwealth Merchant Ship Losses to Axis Submarines 1939-45, A.J. Tennent, Sutton
   Publishing
Cammell Laird, Vols 1 and 2, I. Collard, The History Press
Coastal Convoys 1939-45, N. Hewitt, Pen and Sword
Convoy, J. Winton, Hutchinson
Damned Un-English Machines, J. Hoole and K. Nutter, Tempus
Die Deutschen Kriegsschiffe, E. Groner, 2 vols, Lehmanns Verlag
Die Spur des Lowen, J. Rhode
Dönitz's Last Gamble, L. Patterson, Seaforth
End Game, J. White, The History Press
Hitler's U-boat War Vol. 1: The Hunters, Clay Blair
Hitler's U-boat War Vol. 2: The Hunted, Clay Blair
HMS Thunderbolt – *Vissuto E Morto Due Volte*, C. Freghieri, Mare Alesia
Liverpool and the Battle of the Atlantic 1939-1945, P. Kemp, Maritime Books
Liverpool, the Port and its Ships, M. Stammers, Sutton
Lloyd's War Losses: The Second World War, Lloyd's of London
Mines, Minelayers and Minelaying, Capt J.S. Cowie, OUP 1949
Neither Sharks Nor Wolves, T Mulligan, Naval Institute Press
Pembroke Dock Town Trail, 2007
Pembroke and Pembroke Dock, B. Cripps, Gomer
Q-ships and their Story, E. Keble Chatterton, Conway Press
Royal Navy Trawlers, Part 1, G. Toghill, Maritime Books
Royal Navy Trawlers, Part 2, G. Toghill, Maritime Books
Shore Establishments of the Royal Navy, Lt Cdr Warlow, Maritime Books

Starke Schell, The World Ship Society
Subsunk, W. Shelford, Harrap
Swept Channels, 'Taffrail', Hodder & Stoughton
The Admiralty Regrets, Warren and Benson
The Allied Convoy System 1939-1945, A. Hague
The Battle of the Atlantic and Signals Intelligence: U-boat Situations and Trends, 1941-1945, NRS
The Cross of Sacrifice, Vols I, IV and V
The Headland with the Birches, a History of Birkenhead, A. McCulloch
The Port of Bristol, A. King, The History Press
The Story of Milford Haven, K. McCay
The U-boat Commanders Handbook, Thomas reprint
The U-boat, Evolution and Technical History, E. Rössler
The U-boat War in the Atlantic, G. Hessler
The World's Merchant Fleets 1939, R. Jordan, Naval Institute Press
The War at Sea, Vols I and III, S. Roskill, HMSO, 1963
Type VII U-Boats, R Stern, Naval Institute Press
Warships of World War II, Lenton and Colledge

WEBSITES

http://www.worldnavalsubmarines.com

INDEX

U-BOATS AND SUBMARINES

SELECT INDEX OF FEATURED SHIPS

Although this is a book about submarines and all else is surely incidental, wiser counsels have urged the inclusion of a ship index for ease of reference

Other books in the series:

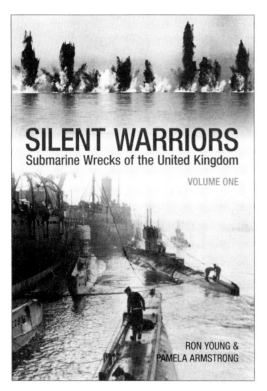

Silent Warriors: Submarine Wrecks of the United Kingdom Vol 1: England's East Coast

In two world wars, the waters off Britain were often a no-go area because of submarine activity as the German U-boats laid waste to coastal shipping, fishing boats and shelled coastal towns. Some of these vessels were sunk and, including British and allied submarines, over 150 submarine wrecks dot the British coastline.

Many are now visited by divers and deep diving has brought a wealth of deep wrecks within the reach of modern divers. Ron Young and Pamela Armstrong tell the story of just some of these wrecks in the first volume of their history and dive guide to every submarine and U-boat wreck of the British Isles. This volume covers the East Coast from North East England to Kent and will prove to be the definitive record of the submarine wrecks of the British Isles.

978-07524-3876-4

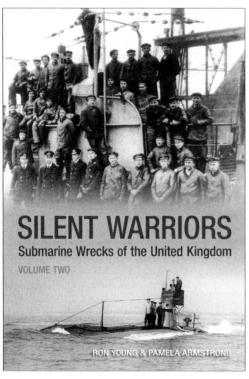

Silent Warriors: Submarine Wrecks of the United Kingdom Vol 2: England's South Coast

Volume Two of Ron Young and Pamela Armstrong's informative trilogy on submarine wrecks of the British Isles, focuses in this edition on the South Coast, from Beachey Head in Sussex down to the Isles of Scilly. Over 150 British submarine and U-boat wrecks in British coastal waters, specifically those in the English Channel, are described in detail, including information on the vessel's type and technical specifications, its voyage history, how it was sunk, a list of crew at the time of loss, details of the wreck site and the current state of the wreck.

978-07524-4789-6

Visit our website and discover thousands of other History Press books.

www.thehistorypress.co.uk